Preface

The essays in this book represent an integrated selection from the many that I have written in ethics since the publication of my *Moral Knowledge and Ethical Character* in 1997. All of the essays concern one or another aspect of practical reason, but they are grouped to provide, in each case, a detailed treatment of an important subfield of ethics or a major moral question. Part I focuses on reasons for action and develops a theory of both their nature and their grounds. Part II presents my own ethical theory, which, though continuous with the view of W. D. Ross, has been called "the new intuitionism" because of its developments beyond Ross's view, particularly in bringing to bear results from my several decades of work in epistemology. Part III presents views growing from those in the previous parts: a conception of rights, especially as applicable to practical ethics; a political philosophy as applied to the realm of religion and politics; and a sketch of cosmopolitanism in contrast with both nationalism and patriotism.

Each part is designed to be usable in teaching in areas of ethics that overlap or coincide with those of its essays. Part I might be integrated into a course on practical reason, the theory of value, or metaethics. Part II can be used both in general ethics and in studies of intuitionism, of obligation, or of virtue. It connects all of these areas, and also formulates a Kantian version of intuitionism that has aroused interest both among those interested in intuitionism and in a number of people working in (or on) Kantian ethics. Part III may be of interest both for ethics courses and for a number of courses in political philosophy.

With one exception, the essays appear in essentially their previously published versions with only the minor corrections that come with a second round of copy-editing. The exception is Chapter 8, which has previously appeared only in Polish and has been shortened and somewhat revised for this book. The introduction provides a sense of both the content and the unity of the book and may be helpful to students as well as to professional readers. My hope, however – which has much influenced my selection of papers for publication here – is that the clarity of the papers and their many concrete examples will make them accessible to educated non-specialist readers interested in the topics.

REASONS, RIGHTS, AND VALUES

A central concern in recent ethical thinking is reasons for action and their relation to obligations, rights, and values. This collection of recent essays by Robert Audi presents an account of what reasons for action are, how they are related to obligation and rights, and how they figure in virtuous conduct. In addition, Audi reflects in his opening essay on his theory of reasons for action, his common-sense intuitionism, and his widely debated principles for balancing religion and politics. Reasons are shown to be basic elements in motivation, grounded in experience, and crucial for justifying actions and for understanding rights. Audi's clear and engaging essays make these advanced debates accessible to students as well as scholars, and this volume will be a valuable resource for readers interested in ethical theory, political theory, applied ethics, or philosophy of action.

ROBERT AUDI is John A. O'Brien Professor of Philosophy at the University of Notre Dame. He has published numerous books and papers, including *The Good in the Right: A Theory of Intuition and Intrinsic Value* (2004), *Practical Reasoning and Ethical Decision* (2006), *Moral Value and Human Diversity* (2007), *Democratic Authority and the Separation of Church and State* (2011), *Moral Perception* (2013), and is Editor-in-Chief of *The Cambridge Dictionary of Philosophy*, third edition (forthcoming, 2015). He is also a past president of the American Philosophical Association and a former editor of *Journal of Philosophical Research*.

REASONS, RIGHTS, AND VALUES

ROBERT AUDI

CAMBRIDGE
UNIVERSITY PRESS

CAMBRIDGE
UNIVERSITY PRESS

University Printing House, Cambridge CB2 8BS, United Kingdom

Cambridge University Press is part of the University of Cambridge.

It furthers the University's mission by disseminating knowledge in the pursuit of
education, learning, and research at the highest international levels of excellence.

www.cambridge.org
Information on this title: www.cambridge.org/9781107480803

© Robert Audi 2015

First published 2015

Printed in the United States of America by Sheridan Books, Inc.

A catalogue record for this publication is available from the British Library

Library of Congress Cataloging in Publication data
Audi, Robert, 1941–
Reasons, rights, and values / Robert Audi.
pages cm
Includes bibliographical references and index.
ISBN 978-1-107-09690-5
1. Reasoning. 2. Virtues. 3. Ethics. I. Title.
BC177.A843   2015
128'.33 – dc23   2014046181

ISBN 978-1-107-09690-5 Hardback
ISBN 978-1-107-48080-3 Paperback

Contents

v

Acknowledgments

Each chapter acknowledges – sometimes incompletely – colleagues and others who have commented on an earlier draft or on one or another aspect of the essay in question. Inevitably, when essays have as much history of presentation and critical response as many of these, one cannot recall everyone one would like to credit for helpful comments or illuminating discussion. I am, however, aware of much benefit from discussions with Robert M. Adams, Karl Ameriks, John Broome, Andrew Chignell, Roger Crisp, Georges Enderle, the late Bernard Gert, Kent Greenawalt, Edwin Hartman, Jill Hernandez, Brad Hooker, Daniel Lapsley, Win-chiat Lee, George Letsas, Joseph Mendola, Christian Miller, Patrick Murphy, Thomas Nagel, Darcia Narvaez, Derek Parfit, Peter Railton, Robert Roberts, Bruce Russell, Jack Sammons, T. M. Scanlon, Russ Shafer-Landau, Walter Sinnott-Armstrong, the late Robert C. Solomon, Marta Soniewicka, James Sterba, Eleonore Stump, Artur Szutta, Natasza Szutta, John Tasioulas, Mark Timmons, Mark Van Roojen, Paul Weithman, Oliver Williams, Linda Zagzebski, and Lorenzo Zucca.

At the Press, I particularly want to thank Hilary Gaskin for her own substantive advice, for securing helpful comments from anonymous readers of the papers (some of which led to changes in the initial plan), and for facilitating the production process. Rosemary Crawley and Emma Collison have also provided able assistance at several points in bringing the book to publication, and I heartily thank Rima Devereaux for the intensive work of copy-editing and Daniel Immerman for preparing the index.

For permission to reprint the essays I very much want to thank the editors and publishers who brought them to their first publication. These are indicated by the following citations of the chapters in question, though some of the editors are no longer with the journals in question: Ch. 1. "Reasons, Practical Reason, and Practical Reasoning," *Ratio* (new series) 17, 2, 2004, 119–49 (John Cottingham, editor); Ch. 2. "Intrinsic Value and Reasons for Action," *Southern Journal of Philosophy*, 41 Supplement, 2003, 30–56

(Nancy Simco, editor); Ch. 3. "The Grounds and Structure of Reasons for Action, from Christoph Lumer and Sandro Nannini, eds., *Intentionality, Deliberation and Autonomy: The Action-Theoretic Basis of Practical Philosophy* (Aldershot: Ashgate, 2007), 135–66; Ch. 4. "Practical Reason and the Status of Moral Obligation," *Canadian Journal of Philosophy*, Supplementary Volume 33, 2010, 197–229 (Sam Black, editor); Ch. 5. "Intuitions, Intuitionism, and Moral Judgment," from Jill Graper Hernandez, ed., *The New Intuitionism* (London: Continuum, 2011), 171–98; Ch. 6. "Kantian Intuitionism as a Framework for the Justification of Moral Judgments," *Oxford Studies in Normative Ethics*, 2, 2012 (Mark C. Timmons, editor); Ch. 7. "Moral Virtue and Reasons for Action," *Philosophical Issues* (*Noûs* Supplementary Volume), 19, 2009, 1–20 (Ernest Sosa, editor); Ch. 8. "Virtue Ethics in Theory and Practice," from Natasza Szutta, ed., *Wspolczesna Etyka Cnot: Mozliwosci I Orgraniczenisa* (Warsaw: Wydawnictwo Naukowe Semper, 2010), 39–66; Ch. 9. "Wrongs Within Rights," *Philosophical Issues*, 15, 2005, 121–39 (Ernest Sosa, editor); Ch. 10. "Religion and the Politics of Science: Can Evolutionary Biology Be Religiously Neutral?," *Philosophy and Social Criticism*, 35, 1–2, 2009, 23–50 (David Rasmussen, editor); and Ch. 11. "Nationalism, Patriotism, and Cosmopolitanism in an Age of Globalization," *The Journal of Ethics*, 13, 2009, 365–81 (Angelo Corlett, editor).

Introduction
Practical reason, moral justification, and the grounds of value

Reasons for action, for belief, and for desire are central in human existence. We regularly stake our future on our reasons. For one or another reason, we promise resources and time, trust other people, buy and sell property. Reasons can be good or bad, conclusive or inconclusive, premeditated or spontaneous. They may arise from inference, but they may also produce it. They may or may not be moral in kind; and when they are moral, they may or may not be based on intuition and may or may not be grounded in some conception of moral rights. Reasons are both central in the constitution of virtue and essential in the motivation of action that expresses virtue. In our political activities, reasons play a special role. How they should figure in the conduct of conscientious citizens, and whether religiously based reasons are on a par with secular reasons is much debated. This is a central question for understanding civic virtue, and that in turn is important for the theory of liberal democracy.

This book is about reasons in all the connections just indicated, and it approaches the topic of reasons with an eye to structure, content, and grounds. The place of reasons in ethics is often directly in view, and the book bears on the nature and scope of moral obligation as well as on the nature and basis of intrinsic value. Related to all these topics is the question of how we can know what reasons we have and what acts are rational on the basis of them. What follows is an indication of the focus of the individual chapters.

I Reasons for action

Reasoning is characteristic of human beings. But what is it? Is it essential for rational action? How is it related to reasons? And how, in turn, are reasons related to value? The essays in Part I provide accounts of all four of these notions and say much about their interconnections. The final chapter in this part, on practical reason and moral obligation, brings the resources of the earlier essays to bear on the perennial question of whether it is rational to be moral.

Reasons and reasoning. In Chapter 1, "Reasons, practical reason, and practical reasoning," five kinds of practical reasons are distinguished and interconnected. These include *normative reasons*, such as reasons there are to keep one's promises; *possessed reasons*, such as *my* reasons to help a student; and *explanatory reasons*, such as the reason for which I in fact do help a student. A natural question about reasons is how they are related to reasoning, and I show why their role in human action does not depend on any process of reasoning in which they figure. Showing why this is so breaks the stereotype of rationality as essentially tied to *reasoning*. The concepts of reasons as supporting elements, of practical reason as a capacity, and of practical reasoning as a process, are all central in the theory of action, and this essay provides a brief account of each. It characterizes practical reason both as a capacity whose exercise is largely constituted by a kind of responsiveness to reasons and as governed by certain normative principles; and it describes practical reasoning as a kind of mental process in which reasons figure as premises and, from those premises, a practical conclusion is drawn. Much of the chapter undertakes three related tasks: to describe the main kinds of practical reasoning, to identify criteria for their assessment, and to formulate some important substantive principles of practical reason. On the theory presented, although any (non-basic) intentional act can be grounded in practical reasoning, the same acts can be performed for the relevant reason(s) *without* being so grounded, and in either case their rationality depends on adequate support by the reason(s) and not on the process by which the reasons lead to their performance. One kind of reason is commonly thought to be captured by Kantian hypothetical imperatives, and the final sections explore what constitutes a hypothetical imperative. A major conclusion is that in the domain of practical reason, if there are no categorical imperatives, there are no hypothetical imperatives either.

The relation between reasons and values. It is natural to think that if there is anything genuinely good in itself, there is reason to realize or in some way honor it. Chapter 2, "Intrinsic value and reasons for action," provides a theory of what kinds of things are intrinsically good (and intrinsically bad) and it clarifies how these things figure in reasons for action. The chapter begins with a brief account of Moore's theory of intrinsic value, assesses some of its central elements, and proceeds to develop a quite different theory. The theory incorporates distinctions Moore did not draw, including the distinction between intrinsic and inherent value; it proposes a revised principle of organic unities (the kind illustrated by the combination of valuable elements in a fine painting); and it avoids commitment to Moore's non-naturalism in metaethics and his consequentialist account of moral obligation. In developing the theory, I consider the question of whether positing intrinsic value precludes acceptance of the idea that to be good is to be a good thing of a relevant *kind*. I also provide an interpretation of the point that some intrinsic goods are (as Kant maintained) not good without qualification. The concluding sections take up the ontology and epistemology of value and the status of normative reasons for action. (It should be noted that a commentary followed this chapter in its initial appearance and that my detailed reply, "Intrinsic Value, Inherent Value, and Experience: A Reply to Stephen Barker" – which was meant to appear in that same issue – appeared in the next issue of the *Southern Journal of Philosophy*, 41, 3, 2003, 323–7.)

The grounding of practical reasons. Chapter 3, "The grounds and structure of reasons for action," develops the view provided in Chapters 1 and 2 by articulating a more detailed account of the nature of reasons for action and also of their grounds. Here the relation between reasons and facts is a central concern, and I argue against the *factivity view* of reasons held by Derek Parfit and others, on which only facts are reasons. Experiences of certain kinds are represented as grounding reasons for action, both causally and normatively. The essay also develops parallels between practical and theoretical reasons. Practical reasons are, however, seen to differ from theoretical reasons in the kind of content they have. This difference is shown to be connected with the different explanatory and normative roles of the practical attitudes, such as intention and desire, and the theoretical ones, such as belief and judgment. The theory of reasons defended here also provides an account of the relation between practical reasons and facts. It describes a kind of dependence of practical reason on theoretical reason, but it affirms their mutual irreducibility and the indispensability of both in the theory of rational action.

Reason and morality. The final chapter in Part I, "Practical reason and the status of moral obligation," considers the question of whether, as so often seems plausible, self-interest is the ultimate source and basis of our reasons for action, hence constitutes the foundation of practical reason and an obstacle to the view that, in broad terms, morality is rational in its own right. Here, drawing on the theory of value articulated in Chapter 2, I distinguish between the roles of the *impersonal* and the *non*-personal in grounding reasons. I also consider the question of how moral reasons are related to practical reasons in general. For instance, if, as I argue, moral reasons can outweigh reasons of self-interest, are moral reasons supreme? This question is best understood in terms of two other dimensions in which we can compare moral reasons with those of self-interest. One is *priority*, which is a matter of one kind of reason's having greater *normative force* than another kind. Priority implies preferability where reasons conflict. The other – not generally noted in the literature of ethics – is *paramountcy*. This is a matter of one kind of reason's being a *better basis of action* than another kind. Paramountcy implies preferability where reasons align. This superiority relation might be said to hold for moral reasons as opposed to self-interested ones even if the former should be normatively of equal strength. Moral obligation, for instance, seems a better reason on which to keep a promise than self-interest even when the latter is aligned with the former in favoring the same action.

II   Intuition, obligation, and virtue

Intuitionism is now widely recognized as a major kind of ethical theory. Much of my work in the past two decades has been devoted to developing an intuitionist ethics that avoids the major weaknesses of earlier intuitionist views and, like virtue ethics, Kantian ethics, and utilitarianism, is a plausible contender for a leading position in contemporary moral theory. The version of intuitionism I propose is intended to approach this status, and Part II introduces it and shows how it accommodates major elements of all three of the other leading kinds of ethical theory. Here is a sketch of the four chapters.

The new intuitionism. The opening essay, Chapter 5 – "Intuitions, intuitionism, and moral judgment" – clarifies a notion important for all the chapters and indeed, in my view, for philosophical inquiry in general: the nature of intuition. Here five cases are considered and interconnected: *cognitive intuitions* – intuitions that *p* (some proposition); *intuitiveness* – *p*'s appearing intuitive, evoking what might be called the sense of non-inferential credibility; *propositional intuitions* – propositions taken to be intuitively known; *objectual intuitions*, roughly direct apprehensions of properties, concepts, or relations; and "*facultative*" *intuition* – a kind of apprehensional capacity by which we know what we intuitively do know. Once the notion of intuition is clarified, intuitionism as I have developed it – now often called "the new intuitionism" – is introduced. This position is more moderate than Ross's and different in important ways. The best elements in his view are preserved, but there are advances in (among other things) the epistemology of self-evidence, the conception of non-inferential justification, and the account of how to determine overall obligation given conflicting prima facie obligations.

Kantian elements in intuitionism. There is little doubt that Kant relied on intuition in his moral theory. Taking this reliance in relation to my conception of self-evidence, I have integrated major elements in Kant with the new intuitionism outlined in the previous chapter. Chapter 6, "Kantian intuitionism as a framework for the justification of moral judgments," briefly presents my integration of a revised, expanded Rossian intuitionism with an account of Kant's Humanity Formula – though I do not claim it is the account Kant would give. I first clarify Rossian intuitionism and, especially, the mistaken notion of self-evidence it employs. My account of self-evidence accommodates Ross's principles of obligation but rejects his conception – shared with Prichard and Moore, among others – of the self-evident as unprovable. The account also explains how the self-evident can fail to be obvious and indeed need not be believed by everyone who comprehendingly considers it. With this much accomplished, the essay meets some recent objections to Kantian intuitionism as I presented it in *The Good in the Right* (2004), and earlier in *Mind* (2001). With the results of this discussion in view, the chapter advances that theory by distinguishing two kinds of moral questions – thick and thin questions – that the theory leads us to stress. Their importance for moral decision is illustrated, and the concluding section formulates a number of principles that are supported by Kantian intuitionism and can aid practical wisdom in making moral judgments in difficult cases of conflicting prima facie moral obligation. In illustrating these principles, I show how the Humanity Formula supports intuitive moral principles even while those principles provide clarity to that very formula. A tree may receive nourishment from roots it does not depend on. This nourishment may affect both its foliage and fruits, but these may each have value independent of that support and may also strengthen the roots.

Virtue-theoretical elements in the new intuitionism. Kant is famous for the distinction between acting *from* duty and acting merely in conformity with it, and this distinction is closely paralleled in virtue ethics and likely anticipated in Aristotle's *Nicomachean Ethics.* Chapter 7, "Moral virtue and reasons for action," clarifies the parallel distinction in virtue theory. It clarifies the way in which actions are performed *from* virtue and explores the extent to which we may have control of how our actions are grounded. Given our having two or more reasons for doing something, as we often do, say where self-interest is aligned with obligation, can we bring it about at will that we act, as would a virtuous person in our position, *for* the moral reason? This seems unlikely. It may still be possible, however, that we have considerable *indirect* control of why we act in such cases. Here and in other cases, there is much we can do to sustain, enhance, and perhaps even develop virtues of character.

Virtue ethics and intuitionist pluralism. In the light of the conception of virtue ethics provided by Chapter 8, "Virtue ethics in theory and practice" (appearing here for the first time in English) considers mainly the structure of moral virtue and, in that light, the normative side of virtue ethics. Moral virtue is characterized in contrast with other kinds, and the role of appeals to virtue in normative ethics is clarified. Here virtue ethics is seen as compatible with reliance on certain rules in practical ethics; its tension with intuitionistic rule ethics is not at the level of endorsements of particular types of action, nor of conditions for the morally creditworthy motivation of action, but only at the level of theoretical explanation of the *grounds* of morally required deeds. This makes possible an extensive use of virtue notions in intuitionist ethics and a high degree of harmony between the new intuitionism and virtue ethics in the practical domain of moral education and applied ethics.

III   Religion, politics, and the obligations of citizenship

Drawing on a number of ideas that govern the theory of reasons, obligations, and values framed in Parts I and II, Part III explores how my overall theory of practical reason and, more particularly, my ethical intuitionism, bear on political philosophy. Here I have been highly selective in choosing representative papers. Its area of application is mainly religion in relation to political activity by both governments and citizens. This is an important area and much debated at present, but I should say here that by contrast with the rather comprehensive ethical theory presented in the first two parts, Part III, though it amply reflects that theory, applies mainly to just one major segment of civic and political life.

Obligation, good character, and rights. Given the importance of rights in political philosophy, Chapter 9, "Wrongs within rights," is an appropriate opening essay in this part. I argue that although many of our major obligations are *rights-based* – such that non-fulfillment of the obligations entails violating someone's rights – not all of our obligations are rights-based. Consider the obligations of beneficence. There are good deeds we morally ought to do that we nonetheless have a right not to do. For even the moderately prosperous, these include charitable donations. And suppose I want to gamble but know that I might waste funds I would otherwise use for morally desirable purposes. I have a right to use more of my resources than I should and may be morally criticizable for doing so. These are examples of wrongs within rights. This chapter defends this position and argues that not all our obligations are rights-based, in the sense that anyone has a right to our fulfilling them. Even rectitude, which some might think is achievable just by living within our rights and respecting the rights of others, is not *fully* achievable thereby; and virtuous moral character certainly requires more. The point is not that the notion of a right is dispensable in ethics, though an adequate set of moral principles may perhaps cover the normative ground indicated by rights – a matter discussed in some detail in the essay. Rather, whatever our principles, if they are to be morally comprehensive, they must call for more than is required by any plausible rights-based ethics.

Reasons and virtues in civic and political life. Given what Chapter 9 argues concerning rights, it should be no surprise that a political philosophy, like normative ethics generally, must contain principles that articulate not only rights-based obligations but also obligations that are more like those of beneficence. These are a kind crucial for civic virtue but perhaps not for minimally tolerable citizenship. Chapter 10, "Religion and the politics of science: can evolutionary biology be religiously neutral?" provides both kinds of principle: first, rights-based principles of the institutional kind that call for respecting religious liberty, to which there is clearly a right; and second, principles addressed to individual citizens. Among these is a principle positing a prima facie obligation (not based on others' rights) to have adequate secular reasons ('natural reasons', in an older terminology) for support of laws and public policies that would restrict the liberty of citizens. To bring these institutional principles to bear on a practical problem, I consider teaching of evolution in public schools. Does doing this violate the religious liberty of parents who do not want it? Is requiring the teaching of evolutionary theory a failure of governmental neutrality toward religion? These questions are treated in detail, and the chapter also proposes some ways in which evolution may best be taught with both governmental responsibility and religious liberty in view.

Transnational ethics and the moral status of patriotism. The final chapter, "Nationalism, patriotism, and cosmopolitanism in an age of globalization," widens the scope of Part III and, implicitly, the ethical position of the book. It considers the matter of our obligations to our fellow citizens in relation to our moral obligations regarding persons in general – at least those in the world as we know it. With this relation in view, the paper addresses a major issue in political philosophy: the extent to which some version of nationalism or, by contrast, of cosmopolitanism, is morally justified. Both may be understood as views on the status and responsibilities of nation states, but the terms may also designate attitudes appropriate to those positions. One problem in political philosophy is to distinguish and appraise various forms of nationalism and cosmopolitanism; a related problem is how to understand the relation of patriotism to each. Nationalists may tend to be patriots, but need not be; patriots may tend to be nationalists, but need not be. Like nationalism, patriotism may also be considered in propositional forms or in related attitudinal forms. But, unlike nationalism and cosmopolitanism, patriotism can exist in the form of an emotion: roughly, love of one's country. This chapter characterizes nationalism, cosmopolitanism, and patriotism in both propositional and attitudinal forms and argues for a conception of patriotism on which it is both distinct from nationalism and compatible with certain kinds of cosmopolitanism. The essay also suggests how, in appropriately moderate forms, nationalism and cosmopolitanism are defensible, even if cosmopolitanism more clearly conforms with the moral requirements of beneficence.

* * *

Every chapter of this book provides a positive view of its topic, but each raises certain questions it does not answer and prepares the way for further inquiry into its subjects. My aim in the book as a whole is to provide much of what is needed in the foundations of a comprehensive ethical theory. Much can be built on what is provided here, but there is also much to be done. Let me conclude with a brief indication of what is needed to extend the work accomplished so far by these essays.

Part I proposes a theory of reasons that grounds them in experience. I have so far only sketched the phenomenology of such experiences. How should we account in detail for the phenomenology of the kinds of rewarding, value-grounding experiences in question? I have also proposed a theory of value that countenances *non*-experiential elements – those having inherent value – as sources of non-instrumental reasons for action. What exactly is the range of connections between things with inherent value, including persons, and intrinsic value as the more basic kind? The final chapter in Part I raises the question of the relation between reason and morality. The theory developed there provides a framework for distinguishing kinds and strengths of reasons for being moral, but it does not show the application of that framework to all of the ten dimensions of moral obligation that, in Part II, are recognized in the categories represented by Rossian obligations. That application is well worth pursuing in detail. My hope is that doing so will confirm the plausibility of the framework I have provided.

Part II introduces the 'new intuitionism', as my intuitionist view has been called, and shows how the view can be integrated with what I take to be a plausible interpretation of Kant's Humanity Formula, but the essay on Kantian intuitionism leaves a great deal to be said regarding just what it is to treat people as ends and to avoid treating them merely as means. This is under study by students of Kant but, quite apart from his use of the two notions, their scope is of major interest to moral philosophy and should be examined in detail (a project I am carrying out in my *Means, Ends, and Persons*, forthcoming from Oxford University Press in 2015). The problem of how to resolve conflicts of prima facie obligations is also addressed by my intuitionist view, but the partial answer provided does not indicate the bearing of two resources that should help with the problem. One – perception of moral phenomena (the subject of my *Moral Perception*, 2013) – is only implicitly treated in the book, but perception as a cognitive capacity has considerable power in determining the overall normative significance of many complex patterns we encounter in dealing with concrete moral problems. The other is the bearing of virtues of character on the resolution problem. In offering a conception of virtue and of action from it, I have gone partway in this direction, but further work is needed to show in detail how the exercise of virtue can lead to resolution of conflicts of obligation. Here my sense has been that the appeal of virtue ethicists to practical wisdom in such matters is quite consonant with the appeal to intuition guided by such standards as the Humanity Formula. Whether this is so is a good question for future research.

Part III extends to the realm of political philosophy the intuitionist, qualifiedly Kantian framework offered in Chapters 1 through 8. In that realm, appeals to rights are common. It is also common (and reasonable) to judge governments and indeed political systems by how well they protect the rights of citizens. I have argued that rights do not exhaust oughts; but the question of how far rights go remains. A related question suggested by at least two of the essays in Part III is this: what differentiates rights to something – say, religious liberty – and a principle calling for its protection? In this connection, I have defended both a right to free exercise of religion and a principle expressing a governmental obligation of religious neutrality, arguing that neutrality does not preclude requiring, in public education, certain curricula that religious people may understandably consider inappropriate for their children. A question remaining here is how neutrality is to be characterized in a way that is both morally defensible and adequate to protecting the rights of all parties concerned. I have gone some distance in that project, but its completion requires further work. The question of the basis, scope, and strength of our moral obligations arises again in the final chapter. If the basis of moral obligation lies, as I believe, in universal elements, can nationalism be squared with a sound moral appraisal of the human condition and justice to all people? This is yet another question on which I hope to have contributed important materials for a resolution but have left room for – indeed invited – further reflection.

PART I

Reasons for Action

CHAPTER I

Reasons, practical reason, and practical reasoning

Reasons are central in understanding both practical reason and theoretical reason. But there are many kinds of reasons. Partly because of this, philosophical writing is often unclear about what counts as a reason and about how reasons are connected with various closely related elements. One of these is *reason*, as a general capacity. A second is reasoning, as an exercise of that capacity. My concern is the practical domain, but much of what I say also applies to the theoretical realm. I begin with the nature of reasons for action, proceed to connect these with practical *reason*, and then connect both with practical reasoning. I am particularly interested in the assessment of practical reasoning and in how such reasoning bears on practical rationality.

I   Three overlapping categories of reasons for action

There are at least three main kinds of reason for action (similar conceptual categories may be identified for belief, which in this respect is analogous to action). The first kind is normative, the second motivational, the third explanatory.

Normative reasons are reasons (in the sense of objective grounds) there *are* to do something. They are reasons for anyone, or at least anyone of a certain general description, to do certain things, for instance (for normal persons) to wear coats in a cold wind and to make amends for wrong-doing. Some normative reasons are *person-relative*: reasons there are for a specific person, say me. The fact that it will help *my* friend can be a reason for me to do an errand.

A second broad category is that of motivational reasons. There are two main kinds. The first is *possessed reasons*: reasons someone *has*, such as my reason to wear a coat, which I have in virtue of needing warmth. The second kind is both possessed and motivating (and is described below). A possessed reason is subjective if based on a desire (which is not to imply that just any desire provides a reason). Reasons based on desires may be called *internal* to contrast them with normative reasons viewed as *independent* of what the agent wants and in that sense external and objective; but 'internal' can mislead because some possessed reasons are also normative, and because normative reasons must be *capable* of being possessed and hence of being in that sense internal. Clearly, a reason we possess may or may not be an actual basis of action. When we act for such a reason, it is not only motivational in kind, but *motivating*, and it plays an explanatory role. The paradigm of a reason's motivating action is one's doing something *in order to* realize the desired state of affairs.

The category of possessed reasons overlaps the third main category of reasons pertinent to understanding practical reason, that of *explanatory reasons*: reasons *why* an action occurs, say why one dons a hat. These are typically also possessed, hence reasons one *has*; but explanatory reasons need not be possessed. Something very different, say certain brain manipulations, might explain why one does something, without constituting or providing a reason one has to do it and without constituting a practical reason even in the widest sense. But typically, explanatory reasons for action are motivating. These are the richest kinds of reasons for action. They are called *reasons for which* we do something.[1] They are not only reasons we have; they actually motivate our doing something on the basis of them and thereby ground a motivational explanation of our doing it. They are explanatory, possessed, and commonly also normative. They are also the kinds of reasons for which we act when we act on the basis of practical reasoning.

One thing common to the three kinds of reasons is that, strictly speaking, they are abstract elements – in the case of contents of beliefs and other cognitive attitudes, propositions, and in the case of the contents of desires and of other conative attitudes, states of affairs. Normative reasons are objective in at least this sense: when a normative reason is propositional, the proposition constituting it is true; when it is not propositional, it in some way corresponds to a truth. For instance, suppose there is an objective reason for me to help a friend and that it is expressed, as it might be, using an infinitive: to fulfill my promise. This reason corresponds to the truth

---

[1] These five kinds of reasons are introduced and discussed in my "Acting for Reasons," *Philosophical Review* 95 (1986), reprinted in my *Action, Intention, and Reason* (Ithaca, NY and London: Cornell University Press, 1993), and, in a different way, in *The Architecture of Reason* (Oxford and New York: Oxford University Press, 2001), esp. ch. 5. I might add that since motivating reasons as here described operate in producing or sustaining action, one might also call them *activating reasons*; and since subjective reasons may or may not activate behavior, but are the appropriate kind to motivate it, we can call them *motivational* as opposed to motivat*ing*.

that it is a promissory duty to give this help. As to the third case, that of reasons one has, these are expressed by one's intentional states, such as desire, hope, and intention, and they are possessed in virtue of being the contents of the appropriate intentional states. These states may or may not exercise causal power on conduct.

In the theory of practical reason, the main focus of analysis is normative reasons for action. These are *practical reasons*, by which I mean the kind that determines what we have (some) normative reason to do. Correspondingly, they determine what it is *rational* for us to do when, in virtue of one or more of them, we have *adequate* (normative) reason for an action, as where we have a practical reason to do something and no such reason not to. (The notion of its being *irrational not* to do a particular thing yields a concept of a *compelling* reason, but I leave this notion aside here.[2])

If reasons are *contents* of such propositional attitudes as desires and beliefs, why is it often natural to say, in answer to 'What was your reason for doing that?' things like 'I wanted to show appreciation', where we cite a desire (though its content coincides with the reason)? For one thing, this reply *both* gives a reason and indicates that it was mine (*I* wanted to show appreciation). For another, 'I wanted' contrasts with different attitudes I might have had that express the same practical reason, all of them different from wanting even if compatible with it; for instance, hoping that the action would show appreciation and feeling obligated to show it. When 'reason' designates desires (and other attitudes) that express the sorts of abstract elements which constitute reasons of the abstract kinds just described, I propose to speak of *reason states*.

It is often thought that desires can provide all five kinds of reason. Some desires do not. Irrational desires, even if they can motivate, provide no normative reasons. Suppose an agent (*S*) can readily see that the desired object is impossible to realize, say because it is internally inconsistent.[3] An irrational desire of this sort surely does not provide any kind of normative reason for action aimed at satisfying it. A normal desire, by contrast, for

---

[2] What about the possibility of a reason so minor that, by itself, it cannot count toward the rationality of an action? I am inclined to think that if a candidate for such a minor reason deserves the name 'reason', then there is a possible action minor enough in some circumstance to enable that reason to count toward its rationality. On a mountain hike, the slightest curiosity about the shape of a leaf can make it rational to examine it.

[3] I do not say that a *desire* whose object the person knows or believes to be impossible is irrational, because I think that, for an object we believe is impossible, we can have only a *wish* rather than a desire (apart from such lapses as temporary forgetting of the belief). We could consider *any* such conative attitude irrational, but I leave open that one might believe, for instance, that one cannot square the circle yet still rationally wish one could. In any case – and this is the main point – such a wish would not render action to achieve its object rational.

instance to read a good novel, can provide (which is not to say it can govern) a normative reason, at least *for* certain people. (It can also provide a subjective, explanatory, and motivating reason, but that point is not my concern here.[4])

II Practical reason

On any plausible view of practical reason, it is a rational capacity, specifically the kind in virtue of which agents respond to (normative) reasons for action. It is also widely agreed to be in some way parallel to theoretical reason, conceived as a rational capacity to respond to (normative) reasons for belief. Theoretical reason is not only analogous to practical reason but also essential to its operation. Beliefs are needed to guide action: desires represent a destination to be reached, but by themselves indicate no routing. An agent will be practically rational, then, at least in good part on the basis of having certain desires and beliefs.

Among the beliefs crucial for practical rationality, instrumental beliefs of a kind that tell us how to satisfy our motivational attitudes are especially important; without such beliefs we could realize our aims only by good luck. Given rationality in these beliefs and in other psychological elements (motivational as well as cognitive), one would expect rationality in practical reasoning and indeed in action. I shall explore rationality in all three cases, but let me first lay out some basic assumptions.

There are several kinds of theory of practical reason. They can be, for instance, subjective or objective, internalist or externalist (about motivation or justification or both), and cognitivist or noncognitivist. The most natural kind, in my view (set out in detail elsewhere[5]) is pluralistic, objectivist, and, in a sense, internalist. It recognizes, for instance, pleasure, pain, and other sorts of rewarding or "punishing" elements as grounds of normative reasons and takes such grounds to be internally accessible to agents in a way that helps to explain their role in motivating action.

---

[4] Beliefs can also provide all five kinds of reason, either for further belief or for action, though they may do so for action only because of what one does or should want, where the 'should' is that of rationality. To be sure, beliefs, by contrast with wants, are not quite as naturally described as reasons for action. I think this is because, apart from what we want or should, in some presumably objective sense, want, there cannot be reasons for action. Even if, e.g., a belief that listening to an aria will be enjoyable provides, by itself, a reason to listen to it, it also provides a reason to want to listen to it, and it could not yield the former reason apart from producing the latter. By contrast, a belief can express a reason for a further belief quite apart from what one wants or even should want, or from any non-cognitive attitudes; and this evidential role of beliefs is usually taken to be their primary reason-giving function.

[5] A comprehensive theory of rationality is set out in my *Architecture of Reason*.

A contrasting theory is Humean instrumentalism: it takes non-instrumental desires as (with special exceptions) grounds of reasons for action almost regardless of their content. To be sure, since desires are internally accessible, the theory is internalist. But it is subjectivist: it takes no particular kinds of contents as providing reasons for action independently of the subjective (conative) disposition of the agent.[6]

One might, however, treat rationality as a virtue concept and then try to understand reasons for actions as the kind that would actuate a person having the virtue of being rational in the relevant sense. One might also frame a procedural notion of practical reason, such as a kind of Kantian constructivism, on one side,[7] or, on another side, a constrained instrumentalism.[8] The former would take the framework of the Categorical Imperative as yielding practical commitments for agents who properly employ it; the latter would have us begin with non-instrumental desires and expose them to reflection guided by factual information and broadly logical standards.

All of the plausible theories of practical reason give theoretical reason a role in practical rationality. For all of them, what actions are rational for us depends on our beliefs – especially our rational beliefs – about the consequences of our alternatives. But on my view instrumental beliefs are not the only kind that bear on the rationality of action. Certain normative beliefs also have practical authority. If we rationally believe that something is good (desirable, valuable, worthwhile), we thereby have a reason for action to realize it, even apart from any independent desire. In virtue of these normative and instrumental roles of belief in determining rational action, one might think that practical rationality is reducible to theoretical rationality. I doubt this (and have argued against it and defended a view on which, although belief has a special role as the connective tissue of rationality, practical and theoretical reason are strongly parallel[9]).

My purposes here do not require denying the *possibility* of accounting for practical rationality in terms of a suitably broad theory of rational

---

[6] I have explicated and critically assessed Humean instrumentalism in "Prospects for a Naturalization of Practical Reason: Humean Instrumentalism and the Normative Authority of Desire," *International Journal of Philosophical Studies* 10 (2002).

[7] For accounts of constructivism, see John Rawls, *Lectures on the History of Moral Philosophy* (Cambridge, Mass.: Harvard University Press, 2000) and "Kantian Constructivism in Moral Theory," *Journal of Philosophy* 77 (1980); Christine Korsgaard, *The Sources of Normativity* (Cambridge University Press, 1996); and Onora O'Neill, "Kantian Constructivism," in Samuel Freeman, ed., *The Cambridge Companion to Kant* (Cambridge University Press, 2003).

[8] For an instrumentalistic view of the qualified kind I have in mind see Richard B. Brandt, *A Theory of the Good and the Right* (Oxford University Press, 1979).

[9] In my *Architecture of Reason*, esp. chs. 3–5.

belief. One might argue, for instance, that, using theological or Platonic or Kantian criteria,[10] we can ascertain what is intrinsically good for us, and that desires and actions are rational on the basis of their role in realizing the good. This intellectualist view allows that our rational beliefs ground our rational desires and rational actions, but it is consistent with the conceptual autonomy of practical reason and does not undermine the distinctions and principles I shall defend. We might, for instance, be able to see that there is prima facie reason to avoid pain even if we lack an intellectualist account of *why* pain is a bad thing in human life. Moreover, the principle that there is better (prima facie) reason to prefer a more efficient means to an end over a less efficient one can be seen to be sound even apart from the kind of grand theoretical claims about action that might justify it from a point of view on which the rationality of "practical" elements like desires is not basic. One intuitive explanation would be that there is reason to avoid wasting effort; but what I say about practical reason will not depend on this explanation.

III Practical reasoning

I have spoken of practical reason as a capacity, and I take it as clear that it is commonly and distinctively manifested in practical reasoning. But – although the literature has long contained instances in which the two are not distinguished – practical reason and practical reasoning are quite different things.[11] Even if all practical reasoning manifests practical reason, the former does not exhaust the latter. To A (where A is an action) or even form the intention to A, when one knows (but has temporarily forgotten) that B is a better way to achieve one's aim is to make a practical mistake,

---

[10] A divine command theory would be an example of a kind that would permit deriving reasons for action from convictions meant to be accessible to theoretical reason. For an account of how such a theory might work, see Robert Merrihew Adams, *Finite and Infinite Goods* (Oxford University Press, 2000). An indication of how a Platonic reduction of practical to theoretical reason might work is provided in my "Moral Judgment and Reasons for Action," in my *Moral Knowledge and Ethical Character* (Oxford University Press, 1997). For accounts of Kantian constructivism, see the work by Rawls cited above. Cf. Christine Korsgaard's view that "The . . . truly Kantian strategy is to first give an account of rationality – as we will see, as the autonomy of the human mind – and then to define reasons in terms of rationality, say as those which can be autonomously willed, or as those considerations which accord with autonomous willing." See "The Normativity of Practical Reason," in Garrett Cullity and Berys Gaut, *Ethics and Practical Reason* (Oxford University Press, 1997), p. 243. This does not entail, though it suggests, the primacy of theoretical reason; but it is clearly a sketch of a top-down strategy for understanding practical reason.

[11] Even as careful a writer as R. Jay Wallace sometimes slides from points about practical reason to points about practical reasoning without noting the difference (though there is no doubt that he does not consider them equivalent). See "How to Argue about Practical Reason," *Mind* 99 (1990), e.g. pp. 356 and 380–1.

but need involve no reasoning; to judge that one is obligated (overall) to do something and have no accompanying motivation is another kind of (prima facie) failure of practical reason, though it need not involve reasoning;[12] and surely a (non-instrumental) desire for pain – say, one induced by post-hypnotic suggestion – is (prima facie) irrational on practical grounds.

The question that naturally arises here is what constitutes practical reasoning and how it manifests practical reason. Such reasoning is widely conceived as reasoning aimed at deciding what to do, by contrast with theoretical reasoning, which is widely conceived as reasoning aimed at determining what is the case. This is broadly correct but must be qualified: first, to account for cases in which reasoning is *exploratory* or has the character of an *exercise*, as where we simply consider a projected plan of action as we might a proposed argument whose premises we do not accept; and second, because 'aim' is metaphorical and chiefly functions here to call to mind the criteria on which practical reasoning is properly judged.

Capturing what is practical about practical reasoning is difficult.[13] It is also difficult to capture what makes it *reasoning*. A good starting point is to conceive reasoning as equivalent to inference. In broad terms, an inference is roughly a certain kind of passage of thought from one or more propositions to another, guided by a sense of some relation of support between the former – call it the premise set – and the latter, the conclusion. It is in part because of this guidance element that we may also take inference to be a kind of transition that – by contrast with, say, free association – is appropriately assessed by deductive or inductive standards. Inferences are typically *belief-forming*, but one can infer something one already believes, or draw an inference from something one disbelieves to something else one disbelieves. Rather than explicate these difficult notions here, I take the idea to be clear enough to proceed to cases. Two preliminary points, however, are needed.

First, both 'reasoning' and 'inference' have uses in which they designate *processes* and other uses in which they designate the abstract *contents* thereof. If you and I each reason from the same premises to the same conclusion, we make the same inference, and do the same reasoning, in the abstract senses of those terms, the senses in which we can speak of valid

---

[12] I have defended these views in "Weakness of Will and Rational Action," *Australasian Journal of Philosophy* 68 (1990) and "Moral Judgment and Reasons for Action," in *Moral Knowledge*. In the former, however, I indicate why the failure – as in certain cases of weakness of will – is only prima facie.

[13] My *Practical Reasoning* (London and New York: Routledge, 1989) contains much discussion of what makes practical reasoning practical. See esp. ch. 4.

inference (and reasoning). But the real mental processes in question are at most qualitatively identical. There are, in my terminology, two inferential *tokenings* of the same inference in the abstract sense. (No sentential tokening is presupposed, though commonly one will occur; the tokens are typed semantically and might be conceived as simply *representations* of an argument in the abstract.) We might also say there are two tokenings of the same argument, bearing in mind that 'argument' also has the same duality of use as 'reasoning'.[14]

Second, if practical reasoning is like theoretical reasoning in being broadly propositional, then its concluding element is not an action or intention, though it may be a practical judgment, say that I must now speak up for a friend, which immediately yields action. Anscombe, following her reading of Aristotle, has taken the concluding element to be the action;[15] but although this view can be accommodated to ascriptions of validity and cogency, accounting for these favors a propositional interpretation of practical reasoning, and it is preferable to work within the latter view. Much (though not all) of what I say below will in any case be re-expressible in some version of the action-as-conclusion view.

IV   The Dimensions of assessment of practical reasoning

It is important to distinguish the assessment of practical reasoning from that of the action (if any) taken on the basis of the reasoning. We can reason quite cogently in favor of an action relative to one goal but lose sight of another goal and hence do something that, though based on a (limitedly) good piece of practical reasoning, is rationally defective. We can also make mistakes in reasoning which we cannot reasonably have been expected to avoid, as where the reasoning is highly complicated; this may result in an action that is rational by plausible standards though based on defective reasoning.

Some patterns of practical reasoning

It will help to note some common patterns – schemata, in my terms – of practical reasoning. It is useful to have a simple kind of basic schema for

---

[14] A further problem is how to characterize the content of a *de se* first-person belief, say that I need an airline ticket, where I conceive myself in an irreducibly personal way. This paper provides room for various ways to deal with this problem, but cannot propose one.

[15] See G. E. M. Anscombe, *Intention*, second edn. (Ithaca, NY: Cornell University Press, 1963).

reference.[16] It has three elements:

1. A purposive (roughly, end-expressive) premise (e.g., I want [need, must achieve, have a duty to realize] *G*, where *G* is a goal);
2. An instrumental premise (e.g., *A*-ing will achieve *G*);
3. A practical conclusion (e.g., I should *A*).

Intention will serve as well as desire in the "major" premise; and the "minor" may indicate not only instrumental means but *constitutive* means: the kind essential in the end itself, as singing is for the pleasure of singing. Let us consider some of the important varieties of practical reasoning.

In one common kind of practical reasoning, the major premise, say that on balance I must accept the invitation, expresses an overriding need, i.e., one taking priority over all competing ends relevant at the time, and the minor premise says that *A*-ing, for example making another trip, is necessary to satisfying the need. This instantiates a *necessary condition schema*. It is plausibly considered valid (though not formally so) because its conclusion simply says that one should, on balance, do something necessary to realizing what one needs on balance – hence something one should on balance attempt to realize. (Rule schemata, such as those representing an action as required by a rule, may also be valid provided the rule figuring in the major premise expresses a similarly overriding demand.)

It is more difficult to identify valid schemata where no such necessary condition is represented. Suppose the major premise sets out a (normatively) overriding end and the minor says that *A*-ing is *sufficient* for it. This would yield a *sufficient condition schema*. It does not follow from these premises that *S* should *A*. An easier alternative might be preferable. Some kind of prima facie judgment does follow, since *S* has *some reason* to *A* (at least where *S*'s belief of the minor is not irrational). I call such judgments practical, but they may often fail to lead to action. Indeed, if there is an obvious alternative means that is far better than *A*-ing as a way to achieve the end, then normally, one would be unreasonable to judge unconditionally that one should *A*.

Suppose, on the other hand, that the minor premise says that *A*-ing is the best way to achieve the end. If 'best' has a suitably broad sense, wider than, say, 'most efficient', then it apparently does follow that *S* should, on balance, *A*. For that is the overall best way to realize the overall best end. The reasoning would exhibit a second kind of practical reasoning,

---

[16] In *Practical Reasoning*, on which I draw substantially in this section, I called this the simplest "basic schema" (ch. 4).

an *optimality pattern*. Depending on whether the end is objectively or subjectively optimal, for instance is "really" best or merely best in *S*'s opinion, the practical judgment will express objective or subjective reason for action.

In the more usual instances of practical reasoning, where the major premise does not represent an end as overriding in the strong sense sketched, even an optimality claim in the minor premise would not suffice for validity. For there might be some competing end in the situation in the light of which, all things considered, *S*'s doing something other than *A* is more reasonable. Granting that we often do posit ends as overriding, we are frequently too cautious to do this and hence can validly infer at best a strong prima facie judgment favoring the action that our minor premise represents as best for achieving our end.

If practical reasoning had only prima facie conclusions, its assessment would be in one way simpler. For these conclusions are often sufficiently weak to follow from the sorts of premises we actually employ, such as that we want to help a student with a paper and, to do so, must work late. However, in the actual context of practical problems, we are trying to determine what to do, and here it is often natural to draw unconditional conclusions yielding a kind of definite directive on which we find it natural to act straightaway.

Often, then, we naturally conclude practical reasoning with an unqualified judgment even if the judgment is not entailed by our premises. Thus, inductive – in the broad sense of 'non-deductive' – standards are more appropriate than deductive standards for appraising the reasoning. In these instances, the basic criterion for good practical reasoning is rather loose. It is the *reasonableness* of the conclusion relative to the premises, by which I mean that given the premises, the conclusion is quite likely to be true, in a sense implying that it is what is commonly called a 'reasonable inference' from them.

The relevant notion of reasonableness is important for the appraisal of practical reasoning. The notion is related to justification as an epistemic concept. If *S* is rational, relevantly informed, and has nothing to go on but the premises, then *S* has at least minimal justification for the conclusion. Reasonableness is normally the appropriate standard for good practical reasoning, and it goes with justification. This point may be taken to imply that the conclusion is probable relative to the premises; but 'probable' is misleading in suggesting that we can commonly assign probabilities here. At best, we are likely to be warranted in saying that relative to the premises, the conclusion is more likely than not; but not even this qualified warrant is clearly entailed by the notion of a reasonable inference.

More must be said about reasonableness. It may imply that the premises make it at least as reasonable to believe the conclusion as to believe its negation (and not unreasonable to believe the former). We might call any pattern that meets this standard a *minimal adequacy pattern*. This is a quite permissive standard. Practical reasoning whose underlying argument only meets, and does not exceed, this standard is not unqualifiedly adequate. For one thing, such patterns allow that it might be *more* reasonable to suspend judgment on the conclusion. Where the premises support the conclusion to the extent that it would be unreasonable *not* to draw it, we might speak of a *standard adequacy pattern*. Here, relative to the premises, it would be a mistake to suspend judgment on the conclusion; and though it might be clear that the premises do not entail the conclusion, they would surely provide adequate reason to draw it.

There is still another gradation. Suppose an argument barely meets the demands of standard adequacy, in the sense that, given its premises, it is only just barely unreasonable not to draw the conclusion. One might say that such an argument is short of being *cogent*. When, on the other hand, the premises give more support than standard adequacy requires, we might speak of a *cogency pattern*. Many such patterns will also be necessity patterns. But there will be disagreement, as with theoretical reasoning, over whether every cogency pattern must be valid. I am inclined to believe that the premises of a cogent argument need not entail, but only give strong support to, the conclusion. I thus characterize a cogency pattern so as to include inductively strong arguments. For most non-skeptics, at least, there are certain good arguments whose premises do not entail their conclusions; cogent arguments may be of this kind.

Consider some examples of adequacy and cogency patterns. Granting that one would not want to base any important judgment on premises that are only minimally supportive, suppose one is choosing between two almost equally attractive small gifts for a friend. Here, believing that one of them is fairly likely to please, and a bit more likely to do so than the other, minimally warrants the judgment that one should give it. It might be slightly more reasonable to suspend judgment, but one would be reasoning in a minimally adequate way if one judged in favor of the more promising gift. If we vary the case so that one believes that the more promising gift is very likely to please, we would have a standard adequacy pattern, though not necessarily a cogency one. Now consider a cogency pattern. Suppose that my end is (normatively) overriding, say to protect my children; I would then like to have a minor premise that decisively favors one alternative over another, say by indicating a means that is necessary and sufficient for my end. If I find such a premise, my practical argument would be cogent. In a situation of forced choice, however, for instance between paying ransom and sending the police, one might have to act on a slim difference in value, say between a certainty of avoiding financial ruin and a low probability of better protecting the children. A cautious reasoner might then infer a weak prima facie conclusion, say that prima facie, one should call the police. This would preserve validity and would yield a cogent argument for a weak conclusion.

Criteria for assessing practical reasoning

In the light of the kinds of practical reasoning noted, the broadly logical assessment of practical reasoning should address at least five patterns it may have – and many distinct subcases. There are necessity, optimality, and adequacy patterns, and two kinds of cogency patterns (valid and inductively strong). Some generalizations may be drawn immediately. Where the underlying argument is valid, the broadly logical assessment may be fairly straightforward. It may be easy to tell that a practical argument is valid, as with a necessity pattern. But formal criteria alone do not suffice for the logical assessment of practical reasoning: it may also involve difficult questions about what kinds of ends and means imply various sorts of practical judgments. In the case of an underlying argument appropriately assessed inductively, there is no question of the conclusion's following from the premises; the logical question is how much support the premises give to the conclusion. The answer will rarely if ever be quantitative, and it may be difficult to determine.

The criteria for a broadly logical appraisal of practical reasoning concern the relations between the (propositional) premise and conclusion elements and thus apply to the practical *arguments* expressed in the reasoning. But there are also non-logical evaluative criteria concerning practical reasoning *processes*. Here the problem is roughly how much support S's believing the premises gives to S's believing the conclusion, where the minimal requirement is that the premise beliefs render S at least as reasonable in believing the conclusion as S would be in believing its negation. We can speak of an *inferential criterion*, since the concern is transmission of support from attitudes toward the premises (typically beliefs of them) to an attitude toward the conclusion (again, typically belief). This is an epistemic matter.

Appraising the overall reasoning process requires using inferential as well as logical criteria.

My main point here has already been suggested: it is that however good the argument underlying one's reasoning, the reasoning process is not successful overall if it does not meet an appropriate inferential standard. For instance, if it is merely a rationalization, and one holds the conclusion on some basis other than the premises, then the reasoning fails to produce knowledge, or justified belief, of that conclusion. One could still know or justifiably believe it, but not through the reasoning. In short, one's conclusion, even if validly *inferable* from the premises, is not *inferential* on the basis of them. Thus, whatever support the premises might give it, it derives none from them. A cognition not *based* on premises is not justified *by* them. (I omit discussion of partial basing, in which case the justificatory power of the premises relative to the conclusion is "proportional" to the degree of basing, other things being equal.) This brings us to the issue of epistemic criteria.

The inferential assessment of reasoning, like its purely logical assessment, is indifferent to the actual truth or falsity of its premises, though not to the agent's justification for them. The overall appraisal of reasoning is not indifferent to truth and falsity; and the rest of this section addresses mainly the epistemic assessment of practical reasoning, including the relations among the truth or falsity of its constituents and S's justification for believing them. Epistemic assessment of reasoning overlaps inferential assessment, since one factor in S's justification for believing the conclusion is the inferential relation this belief bears to the premises. But there are many other aspects of epistemic assessment.

Consider first the premises. There are complicated factors that affect assessment of them. First, these premises may be mistaken without the argument's ceasing to be practical. Moreover, since one may rationally believe certain false propositions, the falsity of a premise does not preclude S's justifiedly drawing the conclusion. If we call a practical argument that is valid and has true premises *sound*, we may say that unsound practical reasoning may nevertheless confer justification on its conclusion, where this implies, minimally, yielding greater warrant for believing it than for withholding it. For S may have excellent grounds for believing the premises (and conclusion) even if they are false. Indeed, even an argument that is not valid may instantiate some adequacy pattern and be inductively strong. Moreover, our having sufficient warrant to *take* an argument to be valid may (given justified beliefs of the premises) justify our believing its conclusion. There may be only a very limited range of cases in which such a logical error concerning a practical argument can have the required degree of warrant (or at least of excusability). But there apparently are some cases. If my premises are true and I justifiably believe them, then if I am mistaken in thinking the argument valid only because I miss a very abstruse source of invalidity, perhaps I can still justifiably believe – though I could not know – the conclusion on the basis of these premises.

We have, then, three dimensions of assessment for practical reasoning. The first, the abstract (argumental) dimension, concerns the embodied argument, viewed logically in terms of its validity or inductive strength, and viewed materially in terms of the truth and falsity of its propositional constituents. The second, the inferential dimension – which is governed by both psychological and epistemic criteria – concerns S's justification for inferring the conclusion from, and for believing it in virtue of, the premises. Roughly, the question is how much justification the reasoning process gives to S's belief of the conclusion – typically by transmitting justification from beliefs of the premises to a belief of the conclusion. The third, the purely epistemic dimension, concerns the overall justification of S's beliefs of each of these propositions (or, if the reasoning is suppositional, the justification *for* believing them, roughly in the sense that if S believed them for the reasons constituting this justification, the resulting beliefs would be justified). In a given piece of reasoning, these dimensions may vary independently. For instance, certain reasonings offered in rationalizing an error may be logically and materially adequate, yet inferentially and epistemically defective.

One would hope that one's practical reasoning is adequate in all three dimensions. When it is sound (or at least has true premises and is inductively strong) and, on balance, S justifiedly believes its premises and, on that basis, also justifiedly believes its conclusion, I shall call it *cogent*. This overall notion of cogent reasoning is quite rich, but the intuitive idea is that in this case our premises provide a cogent reason for our conclusion and we hold it *for* that reason. Such reasoning instantiates some cogency pattern, has true premises S justifiably believes, and yields S's believing the conclusion on the basis of those premises. The reasoning is logically, materially, epistemically, and inferentially adequate. It satisfies all four kinds of criteria and so is adequate in all three dimensions of assessment (three rather than four because truth and falsity are placed in the logical category as crucial for assessing the content of the reasoning). Earlier I indicated how practical reasoning of various sorts may satisfy the logical requirements, and some of the inferential requirements, for cogency. The satisfaction of the (material) truth requirements needs no special comment, but the epistemic requirements for justifiably believing the individual propositions do need it.

Consider the major premise first. We have seen in discussing logical criteria that there is a trade-off: the stronger our premises (in content), especially in representing our goal as overriding, the better the prospect of validity, particularly if our conclusion is prima facie; yet the stronger the premises are, the less likely it is that we justifiedly believe them. If my major premise says only that I want to accomplish something, or simply that I have a prima facie obligation to do something, then (if I am in normal circumstances) it is not likely that I am unjustified in believing the premise. Nevertheless, clearly we are often justified in believing that we want something, or that we have a prima facie obligation to do a certain deed. Often we are also justified in believing that something is currently our overriding end. If I see a child about to ignite a curtain, I would normally be amply justified in believing that on balance I must intervene.

In many cases, however, I would not have a practical problem if I could easily discern my overriding end, or what, on balance, is my overriding obligation. I may be comparing recreational prospects, so the question may be mainly what I most want (or should want in the light of what I enjoy). A week at the beach would be relaxing, but might be too slow; a week in a favorite city would be too expensive; and there may be several other options. If I decide that all things considered, the country would be best, I might be neglecting other prospects, or wrongly appraising my own reactions to the envisaged situation itself. The mere possibility of a mistake does not undermine my justification for settling on the country, but the point is that an avoidable and unjustified mistake is possible here.

This point can also be illustrated with respect to obligations, as where one must devote time and resources to one child as opposed to another, or to a parent rather than a spouse. It is easy to go astray in such cases and unwarrantedly conclude one's reasoning. And just as we sometimes correct an earlier stance, or retrospectively admit an unwarranted view, regarding what we wanted on balance, we may revise our views on what we are obligated to do.

It is one thing to point out basic kinds of mistakes that can be made in holding the major premise; it is another to give criteria for the degree (if any) of the unjustifiability of holding them. No simple formula suffices, and a case can be made for any of a number of standards ranging from demanding to permissive. Plainly, there is a tendency to insist that, as a reasonable person would, one meet a higher standard where more is at stake. Making a change of career is far more important than choosing a birthday cake. Moreover, if the major premise does not represent the end as overriding, the risk of mistake is reduced. However, if the reasoning is undertaken in the normal way in the course of answering a practical question, then even if the words I use, or would use if I expressed the reasoning, do not indicate an overriding end, the belief I actually express by the words indicates one. I may say simply 'I *believe* I'd better concentrate on the older child's problems today' to express the difficulty of being certain what I should, on balance, do, but my belief may well be to the effect that so doing is my overall obligation. The proposition that it is my overall obligation is thus a good candidate for my major premise. Similar points apply to the use of expressions like 'I want', 'my aim', and 'I really should', in expressing practical reasoning. Their common modesty of tone may obscure their frequent unconditionality of intended content.

In assessing S's justification for the minor premise, the task is simpler where the premise represents A-ing as necessary for the end. In that case the question is S's justification for taking certain instrumental or constitutive relation to hold. However, we commonly conclude practical reasoning in favor of actions that we do not consider necessary conditions for realizing our end, but regard only as something like our best bet, or good, or adequate, for achieving this end. In the latter case, in which we do not take the means to be necessary for the end, there are at least three criteria. They parallel those cited for the major premise: we may overlook a relevant feature of the action, say its unpleasantness; we may fail to see one or more relevant consequences of it, such as its eliminating the chance of realizing some other end of ours; and we may neglect a consequence for something that, on reflection, we *would* want. The general point is that where S does not consider the action necessary for the end, and particularly where S believes that it is not necessary, the question of its suitability is comparative. This holds whether or not S actually makes a comparison. Thus, from errors of either commission or omission, S may unjustifiably believe that the action is, say, a good way to realize the end, hence fail to be justified in believing the minor premise.

V   A range of substantive principles of practical reason and practical reasoning

Many philosophers have proposed standards governing reasons and reasoning. I want to consider some of these that bear on all the dimensions of practical reasoning just considered, but particularly on the inferential and epistemic dimensions. I will formulate the standards mainly as principles that do not essentially refer to reasoning. This is because the normative (e.g., evidential) relation between one set of beliefs (or judgments) and another is not affected by the difference between *reasoning* from the content of the first set to that of the second and, on the other hand, simply *holding* the second set of beliefs (or judgments) on the basis of the first set. Reasoning from one belief to a second, for instance, yields justification for holding the second if and only if it satisfies the conditions for being justified in holding the second on the basis of the first.

My main point here concerning the practical domain is that if a practical reason justifies believing one should *A*, it does so whether one simply holds this on the basis of the reason – thereby having a *belief for a reason* – or whether one engages in practical reasoning from a proposition expressing the reason to that belief – thereby having a *reasoned belief*, one based on an inferential process (an inferential tokening) of an argument. A belief (or practical judgment) can have the same foundation whether one has climbed to it by the ladder of inference or reached it more directly, simply propelled, as it were, by the force of the evidence.

It may seem that one is better justified in the former case because, having earned one's conviction through reasoning, one is better positioned to justify it. Perhaps we are often better able, or more readily disposed, to justify a belief when we have reasoned to it than when we have simply formed it on the basis of a reason; but this is a contingent matter. We can forget a premise from which we reasoned, for instance, and we can often readily see what belief of ours grounds one whose justification is queried even if we did not arrive at the latter by reasoning.

Hypothetical imperatives

A good place to start in identifying some basic kinds of practical principles is with Kant's famous hypothetical imperative. In one version, it might be called a *principle of the scope of the will in rational persons*: He who wills the end wills the (necessary) means, at least so far as reason has decisive influence on him. This may be plausibly called an *imperative* because it implies that if willing an end is not accompanied by the corresponding instrumental willing, one is in some way deficient in rationality. Kant also says:

> HI₁ [W]hoever wills the end wills also (necessarily according to reason) the only means to it which are in his power (see the *Groundwork*, esp. sections 417–18).

Both formulations lack temporal variables. Suppose, however, that (as it appears) Kant means to include cases in which we reflect on what to do or in which we will an end *before* being aware of a means. These cases are common, and we need a standard for them. We should add temporal variables that allow the principle to apply across time. A plausible candidate would be

> HI_2 If, at t, S wills an end, E, then, for any necessary means to E which S (a) considers then or over an interval beginning at t and (b) *takes* to be a necessary means in S's power, S wills that means at t or by the end of that interval.

We may assume that the reference is to means that are not *merely* necessary, as with flipping one of two switches jointly required to turn on a light; here presumably S would will to flip both. The principle is plausible only on the assumption that S takes the means in question to have a significant chance of realizing the end. Kant is apparently also thinking of cases in which we are following through on something like an act of will or an occurrent intention. We might call HI_2 a *Kantian principle of volition transfer* (it seems broadly Kantian even if it is not exactly coincident with one of the principles Kant had in mind).

There are other versions of the hypothetical imperative. In a recent account of it, Christine Korsgaard has said:

> [W]illing an end just is *committing* yourself to realizing the end . . . to give oneself a law, hence to govern oneself . . . What about Kant's own formula? If it is to be like my first formula, the one that works [i.e., "if you *have a reason to pursue* an end, then you have a reason to take the means to that end"], then . . . you must think that the fact that you will an end *is a reason* for that end.[17]

This passage suggests (though it does not entail) the principle that

> HI_3 If, at t, S wills an end, E, and believes that the fact that S wills this is a reason to pursue the end, then, for any necessary means to E which S (a) considers at t or over an interval beginning at t and (b) *takes* to be a necessary means in S's power, S wills that means at t or by the end of that interval.

It is not implied (by HI_3 or by Korsgaard) that believing there is a reason entails that there *is* one, only that this belief is required for willing an end to generate (rationally) willing a means and to ground the imperatival

---

[17] Korsgaard, "The Normativity of Practical Reason," p. 245.

character of such principles, in virtue of which those who will the end but not the instrumental means are in some way deficient in rationality.

A counterpart Humean formulation represents reasons for action as arising more directly from a motivational state. Consider this "means/ends rule" (M/E):

> If you desire to A and believe that by B-ing you will A, then you ought to B.[18]

Viewed as a kind of imperative, this is most plausible if the desire is taken to be predominant. For if one had merely a weak desire to A, massively outweighed by desires for objects one knows cannot be realized if A is, 'ought' would be unwarranted (perhaps even understood as prima facie). A principle suggested by this qualification would be

> HI$_4$ If, at t, S has a predominant desire for a state of affairs, E, and believes that A-ing will realize E, then, at t, S has reason to A.

One might claim that M/E or something similar is a basic principle of practical inference and indeed that "Someone who does not accept the M/E principle cannot be given reasons of any sort."[19]

A principle related to HI$_4$ that uses intention rather than desire and is closer to HI$_1$ (on one reading) than is HI$_2$ or HI$_3$, is that

> [I]f you intend to do something and you do not repudiate this intention, your intention normatively requires you to do what you intend. Unrepudiated intentions normatively require to be acted on.[20]

---

[18] James Dreier, "Humean Doubts about the Practical Justification of Morality," in Cullity and Gaut, *Ethics and Practical Reason*, p. 98 (his variables have been altered to correspond with mine). The principle is most plausible if *predominant* desires are intended, but we need not here discuss how to incorporate that idea.

[19] Dreier, "Humean Doubts," p. 98. Cf. Peter Railton's comparison of Moore's "h is true but I don't believe it" with "*E* is an end of mine, but that's nothing to me in my deliberation." See "On the Hypothetical and Non-Hypothetical in Reasoning about Belief and Action," in Cullity and Gaut, *Ethics and Practical Reason*, p. 68, where I would put 'good' or something like it in parallel with 'true'. More tellingly, he says that

> E is an end of mine;
> Means M would secure E;
> So: there is that much to be said for my doing M, or against my having E (p. 77)

is a valid schema *and* defends it by Lewis Carroll's point. He does not raise the question whether having an end provides any reason at all and so licenses inferences. It would seem to provide some reason – something "to be said for" doing M. If it does not, we at best have the prohibition against simultaneously having the end, the belief, and no desire (this would give ends deliberative weight only in a psychological sense).

[20] John Broome, "Are Intentions Reasons? And How Should We Cope with Incommensurable Values?" in Christopher Morris and Arthur Ripstein, eds., *Practical Rationality and Preference: Essays for David Gauthier* (Cambridge University Press, 2001), p. 112.

As explained by Broome, however, the conditional here is material. The requirement is thus that *either* one cease holding an unrepudiated intention or do the intended thing. It is not implied that even unrepudiated intentions generate reasons for action.[21]

Neither M/E nor the unrepudiated intentions principle is temporally qualified. This is important, particularly if reasoning cannot be instantaneous. For then there will be a major difference between normative principles governing practical reasoning and those practical principles simply applicable to agents at a given time, which may govern practical *reasons* but not practical reasoning. I will return to temporal considerations. We should first explore a different dimension of normative assessment.

Three kinds of normative principle

Normative principles differ in a way that is not yet clearly in view. To bring this out, let me contrast two kinds of case, first in the theoretical domain and then in the practical realm. If belief is taken as a counterpart of intention, then a theoretical analogue of HI_1 is

T_1 If, at t, S believes both that p and that p entails q, then, at t (so far as reason has "decisive influence" on S), S also believes q.

Call this *the principle of closure of belief (in rational persons) under believed entailment.* Compare it with a related principle superficially like the unrepudiated intentions principle:

T_2 If, at t, S believes both that p and that p entails q, then, at t, S has reason to believe q.

This is not a closure principle but a *generation principle.* It says in effect that beliefs generate (normative) reasons via entailment. One plausible cross-temporal counterpart is

T_3 If, at t, S believes both that p and that p entails q, then if, at or immediately after t, and with an awareness of holding these beliefs, S considers whether q, S has prima facie reason to believe q.

In appraising T_1–T_3 it is also helpful to distinguish them in relation to time. Call T_1, T_2, and other principles applying at a *given* time *synchronic.*

---

[21] Broome specifies ("Are Intentions Reasons?" 106) that the conditional is material, an important point in distinguishing the principle from the superficially similar one that takes an intention to generate a reason for the action constituting its object. Further pertinent discussion of the kind of principle at issue here is found in his "Normative Requirements," *Ratio* 12 (1999).

Call T$_3$, which applies *across* time, *diachronic*. I believe all three are false. Let us start with T$_1$.

Consider a moment at which S believes that p and forms the belief that p entails q. T$_1$ allows that (a) both beliefs are irrational, and (b) S might, on considering q (which we may assume S can do at the same time), justifiedly find q implausible and thereby acquire a reason not to believe it stronger than any reason S has to believe p. Why, then, must S's belief that p, which is irrational, give S any reason to believe q? One answer would be that since T$_1$ holds, S rationally must (is rationally required to) believe q, given S's believing that p and that p entails q, and that 'must' is the basis of the reason-generating power of the "premise" beliefs in T$_2$ and T$_3$. Is that so?

A principle in this vicinity that clearly *is* true is

T$_4$ At any given time, there is reason *not* to believe: that p, that p entails q, *and* that not-q.

But T$_4$ implies nothing about whether the beliefs that p and that p entails q normatively support believing q. T$_4$ is what might be called a *coherence principle* (or an *in*coherence principle): it prohibits a kind of incoherence. It says nothing about what one has positive reason to believe. Indeed, p might be obviously false. Moreover, this might be discovered by considering its entailment of q, which one might already take to be false or might readily see to be false upon considering the entailment. That point, in turn, helps to show why T$_2$ and T$_3$ are false. Once we allow for S's *considering* q, the possibility arises that through doing it, S will have reasons for disbelieving q that outweigh whatever reason S has for believing p.

Is practical reason different from theoretical reason on the points that have now emerged? I do not think so. Consider a counterpart of T$_2$ suggested by some of the practical principles cited above:

P$_1$ If S intends to A and believes that B-ing is necessary and sufficient for A-ing, then S has reason to B.

Sufficiency is, to be sure, a closer counterpart of entailment than necessity and sufficiency combined; but since, where B-ing is not necessary for A-ing, some other sufficient means to A-ing could be vastly preferable, we have in P$_1$ a more plausible principle than we would without the double-barreled condition. In any case, are there not the same kinds of considerations here that apply to T$_1$? It is true that there is a kind of practical incoherence in simultaneously intending to A, believing that B-ing is necessary and sufficient for A-ing (where one takes it that one can B),[22] and, aware of the intention and belief, intending not to B (or perhaps even failing to intend to B). But this practical coherence principle implies nothing about what one has reason to intend to do.

Now consider the diachronic counterpart of T_3:

P$_2$ If, at t, S intends to A and believes that B-ing is necessary and sufficient for A-ing, then if, at or immediately following t, and with an awareness of having this intention and belief, S considers whether to B, S has reason to B.

P$_2$ does not rule out the possibility that the intention to A, or the related instrumental belief, is irrational. In this case, the consequent may be false. S also might, on considering whether to B, find the act highly objectionable and thereby acquire an overriding reason *not* to intend to A.

We can now see the importance of the distinction between synchronic and diachronic principles. The former apply to a time slice of the agent; they take no account of change. Incoherence is possible at a given time, and there are sound principles that prohibit it; but considering a proposition or prospect *and* forming a belief on the basis of it or an intention to bring it about is at least normally not possible at a single time. Perhaps it is never possible at a single time if we take it to include *beginning* to consider a proposition or prospect and inferentially forming the relevant belief or intention, as opposed to forming it *while* still considering a belief or prospect. The former – call it *episodic inference* – is probably more common than the latter – call it *emergent inference*. If episodic inference is by its nature barely possible at a single time (a matter that can be left open here), the common kind of inference that qualifies as at least a minimal case of *reflection*, is not.

An important general point that emerges is that consideration may lead to change, and change, in turn, may alter the rationality status of an intention. This bears on standards governing practical reasoning. It is doubtful that reasoning is commonly instantaneous. This certainly holds if we think of a piece of (episodic) reasoning, as opposed to just the constituent inference conceived as a passage of thought from the premise(s) to the conclusion. But suppose a piece of reasoning can be instantaneous. This would still allow that at the very moment one considers B-ing in the light of intending to A and of believing that B-ing is necessary and

---

[22] It would be possible to fail to take it that one can B; but if one intends to A and believes B-ing necessary for this, yet fails to take oneself to be capable of B-ing, this would in itself imply some prima facie deficiency in rationality.

sufficient for *A*-ing, one could have the thought that *B*-ing is morally repugnant just as quickly as one could form the intention to *B*. How much the mind can do, or respond to, at a given time, is largely a contingent matter.

More generally, if it is theoretically possible for reasoning to be instantaneous, it is also theoretically possible that, at the relevant time, a thought or realization can occur that provides reason not to form the intention, or do the deed, in question. This bears on how one can avoid the kinds of incoherent triads of propositional attitudes we have been considering. If concluding practical reasoning in the usual way that favors the act figuring in the minor premise can be instantaneous, acquiring a reason to reject one of the premises that favor so concluding can be also. We can instantiate modus tolens just as quickly as modus ponens. The need to avoid inconsistent triads does not by itself favor one pattern of reasoning over the other.

There is another way to put one of my conclusions. Even if reasoning need not be diachronic, it is *dynamic*. It entails a developmental change, at least when it is belief-forming. That change can bring with it new reasons, as where *S* arrives at a new justified practical judgment; these in turn can alter what the agent ought to intend (or believe). There is a sense, then, in which the assessment of reasoning is holistic. This is why so many criteria figure in its proper assessment and why it is defeasible in the light of new considerations.

Toward sound principles of practical reason and practical reasoning

What principles, then, might we rely on in appraising practical reasoning? There are many (including some for each pattern of practical reasoning considered above), but close analogues of simple deductive closure principles do not seem adequate. What the sound principles are can be seen only in the light of the three interrelated dimensions of assessment for practical reasoning and the four kinds of evaluative criteria sketched in Section III. The first dimension concerns practical arguments conceived as abstract structures. We have noted several patterns of argument, representing necessity, optimality, adequacy, and cogency. The arguments corresponding to episodes of practical reasoning may be appraised by logical criteria, whether deductive or, in a broad sense, inductive. Second, assessment occurs in the inferential dimension: the reasoning process itself may be appraised by inferential criteria. These concern both the conditions for justifiably drawing the inference and the requirements for holding the conclusion in virtue of believing the premises. Third, there is the epistemic dimension: the agent's beliefs of the premises and conclusions may be appraised by epistemic criteria that may or may not concern the reasoning process or corresponding argument. These criteria concern both what (if anything) justifies the agent's beliefs and what might defeat that justification. These epistemic criteria leave open whether any of the beliefs is inferentially justified, through either practical or theoretical reasoning. And fourth, there are material criteria, those concerning the truth or falsity of the propositions in question. Ideally, good practical reasoning expresses a valid underlying argument with premises that are true and justifiably believed and with a conclusion that is true and both justifiably inferred from them and justifiably held on the basis of them.

No one manageably simple principle for assessing practical reasoning takes account of all the variables just noted. But we can discern two that are implicit in what has been said and cover a considerable portion of the common kinds of practical reasonings. The first is suggested by a synchronic theoretical counterpart:

> P_3 If, at t, (1) there *is* a (normative) reason for S to realize G, and (2) S has a justified belief, or justification for holding a belief, that A-ing will realize G, then, at t, there *is* a reason for S to A.

This is a principle expressing *closure of practical reasons under instrumentally justified belief* (actual or hypothetical), and it is particularly relevant to appraising practical reasoning having a sufficiency pattern. One counterpart synchronic principle for reasoning would presuppose that inferential and epistemic criteria are met; and a stronger counterpart (of greater interest here) would presuppose the logical and material soundness of the practical reasoning. The latter would yield:

> P_4 If, at t, S does valid practical reasoning, from true premises which S justifiedly believes, to a practical conclusion (say, a practical judgment) which, at t, is held on the basis of them, then, at t, S justifiedly holds that conclusion.[23]

Where truth and validity are not presupposed – as they often cannot be in appraising practical reasoning – we are forced to be less nearly precise. We might perhaps say that

> P_5 If, at t, S does practical reasoning, from premises S justifiedly believes, to a practical conclusion which those premises *adequately* support, then,

---

[23] I take S's justification in P_4 and the principles to follow to be defeasible, but it may still be justification on balance and may be quite strong.

at t, if S holds this conclusion on the basis of those premises, S justifiedly holds it.

Both of these are synchronic; but they differ in that the second does not require either the truth of the premises or their entailing the conclusion. Diachronic versions, allowing temporal passage, require further qualifications. Since reasoning normally occurs over time, we must take account of what may happen if S considers the propositions and prospects in question *after* the time at which S forms (or begins moving toward an inference based on) S's beliefs of the premises. A candidate for a diachronic principle for overall practical reasoning might be this:

> P_6 If, at t, S does practical reasoning, from premises S justifiedly believes, to a practical conclusion which those premises adequately support, then if, at or after t, S holds this conclusion on the basis of those premises and does not acquire grounds which defeat that support, S (on balance) justifiedly holds it.[24]

P_6 will be useful only insofar as we understand what kinds of elements defeat the support supplied by the premises. But for a full understanding of practical reasoning, we need a theory that clarifies that in any case. Whether we have such a theory or not, even synchronic principles like P_6 provide critical standards that are of considerable help in appraising practical reasoning.

VI Practical reasoning and rational action

Implicit in my treatment of practical reason and practical reasoning so far has been the assumption that an action based on good practical reasoning is rational. This section sketches the kind of connection we might expect between a rational action and practical reasoning on which it is based. This is not to imply that rational action *requires* a basis in practical reasoning. Far from it. In broad terms, rational action may be conceived as action that is well-grounded in reasons (including the case of things done for their own sake, say for pleasure).[25] This, in turn, is a matter of its being explainable

---

[24] Suppose there is a long time between the reasoning and the time in question. How can we tell whether the conclusion is held on the basis of its *premises?* It is not sufficient that the conclusion be held on the basis of (belief of) the relevant propositions; the reasoning process itself must in some way figure in the basis or we will have only a judgment based on the same reasons, but not the same *reasoning.* How to tell is a challenge both to philosophical theory and to empirical inquiry, but the task seems possible.

[25] I have developed this view in detail in *Architecture of Reason* and draw on that book in the next few paragraphs.

on the basis of rational propositional attitudes, above all desires and beliefs. The contents of these attitudes represent reasons and presumably do not have causal power; the attitudes, as reason *states*, have explanatory power (and, I assume, causal power).

The rationality of desires and other motivational attitudes, intentions in particular, is practical; that of beliefs is theoretical. This last point implies that the notion of rational action cannot be fully explicated without appeal to epistemological considerations. I cannot here discuss the conditions for rational belief, but there is no shortage of informative theories, and understanding rational belief is a central philosophical problem on whose resolution many special theories in philosophy depend to some degree. If, however, we can presuppose the notion of rational belief, we may plausibly conceive rational action as grounded, by rational beliefs, in rational propositional attitudes.

There are, to be sure, questions of degree. Suppose A is well-grounded in this sense, but S should have seen that B would be far better given everything relevant in the context. This does not imply that S's A-ing is *irrational*, but there is a kind of mistake: choosing B would have been better. Must we, then, maximize some value, to act in a fully rational way? This does not follow. It may seem to follow because, if we are choosing between two otherwise equally acceptable options and it is plain that one conduces more to (say) human flourishing, as where a charity is more efficient than its competitor with the same concerns, then we should choose the better one. That we need not always be maximizing does not permit us to ignore opportunities to advance the good that present themselves in the course of our everyday activity or our discharge of ordinary duties.

It would be a serious mistake to infer, from the defeating role of the perceptible inferiority of an option in conducing to flourishing (or any other value), that we are obligated always to maximize some value or even that we must always positively aim at maximizing some value.[26] Commitment to a *preferential standard* in making concrete choices does not entail commitment to adopt a maximizing standard as either a criterion of rightness or a general policy of deliberation. It is one thing to avoid choosing a lesser alternative when we consider options; it is quite another to take maximization as governing our choices and deliberations at the outset.

---

[26] This is reminiscent of the error in epistemology of inferring, from the capacity of incoherence to *defeat* justification, that coherence is the *ground* of justification. Rejecting the fallacious inferences here does not, of course, commit one to denying that we should ever try to maximize or that coherence never plays a positive role in justification. Analysis of the epistemological case is provided in my *Structure of Justification* (Cambridge University Press, 1993), esp. chs. 3–4.

It will be apparent that on many points my view contrasts with Humean instrumentalism, which conceives non-instrumental desires as grounding reasons for action and hence endorses practical generation principles like P_I and M/E. This is not the place to argue for the superiority of an objectivist view. Moreover, Humeans can grant many of my points: that there is a plurality of basic reasons (even if they consider them all desire-based); that practical reasoning is sound only when the agent rationally believes its premises and is justified in taking them to justify the conclusion; that action in accord with the conclusion of practical reasoning is rational in virtue of that reasoning only if it is based on the reasoning; and that in general action is rational only when grounded, by rational belief, in certain propositional attitudes. The chief difference is that (apart from such defects as internal inconsistency and the obvious empirical impossibility of realizing the desire) for Humeans any non-instrumental desire provides a basis of rational action.

The contrast between the kind of objectivist theory I have sketched and a subjectivistic instrumentalism bears directly on the treatment of hypothetical imperatives. On my view, there are no hypothetical imperatives – as opposed to conditional coherence principles – unless there are categorical ones: nothing is required *given* a condition unless something is categorically required. Similarly, there is nothing we ought to do given what we want, unless there is something we ought to want in the first place. Even conditional coherence principles owe their normative status to the categorical requirement that we avoid incoherence. Kant might well have thought this, particularly if he conceived of what one *rationally* wills as rational in the light of an application of the Categorical Imperative framework.[27]

It might seem that even Humeans may grant the dependence of hypothetical imperatives on categorical ones, since for them the mere presence of a suitable non-instrumental desire "categorically" *constitutes* a ground for a reason for action. But this would be a mistake: Humeans do not conceive reason as categorically calling for our having any desires at all, much less any particular ones. There is nothing intrinsically worth wanting; we are not even rationally required to want desire satisfaction itself.

---

[27] Some of the central passages in the *Groundwork* do not make it clear that this is how Kant sees it, and one might wonder whether here he is influenced by Hume – or at least by instrumentalist ideas – more than is usually recognized. Korsgaard, as quoted above and elsewhere in the same article, seems to take Kant to be presupposing that what we will is in some sense rational; but this is not entirely clear, since autonomous willing is taken to be a source of reasons, rather than reflecting them. This gives autonomous willing a role much like that of desires on an instrumentalist view, though to be sure one that is more like Brandt's constrained instrumentalism than like Hume's instrumentalism in the *Treatise*.

We may seem to be, because it is a truism that given a desire, we want its satisfaction *in the sense that* we want realization of its object. But nothing in the Humean theory requires that we have the relevant *higher-order* desire for the satisfaction of one or more of our desires.

I do not claim to have demonstrated here that hypothetical imperatives depend for any normative power they have on categorical ones or, more accurately, that desires alone do not ground reasons for action and, by themselves, constitute only psychological rather than normative bases for action. But I have shown that there is a subtle difference, which has apparently not been generally noted, between, on the one hand, practical and theoretical coherence principles and, on the other, normative generation principles, such as hypothetical imperatives as usually understood. Coherence principles are not imperatives, except insofar as we may *presuppose* reason to avoid incoherence and take this to be in some sense imperative.

Once the difference between coherence principles and genuinely normative generation principles is noted, hypothetical imperatives like HI_4 and similar principles are less likely to seem normatively sound. It appears that neither desires nor even intentions have independent normative authority. The counterparts of such hypothetical imperatives in the theoretical domain are not plausible; and in that domain, experience – especially perceptual, memorial, and reflective experience – plays a major role in grounding rational belief.

There is a similar range of reasons to think that experiences – particularly rewarding experiences of enjoyment and aversive experiences of pain and suffering – play a major role in normatively grounding rational desires and rational intentions. If this is so, then practical reason is substantive. It supplies criteria for rationality that go beyond those calling for avoidance of incoherence; and these criteria yield a variety of constraints on practical reasoning and, more generally, on rational action. Rational action is action well-grounded in reasons; it may or may not also be based on practical reasoning; but when it is, the standards governing its rationality must take account of the same kinds of grounds that are central in the general theory of practical reason.[28]

---

[28] Earlier versions of this paper were presented at Texas A&M University and at the University of Reading. Comments from the audiences in both universities were of much help in revising. I particularly want to thank John Cottingham, Jonathan Dancy, Brad Hooker, Michael Meyer, Christian Miller, Elizabeth Radcliffe, and Philip Stratton-Lake.

CHAPTER 2

Intrinsic value and reasons for action

The concept of the good – or at least *some* concept of the good – has been a central topic in ethical theory since Plato. Moral philosophers have generally recognized a distinction between what is good only as a means and what is good in itself. The latter, often called the *intrinsically good*, has proved difficult to explicate and, by contrast with the former, seems to many philosophers to be mysterious. G. E. Moore sought to clarify the notion of the intrinsically good, and his theory of value was probably the most influential axiology developed in the twentieth century. The theory is closely tied to his metaphysics, his epistemology, and his normative ethics; but much of what he says about the good can be maintained without commitment to all of his major claims in those three domains. My project here is to set out a theory of intrinsic value that incorporates the best elements of Moore's account of the notion but avoids commitment to his overall view in metaethics.

I   Some major elements in Moore's theory of value

Since my aim is to produce a sustainable account of intrinsic value, I must be brief in introducing the elements in Moore's account that form a good basis for critical discussion and for comparison with my view. I begin with his famous claim

> that 'good' is a simple notion, just as 'yellow' is a simple notion; that, just as you cannot, by any manner of means, explain to anyone who does not know it, what yellow is, so you cannot explain what good is. Definitions of the kind that I was asking for, definitions which describe the real nature of the object or notion denoted by a word, and which do not merely tell us what the word is used to mean, are only possible when the object or notion in question is something complex.[1]

[1] G. E. Moore, *Principia Ethica* (Cambridge University Press, 1903), 7 (references to this book will hereinafter be included parenthetically in the text).

Moore also says that he means by 'good' a property (17). His terminology and his uses of inverted commas vary considerably. Tracking them would be a major task, and rather than undertake that I shall simply be guided by the context in interpreting him. For him, as for most writers on intrinsic value, the phrases 'intrinsically good' and 'intrinsically valuable' are sometimes used interchangeably, though with the understanding that the *theory* of intrinsic value extends to the notion of what is intrinsically bad. (This is sometimes called *disvaluable*.)

Moore is famous for his 'principle of organic unities': '*The [intrinsic] value of a whole must not be assumed to be the same as the sum of the [intrinsic] values of its parts*' (28; cf. 29, 152). He illustrates this with an aesthetic case:

> to be conscious of a beautiful object is a thing of great intrinsic value; whereas the same object, if no one be conscious of it, has certainly comparatively little value, and is commonly held to have none at all. But the consciousness of a beautiful object is certainly a whole of some sort in which we can distinguish as parts the object . . . and the being conscious . . . Now this latter factor occurs as part of a different whole, whenever we are conscious of anything; and it would seem that some of these wholes have at all events very little value, and may even be indifferent or positively bad . . . Since, therefore, mere consciousness does not always confer value upon the whole of which it forms a part, even though its object may have no great demerit, we cannot attribute the great superiority of the consciousness of a beautiful thing over the beautiful thing itself to the mere addition of the value of consciousness to that of the beautiful thing. (28)

I particularly want to bring out here two points whose significance Moore himself (among many others) seems to have missed. First, he is attributing intrinsic value to two radically different kinds of things: consciousness and, on the other hand, external objects, where consciousness is conceived as internal to the mind, or at least as having an element that is. Second, he is exhibiting an awareness that the value, even of a beautiful object, is comparatively little in abstraction from the consciousness of it and, thus abstracted, is 'commonly held' to be nil.[2]

This duality regarding what sorts of things are intrinsically good significantly contrasts with the view Moore held by the time he published *Ethics* nine years later. He says there that "it may, in fact, be held, with

---

[2] Cf. Henry Sidgwick, *The Methods of Ethics*, seventh edn. (London: Macmillan, 1907), 114 and Moore, *Principia Ethica*, 221–5. Moore says in one place that although "the mere existence of what is beautiful does appear to have *some* intrinsic value . . . Prof. Sidgwick was so far right in the view there discussed, that such mere existence of what is beautiful has value, so small as to be negligible, in comparison to that which attaches to the *consciousness* of beauty" (189).

great plausibility, that no whole can ever have any intrinsic value *unless* it contains some pleasure."[3] Pleasure, by contrast with paintings, is or at least entails a form of consciousness. He rejects, however, the ostensibly implied view that "intrinsic value is always in proportion to quantity of pleasure" (*Ethics*, 152; cf. 153). For, on the principle of organic unities, the addition of pleasure to a whole can reduce its intrinsic value; and (in a quite different formulation) he reaffirms this principle in the context (151–2). He also holds that

> whatever single kind of thing is proposed as a measure of intrinsic value, instead of pleasure – whether knowledge, or virtue, or wisdom, or love – it is . . . not such a measure; because it is quite plain that, however valuable any of these things may be, we may always add to the value of a whole which contains any one of them . . . *by adding something else instead.* (152)

His positive view concerning value and consciousness is that "it does seem as if nothing can be of intrinsic value unless it contains *both* some feeling and *also* some other form of consciousness" (153). (A similar view is found in Ross's *The Right and the Good.*[4])

There is one other element in Moore's conception of intrinsic value that I want to bring out before I present my own account. In responding to Frankena (in 1942), Moore says that

> if what Mr. Frankena means to assert is that the propositional function '*x* is intrinsically good' may be *identical* with the function 'the fact that an action which you can do would produce *x* is *some* reason for supposing that you ought to do that action,' then *one* condition necessary for the possibility of this being true is fulfilled . . . there is a two-way necessary connection between these functions . . . But nevertheless I think there is a *good* reason, if not a conclusive one, for doubting whether they are identical . . . Is it not possible to *think* that a thing is intrinsically good without thinking that the fact that an action within our power would produce it would be a reason for supposing that we ought to do that action? It certainly seems as if we can.[5]

The view Moore takes Frankena to attribute to him – roughly, an identification of the intrinsic goodness of something with the existence of a

---

[3] See G. E. Moore, *Ethics* (Oxford University Press, 1912), 148.

[4] See W. D. Ross, *The Right and the Good* (Oxford University Press, 1930), 86. In n. 14 of ch. 11 of *Moral Knowledge and Ethical Character* (Oxford University Press, 1997), I comment on Ross's view of the element of consciousness in the intrinsically good.

[5] G. E. Moore, "A Reply to my Critics," in Paul Arthur Schilpp (ed.), *The Philosophy of G. E. Moore* (New York: Tudor Publishing Co., 1942), 151–2. Note that in treating reasons for action as entailing the production of intrinsic goodness, Moore either presupposes that reducing such evils as pain is producing such a good or simply neglects to take into account that it is with intrinsic *value* rather than with positive intrinsic value alone that reasons for action are essentially connected.

reason for favorable action towards it – is important and represents one way (though not Moore's way) of explicating intrinsic goodness. A theory of intrinsic value should help us appraise this view, and I shall return to the question.

II Intrinsic, instrumental, and inherent value

I have emphasized that Moore attributes intrinsic value both to consciousness of a beautiful object and to that object itself. He also attributes it to such things as knowledge, virtue, wisdom, and love.[6] Aware that it is "commonly held" that a beautiful thing by itself has no intrinsic value, and wanting to do justice to the role of pleasure as an intrinsic good, he expresses sympathy for the view that pleasure is intrinsically good, and (as noted) he maintains that nothing can be of intrinsic value unless it contains *both* some feeling and *also* some other form of consciousness, though (in *Principia*) without suggesting that pleasure must be an element in the consciousness in question. It apparently did not occur to him that a beautiful painting "contains" neither form of consciousness. And consider the other elements in question. Knowledge, virtue, wisdom, and love need not contain any feeling, at least if this means that they can exist over an interval of time only if their possessor has some feeling during at least part of that time. Moreover, when they are not being manifested, they do not even entail the occurrence of any form of consciousness. Granted, all of them may have conceptual connections to consciousness. But nothing about them will sustain Moore's suggested view.

I believe that Moore has not done adequate justice to the data he himself recognizes and that a more fine-grained theory is required to account for them. I propose (as I have in earlier work[7]) that we take the bearers of intrinsic value to be concrete *experiences* on the part of individuals (in this paper I consider only experiences of persons, but I acknowledge the existence of valuable experiences on the part of non-persons). I cannot give a full-scale analysis of the notion of an experience (and will return to the notion), but what I want to say here may be clear enough on the basis of the rough idea that an experience (1) is an occurrent state of consciousness, such as paying careful attention to a painting, or a certain kind of unified set of events in consciousness, such as daydreaming about a vacation trip; and (2) has an object, at least in the sense of a content, hence is not merely

---

[6] See e.g. Moore's at least implicit ascription of intrinsic value to knowledge, virtue, wisdom, and love in *Ethics*, 152.

[7] In ch. 11 of *Moral Knowledge* I have discussed bearers of intrinsic value in some detail.

a matter of one's being awake. An experience cannot be what we might call a period of *empty consciousness*: something like an utterly blank moment in which one has a mere receptivity to stimuli but is aware of nothing.

I am taking the notion of experience central here to be internal in a sense implying that an experience *need* not have an external object, as it does in the case of something that is actually seen and is thus, in an external sense, visually experienced and also experienceable by others. The experience *as of* seeing the same object when one is only hallucinating would be internal and in a sense non-relational, since its occurrence is not even partly constituted by a relation to anything other than the person having it.[8] But suppose one is actually experiencing a symphony. Call this second case experience *in the relational sense*. If one has the latter, one has the former as what might be called its psychological base, but not conversely. It is apparently experiences in the internal sense that are the basic bearers of intrinsic value. This does not imply that enjoying a symphony cannot have intrinsic value. It surely does; the proposal is only that it has that value in virtue of its internal, experiential qualities, hence that what might be called *basic* intrinsic value is wholly experiential. Thus, silently enjoying reciting a poem to oneself would be intrinsically good; being pained at the thought of having cancer would be intrinsically bad. Hallucinatory experiences might also have intrinsic value on this view, and that possibility calls for comment. Before I address difficulties for the view I am proposing, however, let me develop it further.

How can the experientialist account of intrinsic value do justice to the value of a beautiful painting, which is not an experience? Isn't it good 'in itself', hence intrinsically good? The phrase 'in itself' has doubtless been misleading. I find it too crude to serve centrally in understanding intrinsic value. It plainly applies to the goodness of an intrinsically good experience: such an experience is not only non-instrumentally good, it need have no relational kind of goodness. But 'good in itself' also applies to things whose goodness is quite different, in ways I will bring out, from intrinsic goodness. Granted, since the non-instrumental goodness of a beautiful painting resides in its beauty and that, in turn, is consequential (supervenient, in one sense of that term) upon its intrinsic – in the broad sense of 'non-relational' – properties, it is very natural to think of the painting as good

---

[8] I have in mind 'concrete' objects; on some views, an experience of, for example, thinking about a problem or even hallucinating a painting requires being in a relation to propositions or properties. It might also be noted that on a content externalist view, certain experiences are not possible apart from the existence of external objects; but supposing this is so, those objects need not be, as it were, constituents in the experience, rather than suitable factors in the life, of the subject.

in itself. Moore and many others have apparently so conceived such objects and partly for that reason considered them intrinsically good. But here we do well to recall Aristotle. Among the pertinent points he made are these: that one good is more 'final' than another if we seek the latter for the sake of the former, and that *the* good is that which makes life 'choiceworthy'.[9] Surely we (properly) value (e.g. go to see, preserve, celebrate, etc.) beautiful paintings in order to *view* them, and indeed not *merely* to view them but to do so in a way that is aesthetically rewarding. Viewing them in that way yields having an aesthetically valuable *experience* (by which I mean one that is good from the aesthetic point of view, not one that is a good *object* of aesthetic appreciation, though that status is not ruled out for special cases). I take experiences having such value to be intrinsically good. I also take them to be 'more final' in Aristotle's sense than their objects.

A related point emerges when we ask how one should conceive beautiful paintings in relation to Aristotle's thesis about *the* good. Do they contribute to the ultimate choiceworthiness of a life simply by their physical presence in our environment or through our *viewing* them – hence visually experiencing them – in a way that is aesthetically good? Plainly they would not so contribute if we never viewed them or, on viewing them, never had a good experience in doing this or in experiencing anything else in which they figure.

Are beautiful paintings, then, just instrumentally good after all, say means to aesthetic enjoyment? One could call them *constitutive means*; for they are constituents in, and not mere instruments for attaining, such enjoyment. But the term 'means', used by itself, is highly misleading. They are not means in the ordinary, instrumental sense implying a non-constitutive, contingent role in bringing about the intrinsic good in question. They are, in Moorean terms, part of it. We cannot have the pleasures of reciting Shakespeare's sonnets without reciting them. We *can* produce heat in our homes by various alternative means.

A useful term to employ in reference to objects that are good in themselves is 'inherent value'. C. I. Lewis called inherent values those

> which are resident in objects in such wise that they are realizable in experience
> through presentation of the object . . . The value in question is one which is

---

[9] Aristotle says, "We call that which is pursued as an end in itself more final than an end which is pursued for the sake of something else" (*Nicomachean Ethics*, trans. Martin Ostwald (Indianapolis: Hackett, 1962)). Cf. Terence Irwin's translation, second edn. (Indianapolis: Hackett, 1999), which uses 'complete' in place of 'final'. I take Aristotle to be referring not to mere pursuit but to a kind that is 'proper'. The idea of the 'self-sufficiency' of happiness (the good), in virtue of which it makes life choiceworthy, is explicit in 1097b.

found or findable in the object itself. . . in the sense of being one which is disclosed or disclosable by observation of this object and not by examining any other object.[10]

By contrast, he saw "intrinsic value [as] attaching exclusively to realizations of some possible value-quality in experience itself" (389; cf. 390–1). He called this realization the only "ultimately good thing" (390) and went on to advance the experientialist view that "what is *ultimately* desirable is not merely that this object and this property of it called its beauty should exist, but that this beauty of it should illuminate the experience of some beholder" (391).

Lewis does not give a detailed account of intrinsic value or, especially, inherent value. I make no claim to be giving an interpretation of his view; but I find the term 'inherent value' useful, and I want to clarify the notion I have in mind.

First, I seek a wider notion than the one sketched by Lewis. We should allow that an experience of silently reciting a poem can be intrinsically good; but this is not a case of observation. I suggest that we conceive an inherently good thing more broadly, as roughly one such that an appropriate experience of it is intrinsically good. There are many kinds of appropriateness. A mere visual experience of seeing a beautiful painting need not be intrinsically good; some aesthetic appreciation is normally required. A mere walk on a beautiful beach may be dull; a zesty one graced by mild temperature and a fresh breeze may be delightful. And an aesthetic appreciation of a silent poetic recitation can be intrinsically good even if there is no external object thereof.

More must be said to explicate appropriateness (more, unfortunately, than can be said here), but a necessary condition is that an appropriate experience of an inherently good thing be an experience of a suitable subset of its intrinsic properties (though not necessarily of all or only the intrinsic properties of it). This conception suggests that inherent value has at least a great deal in common with what are usually called secondary qualities. But if we take it to be such a quality, we must note that there is no implication that inherent value properties are not 'in' the object. Indeed, they are non-relational, and in that sense intrinsic, properties; but their constitutive manifestations, like those of colors, entail relations to living things.

I also want to allow, as Lewis might not have, that what is intrinsically good can *also* be inherently good. How can this be if the bearers of intrinsic

[10] C. I. Lewis, *Analysis of Knowledge and Valuation* (La Salle, Ill.: Open Court, 1946), 391 (Lewis makes no reference to Moore in the context).

value are experiences? Surely there can be intrinsically good *second-order* experiences. Suppose I view with pleasure my own enjoyable silent recitation of a poem. May I not be taking pleasure in the contemplation of the enjoyable experience, happily noting that I seem to be getting intonations that are difficult to capture? Granted, this could be argued to be not an experience of reflecting on another experience, but simply a complicated first-order experience. It is, however, a reflective experience in which one thinks about a present experience, whereas the recitation (for most poems) involves no such thoughts. This difference in content would seem to warrant countenancing two different experiences; and the content of the former apparently warrants considering that experience second-order.

Perhaps, moreover, we may go further and allow that I can experience, for instance, *your* pleasure in singing a song you audibly delight in singing. If I can, then the intrinsically valuable first-order experiences of *others* can also have inherent value for me: my experience of your pleasure can be intrinsically good. To be sure, I must experience your pleasure through its expression in your behavior; but there is a sense in which I see your pleasure *in* that conduct as well. We may thus take 'inherently good' to apply to certain intrinsic goods constituted by various kinds of first-order experiences. The case also illustrates a kind of relativity possessed by inherent, as opposed to intrinsic, goodness. The latter is experientially realized in the life in which it occurs; the former, though good 'in itself', is realizable in intrinsically good experiences only on the part of beings who can appropriately experience it. Not everyone can enjoy atonal music or abstract art.

The general idea suggested by these reflections is that something is inherently good provided that an appropriate experience of it is intrinsically good, and it is inherently bad provided an appropriate experience of it is intrinsically bad, where the range of appropriate experiences is limited to those that are responses to certain of its intrinsic properties. (These will include at least some of the properties of the thing in question on the basis of which it is plausibly considered good or bad in itself.) Which properties are crucial is, in a certain way, relative to the kind of value in question. If the value is aesthetic, then the appropriate experience must include some sense of the object's aesthetic properties (or at least those they are grounded in). If the value is moral, the experience must similarly include a sense of morally relevant properties, such as harming or helping. If the value is philosophical, the experience must include considering conceptual or other 'intellectual' properties. And so forth. In the light of the kinds of properties in question, an experience may be aesthetically good or bad, morally good or bad, and so on for other kinds of value. An experience of certain harmonious sounds, for instance, can be aesthetically good; an experience of being tempted to cheat can be morally bad, say shameful.

There is another part of my characterization of inherent value that needs comment. Suppose *A*, a bully, maliciously gives *B*, who is timid and much smaller, an unprovoked sharp slap in the face. I want to call this deed inherently (morally) bad. One appropriate experience in response to it is indignation. Is the experience of indignation in such a case intrinsically bad? It is likely to be both unpleasant and morally distressing. Equally important, perhaps, one might quite reasonably prefer that it not have been called for. On the other hand, it is a response that we are glad an observer has in such a case. Our positive attitude toward it is a clue to its status. Perhaps we should say that the response may be, overall, both inherently good and intrinsically bad. As an experience, it may be intrinsically bad overall (though it need not be, depending on the mix of distress and, say, felt righteousness); but in the circumstances, it is good *that* we have it: our having it is a state of affairs that is inherently good and can be viewed, and in that sense experienced, with moral satisfaction.

Similarly, suppose that *A* sadistically teases *B* and greatly enjoys this. *A*'s experience is intrinsically good, at least hedonically; *B*'s experience, let us assume, is one of suffering and is intrinsically bad. Still, the overall concrete event, *A*'s enjoying sadistically teasing *B* and thereby causing *B*'s suffering, seems inherently bad. We properly tend to feel *at least* displeasure, and perhaps a kind of moral repugnance, in the contemplation of it; and its inherent badness can provide sufficient reason to intervene. To say that it *provides* a reason is not to say it *constitutes* a reason; I take providing a reason to entail the existence of a reason, usually either by having the reason as its content, as with desires and intentions, or by virtue of something quite evident in the context, as where it is obvious that intervening would prevent the bad thing from coming to be. Here what constitutes the reason is (generically) the fact that the action would prevent the suffering in question.

III Intrinsic value, inherent value, and organic unity

This case of taking pleasure in someone else's suffering can be used to help in motivating another principle concerning value, inherent as well as intrinsic. Why is displeasure in experiencing a sadist's action and its effect appropriate? And why is it so even if the sadist's pleasure is very great and the suffering in which it is taken is only slight? It seems to me very plausible to say that this pleasure *ill befits* its object; there is a basic inappropriateness in taking pleasure in someone else's suffering – the more so if one is causing it. It is thus appropriate to be displeased upon experiencing someone's taking pleasure in someone else's suffering. On my view, even if the pleasurable experience of the sadist is intrinsically good, it may be inherently bad. I think that (depending on the details) it almost certainly will be inherently bad, even if the pleasure is quantitatively greater than the suffering the sadist causes. For the pleasure has an inappropriate kind of object; and accordingly, an appropriate second-order experience of that pleasure is *intrinsically* bad in the relevant way.

Why is it that suffering is an inappropriate kind of object of pleasure? There is much room for theory here. One answer available to those who countenance intrinsic value and connect it with objective reasons for action in the way Moore and many others do is as follows. Consider the point that there is a basic reason (though not necessarily an undefeated reason) for action to realize or continue the pleasurable thing, whereas there is a basic reason (though not necessarily an undefeated one) to avoid or extinguish a painful or unpleasant thing. Taking pleasure in causing or even observing someone else's suffering, then, provides a reason for producing or sustaining something that there is reason to avoid. The kind of experience in question has properties with opposing valences: one kind, we might say, calls for realization, the other for avoidance. There is no contradiction here, but there is a kind of axiological incoherence, at least on the assumption of the objectivity of the kinds of reasons in question.[11] This in part accounts for the intuition that such pleasure ill befits its object. If we extend this idea, it can be applied to taking pleasure in *thinking* about causing someone suffering. Envisaging or imagining suffering is still a case of having before the mind something of negative valence and taking a positive (non-instrumental) attitude toward it. It mirrors, in a sense, the enjoyment of actual sadistic conduct.[12]

I am suggesting that sadistic pleasure is (perhaps with special exceptions) inherently bad in part on the basis of its intentional object, the kind such

---

[11] That pleasure and pain (whether actual or in prospect) provide, as Moore thought, objective reasons for action is of course controversial; I assume it in this paper, but have argued for it in detail in *The Architecture of Reason* (Oxford University Press, 2001), esp. chs. 4–6. Cf. *Principia Ethica*, where Moore says, "when I talk of a thing as 'my own good' all that I can mean is that something which will be exclusively mine, as my own pleasure is mine (whatever be the various senses of this relation denoted by 'possession') is also *good absolutely*; or rather that my possession of it is good absolutely . . . everyone else has as much reason for aiming at it as I have myself" (99).

[12] The attitude must be non-instrumental to rule out cases in which one takes pleasure in someone's suffering because it is a means to, for example, the person's recovery from depression or a cleansing penance for a wrong.

pleasure has even if the sadist only mistakenly thinks the other person is suffering or, somewhat similarly, is taking pleasure in the mere *thought* of someone's suffering. I am not assuming, but am allowing, that, overall, the pleasure is also intrinsically bad. It may seem that it *must* be so at least where the suffering caused is greater than the pleasure taken in causing it. But perhaps it need not be so in special circumstances, such as causing suffering in administering deserved punishment, as where the jailer – within limits – takes pleasure in causing the pain that an unrepentant violent criminal feels in being locked up. In any event, the *intrinsic* value of the pleasure cannot be decided on the basis of how much suffering the pleasurable action causes; for in that case we have an experience with an external effect: the having of that object is a relational property of the experience, whereas I am assuming, as Moore and others have, that the bearers of intrinsic goodness have it in virtue of at least one of their non-relational properties. The complex consisting of an experience and its external effects can have inherent but not intrinsic value.[13]

The sorts of cases we are considering make it natural to posit Moore's principle of organic unities. I prefer, however, a broader formulation that specifies parts *or aspects* of the bearer of value. I also think that the resulting principle should be applied to inherent as well as intrinsic value. Recall the sadist's taking pleasure in someone's suffering. Even if the pleasure is much greater than the suffering, the inherent value of the complex whole can be negative, illustrating that the inherent value of the whole is not the 'sum' of the inherent values of the 'parts' (I assume that these are the only parts, or the only relevant ones, and that the relevant notion of a sum is not strictly quantitative).[14]

As to the case of intrinsic value, we can speak of one aspect of the experience of pleasure in someone's suffering as the pleasant quality of the experience and of another as its content, in the sense of its being directed

---

[13] If one wonders how a relational experience, such as pleasure in a symphony, can have intrinsic value at all, given that the symphony is not intrinsic to its internal side, two points should be stressed: first, the symphony *is* intrinsic to the experience qua *relational*; but, second, the internal side of that experience is also intrinsic to it, and it is in virtue of this (which includes intentional content) that the overall experience has intrinsic value.

[14] The non-additivity claim in the principle of organic unities does not entail that there *cannot* be a case in which intrinsic or inherent value is additive. Consider two qualitatively identical experiences. Might we say that – provided one has a determinate value – the pair has twice that value? This would be important for the theory of rational action as well as for the theory of value. Extensive discussion of the principle and a defense of it are provided by Noah Lemos in *Intrinsic Value: Concept and Warrant* (Cambridge University Press, 1994) and "Organic Unities," *Journal of Ethics*, 2 (1998): 321–37. For criticism of the principle, see Michael A. Zimmerman, *The Nature of Intrinsic Value* (Lanham, Md.: Rowman & Littlefield, 2001).

at the suffering. We can now say that the pleasant quality of the experience is inappropriate to this content and that even if the former is intense, the *overall* intrinsic value of the experience is either negative or at any rate much less positive than that of an experience differing from it only in the pleasure's being taken in something neutral. The same point applies even if we suppose the person only mistakenly thinks the other is suffering and we hold all else fixed. It is important to see, however, that even if inherent badness is the only kind of badness possessed by these experiences, it may have sufficient magnitude to warrant the kinds of negative appraisals we require, for instance judging that such experiences are non-instrumentally bad and that one should avoid bringing them about.

Aesthetic cases more readily illustrate the organicity of inherent and intrinsic value. Consider paintings and poems. Both can have parts and aspects that have no inherent value, such as a blank white space in a painting, a certain rhythmic shift in a musical composition, and ellipsis marks in a poem. But the overall inherent value of these artworks may be very positively affected by such elements, so that the value of the whole is greater than the sum of the values of the parts or aspects. This can hold even if all of the parts and aspects are inherently good. Similar points apply to intrinsically valuable experiences. Consider a pause in musical work: as experienced in itself, it may be aesthetically empty but, as part of the overall musical experience, valuationally important.

IV   Some problems of specificatory incompleteness

An apparent difficulty for my view may seem to arise in the light of some important points made by Aristotle in the *Nicomachean Ethics*:

> Good is spoken of in as many ways as being . . . as God and mind; in quality, as the virtues; in quantity, as the measured amount; in relation, as the useful . . . Hence it is clear that the good cannot be some common [nature of good things] that is universal and single; for if it were, it would be spoken of in only one of the categories, not in them all. (1096a 24 ff.)

Following Aristotle, one might point out, as Peter Geach and Judith Jarvis Thomson have, that, contrary to the impression Moore sometimes invites, a thing cannot be just good.[15] It must be a good *F*, for some appropriate *F*, or good in a way, or good as a thing of a certain sort, and so on. Is Moore committed to denying this? I do not see that he is; in any case,

---

[15] See Peter Geach, "Good and Evil," *Analysis*, 17 (1956): 33–42; and Judith Jarvis Thomson, "The Right and the Good," *Journal of Philosophy*, 94 (1997): 273–98.

he *need* not be if, like many others (including me), he takes goodness to be a consequential property, as he seems to.[16] By this I mean roughly that things are good in virtue of other properties they have, in a sense of 'in virtue of' that implies (but is not equivalent to) the impossibility of two things differing in their goodness though they are alike in *all* their other properties. For intrinsic and inherent value, the relevant base properties are, in my view, intrinsic and, in some intuitive sense to which I shall return, 'descriptive'.

If this view is correct, then we might expect the context of a predication of goodness, especially inherent on intrinsic goodness, to indicate the relevant kind of thing.[17] Call this a *value-anchoring kind*, since specifying it anchors the use of 'good' in question. The ascription 'She is good' implies goodness as a person in one context, goodness as an athlete in another; 'Beautiful paintings are among the good things in life' implies that viewing them is (intrinsically) good; and so forth. When we know what kind of thing is being called good and what kind of goodness is attributed to it, we can begin to figure out what sorts of experiences of it are intrinsically good and what sorts of qualities it must have to yield those experiences.

If, however, the bearers of intrinsic value are experiences, don't we need to make sense of the locutions 'a good experience' and 'a bad experience' even apart from any context? Not entirely apart from any context, for there are at least two commonly accepted constraints on a theory of intrinsic goodness – and perhaps on any normative discourse embodying notions of intrinsic goodness – that can help us here. First, it must be clear how what is properly thought good in itself (whether intrinsically or inherently) can contribute to making life choiceworthy. Second, and related to this, it must be clear that what is intrinsically good can provide reasons for action. This is not to say that the goodness itself *constitutes* a reason; what constitutes a value-based reason for action is typically, and perhaps will always be, something connecting the action with that in virtue of which the relevant experience is good (or bad), say the fact that doing the thing

---

[16] Moore's term for 'consequential upon', at least in what I believe is his last published essay on intrinsic value, is 'depends on'. He says, for example, that whether and to what degree anything possesses intrinsic value "depends *solely* on the intrinsic nature of the thing . . . anything *exactly like* it, must, in all circumstances, possess it in exactly the same degree." See "The Conception of Intrinsic Value," in G. E. Moore, *Philosophical Studies* (Patterson, NJ: Littlefield, Adams, 1959), 265 (originally published by Routledge & Kegan Paul in 1922).

[17] Indeed, if the consequentiality of goodness is a priori and necessary, a thing absolutely cannot be just good, rather than good by virtue of being something else, whereas it is not a priori that a thing can't be (say) yellow but not in virtue of anything else true of it (this does not hold for all descriptive properties, such as being colored, since it is a priori that a thing cannot have this property except in virtue of having a specific color property). I am not sure whether Moore noticed this contrast.

in question will be enjoyable.[18] I take a choiceworthy life to be (roughly) one constituted by a favorable balance of good experiences relative to bad ones.

Moreover, I take it to be a non-contingent and probably a priori truth that the fact that an experience would be intrinsically good provides a reason – some reason, at least – to seek it (in a very wide sense that can include trying to bring it about for someone else) and that the fact that an experience would be intrinsically bad provides a reason for avoiding it. More specifically, the kinds of qualities of experiences in virtue of which they are good or bad experiences – most obviously being enjoyable or painful – constitute grounds for desire and thereby for action. Is there, then, reason for the sadist who would enjoy torturing a terrorist to death to do so? If we keep in mind that there can be a reason that is defeated by the presence of better reasons for something else, I believe we should answer affirmatively. How such a question is to be decided will be addressed in Section VI.

Countenancing things that are inherently good but not intrinsically good can be seen to cohere with this partial account of intrinsic goodness. There is, for instance, non-instrumental reason to preserve a beautiful painting because it is a potential constituent in an intrinsically good aesthetic experience of it. The account is also sufficiently pluralistic to accommodate the variety of inherent and intrinsic goods we should countenance. For each inherent good, we can imagine intrinsically good experiences in which it is a constituent; and each such experience grounds reasons for positive action regarding the inherently good thing.

To be sure, if, in requiring a specification of the kind of object said to be good – the specification of a value-anchoring kind – as a condition of the intelligibility of predicating intrinsic value, one seeks to *reduce* the predication to a 'descriptive' statement, then my view may not be

---

[18] I am again allowing that an intrinsic good might 'provide' a reason without *constituting* one. Suppose, for example, that we adopt T. M. Scanlon's "buck-passing" view of goodness and value (hence presumably of basic reasons for action as well), on which reasons are constituted by the specific things in virtue of which something is good – say, being enjoyable – not by its goodness as such. See *What We Owe to Each Other* (Cambridge, Mass.: Harvard University Press, 1998), esp. 95–100. We can still speak, however, of intrinsically good experiences as providing the reasons, though in *virtue* of their grounds, such as pleasurable qualities of experience. We could also distinguish between elements' directly and indirectly constituting reasons and between specific and general reasons. I might do a thing because it is good even if I think it is good only *because* of some particular property of it. Suppose, moreover, that I do it only because, entirely on your testimonial authority, I believe it will be good. It would appear that even if I would pass the buck to you given an enquiry into the status or basis of my reason, my generic reason – to do something good – is where the buck stops for me. To be sure, it stops there *on* your authority, but that does not make my reason *doing what you suggest*.

accommodating. A good knife may be simply one that cuts certain things easily and retains its edge through multiple uses, but it is not at all clear that a good person is simply (say) one who performs certain tasks efficiently and tries to help, and never to harm, others (this gains some plausibility, however, if we take 'help' and 'harm' to be richly normative terms, as where helping people is understood to imply contributing to their moral well-being). Perhaps 'good knife' admits of a descriptive, if vague, analysis; but 'good person' surely does not. If we distinguish between *reductive* and *identificational* uses of phrases in which 'good' is anchored by a specification of the relevant kind, then, for ascriptions of intrinsic and inherent goodness, my account welcomes the latter uses but makes no commitment to the former.

If predications of goodness are intelligible only relative to some value-anchoring kind, are they also implicitly comparative, and might they be analyzable in terms of comparative, perhaps even 'descriptive', statements? Granted, *knowledge* of intrinsic goodness may require comparing the thing in question with other things of the relevant kind, or at least a readiness to make such comparisons. But it does not follow, and I think is not true, that the attribution of intrinsic goodness is equivalent to a comparison of the thing with others or, especially, to a ranking of it in relation to them on the basis of some descriptively specifiable property such as efficiency in producing a certain effect. One can know an experience of a beautiful painting to be intrinsically good without being committed to this experience being, say, at least as enjoyable as most of one's pleasurable experiences of viewing paintings.

There is another kind of incompleteness we must consider: 'evaluative incompleteness'.[19] Consider someone's experiencing pleasure. How should we evaluate such an experience? If, as hedonists and others hold, pleasure is intrinsically good, it would seem to follow that we must call this experience intrinsically good; but, as we saw, the pleasure may have an object which pleasure ill-befits.

It is useful here to view intrinsic goodness on the model of prima facie duty as understood by Ross. Consider promising. If all I know is that you promised to do something, I am not entitled to infer that you ought (in

---

[19] See Michael Zimmerman, "Evaluatively Incomplete States of Affairs," *Philosophical Studies*, 43 (1983): 211–24, and *The Nature of Intrinsic Value*. He says in the latter, regarding the state of affairs, John's being pleased at time t, "Is there *any* reason to think that contemplation of a state of this form as such requires that you favor it? ... If it occurs in virtue of a state of the form [John's being pleased at Mary's pain] ... What reason is there to think that *anything* good has happened?" (145). Here intrinsic goodness is "defeated."

the sense of final obligation) to do it. But surely I can know that you
have a prima facie obligation, in a sense that implies final duty if no set
of other duties overrides this one.[20] In this sense, we might say, promising
is *intrinsically obligating*. Similarly, suppose I can tell that you are taking
pleasure in something, but I do not know what it is. May I not infer that
there is something *intrinsically good* (good-making) in your experience,
indeed something such that, if nothing in or regarding your experience
defeats this good, the experience is, in an overall way, intrinsically good? I
think so; and if this is so, then just as promising is intrinsically, though not
necessarily *finally*, morally obligating, pleasure is intrinsically normative –
since it is *good-making* – and, where its value is not overbalanced by some
other element(s) in or regarding the experience to which it belongs, renders
that experience intrinsically good overall. Moreover, pleasure, like moral
obligation, is 'practical' in implying a reason for action.

We now face another question. Why should we not say that pleasure is
only prima facie good? Let me make two points about this.

First, we *may* say that pleasure is prima facie good, so long as we take
prima facie goodness to be a kind of intrinsic goodness: the pleasure
cannot fail to be good qua pleasure, even though the whole of which it
is an aspect can fail to be intrinsically good, just as an action cannot fail
to be obligatory qua promised even if other facts about it prevent it from
being obligatory on the whole. This kind of defeasibility does not imply a
relational status; that pleasure does not necessarily make the experience it
characterizes intrinsically good *overall* does not imply that the pleasure itself
is good only in relation to something else, *or* only when certain conditions
are met.

One way to see this point about pleasure is to note that we recognize,
as a basic reason for performing an action – even if a defeated reason –
that one will enjoy it. Another way is to note why it is that we do not look
favorably on pleasure on the part of a malicious person who in no way
merits it (here I vary a well-known example Kant used in the *Groundwork*).
The best explanation of this is that we take the pleasure to be a good the
person should not have. The explanation of this, in turn, is not, or not
only, that the pleasure itself is inherently bad; we might think the person
should not have it even if we believe that the pleasure is not the kind that
ill befits its object. Virtually regardless of the object, we take the pleasure

---

[20] I have argued for this in "Moderate Intuitionism and the Epistemology of Moral Judgment,"
Ethical Theory and Moral Practice, 1 (1998): 14–34. For a treatment of Ross's analogy between
goodness and prima facie duty, see Lemos, "Organic Unities" (I take Lemos's defense of intrinsic
value here to be at least largely compatible with my response to the analogy).

to be a good that the person should not have.[21] More specifically, the state of affairs, that malicious person's having it, is (as indicated earlier) virtually always inherently bad. Pleasure can ill befit its possessor, just as it can ill befit its content.[22]

The second point is that the experientialist theory of value I am proposing is not as such committed to taking any particular kind of experience to be intrinsically good *overall*. It may be combined with the view that the overall intrinsic goodness of an experience cannot be determined until its relevant content, particularly its phenomenal and intentional properties, is taken into account. Overall intrinsic value would then be what Ross calls a "toti-resultant attribute."[23]

A complication here is that individuation of experiences is no easy matter. If I read a beautiful poem while hearing crude, ugly music, am I having a single, mixed experience or two experiences, a good literary one and a bad auditory one? There is no simple way to determine plausible criteria here, but that is not crippling. We can say that there is one experience with good and bad qualities and seek to determine its overall value, or we can countenance two simultaneous experiences, one good and one bad. On the latter alternative, we can ask whether the person's experience is *overall* (intrinsically) good or bad. This is not to posit additivity of intrinsic value and abandon organicity but to recognize a kind of *combinability* of the separate intrinsic values of experiences over moments of life. Such combination is something we must reckon with in any case to assess how good a life is.[24]

---

[21] I say 'virtually' rather than always to allow for the possibility that such people of bad character might take pleasure in the thought of doing things to make amends for their past wrongs and to improve their character. But if we are happy to see them have this kind of pleasure, it seems in part because we take it to show at least that they have enough decency to look with pleasure on what morality calls for. Cf. Moore's view that "When I talk of a thing as 'my own good' all that I can mean is that something which will be exclusively mine... is also *good absolutely*. The *good* of it can in no sense be 'private'... The only reason I can have for aiming at 'my own good' is that it is *good absolutely* that what I so call should belong to me... which, if I have it, others cannot have" (*Principia Ethica*, 99). On the surface, this precludes Moore's holding that an experience of pleasure might be intrinsically good, yet I should not have it. But perhaps he could here invoke the principle of organic unity and claim that enjoying causing someone pain would not normally constitute my own good. In any case, my theory allows us to say both that sadistic pleasure may be intrinsically good, qua pleasure, but not good, considered overall, *and* that it may in any case be inherently bad. The latter point alone might imply that there is adequate reason to oppose it.

[22] In "Organic Unities" Lemos uses this kind of example to show that evaluative incompleteness does not undermine the view that intrinsic value (construed as encompassing inherent value) is organic. He notes that (on highly plausible assumptions) *S*'s being wicked, deserving no pleasure, and having none is, in itself, better than *S*'s being wicked, deserving no pleasure, and *having* it, even apart from the content of the pleasure. See pp. 330–1.

[23] Ross, *The Right and the Good*, 28.

[24] For a defense of the additivity of intrinsic value (once we have 'basic' intrinsic values to work with), see Zimmerman, *The Nature of Intrinsic Value*, esp. ch. 5.

One further point is appropriate here. My positive intuitive notion of a good experience has been partially explicated by appeal to the concept of the kind of experience that makes life choiceworthy. Is my account circular because I define 'intrinsically good' in terms of, in effect, 'intrinsically good life'? I am not giving a definition or analysis of 'good life' in any sense, as opposed to an explication (and I am willing to leave open whether Moore was right in thinking that there is a significant sense of 'indefinable' in which 'good' is indefinable). But one point to note is that if only experiences are intrinsically good, then one's life, not being an experience, cannot be intrinsically good, as opposed to inherently good. Still, this is only because a succession of experiences is not necessarily an experience. It is, however, in a broad sense *experiential*. We need a term for a good life or indeed for any desirable whole made up of intrinsically good experiences, or of a kind and proportion of them such that it is overall desirable to realize that whole. 'Choiceworthy' might do for lives, and perhaps also for sequences of experiences, say those constituting an evening. But it must be understood in terms of the things we intuitively take to be good, such as enjoyable social and aesthetic experiences. Another possibility is the term 'compositely good' (or 'compositionally good'); not all goods are such, and basic ones cannot be.[25]

It may help to draw an analogy to epistemology. The general idea is to explicate intrinsic goodness intuitively, in terms of experiences, as we do grounds of justification, and then to provide a way to use the notion to guide choice as we use the notion of justification to guide the formation and criticism of belief. Certain social, hedonic, and aesthetic qualities of experiences are the sorts of things for which we (rationally) choose to have experiences; the choiceworthy experiences are the kinds of thing for which we ultimately choose lives themselves.

V   The ontology of intrinsic value

Nothing I have said entails that intrinsic or inherent goodness is a non-natural property. If, however, they are consequential in the way I have suggested, then they are indeed properties, and thus a kind of realism is implied. This realism is of a special sort, however; for experiences of the kind that have intrinsic value are *mind-dependent*, or at least *life-dependent*.

---

[25] For support of the idea that we must rely on intuitive starting points in the theory of value and discussion of how overall value is to be understood in the light of those he chooses for his base clauses in a recursive value theory, see Thomas Hurka, "Two Kinds of Organic Unity," *Journal of Ethics*, 2 (1998): 299–320.

Hence there cannot be anything of intrinsic value in a world in which there are no persons – or minds or at least living things capable of experience.

By contrast, an *inherently* valuable thing can exist in an otherwise empty world. But there is a sense in which such a thing is axiologically unfulfilled. It is, to be sure, good 'in itself', as non-relationally and non-instrumentally good.[26] Inherent goodness is a significant status, but inherently good things do not *directly* provide reasons for action nor, simply as unexperienced inherent goods, contribute to the experiential goodness of any life. This is not to deny that a life in which one's friends flourish is better than a life experientially just like it in which one has the same evidence that they do, but is wrong. The former life is even better in itself – inherently. We could also call the former more choiceworthy if we are thinking of choosing in the light of knowing the important facts about each, including the error in one of them. Its inherent superiority makes it preferable in the contemplation of it; its entailing the realization of additional intrinsic value – which it does since the friends' flourishing entails that realization – provides an other-regarding reason to choose it over the alternative.[27] But for the person in question, neither life is better in the living of it. We can and indeed should insist that the point of view of the subject living a life is not the *only* one from which to make assessments of its goodness; but this does not require treating all non-instrumental goodness as intrinsic or taking the inherent to be as basic as the intrinsic.

What about Moore's idea that (the property of being) *good* is simple? Butchvarov has suggested that it is a generic property, presumably a determinable such as shape.[28] There are indefinitely many shapes, as there are colors. Are these determinable properties simple? There is a sense in which they may be: one does not define them (or the determinates under them)

---

[26] Arguably, we may say non-relationally *hence* non-instrumentally good. But suppose one makes a device for capturing emissions that do not and may never exist. Could we not say it is a good pollution-control device, where the goodness is plainly instrumental? We might reasonably rule that this is *potential* instrumental goodness and that actual instrumental goodness requires the existence (past, present, or future) of something to which the instrumentally good thing is a means. I cannot here explore the merits of the main alternatives on this matter; the contrast between inherent and instrumental value that I make use of is that the former, but not the latter, is strictly (presumably even conceptually) necessary for that to which it is a means.

[27] Suppose we know that creating something of a kind that has inherently good instances *could* not lead to anyone's having a valuable experience of it. Perhaps a painting could be created such that the attempted viewing of it immediately destroys it (nor does it have any other way of figuring in a valuable experience). Does it (as opposed to, for instance, the intrigue of producing it) provide any reason to create it? (If the impossibility is *logical*, of course, the thing in question is not inherently good.)

[28] For a detailed account of goodness along these lines see Panayot Butchvarov, *Skepticism in Ethics* (Bloomington, Ind.: Indiana University Press, 1986), esp. 63–6.

by genus and difference. Something at least highly analogous seems to hold for the property of being a good experience.

Shapes and colors, however, are apparently natural properties; why not, then, conceive value properties as natural? Moore said one thing on this score that impressed C. D. Broad and needs examination.[29] It is that there is a sense in which what we intuitively call natural properties are *descriptive*, and goodness is not. Insofar as 'fully' describing anything makes sense, can we not fully describe something that is intrinsically good without saying whether it is intrinsically good? This would seem so if, from our description, as with a description of a painting, it does not 'analytically' follow (as Moore could plausibly claim it does not) that it is good or that it is not good. For in that case we cannot be plausibly thought to have 'implicitly' described it as good or as not good. That will remain, in *one* sense, an 'open question'.

To look at the matter from the other direction, if I tell you that a painting (for instance) is good, have I even partially described it? One plausible reaction is that I have not; but another, perhaps as natural, is, 'You've described it as good, but now tell me more about it'. Still another is 'I know what sorts of things characterize a good painting; which do you have in mind?'

Pushing this line further, we might get something it is natural to call *normative disjunctivism*, the view that an attribution of a normative property is equivalent to an ascription of a disjunction of relevant grounding properties. If we suppose that for each normative property, there are certain natural properties on which, as a matter of conceptual truth, it is consequential, this view gains some support. The supposition also provides for a contrast with natural properties, since, so far as the notion of a natural property is clear, the counterpart point apparently does not hold for them. But must there be a definite list of base properties for each normative one? And, if not, do we, for any context of normative attribution, have a way to determine what base properties are implicitly ascribed? We need at least a theory of normative properties and a theory of kinds of description, and apart from such theories it is not clear how much weight to give to Moore's initially plausible claim that goodness is a non-natural property.

---

[29] Explicating Moore, Broad said, "a description of a thing can be complete even if it omits those characteristics of it which, though determined solely by its intrinsic nature, are not themselves intrinsic. E.g., a pleasant experience, which is also good, could not be completely described unless its pleasantness was mentioned. But it could be completely described without its goodness being mentioned. I find it most difficult to follow or accept this." But he does admit that goodness is a "derivative characteristic" ("Moore's Ethical Doctrines," in Schilpp (ed.), *The Philosophy of G. E. Moore*, 60).

There is something further we should note, something perhaps more controversial. It is not clear that the properties of being intrinsically or inherently valuable or, for that matter, any broadly normative properties, have causal power. Their non-normative base properties do. If this is correct – if, for instance, injustice's causing a revolt is a matter of the elements underlying the injustice doing the causal work, then the point may help to explain why normative properties are not plausibly considered natural or, perhaps, even descriptive.[30] (One might also take it to imply that they are not really properties at all.) But, one might reply, does shape, as such, have causal power, as opposed to the circularity, say, of a wheel's having it? One answer is that a circular thing may have causal power qua circular, where *being circular* is a shape property. Does injustice, for instance, have causal power qua normative property, say as a moral evil? The reality of moral intrinsic value, like that of other kinds of intrinsic value, does not self-evidently entail that *as* intrinsically valuable, such things have causal power.

If intrinsic value properties (of which the most generic are being intrinsically good, being intrinsically bad, and being intrinsically neutral) are natural properties, they are then certainly real. But surely they can be real without being natural, and they can perhaps be natural without being causal. I leave open whether they are causal, but I am taking them to be real properties. Are they, however, as Moore and others have thought, *essential* to their possessors?[31]

If intrinsic value properties belong to *experiences*, and if the (intrinsic) value properties of experiences are (necessarily) consequential on their phenomenal properties, then there is reason to take the former to be essential. For the phenomenal properties of an experience are plausibly considered essential to it. What about thought properties, such as silently reciting a certain Shakespearian sonnet? If these are not phenomenal, they in any event seem essential to the experiences that have them. But we again find difficulty regarding criteria of individuation. An experience of a painting in which I am conscious of a yellow patch in that painting is not of the same experience-type as one in which I am conscious of red in the same spot. Asked which color I like better, I might respond by saying I can answer only on the basis of experiences of each. Suppose, however, that a painting is designed to have that spot go from yellow to red with

---

[30] In "Ethical Naturalism and the Explanatory Power of Moral Properties" (in *Moral Knowledge*) I have explored in detail the question of whether moral properties are causal.

[31] For discussion of the apparent essentiality of intrinsic value see Zimmerman, *The Nature of Intrinsic Value*, e.g. 47–9; and Lemos, *Intrinsic Value*, esp. ch. 3.

each viewing. Then one might be inclined to speak of a single, changing experience of the painting rather than of two experiences differing in respect of the difference between yellow and red.

We might, then, speak of a *qualitative, fine-grained mode of individuation* and of a *coarse-grained, temporal unification mode*, the kind illustrated by the second case. In the second case, pragmatic factors may also enter in. If, for instance, we are concerned with viewing paintings, then even two viewings in rapid succession with only a movement of the head between them will yield two experiences; if we are concerned with how a person likes the experience of entering a newly decorated room, then a view of paintings, furniture, and rugs may count as a single experience.

In replying to his critics Moore said something quite pertinent to this question: that there is a sense in which pleasure is not intrinsic to an experience. For you and I can have the same experience of the taste of caviar and one of us like it, the other not. He does not, however, take up criteria of individuation at this point. Presumably pleasure is not intrinsic to any experience *non-hedonically*, say gustatorily, characterized, since any such experience could be enjoyed or not; but on a qualitative standard of individuation, pleasure is surely an intrinsic experiential property.[32] Indeed, he goes on to say that if we speak of an experience of being pleased by the taste of caviar, then the pleasure in question *is* intrinsic. Calling an experience one of being pleased is giving it a hedonic characterization. (Perhaps he is thinking of experience-*types*. Doubtless pleasure is not intrinsic to an experience-type unless it is essential to it, and pleasure is not intrinsic or essential to the type, tasting caviar. But Broad, to whom Moore was responding here, was presumably thinking of experience-tokens, as I am when I speak of experiences as the bearers of intrinsic value.)

A further point is that, plainly, to call an experience one of the taste of caviar is not to give a phenomenally 'complete' description (whether we speak of types or of tokens). Perhaps we can say that if a description of an experience (token) is phenomenally complete, it will include any hedonic properties the experience has, and if one of them is pleasure, then the token necessarily has that property, presumably in virtue of (another set of) its intrinsic properties. In that case, if a pleasurable experience is necessarily good, then its goodness is also essential to it.

---

[32] This would be denied by a proponent of the conative (intrinsic desire) theory of pleasure suggested by Richard B. Brandt. I have noted serious difficulties for that theory in "Prospects for a Naturalization of Practical Reason: Humean Instrumentalism and the Normative Authority of Desire," *International Journal of Philosophical Studies*, 10 (2002): 235–63.

Moore must have seen something we need not deny: we *can* specify a type of experience in a coarse way by specifying what its object is; and when we do this, we do not foreclose whether it is pleasant or not, since an experience even of, say, a backrub may not be pleasant. But this is quite compatible with saying that when an experience is pleasant, its pleasantness is an intrinsic property of it. For calling the experience one of a backrub is a coarse specification in terms of a single object (note that one can have an experience that is of both the taste of caviar and the sound of crude music, but we may refer only to the former if that is the *focal* object or is salient), whereas calling an experience pleasant is (in one way) a more fine-grained – and is a phenomenally more specific – characterization.

Inherent value properties might seem to admit of the same treatment as their intrinsic value counterparts. But there is at least one important difference. An inherently valuable thing can retain its identity across changes that alter its inherent value. A beautiful painting can be damaged without ceasing to be the painting it is; this is clear, at least, where it is fully restorable. If, however, we specify inherent value *given the exact (non-relational) condition of the thing in question*, then there is the same kind of reason for saying that the inherent value properties of a thing are essential to it as for saying that intrinsic value properties of a thing are. I do not, however, claim that it is clear that we *must* consider either kind of property to be essential.

VI The epistemology of intrinsic value

I will be brief in discussing the question of how we know propositions about intrinsic value. This is in part because I have addressed the topic in some detail elsewhere[33] and in part because my most important points are neutral with respect to the various plausible positions on the epistemology of value.

In *Principia Ethica* Moore made the sweeping claim that propositions about the good are all synthetic, and he clearly took some of them to be a priori as well.[34] Here again the concept of goodness as a determinable is a useful focus. There is some reason to think that the domain of determinables and their determinates is one where synthetic a priori truths occur. But do they? I doubt that anyone has shown that the proposition that nothing is red and green all over at once is either analytic or empirical, and the proposition that if something is square, then it is not round

---

[33] In e.g. ch. 11 of *Moral Knowledge* and in "Moderate Intuitionism."

[34] He said, for example, that "propositions about the good are all of them synthetic and never analytic" (7).

seems quite similar on this score.[35] Do we, however, know a priori that, for instance, pleasure is (intrinsically) good and that burning people to death is morally bad? We need a lot of experience to be in a position to know these things; the background knowledge needed, involving such notions as that of the intrinsically good and the morally bad, requires considerable conceptual sophistication. But arguably the required experience is only that needed to acquire the concepts and is not evidential. Could we know general propositions about value, say that pain is intrinsically bad, in the way we know empirical truths, such as laws of nature? I doubt this, largely on account of the different kinds of grounds appropriate to each; but I will not pursue the matter here.

There is another way to approach the epistemological issue. Suppose it is not only necessary but a priori that, as Moore held, between "the propositional function 'x is intrinsically good' . . . and the function 'the fact that an action which you can do would produce x is *some* reason for supposing that you ought to do that action' . . . there is a two-way necessary connection." Then, if we know a priori that producing pleasure is a basic reason for action, we may conclude by a priori reasoning that it is intrinsically good. This does not presuppose that the notion of a reason for action is more basic than that of the intrinsically good, though it is compatible with that view.[36] Indeed, we can treat both goodness and reasonhood as common consequences of the same supervenience bases, including pleasure and pain. For Moore, however, reasonhood implies intrinsic goodness; and unless he countenances moral goodness, he could not (as I would) take the fact that an act would be, say, a breaking of a promise or a deprivation of liberty as a basic reason for action.

Suppose, on the other hand, that basic axiological knowledge is empirical. If value properties are causal, or indeed natural in any sense, this would seem possible. Might one not still have a kind of intuitive knowledge of such propositions as that enjoying viewing a beautiful painting is intrinsically good? And might one not still be able to have non-inferential knowledge of some propositions attributing intrinsic value to experiences? I cannot see why these possibilities must be ruled out. It is not as if only a priori knowledge could be intuitive and non-inferential.

---

[35] This position is defended in ch. 4 of my *Epistemology*, second edn. (London: Routledge, 2003).

[36] This view is suggested by some (but only some) of what Thomas Nagel says in *The View from Nowhere* (Oxford University Press, 1986). See e.g. ch. 8, sections 5 and 6. A position further in the direction of taking rationality to be more basic than value is Elizabeth Anderson's view that "to be intrinsically valuable is to be the immediate object of such a rational attitude" (she refers to "love, respect, consideration, affection, honor and so forth"). See *Value in Ethics and Economics* (Cambridge, Mass.: Harvard University Press, 1993), 20.

Moreover, even apart from whether principles of practical reason can be known non-inferentially, the most important point here is that much the same ones may be retained as on a rationalist epistemology. I refer to principles indicating that there is reason to avoid pain, to seek pleasure, to weigh future goods on a par with present ones other things equal, to take account of probabilities in deliberation, and so forth. Thus, although I favor a moderate rationalist conception of such principles, I do not think that the kind of theory of intrinsic value I am developing requires it in order to sustain highly similar principles for guiding and appraising conduct. Those principles could also be retained if, instead of distinguishing intrinsic from inherent value, we took inherent value to be a kind of intrinsic value. Neither my preferred epistemology nor my proposed taxonomy interferes with the selection and defense of plausible normative principles.

VII   The intrinsically valuable as a basis of reasons for action

Suppose that there is a close connection between intrinsic value and reasons for action. More must be said to indicate how my account of intrinsic value may contribute to the general theory of practical reason. Let me first bring out the advantage of conceiving the bearers of intrinsic value as experiences rather than concrete objects or even such dispositional elements as knowledge and virtue.

I assume that reasons for action are always expressible in (though not only in) the kind of infinitive clause that indicates the content of an intention or follows 'in order to' in an explanation of action, as in 'I agreed to read the book in order to satisfy a long-standing curiosity'.[37] The contents of these clauses are apparently types of events, especially act-types, all of which are things that can be realized (and in that sense brought about). More important, if their being realized (tokened) in a certain way has intrinsic value, then – as indicated earlier – there is some reason for the agent to act to realize them, though the ascription of intrinsic value does not specify just what it is that has that value. Now experiences, like actions, admit of a type-token distinction, and to bring either one about is to token it. Might we not say, then, that experiences of performing actions are among the bearers of intrinsic value? Surely the experience of conversing, of singing, of swimming, and of many other actions can

---

[37] I argue for this view in ch. 5 of *The Architecture of Reason*, where I also suggest some contrasts between the propositional and infinitival forms of expression of reasons for action.

be intrinsically good. These often prominently include the experience of *producing* something inherently good, such as a fine poem or a beautiful sculpture.

To see how this idea is best understood, consider what it is to do something 'for its own sake'. This is to do it for qualities of performing it that attract us on their own account. These are always experienceable qualities; and there is much plausibility in taking the experience we have in acting, particularly in respect of these qualities, to be the bearer of any intrinsic good we seek in performing the action. If I want to satisfy my curiosity for its own sake, I want to experience the acquisition of the relevant knowledge, not merely to acquire it. To have a machine implant the relevant knowledge in me by brain manipulation while I sleep would not fulfill the particular desire I have. It is the experience of gaining the knowledge that I specially want, and if that experience is rewarding in a certain non-instrumental way, it will be intrinsically good.

In part, the general idea is this. If there is anything intrinsically good (or intrinsically bad), it provides a basic (if defeasible) reason for action to bring it about (or continue its existence, which is roughly equivalent to bringing about a later stage of the thing in question). Intrinsically good things should thus be the *kinds* of things that can be realized in the way the act-types (or at least experience-types), which are (or are specified by) the contents of reasons for action, can be realized. Experiences can be realized in that way; paintings, as opposed to the actions of producing and viewing them, cannot. If intrinsic goodness belongs to certain kinds of experiences, it can accordingly figure in the content of reasons for action, and intrinsically good experiences will figure centrally in the content of the most basic kinds of reasons for action: to enjoy a symphony, for instance, or to swim in cool waters, to talk with a loved one, or reduce the pain of a headache.

The suggested view of reasons is connected with the idea that the intrinsically good is that in virtue of which a life is choiceworthy. Surely a life is choiceworthy on the basis of the experiences that – as I would put it – constitute that life. Knowledge and virtue are, to be sure, good 'in themselves' – where that means *inherently good*. But would they make a life good apart from experience? In principle, a person could be created with a great deal of both, but in a deep sleep; if such a person ceased to exist before experiencing anything, would the person's life be good? Inherent goods provide non-instrumental reasons for action because of their constitutive place in intrinsically good experiences. This gives them incalculable normative importance. But their existence in itself, as opposed to the experiences we bring about in which they essentially figure, does not make anyone's life, as lived, better.

Might the *only* reasons for action be grounded in considerations of intrinsic value, for instance of pleasure and pain? Suppose this is so. It would not follow that the *notion* of intrinsic value, as opposed to that of something which *has* it, must come into the concept of a reason for action. Still, not only instrumental reasons, but also non-instrumental reasons deriving from inherently good things, might ultimately depend on a relation to what *is* intrinsically good or intrinsically bad. We can say this without treating the concept of value as a constituent in that of a reason for action. I do not want to presuppose, however, that all reasons for action are grounded in considerations of value. I leave open, for instance, that a deontological reason such as that a deed would be dishonest can provide a reason independently of intrinsic value (at least of non-moral intrinsic value).

I am supposing, however, that some experiences are *moral* and have moral intrinsic value. Moral reasons, then, need not derive from non-moral grounds even if they do ultimately depend on considerations of intrinsic value (including disvalue), and they can be a kind of basic reason for action. I have mentioned indignation; an experience of this emotion can be intrinsically good qua moral, as well as inherently good on the basis of its overall moral character, yet intrinsically bad hedonically. The *experience* of being done an injustice can be not only painful, and in that way intrinsically bad, but also (intrinsically) morally bad; and in my view even the felt attraction to doing an injustice is an intrinsically morally bad experience.[38]

To be sure, to say that some basic reasons for action derive from considerations of moral value leaves open whether all moral reasons for action so derive. I have said nothing implying that the good is more fundamental than the right, as it in some sense would be if all moral reasons derive from considerations of intrinsic moral value. But my view certainly makes that position intelligible and indicates some of the questions that must be pursued in appraising it.

One further matter needs attention to fill out my sketch of the connection between intrinsic value and reasons for action. Is there, in the domain of such reasons, an analogue of the organicity of intrinsic value? Recall the case of *schadenfreude*. If I enjoy teasing someone, I thereby have

---

[38] It is of course not self-evident that experience (or anything else) can have moral intrinsic value; that it can is argued in my "The Axiology of Moral Experience," *Journal of Ethics*, 2 (1998): 355–75.

a (normative) reason to do it; but if I am pained by (the experience of) causing someone else to suffer and believe that the person in question will suffer from my teasing, I thereby have a (twofold) reason not to do it. Now suppose that my pleasure will (quantitatively and qualitatively) outweigh her suffering. Do I thereby have better reason to tease her than not to? Not if, as is quite rational, I believe that pleasure taken in something that one knows causes pain as this does is unbefitting to its object in a way that renders the pleasure inherently bad. Experiencing such pleasure even in prospect is intrinsically aversive, say repugnant; this kind of experience provides reason to avoid realizing that prospect. Indeed, I do not have to believe anything this theoretical in order to have non-instrumental reason to avoid the teasing. As I have described the case, then, I apparently have better reason not to tease. Suppose this is so. Is it something I know by summation of the values in question? I think not.

Indeed, summation, so far as it is possible in a rough-and-ready way, would not work to give me a decision even apart from considerations of fittingness. We must use practical judgment to decide how to weight the good against the bad or, more generally, sets of positive against sets of negative intrinsic values. This is something Ross insisted on in connection with conflicts of prima facie duties. It applies to what we have overall reason to do, as well as to ascertaining what is intrinsically good overall.

If basic moral reasons for action depend entirely on things of intrinsic value, then the kind of organic composition of prima facie duties Ross saw as yielding final duty is to be expected. It might in fact be expected even if values play a lesser role in grounding duties, say because some duties are purely deontological. For instance, if there are duties of beneficence and also of self-improvement, each set concerns promotion of good things and elimination of bad ones in the lives of others or in one's own life. The best overall result will often be determinable only by taking into account the organicity of the values in question. Reading all afternoon might best promote my knowledge; helping a friend might best reduce his suffering; and there may be many other considerations pertinent to my decision regarding the same period of time.

Conclusion

The theory of intrinsic value sketched here is experientialist, pluralistic, internalist but not subjectivistic, realistic about values, and, in the way the most plausible kinds of intuitionism are, moderately rationalist about knowledge of certain propositions about value. It takes what is intrinsically good to provide basic reasons for action, but does not imply that every basic reason for action is grounded in intrinsic value. The theory is consonant with the idea that goodness – whether intrinsic or inherent – is unanalyzable, but it is not committed to that view. It is also consonant with the idea that value properties are not natural properties – so far as that idea is clear – but is not committed to that either. It is committed to the view that value properties are consequential on non-value properties. If these are properly characterized as natural or, as seems plausible, 'descriptive', value properties can be consequential on them whether or not they themselves are natural. Although a property cannot be identical with the set of properties on which it is consequential, it may or may not be of the same ontological kind.

How Moorean does all this make the position? This depends in part on how much significance attaches to distinguishing between intrinsic and inherent value and attributing, to many things Moore considered intrinsically valuable, inherent value instead. It also depends on how much significance attaches to avoiding Moore's commitment to non-natural properties. Another difference is that moral value is specifically posited by the theory I have introduced, but not by Moore's;[39] nor does Moore's view provide for basic deontological reasons for action. I have also broadened the principle of organic unities both in considering aspects of the valuable as well as parts of it and in applying the principle to the inherently as well as the intrinsically valuable.

Still another difference between my view and Moore's concerns the connection between the right and the good. He holds a kind of maximizing consequentialism. No such position follows from the theory of value I have sketched here (and I do not endorse it). It may indeed not follow from Moore's theory of value either, but the idea that the right is, in a quasi-quantitative way, derivable from the good is a major strain in his ethical thought.[40]

There is a great deal more that must be said to appraise the theory I have presented. The sketches of the relevant notion of experience and of criteria for individuating experiences need extension; the revised principle of organic unities and its application need further explication; and the nature of value properties and of their grounding in what seem to be

---

[39] I do not take this to be obvious. But given Moore's presentation of his utilitarian view of goodness and such remarks as that "so far as definition goes, to call a thing a virtue is merely to declare that it is a means to good" (*Principia Ethica*, 173), this is a plausible reading.

[40] In e.g. *Ethics*, Moore says that "the total consequences of right actions must always be as good, intrinsically, as any which it was *possible* for the agent to produce under the circumstances" (98).

natural properties is an unending philosophical problem. But I believe that at least if a cognitivist view is sound, then the kind of experientialist, pluralistic axiological intuitionism presented here is a major option for ethical theory.[41]

---

[41] This paper has benefited from comments by Stephen Barker, Panayot Butchvarov, Roger Crisp, Jonathan Dancy, James Dreier, Brad Hooker, Derek Parfit, Robert Stecker, Judith Thomson, and Mark Timmons, and from discussions at the Universities of Georgia, Memphis, Missouri, Notre Dame, and Oxford. In *Southern Journal of Philosophy*, 61 (2003 supplement) where this paper first appeared, Barker published a commentary immediately following my paper. My reply is in "Intrinsic Value, Inherent Value, and Experience," *Southern Journal of Philosophy*, 61 (2003): 323–7.

CHAPTER 3

The grounds and structure of reasons for action

We enter the world with a multitude of needs, entirely dependent on others, and utterly ignorant. But needs give rise to desires, experience remedies ignorance, and we learn to act on our own. Desire is essential for full-blooded action: nothing wanted, nothing done. Belief is also essential for full-blooded action,[1] but desire is a ground of action, in a way belief is not. For one thing, we act in order to fulfill desire, but not in order to fulfill belief. I will say more about this, but I want to begin by showing how even basic desires – those not grounded on other desires – can be grounded, and by comparing this kind of basis with that of their counterpart beliefs.[2]

I Experience, desire, and belief

Experience is the fabric of our lives. Life as *lived*, by contrast with mere biological animation, is constituted by experiences. This is largely why a good life is one in which good experiences, those having intrinsic value, predominate.[3] As we are naturally constituted, good experiences are central among those we want, though there is no particular description under which we must want them. In the content of our desires for things that are good, plurality reigns, and the good things we want need not bear that generic name.

It is clear that desires arise from experience, even if not solely from that source. Take an elemental case. The experience of eating a normal, satisfying

---

[1] It is true that if an action is basic for the agent (S), it may not be necessary for S to have a belief to guide it (though arguably S must believe at least something to the effect that to *A* one just does it – or does *this*). But for non-basic (intentional) action, some kind of instrumental belief seems required. This matter is discussed in some detail in my (1986a), pp. 511–46.

[2] My terminology may suggest to some readers that 'desire' and 'want' are normally used interchangeably. They are not; but the subtle differences between their uses will not cause trouble in my sometimes shifting from one to the other for stylistic reasons.

[3] The distinction between inherent and intrinsic value is developed at some length in my (2003a). This paper also makes a case for experientialism regarding the basic bearers of intrinsic value.

kind of food (particularly where one needs food) commonly produces a desire for the sort of experience in question. To be sure, before children can develop concepts adequate for desire – which has a content that is in some sense conceivable to the subject – they must go through predecessor states of discrimination. In these states, although children respond differentially to the different properties that their experience reveals to them, they do not apprehend the corresponding concepts.

There is no sharp distinction between these developmental stages. Consider a desire for, say, milk. This is distinct from a tendency to ingest it when it is offered; the desire requires at least a minimal concept of milk as opposed to other consumables. This kind of discriminative consummatory tendency may be a natural precursor of desire; but in either case, experience seems to be the most elemental (psychological) determinant of desire.

Given this picture, we can say that experience is a *source* and sustainer of desire and hence a ground of it in at least that genetic sense. But it is important to see *how* experience grounds desire. For it is possible simply to want to drink milk and have no reason for this, nor even any sense of why one wants it. Even a desire that is (at least ultimately) genetically grounded in experience need not be one for which the person has a reason.[4] But in normal cases of desire, we want the objects of our desire *for* something: either for qualities that are intrinsic to them (or that we take to be so) or for their contribution (or believed contribution) to something else we want.

My interest here is in the basic conative case: in what may be called *intrinsic desire*. This is desire for the wanted object *for its own sake*. Intrinsic desire is, roughly, wanting the object on account of its intrinsic qualities (or qualities one takes to be intrinsic to it – a qualification I will hereafter usually omit). Thus, we might want to converse for the stimulation we find in the exchange, to drink wine for its flavor, and to feel a soft breeze for its cool gentleness. There are two kinds of grounds important here: causal and normative. The experience of enjoying wine can produce desire to sip it, and in that (genetic and causal) sense can ground the desire. The experience apparently does this causal work *through* our consciousness of certain of its qualities. Those gustatory qualities are enjoyable (or perhaps in some other way rewarding). In virtue of our enjoying them, we tend to want to drink the wine. The appeal to enjoyment, then, can explain why we want to drink it. But surely experiencing these enjoyable qualities can *also* normatively ground our desire. Roughly, to ground it normatively is to support its rationality. This is easier to see where desire seems irrational

---

[4] This is argued in my (2002).

than in a case of natural, perfectly rational desire like wanting to sip wine for its enjoyable flavor. Imagine a man combing his hair with a brass clothes brush. Thinking he may be causing himself pain, we ask why on earth he wants to brush his hair with *that*. If he replies, 'It feels good – it relieves a terrible itch', we can see his desire as rational in the light of the qualities for which the action is (intrinsically) wanted.

Since belief as well as desire is essential for action, it is also important to consider the grounding of belief. The parallel between belief and desire is striking here.[5] It is plain that experience is a source of beliefs. "Seeing is believing," we often hear, and comparable points might be made for the other senses.[6] The parallel holds not only for causal grounding but also for normative grounding. Seeing lightning is a sensory experience, and it tends to produce (in those with concepts adequate for it) belief to the effect that lightning is occurring. Such beliefs, moreover, are rational on the basis of (and justified by) the sensory experience in question.

We might generalize. In virtue of certain evidential or, we might say, *truth-indicative* qualities of experience, beliefs are rational. There is, for instance, the flashing, jagged brightness of lightning, the roaring sound of a motor, the furry feel of a cat. Similarly, we might say that in virtue of certain *value-indicative* qualities of experience, desires are rational. There is, for example, the pleasantly tangy quality of sipped wine, the relief from heat that comes with a cool breeze, the sense of free movement and high muscle tone we can have on a mountain hike. As the examples suggest, the value-indicative properties need not indicate value as such; at least in typical cases, they indicate something *having* or *conferring* value. They do not directly point to the property of being valuable (if they point to it at all), but rather to something that has or indeed underlies that property. Believability and desirability, I suggest, and not just belief and desire, are (in the basic cases) grounded in experience.

II   The mutual irreducibility of practical and theoretical reason

For philosophers seeking understanding of a complex kind of thing, it is natural and proper to want the most economical account that does justice to the data to be explained. The more extensive the analogy between any two kinds of phenomena under investigation, the stronger the pull toward economy of analysis. In the case of normativity, must we countenance two

---

[5] I have discussed parallels between desire and belief in great detail in (2001), esp. chs. 3–6.
[6] This adage is critically discussed in some detail in my (2003b), ch. 1.

ultimately different dimensions, the practical and the theoretical? Could rational belief, for instance, be fully explicable in terms of rational desire or conversely?

Few if any plausible attempts have been made to reduce theoretical to practical rationality, and I will not address this possibility here.[7] But philosophers at least since Plato have been attracted to the idea that the will should be subordinate to the intellect. This idea may generate reductive efforts of two kinds, one causal, the other normative. First, one might argue that beliefs (or other theoretical attitudes) can adequately motivate action; second, one might argue that beliefs – or at least those that are justified – can render action rational. If these points hold, one might go on to argue for two reductive claims: that desire is not essential either for the performance of action or for its rationality, and that our practical rationality is a matter of the content and rationality of our beliefs.

The first, broadly causal claim has been associated with motivational internalism, which, in its most general form, I take to be the view that some degree of motivation to do a deed is internal to the judgment that one ought (on balance) to do it. That view as usually understood concerns moral beliefs rather than normative beliefs of all kinds, but the difficulties confronting it suggest why normative beliefs alone cannot account for all human motivation. I have elsewhere argued at length that they cannot, and I will not pursue the matter now.[8] But it is central to my purposes here to consider whether, *normatively*, belief is the basis of desire: specifically, whether the rationality of the former is the ground of the rationality of the latter.

If desire is essential to motivating at least some human actions (and my concern here is human action), then the theory of action must countenance desire, and there is less incentive to eliminate it in our normative theory. But the further question whether the *rationality* of desire is analyzable in terms of, or at least depends on, that of belief is important in its own right. Some of what I have to say about this will be implicit in the case to be made shortly for a difference in the kinds of objects of the practical and theoretical attitudes. But two points are appropriate immediately.

First, the analyzability claim is surely too strong. A desire to drink milk can be rational on the part of a child without the child's believing anything to the effect that drinking milk is good. Indeed, it seems likely that if, when we are conceptually capable of (rationally) believing drinking

---

[7] I have addressed the possibility in ch. 5 of (2001).

[8] Motivational internalism is assessed in detail, and much literature on the topic is considered, in my (1997b), which contains other papers pertinent to the subject of this one.

something to be intrinsically good, say as pleasantly refreshing, we do rationally believe that, this is very likely *on the basis of* enjoying it; and if one (rationally) believes it to be instrumentally good, this is very likely on the basis of enjoying (or suffering from the absence of) something to which one believes it is (in some way) a means. The point is also apparent in relation to aesthetic experience. I may enter a gallery not expecting to enjoy, and even thinking ill of, the unconventional works on display. Suppose I am surprised and I find viewing them intriguing and, after a time, enjoyable. This response can render rational *both* my wanting to continue viewing them and my believing they are good. I need no antecedent or concurrent belief that they are good to render my desire rational.

My second point concerns the cognitive dependency claim: the thesis that the rationality of one's desire depends on that of one's beliefs. There are two relevant kinds of normative dependency that are not always distinguished. One is negative, a kind of defeasibility, a vulnerability to defeat. The other is positive, a kind of grounding. Suppose I want to do something, say to sky-dive, for what I take to be its enjoyable qualities. This may be a rational desire, but its rationality (and certainly the rationality of wanting on balance to sky-dive, or of intending to do it) can be defeated by my discovery that the experience would only be unpleasantly dizzying. The normative ground of my desire is the anticipation of enjoyable qualities;[9] but its rationality negatively depends on what I do or should believe.

In this way, practical reason has a negative dependence on theoretical reason. A necessary condition for rational desire, then, is the *absence* of certain beliefs or of other 'theoretical' elements. But it does not follow and is not true that, for desires, practical rationality is *constituted* by possession of, or grounding of desire in, such elements. Defeasibility is a kind of necessary condition dependency; it is not a constitutive dependency.

This defense of the irreducibility and (qualified) autonomy of practical reason should be balanced by two further points, one negative, one positive.

First, theoretical reason does not have a like dependence on practical reason. The rationality of belief, for instance, is not comparably defeasible by the presence of even rational desires (not *comparably*, but possible in one way, since a belief that I do not want x could have its rationality defeated by the perceptible presence of a desire for x). Even rationally wanting to believe that *p* is false – for instance, that it is false that a loved one has

---

[9] Perhaps the relevant anticipation of an experience can serve as a normative ground for wanting it, only if I have *actually* experienced something I take to be appropriately similar, but I want to allow that anticipation, like memory impressions, can be among experiential elements that qualify as normative grounds.

died – cannot undermine the rationality of believing it; and rationally wanting *p* to be true, though it can lead to excusable wishful thinking that it is true, does not make that belief rational (I here conceive wishful thinking that *p* as believing that *p* because of wanting that it be true).

Second, on the positive side, even though belief is not required as a ground of rational intrinsic desire, belief *can* render even intrinsic desire rational. Believing that I would enjoy viewing the unconventional paintings can render rational my intrinsically wanting to view them. A belief can do this, however, only if rational, and its rationality in such a matter (where one has not experienced the type of thing in question) will normatively depend in some appropriate way on some experience relevantly similar to the kind of experience in prospect as an object of desire.

There is another source of reasons for resisting a reduction of practical to theoretical rationality and for taking the former to have a significant kind and degree of independence of the latter. If desire and belief, as paradigms of practical and theoretical attitudes, have different kinds of objects that, in turn, differ in the criteria for their appraisal, this would support (though it does not entail) the mutual irreducibility of practical and theoretical rationality. How this is so will become clear as we examine their objects. I begin with intuitive data and, in the next section, proceed to an outline of a theory of reasons for action.

Beliefs, but not desires, may be said to be true or false (I do not mean to rule out a third value here, for even if a belief is neither true nor false, there is no semantic impropriety, as there is with desires, in calling it true or calling it false). Moreover, where the objects of desires are one's own actions, then, as in the case of intentions, these objects are most naturally identified infinitivally: schematically, *to A.* Even where a desire is not for action, in English, at least, the subjunctive is preferable to the indicative for specification of its object. I have a desire *that you visit me* (not that you will do so), a desire *that my students prosper* (not that they will prosper), a desire that my concerns *be* (not are) heard by my congressional representative. These phrases are not used in a way that calls for assessment of what they express as true or false. That fact goes with the point that the attitudes themselves are never properly called true or false in the way beliefs are (a true intention is a *genuine* one, to be sure, but there 'true' contrasts not with 'false' but with 'apparent').

Intention should also be mentioned as a central practical attitude. If (in English, at least) the infinitive is not used to express the object of an intention, the subjunctive is the norm: I intend that there *be* plenty of food at my party, not that there *will* be. Granted, there is the stilted 'I intend that my children shall run my company after my death', but the sense of this is something like 'I intend to see to it that my children run my company'.

None of this is to deny that all of the attitudes in question are propositional in the wide sense that they are individuated by content in a broadly propositional way. For instance, intending to *A* differs from intending to *B* in the way the proposition that one *A*'s differs from the proposition that one *B*'s. As this suggests, the practical attitudes are *intentional* and their objects correspond to propositions in a way I shall soon indicate.

What sorts of things, then, do constitute the objects of desire, where 'object' has the content sense appropriate to propositional attitudes? Wanting the flower to be replanted to the left may be conceived as having the state of affairs, *the flower's being replanted to the left*, as object. I have long thought that the most natural generic category – though not the only category – to use in describing these attitudes is that of states of affairs, understood roughly as what is designated by certain kinds of descriptions of acts, situations, or occurrences that the desire represents and that may or may not ever be actual. Roughly, I am speaking of states of affairs in the sense in which (unless impossible or necessary) they may or may not obtain, just as (normally) the object of a desire or intention may or may not be realized. If I want to view paintings, the relevant state of affairs is (my) viewing paintings; this may or may not occur. The act-type in question may or may not be tokened.

The mention of an act-type here suggests a plausible direction in which we might go to achieve greater specificity. We might plausibly hold that the *basic* cases of intention and all cases of action-desires (desires to do) have act-types as their objects. These act-types are abstract enough to do justice to the many different tokens that can realize the objects, but are narrower than states of affairs conceived generically. We would say, then, that intending that there be plenty of food at my party is equivalent to some intention *to do*, say to supply plenty of food. That is plausible; but wanting may be wider: wanting to possess a painting, for instance, is not equivalent to wanting to do something. We need states of affairs or something similar to do justice to the object of that kind of desire.

One might think that since, in any of these cases of practical attitudes, the proposition that the relevant state of affairs does occur *corresponds* to the state of affairs and is true if and only if that occurs, we might simply speak of propositions and avoid complicating our terminology (and possibly our ontology). But whereas the proposition has truth value – presumably even before I act – act-types and states of affairs, when they figure as objects of intentions and certain desires, are instead viewed, at least by the agent, as *to be brought about*. The significance of this contrast will emerge in the next section, which concerns the structure of reasons, especially practical reasons: normative reasons to act.

III   Normative reasons

During the years when the controversy over whether reasons are causes raged, reasons for action were taken to be intentional attitudes or, not infrequently, desire–belief combinations of the kind Donald Davidson called *primary reasons*.[10] More recently, reasons have been taken to correspond with the *contents* of such attitudes. This seems a more natural view. The most basic specification – though not the only kind of specification – of a reason to act seems to be of the form of 'to x', where the infinitive clause is of the kind that follows 'in order' when an action is explained as performed in order to bring something about. The most basic specification of a reason for belief, by contrast, is of the form of 'that p', where p is a proposition.

It is true, however, that we can properly say, in answering 'What is your reason?' as applied to action, things with the forms of 'I want to . . .', 'I intend to . . .', and 'I believe . . .'. Recognizing this, I have distinguished, in earlier work, between *reason states* and *reasons proper*.[11] The former are intentional attitudes, the latter their contents (also often called their *objects*). Thus, asked for a reason for driving rather than taking a fast, comfortable train, I can say 'I wanted to take a great deal of luggage' or 'to take a great deal of luggage' or even 'I believed I had too much luggage for the train', or simply 'I had too much luggage'.

Often, citing the reason state is felt to be equivalent to citing the reason proper; but the former ascription is often preferable where one is uncertain, for instance unsure whether one was correct in thinking there was too much luggage for the train. If, as I suggest, we distinguish between reasons proper and reason states, we can leave open whether reasons in either sense are causes, though few would argue that the abstract contents of intentional attitudes are the right sorts of things to be causes.

Normative reasons may be practical or theoretical. The practical kind of normative reasons are broadly speaking reasons for action, roughly, reasons that favor performing some action and support the rationality of doing so. The theoretical kind are broadly speaking reasons to believe, roughly,

---

[10]   In Davidson (1963).

[11]   "Acting for Reasons" (1986a) is probably my earliest published work developing the distinction between reasons and reason states in detail.

reasons that favor believing some proposition and support the rationality of believing it. The remainder of this paper will suggest an overall conception of these two kinds of normative reason and connect it both with the sorts of normative grounding sketched above and with the different structures of the objects of the practical and theoretical attitudes.

One way to conceive practical reasons connects them with the theory of value. Speaking in quite general terms, we might say that a practical reason is (in good part) *a projection of something of value* (something good, if we simply treat reduction or elimination of pain or suffering as good): something of intrinsic value if the reason is basic, something of instrumental value if the reason is non-basic. Thus, someone might say that a good reason to go into medicine is *to reduce suffering*. I suggest we think of the phrase 'to reduce suffering' projectively and conceive *affirming* the reason, as in saying it is a good one (or, e.g., is one's reason for wanting to *A*), as *making* the corresponding projection. Such (sincere) affirmation does not entail having the intention to *A*, though it would naturally give rise to it. Practical reasons (roughly, normative reasons for action) are commonly expressed by rational desires, since these commonly project something of value. But not *all* desires express reasons; a sufficiently ill-grounded desire, say a hypnotically induced (non-instrumental) desire to be slowly burned to death, would not (though it might provide a *motivational* reason why someone lights a match in the absence of anything to be ignited).[12]

The notion of desirability (as applied to states of affairs) may be taken to be approximately equivalent to that of goodness, and it may help to describe the suggested conception of a practical reason as an invitation to view it as projecting something that is in some way desirable. Why speak of projection rather than simply of representation? A practical reason may be conceived as a projection because the agent (actual or hypothetical) sees the object as realizable in the future by *A*-ing. We could regiment and say that the projection must be correct (factual). But it is more natural to hold that if the projection is (sufficiently) plausible, it yields a good reason, and if not, a bad one. Where it is both plausible and correct,

[12] Indeed, even if an ill-grounded desire has a content that describes something of value, as where a hypnotically induced desire is for good conversation, it may not provide the agent with a normative reason for action. There *is* (normative) reason to pursue good conversation (on the plausible assumption that it is an intrinsically good thing), but not just any desire for it *provides* the *agent* with normative reason to pursue it. The agent may (say, because of narrow experience and poor education) lack an adequate conception of good conversation. A *merely non-instrumental* desire, moreover – one that is neither intrinsic nor instrumental – projects neither kind of value. When I have forgotten why I want to go to the backyard, but still want to and find myself doing it, my desire at the time points neither to any intrinsic good in the action nor to any good it leads to. This is supported by the arguments of my (2002).

we might speak of a sound reason. The reason is *provided* (expressed, carried, etc.) by a desire or intention; it is *grounded* – strictly speaking, its normative force is grounded – ultimately in the *good-making* properties of the relevant experience, for example pleasurableness. (For convenience I construe "badness-reducing" properties as good-making.) The projection is fulfilled, or realized, if the relevant experience occurs.

To be sure, the presence of one or more good-making properties of an experience allows that it have bad-making properties too. Hence, desire grounded in experience of one good-making property need not be rational on balance, and its object need not be good overall. (This projectivist notion of a reason does not depend, however, on the experientialist view that fulfillment of the relevant projection is constituted by the occurrence of an experience; the notion would apply to non-experiential states of affairs as well.)

By contrast, a theoretical reason, conceived as a normative reason for belief, is (in good part) a *representation of something as true*. Someone might say, for instance, 'That she always sneezes around my cat is a reason to believe she has an allergy to cats'. The kind of representation in question is apparently truth-valued and admits of justification. We might say that if it constitutes a basic (normative) reason for the subject, it is non-inferentially (prima facie) justified for that person; otherwise it is in some sense inferentially justified for the person.[13]

Again, we could regiment and say that the representation must be or express a fact, but we could also do as above. Here, however, the representation need not concern the future and, a fortiori, is not constituted by a projection into the future. It concerns how things are (or were); and it is grounded (strictly speaking, its normative force is grounded) in a *truth-indicative* property such as the sense of a hard, cool, smooth surface beneath one's fingers (as indicating glass). If the reason is factual (hence externally sound), and its relation to what it is a reason for is entailment, then the factuality transmits and the entailed proposition is true. If the relation is inductive, then probability, a "measure" of truth, transmits.

It is natural in speaking of propositional attitudes to talk as if they were relations to objects, and I will continue to do so. But my account of reasons can leave open the possibility of taking those attitudes to be properties of

---

[13] Two points will be clarifying here. First, I take it that a *merely* non-inferential belief – one that is neither experientially nor inferentially grounded – does not supply any theoretical reason. The case for this is similar to the case regarding merely non-instrumental desires and is outlined in my (2002). Second, I include, under 'inferential' construed broadly, any justification coherence might supply.

persons, projective or representational as the case may be. The attitudes would still be individuated in a fine-grained way, and the practical ones would still differ from the theoretical ones in the kind of content they have. On either the relational or non-relational construal of the propositional attitudes, having such an attitude puts the possessor in different functional relations to the world. Roughly, in virtue of beliefs we are disposed to make corrections as a result of certain sensory inputs and relevant inferences; and in virtue of intentions we are disposed to perform actions that, on our instrumental beliefs, will bring about the state of affairs represented in our projections. My account does presuppose some role for intentional psychological properties, then, but does not strictly require that these be relational.

IV Intellect and will and the functioning of practical and theoretical reasons

The proposed conceptions of the structure of reasons are highly consonant with a venerable idea that still has much to recommend it: the idea that the function of the intellect is to pursue truth, and the function of the will – the practical "faculty" – is to pursue the good.[14] Theoretical reasons at their best reflect how the world is – or even how all possible worlds are. Practical reasons at their best project how the world may be made better. There have been many versions of this idea, and there are numerous views about how intellect and will are related, including the famous Socratic doctrine that (baldly stated) knowledge of the good implies willing (or at least wanting) its realization.[15]

In contemporary philosophy, this conception of intellect and will seems to have reappeared in the view that belief and desire – and more generally the theoretical and practical attitudes – have different directions of fit to the world.[16] Roughly, beliefs and other theoretical attitudes (those with truth-valued objects) succeed (in an external objective sense) when they fit the world; desires and other practical attitudes (those with the kinds of objects intentions have) succeed when the world fits them (at least typically, the future world, but otherwise the world contemporaneous with the desire).

---

[14] As Aquinas puts it at one point, "The object of the reason is the true . . . the object of the appetitive power is the appetitive good." *Summa Theologiae* question 60, article 1.

[15] This kind of view survives in ethical theory under the name 'motivational internalism'. For a detailed appraisal and many references to relevant literature, see my (1997a), reprinted in Cullity and Gaut (1997), which contains several other papers bearing on motivational internalism.

[16] This version of the contrast is apparently due to Anscombe (1956).

The normatively central point here is that different standards of appraisal are appropriate. The point does not commit us to attributing any particular sort of content to either kind of attitude.

To be sure, true but unjustified beliefs, and similarly, realized but irrational desires, are not unqualifiedly successful. We might call them internally unsuccessful insofar as we think that despite their positive status in one respect – in virtue of the agent's being correct and getting what is wanted – they violate standards that the person accepts or, if sufficiently rational and adequately reflective, would accept. Still, we may contrast beliefs and desires at least in this: being *false* is clearly a kind of defect in beliefs, whereas being, even at all times, *unrealized* (and thereby arguably instantiating a counterpart of falsehood) is not a defect in desires.

What has generally not been noticed is that there is apparently a connection between the kinds of *contents* appropriate to the theoretical and practical attitudes and, on the other hand, their different directions of fit and, more broadly, their different functions as basic elements of intellect and will respectively. In spite of these differences between beliefs and desires in function and directions of fit, a number of philosophers have taken them to have the same kinds of contents – truth-valued ones – and many other philosophers have been at least casual about distinguishing these kinds of contents.[17] Perhaps it need not be argued that (de dicto) beliefs have propositional contents, in the sense of items that are true or false (we can leave open whether some kind of linguistic entity could serve here). But something must be said about contents of desires, intentions, and other practical attitudes.[18]

As I have stressed above, truth value may always (without semantic impropriety) be ascribed to beliefs, but never to desires. We express the content of desires using (primarily) infinitives or subjunctives, not indicatives: I can want *to* talk with you, or *that* we talk, but I cannot want that I am talking with you, or that I will talk with you, or even that it is true that I am talking with you.

There is a parallel set of data regarding theoretical and practical reasons, roughly, reasons for believing and reasons for action (or at least for desire). As suggested earlier, a reason for action is always expressible in a phrase

---

[17] Davidson, e.g., has taken intending to be a kind of belief. See his (1980). Others have supposed there are attitudes (sometimes called *be*sires) with the function of *both* belief and desire.

[18] In (1975) Hector-Neri Castañeda construed the objects of the practical attitudes as "practitions," which he contrasted with propositions as objects of the theoretical attitudes. Although I do not adopt his terminology (or his specific views on this issue), I have benefited from his far-reaching work on the ontology of the intentional attitudes.

of the form of 'to *A*' (or 'in order to *A*' where the action has occurred), where '*A*' ranges over action-types, though a reason for action may also be expressed in other ways.[19] A reason for believing is never so expressible. A reason *why* one believes might be claimed to be expressible in that way. A doxastic voluntarist might say, for instance, that it was in order to save his life that James believed he could jump across a precipice (where he *brought* himself to believe this to increase his confidence of success). But this apparently makes good sense only where we think of the 'in order to' as expressing a reason to *cause* or sustain the belief. That is a reason for action.[20]

The positive side of reasons for believing is more complex. If a reason for believing is conceived strictly, as expressible in a sentence of the form of 'My reason for believing that *p* is that *q*', then such a reason is always a proposition (or similar entity, such as, on one conception, a fact conceived as a true proposition). This is because *q* must express something believed by the speaker (assuming the overall statement is true). Moreover, if what is cited as a reason for believing *p* really is a reason for believing it, one can at least sensibly ask whether it supports (e.g., entails, explains, or probabilistically implies) *p*. There are, however, *grounds* for believing a proposition that are not reasons in the strict sense for believing it (though I do not mean to overstress this distinction, since the *proposition* that a ground obtains *is* a reason for believing a proposition the ground supports). Simply seeing a flash of lightning is a ground, not (I think) strictly a reason, for believing there really is a flash. We can call seeing it a reason, particularly if we are thinking of the point that once we *believe* we see it, we *have* a reason, in the strict sense, for believing there is lightning: namely, the proposition that we see it.[21] But we would not normally cite just our seeing a flash of lightning as a reason for believing there is one, but rather the proposition *that* we see it. Non-propositional grounds do not even seem to constitute reasons for believing (except in the sense of reasons *why it is* that one believes) until they are believed to obtain. They are, to be

[19] As noted in the text, in answering 'What was your reason for doing that?', one may answer 'I believed . . .' or (especially) 'I wanted . . .'. I call these attitudes *reason states* and distinguish them from reasons proper, which are their contents. A partial account of this distinction is given in my (1986a). That paper also deals with the special case of things we do for their own sake, for which 'in order to' is perhaps not entirely appropriate in giving an explanation. In any event, I suggest that where a belief provides a reason for acting, it does so at least in part because there is a suitably related want or a reason for having such a want, as where one's reason for telephoning is given by citing a belief that one has too little time for email.

[20] Cf. Harman (1999), esp. chs. 1 and 4; and Foley (1993) on this point.

[21] One epistemologist who uses 'reason' to encompass grounds is Swain (1981). A sorting out of different uses of 'reason' is given in my (1998).

sure, *evidences*; and reasons for believing, on my view, are propositional *expressions* of evidence (or at least apparent evidence).

In any event, for both reasons proper and grounds, we may say that when they figure as reasons or grounds for believing, they support believing *as* truth-valued. A premise, as well as an experience or memory impression, may *be* a ground, and a belief of a premise may *express* a reason (an inferential one). In the case of non-propositional grounds, such as a visual experience of lightning, the counterpart reason for belief is also a proposition: one that expresses the state of affairs experienced. Reasons for believing (and for other theoretical attitudes) are in this way unlike practical reasons, which are not truth-valued though they express a content that may be said to be realized or unrealized. A desire that one's friend receive an honor, for instance, expresses (and projects) a content to be realized.

With this much theory in view, we can see something important. Suppose we think of the will – or, in my terminology here, of practical reason – as properly functioning to change the world in the direction of either some good (whether it is objectively or subjectively conceived does not matter at this level of generality) or at least some desired state of affairs. And suppose we also conceive the will as guided in exercising this function by practical reasons and as successful when its functioning – by its acts, we might say – produces the changes. If the guiding reasons are practical, they must point to acts. This is exactly what practical reasons, in the central cases of their operation, do. For intention, and equally for action-desires, the content of practical reasons is expressible by an infinitive clause designating an act-type, say 'to signal my vote'. This clause expresses my reason for raising my hand; my will produces that action; and the action changes the world (or so one may hope).

By contrast, think of the intellect as properly functioning to provide a true representation of the world – or the part of it relevant to the subject, or at least to the subject's survival. The intellect is properly guided by theoretical reasons. Insofar as it represents the world correctly, it is externally and objectively successful. If the guiding reasons are theoretical, they must point to truths. (Whether the pointing must be conceived in terms of epistemically internalist or externalist standards may be left open here.) If the content of the reasons is propositional, they can do this; if it is not (at least in the indirect way a ground is) – if, for example, the content is practical, as where 'to make life bearable' expresses a presumptive reason for believing one's friend is honest – they cannot. Thus, suppose my reason for believing there is lightning nearby is that a flash and loud cracking sound have occurred. This clause expresses a proposition that constitutes a reason for my belief; my coming to believe that evidential proposition produces, and my believing it causally grounds, my believing that there is lightning; and my intellectual state changes to reflect the world.

The first thing that may come to mind in the comparison is the different directions of causation: from the will to the world in the first case, and from the world to the intellect in the second. This is as it should be: if the will succeeds when it changes the world, it must produce a causal condition sufficient for the change; and if the intellect succeeds when it truly represents the world, it must achieve such a representation through a causal connection running from the world to it.[22] If, however, the broad perspective on intellect and will so far presented is correct, there is something more. It bears on the causal contrast just drawn, but, as the next two sections will show, it has more to do with the ontology of the objects of intentional attitudes.

V　The relation between reasons and facts

I have described practical reasons as non-truth-valued and best represented by contents of infinitive clauses, and I have characterized theoretical reasons as truth-valued and best represented by contents of truth-valued propositional clauses. If I am correct, then I am bound to show how my view can take account of two points that may suggest a univocal conception – specifically, a *facticity view* – of the nature of reasons.[23]

Let us begin with the notions of a person's reasons for believing and for doing something. The first thing that may strike one here is that there is at least an oddity in saying that p is a person's reason for believing or doing something if the person takes p to be false. Second, it appears that reasons for action *can* always be expressed in a propositional mode and, when they are, also seem subject to this same kind of constraint: if p is false, we find it

---

[22] We cannot say 'causing it'; beliefs about the future are not caused by future events. But there is still a causal connection: from causes of the relevant events, such as my decision to do something tomorrow, to the belief representing those events.

[23] In epistemological literature, something at least close to this view has been affirmed as early as 1975. Unger said that "[I]f someone's reason for something is that p, then it follows that it is true that p." See (1975), p. 208. A similar view regarding evidence has been recently defended by Williamson: "Although we may treat false propositions as evidence, it does not follow that they are [evidence] . . . If e is evidence for h, then e is true" (2000), pp. 186 and 201. In the domain of practical reason, Stampe has held, "Reasons are what we mean to reason from, and reasons are facts . . . Thus the sailors who, believing that the earth is flat, declined to sail with Columbus had *in* that belief no reason to decline: since the earth is not flat, its being flat was no reason." See Stampe (1987), p. 337. Cf. Parfit (1997) and Dancy (2000), esp. ch. 5.

at best odd to call it the person's reason for doing it. These worries require considerable analysis.

Let me start with the theoretical case. Why is it odd to say (at least in English) that someone's reason for believing p is q, where one does not think q is true, and especially where one thinks q is false? Is this because, if q is false, we would be referring merely to a case of believing for a (cognitively) *motivating*, as opposed to *normative*, reason? Surely the reason need not be merely motivating. One can have excellent evidence for q, say joint testimonial and inductive evidence, even if q is false. I think that when, speaking sincerely, *we* give our own reasons for believing p, we believe the proposition(s) we cite; and the most common case with others – we normally assume – is their having truths as their reasons. We so regard our own reasons; and we tend to give others credit for getting such things right unless we have reason to think otherwise.[24]

This pragmatic point is sufficient to explain why it is odd to say such things as that his reason for believing that (e.g.) there has been life on Mars is that there was once water there (where we think there was not, though there is evidence of water). We want to say something like 'His reason is that – as he sees it – there was once water there'. Notice, though, that – speaking as we commonly do in giving our reasons – he might say his reason is that there was once water there. This explanation is equivalent to 'The reason for which he believes that there has been life on Mars is that there was water there'. This is a similarly odd thing to say if we think there has never been water there. But consider the following equivalences. The proposition that someone believes that p (wholly) on the basis of (the proposition that) q seems equivalent to the proposition that the person believes that p (wholly) on the basis of *believing* that q *and* to the proposition that the reason for which the person believes p is that q.[25] But the second of these, employing the basic locution, clearly does not imply that q is true. If so, neither do the others.

I think that the best explanation of the data here is again that pragmatic considerations heavily influence what reason-ascribing locutions we use and that, as is not uncommonly the case with equivalent locutions in English, some ascriptions are odd where their equivalents are not. Equivalents may

---

[24] We might speak here of true propositions rather than of truths. But suppose a truth is not just a true proposition but one that is undergirded by a corresponding fact. This might be so and may be why some people think of true propositions as facts. Nothing in this paper will turn on my conceiving truths as true propositions and leaving open how they are related to facts.

[25] This equivalence is argued for in my (1986b).

also differ in what their common *uses* imply, as distinct from what their content entails. This pragmatic difference is consistent with the view I am presenting, on which we can believe for reasons in the same sense of the term whether the propositions in question are true or false.

It should also be noted that on the facticity view, if I am asked my reason for believing p (or for what reason I believe p), and I sincerely say that my reason for believing it (or the reason for which I believe it) is q, I can be corrected – by being told that q is not my reason – (1) without being thought insincere or mistaken about why I believe p and (2) on the ground that q is false. But we do not correct self-ascriptions of (actuating) reasons for believing in this way. We normally presuppose that others (apart from self-deception and other special cases) know for what reasons they believe what they do (when they do believe for a reason rather than simply on the basis of, say, perception or memory), and we normally do not take the falsehood of p to falsify this presupposition of self-knowledge. Suppose, for instance, that I am told by a credible person that q is false. Assuming that I now doubt that q but do not immediately cease to believe q, I will *not* now doubt that q is the reason for which I believe p, but rather will think that perhaps I ought not to believe p on the basis of q (and may also come to doubt that p is true).

A further point is this. Suppose that, as is common, I formed my belief that p on the basis of *reasoning* from q, I will find it especially strange to think that I believe p for no reason. My reasoning might even be valid, hence formally good. In one terminology, the trouble with my reasoning (hence my inferential ground for p) is external; it is with the *inputs* to my reasoning. This defect does not preclude my conclusion's being reason-based. To be sure, we might perhaps say that in second- and third-person *ascriptions* of reasons for belief, whether of (a) reasons for anyone at all to believe p, or (b) reasons for a specific person to believe it, or (c) reasons *for which* a particular person *does* believe it, *a (defeasible) presupposition of objectivity predominates*. Hence, if we think q false, we normally do not cite q as someone's reason for (holding the belief that) p, unless we cancel the predominance presupposition, for example with 'that – as he claims – q'. Suppose the question is 'What reason does Sally have for her belief that p?' We usually would not say 'that q' if we disbelieve q – though we might cite the corresponding reason state, saying that she believes q. If we are thinking of q as false and only as a subjective or a motivating reason or both, we are likely to say 'She believes that q', or use 'as she sees it', or in some other way distance ourselves from the objectivity presupposition.

It may help in understanding such cases to notice that in the kind of context in question, where the inquirer presumably seeks an *objective* reason, the notion of a *reason there is to believe p* seems to be operating. And it is no surprise that such an external reason must be true (factive). Suppose that one could have a reason to believe *p* only if one had an external one – a reason that is factive. Now consider a person with excellent basis for believing *p*, say *q*, for which the person has evidence in the light of which any rational person would make the (objective) mistake of believing *q* (which is false). We would have to conclude that the person has *no* reason to believe *p*. This holds even if good evidence, or indeed any genuine evidence, must be true (on the plausible assumption that some evidence is inductive and hence non-truth-entailing).

This consequence of the facticity view not only forces us to draw what is at best an implausible conclusion about beliefs based on excellent though ultimately misleading evidence. It also drives a wedge between, on the one hand the notion of rational belief and, on the other, the notion of reasons for believing a proposition as constituted by something that, at least given the evidential resources of the subject, supports that proposition and renders believing it *rational.* Similarly, the view would sever the connection between reasons for belief and reasoning as a process normally understood to supply them (even if not always good ones). (Parallel points hold for practical reasons.) It is neither plausible nor theoretically desirable to hold that the kinds of considerations on the basis of which it is rational to hold a belief cannot be reasons for it unless they are facts (or true propositions). This view seems to lead to an avoidable paradox.

Granted, on my view we must acknowledge that a reason one has, a possessed reason, need not be external or objective – a reason there *is* to believe *p* (or to *A*) – and that reason-ascriptions for beliefs tend to presuppose truth and so, apart from qualifiers like 'as she sees it' which select subjective (or at least internal) reasons for *p*, are odd and misleading given the ascriber's disbelief of the proposition in question. But granting this point sacrifices nothing major if anything at all. For many truths, there are some contexts in which any unqualified affirmation of them is odd or misleading.

Let us now see how nearly parallel the practical case is and then proceed to further considerations favoring the distinction I earlier suggested between the kinds of objects of the practical and theoretical attitudes. Consider the most general kind of ascription of a reason for action: the kind employing the purposive locution 'in order to'. Every intentional action for a further end – and arguably every intentional action – admits of an in-order-to explanation in which the agent's reason is expressed by the infinitive clause.[26] We raise our hands in order to greet others, open books in order to find information, make appointments in order to meet people, and so forth. These locutions imply both a desire, in a very wide sense encompassing (though not entailing) intending, and, except possibly where the action is basic for the agent, an instrumental belief. But they do not presuppose that the instrumental belief is true. Thus, even if the same explanation can normally be given by citing the belief, for instance by saying that she opened the book because she believed it would contain a map of Siena, this equivalence would not hold if that mode of explanation presupposed a true belief.

One might reply that if the instrumental belief is false, then both explanations cite only a motive, not a reason. But an instrumental belief does not by itself constitute a motive: the agent may have no desire for the state of affairs to which the belief represents the action as a means. One might go on to claim that the explanation cites only a motivating reason. But what would this come to, if it implies any more than that the instrumental belief is false? Not that the action or agent lacks rationality; not that the goal sought is not desirable; not that there is *no* sense of 'reason' in which the agent had a reason to act and acted for that reason; not – so far as I can tell – anything implying that practical reasons must be true or in any other sense factive.

Connected with these points are other untoward consequences of taking reasons for action – not just objective or sound or "external" reasons for action – to be factive. Let us focus on the practical case (the theoretical one is quite parallel). If my reason for action must be factive, say, constituted by some truth connecting my action with its goal (what I want in performing it), three untoward consequences follow. First, I cannot, in a way that seems plainly possible,[27] know what my reasons are without knowing the relevant propositions to be true, say cannot know that my reason for signing a check is that it will discharge a debt (where the check will be lost in the mail). Second, I can do something in order to achieve some end, yet either do it for no reason or do it *for* a reason though I *have* no reason for doing it. Third, others who see that my relevant belief is false can tell me that I acted for no reason or acted for a reason though I had no reason. But all of these implications seem quite mistaken. If, for instance, you take a medicine in order to relieve a headache, I may not say to you, simply on the ground

---

[26] This is argued in my (1986a), which admits a possible exception for explanations of basic actions.

[27] There is a subtlety here that I cannot discuss: if I do not *believe* that reasons are factive, I might know that R is my reason for an act but not believe, hence not know, that R is true. (I cannot believe it false; but I might, e.g., believe only that it is probably true.)

that the medicine will have no effect, that you had no reason for taking it, or that you were not acting for a reason. I can perhaps say to you that despite appearances, there was no *good* reason to take it, where now (if this paper is correct in the matter) I invoke the notion of an objective reason, an external reason there is, for an action. But this is neither the only notion of a reason for action nor – even more important – the only kind that bears on the rationality of action.[28] The contrast with appearances prepares us to take 'good reason' to entail truth, but ordinarily the notion of a good reason is not this narrow.

I think, then, that the external, objective notion of a reason does not even reflect the only notion of a *good* reason for action. Regarding the medicine that I have excellent but ultimately misleading reason to think effective, I could reply that since I had excellent evidence that the medicine would work, I had a good reason to take it: one that was evidentially good even if factually mistaken. To suggest that my reason was only motivating fails to do justice to its role in rational assessment of the action.

VI Facticity versus factual groundability

Nothing I have said requires denying that there is an important connection between objective reasons for action (and belief) and facts. In my view, which is an axiological objectivism, unless it is true that there is something good about a state of affairs – in which case it is a fact that there is – there *is* no (objective) reason to bring it about. Moreover, if there *is* (objective) reason to believe p, say that q, then the proposition that q is a truth. We must grant, then, that if someone believes that p on the basis of a false proposition, this false proposition, though it is the *person's* reason, is not an objective (external) one. Thus, we can say such things as that, though his reason for believing that there is life elsewhere in our galaxy is convincing to him and backed by some reflection, it is mistaken (not a reason for the rest of us, not a good reason, not objectively sound, not in line with the facts, and so on). Indeed, on the kind of experiential groundedness view I have sketched, there is a still deeper connection between reasons and facts. Apart from the reality, hence the factual character, of the qualities of

---

[28] Another problem with the facticity of reasons view arises on the plausible epistemically internalist view that we have internal access (roughly, access by reflection or introspection) to our justifying reasons, hence to their content: we do not have internal access to all the relevant facts. I may have such access to my believing that p and hence to p as an object of thought. But apart from facts about my own inner life (and perhaps certain a priori facts) I do not have such access to the fact that p (assuming p is true).

experience (including abstract thinking as a kind of intellectual experience) in virtue of which experience renders desires and beliefs rational, there are no rational propositional attitudes to provide good reasons for action or belief, objective or other. Neither true beliefs nor desires for something objectively good provide normative reasons for action if these attitudes are ill-grounded. Wishful thinking may by good fortune lead to my truly believing that a medicine will cure me, and a lucky post-hypnotic sugges-tion may lead me to want to do something that is desirable but could not be known by me to be so given my limited experience. In neither case do I have good reason for acting.

We can now see that just as normative reasons for action, in the wide sense of reasons for the agent in question to act, need not themselves be true propositions (or facts, conceived as entailing the relevant truths even if different kinds of entities), not all factive propositions that are a person's de facto reasons for action are genuinely normative. It is not *only* factive propositions that can support the rationality of action, nor is it supported by *every* factive proposition that constitutes a reason for which a person acts. I believe, however, that in a certain way practical reasons *depend* on facts. Reasons there are to do something (practical reasons in the external, objective sense of 'reason') depend on something's in fact having value; and even a *person's* reason for doing something, if it is a good reason for the person to do it, must be well-grounded in certain facts of experience. We can retain a facticity view regarding ultimate (normative) grounds, then, even if we reject the overall facticity of reasons view.

To see more clearly how normative reasons depend on facts, recall the case in which one takes a medicine in order to reduce pain but is mistaken, though well justified, in thinking that it will reduce pain. I have already noted that if reducing pain is an objective reason, then reducing pain – to reduce pain, to put it in projective language – is in fact good. But now consider the false belief. It provides a normative reason for the act (sup-ports the rationality of performing it) only if there *are* facts appropriately accessible to the agent in the light of which there *is* objective reason for the act. One such fact would be that there is evidence making it probable that the medicine will reduce pain. If there is no evidence, then the agent is not well justified in the instrumental belief.

On my view, the justificatory bearing of the evidence in such a case of mistaken belief is supported by an evidential principle that the agent can in principle see to be true: that when there is information of the relevant kind (say, a high proportion of positive instances in a variety of circumstances, and no negative instances) regarding a proposition, it is likely to be true. I would myself argue that epistemic principles of the relevant kind are a priori, but that need not be assumed here. It also need not be assumed that the agent believes (as opposed to being disposed to believe) such a supporting principle or can even formulate one, at least apart from Socratic prodding. The kind of questioning that may lead to formulation may also lead to belief formation.

The general point here is that, although the agent's (normative) reason for action, propositionally expressed, need not be true, it *is* such as to render the action *truth-groundable* – factually groundable, if you like. (The counterpart point holds for normative reasons for belief, but I will not pursue the analogy now.) A proponent of the facticity view could insist on regimentation and claim that the agent's "real reason" *is* the true proposition (or the fact) that there is evidence that the medicine will reduce pain. But this seems inadequate both to our actual thinking about what our reasons are and to our discourse in which they figure. I believe, then, that practical reasons as most perspicuously expressed – infinitivally – are not truth-valued, and that normative reasons for action that are propositionally expressed need not be factive. But basic practical reasons correspond to axiological truths, and propositional expressions of practical reasons, if not themselves true, are so connected with facts as to render the actions in question truth-groundable.

It should now be clear that denying that practical reasons must be construed as facts does not commit one to denying the plausible idea that every practical reason has a propositional *expression* and that, if this proposition is true, the reason is indeed factive (either because a true proposition *constitutes* a fact in the relevant sense or because there must be a fact in virtue of which it is true). Suppose the reason for *A*-ing is to bring about *G*. This reason can be expressed by an instrumental proposition. The "simplest" kind expresses a sufficient condition relation between the act and the goal: that *A*-ing will bring about *G*.

VII   Moral reasons

So far, I have not explicitly brought moral reasons into the account I am outlining. Moral reasons can be theoretical or practical. Both are of concern here, particularly the latter. But even when a moral reason is truth-valued and in that generic way theoretical, as where it is a judgment that one is morally obligated to do something for a friend, it supports one or another type of action. As I view morality, its basic principles are epistemically autonomous: they can be seen to be true on the basis of adequate reflection on their content, even if they can also be known on a non-moral basis, such as an appeal to a sound general theory of practical reason. There is, then, a cognitive basis, a grounding in theoretical reason, on which they can be known.[29]

I have maintained that theoretical reason has a special authority in the practical domain. The epistemic autonomy of moral principles seems to me to constitute one case in point. If I know that I ought to keep my promises, I thereby have reason to do so. As a result of knowing this, I may also want to do so. Even a justified false belief of this kind could provide a reason to act accordingly that can both motivate doing so and is good enough to render such action rational. But quite apart from whether motivation is implied by self-addressed moral knowledge, the existence of objective reasons for action is implied by the truth of moral principles. The moral principles that underlie one's knowledge and belief ascribing obligation to oneself, then, have considerable normative authority in the practical domain. These points do not entail that moral facts, as opposed to normatively authoritative facts of experience, are required as a ground for the existence of moral reasons (though I think this may well be true, depending on what constitutes a moral fact). I have argued that there can even be instrumental reasons good enough to sustain rational action without the reason-constituting propositions being true, as opposed to being believed in a sufficiently rational way. But even if *moral* facts (in some special, specific sense) are not necessary in grounding good moral reasons, there are *morally significant* non-moral facts that are sufficient. Just as an action's reducing pain (a non-moral fact about it) makes the action desirable and yields a reason for performing it (where the reason is *to reduce pain*), an action's fulfilling a promise or avoiding an injury (a non-moral fact about it) makes it morally (prima facie) obligatory and yields a reason for it: to keep the promise or to avoid injuring someone.

Maintaining the epistemic autonomy of moral principles does not, however, require maintaining their isolation. Indeed, I think, as Plato and Aristotle and Kant (among others) have, that there is a route to seeing their truth from considerations about practical reason. But this is not the place to argue for that.[30] My main concern has been to indicate how actions are grounded in desires and beliefs, which in turn are both causally grounded in experience and, when rational, also normatively grounded therein. Experience has qualities in virtue of which desires can be rational and can thereby

---

[29] I defend the moral epistemology suggested here in (2004), esp. chs. 1 and 2.
[30] In ch. 6 of (2001) I have made a case for the view that considerations of practical reason support the rationality of being moral.

provide (which is not to say desires can constitute) reasons for action. The reasons that desires can provide are objectively good when the object of the desire is also objectively good, whether intrinsically or instrumentally. We can speak of reasons for action as grounds for it – specifically, of reason states as in some sense *causally* grounding it and of reasons proper as *normatively* grounding it. This point holds for moral reasons as well as for other kinds of reasons for action.

* * *

The overall picture I have offered represents experience as grounding reasons, both causally and normatively, and whether they are practical or theoretical, or external or internal. This foundational commonality implies many parallels, but, even on the assumption that non-factive normative reasons are truth-groundable, it does not imply that either of our rational capacities is reducible to the other. I have granted one kind of dependence of practical reason on theoretical reason – a kind of defeasibility of practical considerations by theoretical ones – but have also affirmed their mutual irreducibility. I have maintained not only that neither dimension of rationality can be reduced to the other, but also that, connected with this difference, the two sorts of attitudes have different kinds of objects. Only the objects of theoretical attitudes are truth-valued. This does not imply, however, that truth plays no role in the notion of practical reasons. The sound ones, the reasons there are for *any* of us to do certain kinds of things, correspond with truths.

These objective, external reasons for action may be seen as projections of something good, rather as sound theoretical reasons may be seen as representations of something true. Experience supplies grounds for reasons of both kinds. When it supplies grounds for normative beliefs, and particularly for moral judgments – all of which have a certain future-oriented element – it may, in that way, provide grounds for action that accords with those judgments. But this does not entail that theoretical grounds exhaust the basis of practical reasons.

Experiential grounds are not reasons, but I do not deny that the category of grounds includes reasons, actual or potential, for action or belief. The ultimate grounds, which on my view underlie reasons, are experiential. The enjoyable and painful qualities of experience that are the readiest paradigms of practical grounds, like the qualities of sensory experiences that are the readiest paradigms of theoretical grounds, confer rationality but do not admit of it. Experiences and their qualities are not as such rational or irrational. The two kinds of grounds, most prominently sensory grounds for belief and hedonic grounds for desire, go with the different roles of belief and the other theoretical attitudes and, on the other hand, of desires, intentions, and the other practical attitudes. The theoretical attitudes give us our map of the world, and the normative beliefs among them can tell us what destinations are worth visiting, as well as, in the moral case, which ones we must, or must not, visit. The practical attitudes, when they are well-grounded in good experiences, will at once help us to discover worthwhile destinations and motivate us to reach them.[31]

References

Anscombe, Elizabeth (1956), *Intention*, Oxford: Basil Blackwell.
Audi, Robert (1986a), "Acting for Reasons," *Philosophical Review 95*, 511–46.
    (1986b), "Belief, Reason, and Inference," *Philosophical Topics 14*, 1, 27–65.
    (1997a), "Moral Judgment and Reasons for Action," in *Audi* (1997b), 217–47.
    (1997b), *Moral Knowledge and Ethical Character*, Oxford University Press.
    (1998), "Reasons for Believing," in *Craig* (1998), 127–30.
    (2001), *The Architecture of Reason*, Oxford University Press.
    (2002), "Prospects for a Naturalization of Practical Reason: Humean Instrumentalism and the Normative Authority of Desire," *International Journal of Philosophical Studies 10*, 3, 235–63.
    (2003a), *Epistemology*, 2nd edn., London: Routledge.
    (2003b), "Intrinsic Value and Reasons for Action," *Southern Journal of Philosophy 41*, 30–56.
    (2004), *The Good in the Right*, Princeton University Press.
Castañeda, Hector-Neri (1975), *Thinking and Doing*, Dordrecht: D. Reidel.
Craig, Edward (1998) ed., *Routledge Encyclopedia of Philosophy,* London: Routledge.
Cullity, Garrett, and Berys Gaut (1997), *Ethics and Practical Reason*, Oxford University Press.
Dancy, Jonathan (2000), *Practical Reality*, Oxford University Press.
Davidson, Donald (1963), "Actions, Reasons and Causes," *Journal of Philosophy 60*, 685–700.
    (1980), "Intending," in Davidson, *Essays on Actions and Events*, Oxford University Press.
Foley, Richard (1993), *Working without a Net*, Oxford University Press.
Harman, Gilbert (1999), *Reasoning, Meaning, and Mind*, Oxford: The Clarendon Press.

---

[31] For helpful comments on this paper I am grateful to audiences at Northwestern University, the Oxford Moral Philosophy Society, the State University of New York at Albany, the Siena Conference on Intentionality, Deliberation, and Autonomy, and to Christoph Lumer, Hugh McCann, and Derek Parfit.

Parfit, Derek (1997), "Reasons and Motivation," *Proceedings of the Aristotelian Society*, Supplementary Volume 71, 99–130.

Stampe, Dennis (1987), "The Authority of Desire," *Philosophical Review* 96, 335–81.

Swain, Marshall (1981), *Reasons and Knowledge*, Ithaca, NY: Cornell University Press.

Unger, Peter (1975), *Ignorance*, Oxford University Press.

Williamson, Timothy (2000), *Knowledge and Its Limits*, Oxford University Press.

CHAPTER 4

Practical reason and the status of moral obligation

The power of skepticism depends on the apparent possibility of rationally asking, for virtually any kind of proposition commonly thought to be known, *how* it is known or what justifies believing it. Moral claims are among those commonly subjected to skeptical challenges and doubts, even on the part of some people who are not skeptical about ordinary claims regarding the external world. There may be even more skepticism about the possibility of justifying moral *actions*, particularly if they are against the agent's self-interest. Both problems – how to justify moral claims and how to justify moral action – come within the scope of the troubling question 'Why be moral?' Even a brief response to moral skepticism should consider both kinds of targets of justification, cognitive and behavioural, and should indicate some important relations between the two types of skeptical challenge. I will begin with the cognitive case – with skepticism about the scope of theoretical reason in ethics – proceed to practical skepticism, which concerns the scope of practical reason, and then show how an adequate account of rationality may enable us to respond to moral skepticism.

I Skepticism: general, moral, and practical

There are many kinds of skepticism, far more than can be even catalogued here.[1] Call the view that there is no knowledge or justification, whether theoretical or practical, *comprehensive general skepticism*. This has rarely been held, but the view that no one has knowledge or justified belief regarding the external world – a kind of *general cognitive skepticism* – is an arguably defensible position. (*Comprehensive* cognitive skepticism – the

---

[1] For general discussion of skepticism and many varieties of it see ch. 10 of my *Epistemology* (London: Routledge, 2003). For a theory of the status of morality on which moral justification is reconciled with Pyrrhonnian skepticism, see Walter Sinnott-Armstrong, *Moral Skepticisms* (Oxford University Press, 2006).

view that there is no knowledge or justified belief whatever – has not been plausibly defended.) Most who are inclined to hold this version of external world skepticism would also tend to maintain that there is no moral knowledge and no justification for holding moral views. Call that position *cognitive moral skepticism*. This position is distinct from *behavioral moral skepticism*, which is the view that there are no fully justifying moral reasons for action (in a strong form this view would entail that there are no moral reasons for action at all). Moral skepticism of both kinds is implicit in *comprehensive practical skepticism*, the view that there are no justifying reasons, moral or other, for *any* sort of action.

One might think that any kind of cognitive skeptic would have to be a practical skeptic as well; but since a certain kind of normative (say, ethical) noncognitivist would hold that there are no moral propositions, such a position opens up the possibility that there could be justification for *action*, say in terms of rational desires, which is *not* dependent on justification for any moral proposition concerning the action. Noncognitivism entails that there are no moral properties and, correspondingly, that there are no moral propositions to be known or justifiedly believed. This implies skepticism about moral knowledge, and indeed about cognitive moral justification; but such skepticism does not obviously rule out non-cognitive justifiers of action as distinct from belief.

In broad terms, skepticism presents a challenge to one or another view of the power of reason, usually some common-sense view. My concern here is the power of skepticism in the moral domain. To simplify matters, I propose to say that reason has *cognitive normative authority* provided it enables its possessor – and I have in mind normal adult human beings with a mastery of a language having approximately the expressive power of English – to be justified in *believing* normative propositions. These include ascriptions of justification to beliefs, but in ethics the chief cognitive focus is "practical": it includes both deontic propositions – roughly those to the effect that some act or kind of act is right, or wrong, or obligatory – and axiological propositions, roughly those to the effect that something is good, or bad, in itself.

I propose to say that reason has *practical normative authority* provided it enables its possessor (say, a rational adult) to have normative reasons for action. This formulation leaves open how much practical authority is in question; but I will be concerned only with versions claiming that the authority suffices for a rational person to have reason for action *sufficient* to render an action performed *for* that reason rational. There is no implication, of course, that someone's having sufficient reason for action requires nothing empirical, such as some experience – say of an advancing forest fire – that yields an occasion or need for action.

Similarly, reason may be said to have *cognitive moral authority* provided it enables its possessor to know or justifiably believe moral propositions, and it may be said to have *practical moral authority* provided it enables its possessor to have specifically moral reasons for action. One could hold that reason has practical but not moral authority if one held that the only practical reasons are self-interested and that moral reasons (even if they should call for the same actions) are not self-interested. I am particularly concerned with the relations between cognitive and practical authority and with whether reason has moral authority and, if so, how much.

II   Basic elements of practical reason

My strategy in examining the moral authority of reason is to begin by considering the practical authority of reason and then proceed from there to assess what seems the best skeptical case against its also having specifically moral authority – call it the case from egoism. I will start by extending an account (proposed elsewhere)[2] of the foundations of practical reason. I will also indicate some connections between practical and theoretical reason, connections we must see if we are to appreciate the full bearing of the account on the moral authority of reason.

Let us begin with an example. Consider an advancing forest fire. As it approaches Janet, a beleaguered homeowner wielding a garden hose, she feels pain from the first burn on her outstretched hand. She now has both a reason for retreating – to reduce the pain – and a reason to jump into a nearby swimming pool: to have the relieving experience of being cooled. This alone does not entail that if she jumps in, she will be doing it *rationally*. Having a reason, even having sufficient reason, for acting is one thing; acting rationally is a different though related matter. In this case it requires (for one thing) that she rationally *believe* something to the effect that doing the thing in question will relieve the pain.[3]

We can already see, then, that even if the practical authority of reason extends to reasons for acting, it remains true that if its authority is to be sufficient for rational action itself, we must at least sometimes *respond* to reasons in the light of rational beliefs. Suppose this requires rational instrumental beliefs concerning the act in question, say, that jumping in

---

[2]   In Robert Audi, *The Architecture of Reason* (Oxford University Press, 2001), esp. Part II.

[3]   The phrase "to the effect that" is used to allow great breadth. Indeed, I want to leave open that even a rational *de re* instrumental belief might serve here.

the pool will relieve the pain. Then any cognitive skeptic who denies that we have rational beliefs about the world will likely hold a corresponding version of practical skepticism, to the effect that, even if there are reasons for instrumental actions – arguably the most important type of action for human well-being – no concrete actions (act-tokens) of this type are rational. There would be no rational instrumental beliefs to guide them.

Sources and grounds of reasons

On my view, the sources of *normative reasons for action – practical* reasons, as distinct from mere *motivational* reasons – are both experiential and (as this suggests) internally accessible to the agent, in the sense that the agent can become conscious of them by introspection or reflection. As this indicates, my theory of basic practical reasons is both internalist and experientialist. It allows, to be sure, that non-experiential elements, such as (non-occurrent) desires and beliefs, can provide practical reasons, but entails that they do so only on the basis of their having an appropriate connection to experiences. Since many practical reasons are for future conduct, the experiences may ground them via memory or, in some cases, may themselves be future-directed, as in the case of anticipatory distress at the thought of breaking one's word. Hedonism is also experientialist, but (unless the notions of pleasure and pain are taken with extreme breadth) my view is more pluralistic than hedonism.

Three related notions important for my view are these. First, by virtue of certain of its qualities, most clearly its hedonic qualities, experience, say of pain, is a *source* of practical reasons. The experience of pain, as where dental drilling is excruciating, directly provides a reason to take an anesthetic. Second, prepositional attitudes, above all desires and beliefs, can indirectly provide practical reasons, in the sense that, by virtue of their content, they *express* practical reasons. Third, reasons themselves are the kinds of entities that can be *contents* (objects, in another terminology) of prepositional attitudes. Janet wants (say) *to stop the pain* (a kind of basic reason, since this is properly wanted intrinsically) and *to escape the hot flames* (an instrumental reason, since this is wanted as a means of stopping the pain), and she believes *that retreating will suffice to escape.* The want and belief are *reason states*, and indeed they can be reasons *why* an agent does something. Thus, given their broadly causal explanatory power, these states are quite properly called motivational reasons. But they are not reasons proper – a kind that, as abstract contents, are not good candidates to be causally explanatory. Desires and beliefs, but not their contents, are causal elements.

A major question for this paper may now be broadly expressed in at least two ways. First, are moral reasons ever (to some degree) good? Second, are actions performed *for* a moral reason ever thereby rational? A positive answer to the first question entails that moral reasons have some practical authority; a positive answer to the second entails that its normative authority is substantial. If we can see how these questions may be correctly answered in the affirmative, then we will have at least one kind of plausible answer to the question of why one should be moral.

The two kinds of reasons, reasons proper and reason states that express them, work together in at least this way: when a normative reason, say that running westward will escape being burned, motivates and explains an action, for instance Janet's running westward, (1) that fact bears a normative or at least conceptual relation, say making-intelligible-in-the-context, to the act-type in question, namely, running west, and (2) the agent's belief with the content given by the reason-expressive that-clause, together with a desire for (hence having as its content) the indicated state of affairs, say escaping being burned, causally explains the agent's tokening that act-type, i.e., the agent's actually running west, the action is motivated by the desire and, in the context of that desire, may also be said to be motivated by the belief; the two together causally explain it; and, in the light of their content, they render it prima facie rational.

Regarding reasons proper, which are abstract elements such as contents of prepositional attitudes, such reasons for action can be referred to in either of two ways: as states of affairs to be realized and as propositions that instrumentally connect the action in question with the relevant state of affairs, say by representing the action as sufficient for escaping a fire. Some philosophers take the prepositional expression to be more basic, and indeed take reasons to be a kind of fact.[4] I have argued that the former, infinitival locution is more plausibly considered basic for practical reasons *if* either must be considered more basic.[5] But quite apart from how this question is settled, the more important questions for our purposes are whether

---

[4] Derek Parfit is an influential proponent of the view that reasons are facts. See, e.g., his *On What Matters* (Oxford University Press, 2011). Cf. Timothy Williamson's view that evidence is constituted by knowledge (hence is always factive). See *Knowledge and Its Limits* (Oxford University Press, 2000).

[5] In "The Grounds and Structure of Reasons for Action," in *Intentionality, Deliberation and Autonomy: The Action-Theoretic Basis of Practical Philosophy*, ed. Christoph Lumer and Sandro Nannini (Aldershot: Ashgate, 2007), 135–66 (Chapter 3 in this volume).

conative states, most significantly intrinsic desires (desires for something "for its own sake"), can be rational and whether the rationality of action requires *both* the rationality of some explanatory (instrumental) belief and that of an appropriately explaining desire. If, as I hold, it typically requires both, there is even more room for skepticism. Skeptics may challenge both the rationality of the relevant desires and that of the needed beliefs.

Normative externalism

Since our desires and beliefs and their experiential and intuitive grounds are accessible to our consciousness in the appropriate way, the theory so far presented is, in that epistemic sense, internalist. The idea is roughly that it takes such normative properties of action as rationality and justification to be grounded in elements accessible to the person in question by introspection or reflection. Hedonic qualities of experience are plausibly taken to be major examples of such elements. Might there be a plausible externalist theory of practical reasons, as there is for theoretical reasons (reasons for belief)? Outlining a contrasting externalist view may add clarity to the kind of internalist view I propose. Consider believing that one needs water, and take "reason" in the wide sense that includes non-inferential grounds, such as sense experiences, which are not ordinarily called reasons. Normally, our ground for such a belief is thirst, which is internally accessible. But could we not be built so that there is a highly reliable connection between our physiological need for water and our belief that we need it? If there were a sufficiently reliable connection, we would likely say that (normally) people who are so constructed *know* they need water when they believe they do.[6] They could know this even if their "ground" for the belief is inaccessible to them (our own basis for ascribing knowledge to them would be inductive).

To see the counterpart view for action, imagine an evolutionary theorist holding that since drinking when one needs water has survival value, doing so even when one simply finds oneself intending to – provided intending to drink is reliably produced by the need for water – is rational, and the neural basis of the intention, though inaccessible, is a reason. This reason would be external: it would work through a mechanism that, though not internally accessible, reliably generates behavior that conduces to survival. I am not aware of anyone's holding such a view of practical rationality, but

---

[6] The possibility of knowledge without internally accessible grounds is defended in ch. 8 of my *Epistemology*. The example does not mention justification, which seems less plausibly attributed on the indicated basis; but there are externalist views on which it, like knowledge, would be implied by the kind of reliable connection in question.

it is intelligible. It may be plausibly said to assimilate practical reasons to merely explanatory as opposed to normative ones, but to appraise it in any detail is not possible here.

Experiential reasons are not only accessible but *intrapersonal*. If my basic practical reasons are grounded in (qualities of) *my* experience, should they not be egoistic? If they are, how can I have moral reasons, since at least some of those are not egoistic and indeed call for overriding my self-interest? I can, to be sure, have reasons *aligned* with moral ones; many egoistic reasons will be so aligned, given the need for cooperation and friendly relations with others as a condition of survival at a level of well-being that accords with self-interest. But should we not conclude that all *basic* normative reasons are egoistic?[7]

The intrapersonal vs. the egoistic

It is essential here to distinguish what is intrapersonal from what is *personal* in a sense favorable to egoism. To see the difference, consider what it is about the pain of being burned that yields my reason to reduce it. Is it that the pain is (say) awful, in a phenomenal sense we all understand, or is it, at least in part, that this awful experience is mine? Surely the pain's being mine is not an aspect of its awfulness. Do I even experience its being mine, say by awareness of a possessor-indicative property of it? I can *think* of it as mine; yet its self-possession is not a phenomenal property of it but a matter of who has it – i.e., who instantiates the relevant pain property. My phenomenal sense of what *it* is and how bad it is – by contrast with, say, a self-focused sense of how much *I* am suffering – is a matter of its phenomenal qualities and in no way depends on my regarding it as mine.

Given this and related considerations, I suggest that the basic grounds of practical reasons are, on the one hand, impersonal but, on the other hand, as phenomenal qualities, both internal and experiential. They are, then, impersonal without being *non*-personal. For concreteness, recall the case of the burning pains. It is because of their qualities as painful that one

---

[7] If our basic reasons for action are grounded in qualities of experience, one might wonder whether there are *any* non-experiential sources of practical reasons. My view is that there are, though their normative force is essentially connected with experience. Consider the aesthetic value of a painting. This is not an experiential property of it, but it provides a non-instrumental reason to view the painting in virtue of the experiential value of, say, rewardingly contemplating it. I call such value as artworks or natural landscapes have *inherent*. A partial theory of inherent value is provided in my "Intrinsic Value and Reasons for Action," *Southern Journal of Philosophy* Supplementary Volume 41 (2003): 30–56 (Chapter 2 in this volume).

has reason to stop them and wants to do so. We need not think of the pain as ours in order to have such practical reasons or such desires in response to them. Compare my seeing print here. My visual impression of print is my normative basis for believing that there is print here. But I do not conceptualize the experience as mine, and I certainly do not need to do so in order to have a normative experiential ground for believing the print is here. There is no reason to think that practical reason should differ from theoretical reason on this count.

It is instructive to compare the case of children (and, on some theories, of animals). Even before children have a self-concept, hence before they can even think of their pains as their own, they can want the pains to stop and want this on the basis of good ground for wanting it. They can also have a similarly impersonal ground for believing Mama to be approaching. Granted, we adults are *disposed* to believe, of pains we suffer, that they are ours, but we do not have to *form* such a self-referential belief in order to act in response to the pain; and even when we do believe a pain to be ours, its being ours, as opposed to its being experientially awful, is not essential to its providing a reason to avoid it.[8]

One might object that even granting that the awfulness of Janet's pain may explain why there *is* reason for *someone* to reduce it – in the impersonal sense in which we can say there ought to be less pain in the world and *anyone* who can reduce it should do so – it does not explain why (1) there is reason *for her* in particular to reduce it by jumping into the pool. And does it explain why (2) she *has* reason to reduce it by doing so? I have not been claiming that the awfulness of her pain explains these two facts apart from her (a) believing, or (b) having sufficient reason *to* believe, something to

---

[8] A recent commentator misses the subtlety of the main point here: "As Audi sees it, underlying his desire for *him* to experience a swim is a desire for there to *be* an experience of a swim." See Jason Bridges' review of *The Architecture of Reason*, *Mind* 116 (2007): 1083–8 (1086). My view is that in the primitive case the desire is *de re*, e.g., wanting this pain to stop; it is not a *de dicto* desire *that* there be a cessation of this pain. The crucial distinction is between ascribing a property to something (here something experienced) and having a propositional attitude toward something identified in terms of some self-concept. To illustrate, I said "I can believe the man in the mirror to have a stain on his coat, without conceiving him as me," even when he is (*Architecture*, 91). Bridges replies, "But if I believe that *that* man – the man I see in the mirror – has a stain on his coat, then I have a belief that predicates a property of a specific person" (1086). Bridges has assimilated a *de re* belief to a *de dicto* one and a *person's* predicating a property to a *belief's* doing so. In the latter case the subject must exercise the predicative concept – hence Bridges' phrase within dashes. My view allows responses to properties that imply a disposition to form such predicative beliefs but do not entail their formation. The view also allows for *responses* to the properties ascribed even before development of the concepts of those properties. In the primitive hedonic cases I cited, an elemental rational response to experiencing painful qualities does not require conceiving them as one's own. But of course we are "wired" so that, once we have the appropriate concepts, we are disposed to believe their references to be ours.

the effect that her doing something (say, jumping in the pool) will reduce the pain. (b) does not entail (a), and even (a) need not be egoistic.

Compare the grounds of reasons in the cognitive case. If, in a being structured sufficiently like me, there is a visual impression of print qualitatively like the one I now have, then there is reason for someone to believe there is print in the visually indicated place. Moreover, where the impression is mine, there is reason for *me* to believe there is print here, and I would not *have* reason to believe that the print is *here*, the place I would point to if asked where I believe it to be, apart from a connection or apparent connection to me, such as a visual sense of the print as at a short distance from my body. Nonetheless, I can have such a visual sense without believing that it is mine and without in any way exercising a self-concept. Similarly, the pain's being Janet's is essential to *her* having reason to reduce it by jumping in the pool. Still, the conditions for a reason's being hers, as opposed to someone else's, do not require her exercising a self-concept, nor is such an ascription part of the ground of the reason even when the reason is hers. Granted, that an act would relieve *my* pain (where this is the content of my own self-referential belief) is a self-interested reason for it and one which only I can have; but this does not make it an egoistic reason if that is taken to imply that the normative force of the reason is *based on* the pain's being mine. That an act would reduce the very same pain, say described as 'the pain hurting RA', would also be a reason for someone else to perform an act of the same type.

The metaphysics of normative properties

The view I have expressed can be supported in the light of some metaphysical points about normative properties. For brevity I will consider just moral properties and will make the plausible assumption that having an obligation to do something entails having a reason to do it. Consider the property of being obligated to *A*, say to present a paper at a conference. It is widely agreed (and I assume here) that moral properties are consequential on non-moral, natural properties, in the sense that the former are possessed in virtue of the possession of one or more of the latter. Thus, the obligation to present a paper might be consequential (based, in a sense) on promising to do so. The idea is roughly this: if it is a fact that someone has this kind of obligation (a promissory one), this is so *in virtue of* the fact that the person has promised to. On this view the consequentiality of a property on one or more other properties is best understood on the basis of the corresponding grounding relations between the fact constituted by a particular thing's having the first property and the fact constituted by its having the other(s).

To see the significance of this consequentiality relation more clearly, we should distinguish between the generic property of having an obligation and the specific (though not maximally specific) property of being obligated (e.g.) *to present a paper.* It is natural to speak here of the generic (deontic) property of being obligated (being such that one ought to do something) and to specify the content of an obligation on a particular occasion of its possession by citing *what* the agent in question ought to do. Consider the relevant base property for promissory obligation: promising is an act-type and, as such, a property, and, where a promissory obligation is instantiated, the concrete promise instantiating it may be said to have a content, here the same one as the obligation, say, to present a paper.[9]

More generally, if an obligation is to A, the relevant base property will correspond to the obligatory content, i.e., to A. Take being obligated to abstain from falsifying a record. This obligation is grounded in a property something like this: abstaining from making a lying – a record-falsifying – assertion that p, where p is the kind of false statement in question. The property of being a lying assertion is, on my view, a priori wrong-making; the prima facie wrong-makingness of such assertions underlies the obligation to abstain from falsification (as in making a lying assertion); the content of the obligation in question is abstaining from asserting p. Similarly, being obligated to help someone escape a fire is consequential on someone's having the property of needing one's help to escape the fire. The relevant base property is someone's needing help; the content of the obligation in question is to help someone escape the fire, and this content corresponds to the content of the underlying need – to escape the fire.

What I propose to add to the picture so far drawn is the thesis that moral properties are consequential on properties that are not only non-moral but also purely qualitative.[10] The notion of the purely qualitative is not easy to

---

9 I here construe "being obligated" as a variable-place predicate. Being obligated not to falsify records is a monadic property – the reference to records specifies its content but does not entail that there are any records; being obligated to you to A is representable as a dyadic relation between us. What of being obligated to someone to return a book? Perhaps this might be represented as either a triadic relation or a dyadic one with external content referring to the book. In any case, the notion of consequentiality may be applied to purely qualitative relational properties, such as one person's being obligated to another (which I take to be a universal). Where a relation is between particulars, we may speak of it as a fact (the fact that the first bears it to the second) and the relation may be *grounded* in another relation.

10 The same holds for normative properties, but my main focus here is on the moral subset of those. I should add that I am taking natural properties to be simply "descriptive" and so am allowing mental properties even if they are not reducible to physical ones.

explicate, but for our purposes it is enough to say that purely qualitative properties are universals and are certainly both general – being in principle instantiable by more than one individual – and non-indexical, having no essential reference to a particular concrete individual. Relational as well as monadic properties can be purely qualitative, as will be illustrated.

To see how this thesis bears on the question of whether the grounds of moral obligation are egoistic, consider first the case of the obligation of self-improvement. One might think that there is no such obligation and that only prudence calls for self-improvement. Here I will assume that there is such a prima facie obligation,[11] and focus on its ground. Is my obligation of self-improvement grounded on the relevant improvements being in *me* or in their being in a person over whom I have (among other things) a kind of direct control, and of whose mental life I am non-inferentially conscious? This person is of course identical with me, but we can imagine a world in which I have such control and consciousness regarding a double, yet *not* regarding myself. Would I not then have an obligation of "him-improvement?" Given this point, one might argue that the obligation of self-improvement is derivative from that of beneficence, but that is not at issue here. Even if having the same basis should imply derivability in one direction or the other (or of both obligations from some common ground),[12] the point is that the need for improvement's being *mine* is not its basis.

If the ultimate grounds of practical reason are not egoistic, are they not agent-neutral in a way that implies an apparently unacceptable consequentialism on which we should all seek to *maximize* intrinsic value – which, in a world like this one, is a highly burdensome imperative? This demandingness problem is certainly raised by at least most versions of utilitarianism and also by the kind of maximizing view expressed by Moore in *Principia*, an "ideal utilitarianism" on which we should seek to produce "the greatest sum of good."[13] If, however, we take intrinsic value to be organic (as Moore himself did), in the sense that the overall value of a complex state of affairs need not be the sum of the value of its parts or aspects, then

---

[11] For a criticism of the idea that there is a moral obligation of self-improvement, see Bernard Gert's "Two Conceptions of Morality," in *Rationality and the Good: Critical Essays on the Ethics and Epistemology of Robert Audi*, ed. Mark Timmons, John Greco, and Alfred R. Mele (Oxford University Press, 2007), 54–63.

[12] The relation of a basis for Rossian principles to those principles and the implications of the derivability of the principles from a set of propositions constituting a basis for them is discussed at length in my third chapter ("Kantian Intuitionism") in my *The Good in the Right* (Princeton University Press, 2004), 139–51.

[13] See, e.g., G. E. Moore, *Principia Ethica* (Cambridge University Press, 1903), 149.

if – as I do – we consider some kinds of intrinsic value to be moral, we *need* not conclude that morality demands extreme self-sacrificial beneficence. A second important point here is that an experientialist view of the grounds of reasons for action is consistent with taking some of our basic reasons for action to be deontological. My project here is not, however, to show that moral reasons are not *overdemanding*, but rather to make a case for their being *sufficiently* demanding to make it reasonable for a certain kind of rational person to be moral.[14] If the demandingness problem is insoluble, this might show that morality is a harsh taskmaster, but not that it lacks normative authority.

Another important kind of case to be considered in relation to the qualitativeness view proposed here is that of an obligation to a particular person, say to deliver a paper. Ascribing this specific obligation to me *does* entail dependence on indexicals, since there is an essential reference both to me and to that person. Note, however, that this particular obligation is a relation between concrete individuals. The crucial property constitutive of it, however, that of being obligated (a case of having a reason), is purely qualitative; it is the relata that cannot be specified without ultimate dependence on indexicals. Compare Jeff's being heavier than Margaret. Must we say that the (relational) property of being heavier is not purely qualitative because we cannot specify the relata in particular cases without dependence on indexicals? I see no reason to say so. The twofold basis of the relation itself is the property of weight and the relation *being greater than*.

Constitutive conditions and possession conditions

What these considerations show is that the question of how to determine the basis of obligation in general – or of reasons for action in general – must be distinguished from the question of how to determine who has the obligation or reason. To be sure, if we look for the basis of *my* obligation to *A*, we must look to some property that *I* instantiate which grounds the obligation or reason to *A*. Moreover, where the moral property in question is relational, as with my being obligated to you, the relational fact that one particular person has the relation to a second is grounded on the more basic relation – here, my promising, to you, to *A*. I stand in the obligation relation to you by virtue of standing in the promising relation to you. The broad obligation relation is consequential on the specific promissory one.

---

[14] This beneficence problem is treated in detail in *The Good in the Right*, ch. 3 and esp. ch. 4.

But although the particular relational facts are not specifiable without dependence on indexicals, it does not follow that the grounding property (in this case promising) may thereby be taken to be indexical, and there is no good reason to think that it is. If it is not indexical, it is not essentially egoistic.

The main distinction I am making here is between constitutive conditions for obligations and possession conditions for them. In the practical case, possessing an obligation to A requires that there be some kind of instrumental connection between A-ing and the ground of the obligation; in the theoretical case, there must be some kind of cognitive connection between a justified belief and its ground. For particular persons, these connections cannot be specified without dependence on indexicals, but that point stems from a requirement for determining who *has* an obligation or other kind of reason, not for there *being* an obligation or reason. The grounds of our reasons for action are intrapersonal in belonging, in a purely qualitative way, to our experiences, and our having those reasons depends on our beliefs (or grounds for beliefs); but the grounds of those reasons – the experiential qualities that determine the desirability of acts – are impersonal and can yield reasons for others to act provided they have an appropriate cognitive relation to these grounds. My knowing that Janet is suffering pain that I can reduce provides a reason for me to help her get into the pool.

In the light of what has been said in this section, it should be apparent that although the basis of normative reasons is in a sense internal, that point does not support egoism. Even in the uncontroversial case in which, on the practical side, pain or, on the theoretical side, visual experience, provides reasons *for me*, their being mine is not what explains their normative authority. Their being mine is essential, via instrumental or other cognitive connections, for explaining how these grounds of reasons yield specific reasons actually possessed by me. Those reasons and their grounds are intrapersonal, but their grounds are also impersonal, in the sense that they are not essentially egoistic.

Does the proposed view imply that there might be normative reasons that no one has? It does not imply this if *hypothetical* reasons are included. Consider a world with nothing but an animal suffering from burns on the edge of a cool pond it has no notion is there. If it has no sense of any act that would reduce the pain, there still *is* a reason for the animal to jump in the pond and it *would* have this reason if it could connect immersion with relief. Hypothetical persons, moreover, do have reason to help it. Note an analogy. There are normative reasons, for example evidential ones, why something is or will be the case, such as reasons why there is or will be an earthquake, that no one has. That there are reasons of this kind can be seen from our properly speaking of such reasons as *discovered*. Note too that, on the proposed view of normative reasons, practical and theoretical alike, they are essentially related to reasons persons have in this sense: they are essentially capable of being someone's reasons. If normative properties depend for their grounds on non-normative ones, the latter are also not wholly independent of the former: it is impossible that there be pains and pleasures, or promises and killings, without the consequent reasons.

Now if what is bad about my pain, and hence what grounds reasons to eliminate it, is its awfulness, and if its being mine is not a basis of its normative authority – its power to ground reasons for action – then the same should hold for a pain of yours that is qualitatively just like mine. I think it does. This point surely supports the rationality of altruistic desires. These are (very roughly) intrinsic desires to do something for the good of someone else. It can be rational for me to want (intrinsically) to reduce your pain. To be sure, my knowledge of it is indirect, and my motivation to reduce it is not, like my desire to reduce mine, a direct response that is, as it were, wired in. These and other points may explain why it is rationally permissible (hence not irrational) to prefer eliminating one's own pain to eliminating someone else's qualitatively similar and at least equally strong pain. But surely it is also rationally permissible (hence not irrational) to have the opposite preference. That point (to which I return below) is best explainable on the basis of the impersonal grounds of normative reasons.[15]

III   The relation between practical and theoretical reason

I have already suggested that practical reason has a certain dependence on theoretical reason. It is in part an instrumental dependence. Whatever the conditions for the existence of a normative reason for someone to act (a kind of practical reason), specific agents cannot *have* such reasons for particular actions without having instrumental beliefs or sufficient reasons for such beliefs. In particular, we cannot have *good* practical reasons for particular actions without *rational* instrumental beliefs (or grounds sufficient for them), and we cannot act rationally (as opposed to intelligibly and excusably) without such beliefs.[16]

---

[15] The problem here is again to explain why morality is not too demanding. This difficult problem is treated in part in *Architecture*, e.g., ch. 6, and in *The Good in the Right*, esp. ch. 4.

[16] Two qualifications are needed here: (1) there may be an exception for cases of basic action, e.g., moving a finger, where desire alone seems sufficient. I am also leaving open whether certain *de re*

The instrumental dependence just sketched is positive. Practical reason also has a negative dependence on theoretical reason: a vulnerability to defeat given certain beliefs (or given justification for them). There are basic grounds of reasons for action, such as experienced pain or pleasure, that indefeasibly yield reasons for action, in the sense that their presence confers prima facie rationality of the actions in question. But an element's indefeasibility *as* a ground of action – necessarily normatively supportive of the action – entails only that it necessarily yields a reason; it does not entail the indefeasibility *of* the reason, in the sense that the reason it provides cannot be overridden or undermined. In virtue of her pain, Janet has a reason to do what she believes will reduce it. But suppose she has a pain that she has excellent (and overriding) reason to think she cannot reduce. Then, even if there is in fact something she can do to reduce it, she may justifiedly believe there is no such thing and so either *have* no reason to do that or, at best, a defeated reason to do it. A different kind of case is one in which an intrinsic desire, say to ride a roller coaster, would ordinarily express (and in that sense provide) a reason for action but does not do so because the agent rationally believes that the experience will be highly unpleasant overall. Here the desire not only does not provide a reason but may be rendered irrational by a justified belief concerning its object.

It is important to see that the dependency of practical on theoretical reason is asymmetrical on both counts. First, an experiential state, such as a visual impression of printing, can provide an overall reason for belief regardless of our desires or practical reasons. Second, apart from beliefs whose content involves desires in certain ways, the rationality of a belief is not dependent on desires or even the rationality of desires. The asymmetry of this dependency relation between practical and theoretical reason does not, however, imply that practical reasons are derivative from theoretical ones. It is true that believing that an experience would be, say, enjoyable can provide a reason to act to bring it about and that wanting something cannot provide a reason for belief in any similar way. But the desirability of enjoyable experience – roughly, its reason-grounding power – does not depend on prior or contemporaneous beliefs about its goodness or good-making qualities. The basic grounds of practical reasons do not depend on intellectual recognition or endorsement.

beliefs might do the relevant instrumental work. But these fine points of action theory need not be pursued here. (2) One might argue that merely true instrumental belief is sufficient for a good reason, even if irrational. Nothing in this paper will turn on that issue or certain other controversies about what counts as a good reason. All parties agree that it is rationally preferable for the relevant instrumental belief to be rational and for one to have grounds for rationally holding it rather than merely a disposition to hold it on non-rationalizing grounds.

The priority of theoretical over practical reason, then, is quite limited. It is chiefly a matter of the positive instrumental role of the former in guiding action and its negative role in defeasibility. But even its capacity to defeat practical reasons depends on using the weight of some of them, such as anticipated pain, to override others, such as anticipated pleasure. Without a practical footing of this kind, theoretical considerations cannot justifiedly override practical ones. Furthermore, the global notion of a rational person requires the rationality of both kinds of elements, theoretical (above all beliefs) and practical (above all desires), and an integration between them. This idea is important for the overall question of the authority of practical reason in the moral sphere, and it will be pursued below.

IV The status of moral reasons

I have pointed out that the rational belief that something will be unpleasant can provide a practical reason, say to avoid it. If theoretical reason can have this kind of normative power (through the authority of cognition), might we expect it to have moral authority as well? The answer may be seen if we consider how it is that, in general, rationally believing an experience will be unpleasant provides a reason to avoid it. Is this an empirical truth? I doubt that. Granted, one might not have an adequate understanding of the relevant concepts apart from having experience of the phenomena in question. But that does not preclude a priori status of the proposition in which they figure. On my view, both basic practical principles and a number of basic moral ones are not only a priori but self-evident. Let me explain.

I am employing a notion of the self-evident on which self-evident propositions are truths such that (a) in virtue of adequately understanding them one has justification for believing them (which does not entail that all who adequately understand them *do* believe them), and (b) believing them on the basis of adequately understanding them entails knowing them.[17] This account is moderate in a number of ways that support its applicability to substantive principles. It allows for *defeasibility* of our justification for believing a self-evident proposition; it does not entail that such propositions are (psychologically) *compelling*, in the sense that comprehendingly

---

[17] My "Self-Evidence," *Philosophical Perspectives* 13 (1999): 205–28 contains a more detailed account of self-evidence than *The Good in the Right*, and some extensions of both treatments are made in my "Skepticism about the A Priori: Self-Evidence, Defeasibility and *Cogito* Propositions," in *The Oxford Handbook of Skepticism*, ed. John Greco (Oxford University Press, 2008), 149–75. The term "fully" may be preferable to "adequately" provided one does not take it to imply maximality.

considering them entails believing them; and it does not preclude their *provability* in terms of something else, possibly something more basic. Given these points, it should be no surprise that there can be rational disagreement on self-evident propositions.[18]

What moral principles might be self-evident in this sense? I have argued for ascribing this status to *Rossian* principles. These include principles expressing prima facie obligations of justice and non-injury, veracity and fidelity, beneficence and self-improvement, and reparation and gratitude. Showing that these are self-evident, even in the moderate sense just indicated, is difficult; but once we understand the self-evident as I propose and so reject the stereotype on which it is *obvious* or compelling or both, the way is open to appreciate the case for their self-evidence. Consider, for instance, the proposition that there is a prima facie obligation not to burn infants to death. Is there any good reason to doubt this? And is it merely an empirical truth? Such examples provide no conclusive argument, but they do have heuristic value.

If such principles are even empirically true, then there are at least weak prima facie reasons for the relevant types of action in any case in which the specified ground exists, such as making a promise or finding someone who will die without one's help. It is clear (I think self-evident) that a prima facie obligation implies a prima facie reason to do the thing in question. What is not self-evident, though clearly true, is that there can also be *final* moral reasons for action, i.e., prima facie reasons that are not overridden, as where only I can save a child's life and I need only restrain it for a moment until a speeding vehicle that will otherwise hit it has passed. Whether there are cases of final moral obligation is at most rarely doubted; but the absence of overriding moral reasons is not self-evident, and a strong skeptic might raise the question how we ever know there are none. I assume that we can know, or at any rate quite justifiedly believe, they are absent. Let us suppose so. This still leaves the question of whether any *non*-moral overriders might exist.

The question is important for the issue of the authority of practical reason because we should not simply assume that moral reasons are supreme from the practical point of view – something egoists (among others) will deny. For a moral reason to be *supreme* is for it to have sufficient force to outweigh any combination of opposing reasons, whether of the same or of different kinds, such as reasons of self-interest. (Religious reasons, say that an act

---

[18] How there can be rational disagreement on the self-evident is dealt with in my "Rational Disagreement as a Challenge to Practical Ethics and Moral Theory," in *Epistemology: New Essays*, ed. Quentin Smith (Oxford University Press, 2008), 225–47.

is commanded by God, and aesthetic reasons, for instance that a certain dominating treatment of another person would be beautiful, might also be cited as possibly conflicting with moral reasons, but I shall ignore them here on the ground that reasons of self-interest are the clearest candidates of normative reasons whose authority might be considered greater than that of any moral reasons.) I also believe we should not assume that moral reasons even have *priority* over other kinds, in the sense that a moral reason for doing something outweighs any set of competing reasons of any other single kind.

These limitations on what may be assumed concerning the normative authority of moral reasons increase the difficulty of the perennial question of whether it is rational to be moral. We cannot support a positive answer by showing that there *are* moral reasons, even final as opposed to only prima facie ones, because we must not assume that moral reasons must be supreme or even have priority over all other kinds of reasons. Even if we make the plausible assumption that if an agent has a *morally* final reason for an action – one not overridden by any conflicting moral reason(s) – then performing an action for that reason is at least not *irrational*, this leaves open that it might be *more* rational to do something else. We must, then, pursue the question of the rationality of moral action in a more nuanced way if we are to provide even a partial account of the normative authority of standards of moral obligation.

V   Rationality, reasonableness, and moral judgment

The outlined account of reasons for action is at once internalist and objectivist. The grounds of practical reasons are internal, but there really are such reasons and there are intersubjectively knowable, even self-evident, truths connecting them with their grounds. This view does, however, imply a kind of relativity and, for that reason, is quite latitudinarian. Let me explain:

The relativity and permissiveness of rationality

The rationality of an action (or belief) for a person is relative to the person's experiences. Given how different people's experiences can be, this implies that there may be at most a few propositions that all rational persons must believe and (apart from the contingent requirements of sustaining life) only a few act-types they all must token. Granted, perhaps *if* one comprehendingly considers the obvious proposition that if A is under ninety years of age and B is over that age, *then* A is younger than B, one must believe it. But must every rational person comprehendingly consider this proposition? The case with action is perhaps more complicated. Perhaps a rational human being with experience anything like ours must, even in a short time, perform acts of certain broad types, say the type, moving one's attention from one thing to another.[19]

Consider a thought experiment. Imagine a kind of cognitive amnesia wherein people simply cease to have beliefs, though they retain the capacity – including the conceptual capacity – to form them as soon as they have appropriate experiences: call these *eliciting* experiences. This possibility apparently shows that there are no propositions a person need believe at a given time in order to be rational at that time. Even if what is possible is only a limited cognitive amnesia – say with respect to propositions one need not believe in order to retain the conceptual skills sufficient for being rational – it still appears that no particular propositions need be believed by all rational persons in every moment of their existence.

Even if there are some *categories* of propositions, such as simple logical truths, of which every rational adult person must believe an appropriate subset, the minimal rationality of persons apparently does not entail their holding moral beliefs. But suppose it did. They might still never have moral reasons for action. It is not just that a person might never see, for instance, a child who can be saved from an approaching car. A person could be kept alive without ever having any relations with others. This might make it possible to have general moral beliefs (e.g., partly through cinematic exposure to experiences), yet no moral reasons for specific actions (at least toward others). One might say that, by virtue of holding those beliefs, such a person would still be *moral in character.* Perhaps, but having those beliefs does not entail any particular moral motivation. Indeed, it is doubtful that rationality alone entails such motivation on the part of an (adult) agent – or entails enough such motivation to qualify the agent as moral. Even

---

[19] The relativity in question is compatible with a full-bloodedly rationalist moral epistemology and theory of action. Cf. the claim of Lionel K. McPherson that his "account of moral normativity is nonrationalist: (1) it denies that all rational persons as such have reason to do what morality requires; (2) it denies that moral motivation can derive solely from a rational person's acknowledgment of moral reasons." See "Normativity and the Rejection of Rationalism," *Journal of Philosophy* 104 (2007): 55–70 (67). There is no reason why a rationalist should deny that what we have reason to do depends on our experience or insist that rationality as such requires having – as opposed to there being – reasons to act morally. This is argued in detail in ch. 7 of *Architecture* (with much of whose account of rationality, however, McPherson's views are compatible). Regarding (2), a rationalist can be a belief-desire theorist concerning the motivation and explanation of action. McPherson, like others, is perhaps attributing to rationalism the rejection of this view found in, e.g., Thomas Nagel's *The Possibility of Altruism* (Oxford University Press, 1967), but rationalism does not entail rejecting it nor is one committed to rejecting it *by* denying Humean instrumentalism about practical reason.

people who have certain moral beliefs to the effect that they ought to do something need not be sufficiently motivated to act on those beliefs. This is to affirm a version of motivational externalism.[20]

Rational agents and moral reasons

If I have been right so far, it is not true that simply being rational entails being moral in any general sense or even that simply being rational entails acting morally when one judges one ought to act so and is capable of it. We should not, then, answer the question "Why be moral?" by maintaining that being moral is entailed by being rational. This, however, is a rather narrow conclusion. It does not imply, for instance, that we normal human beings might never have overriding moral reasons for action or even that moral reasons do not generally have a high degree of normative authority for us. To see the importance of this point, let us focus on persons who are rational in the relevant capacity sense *and*, like most rational adults, live with others in a social context in which they are exposed to and understand at least rough formulations of all or most of the Rossian moral principles, say that we have prima facie obligations not to lie, not to kill, not to break promises, and, positively, to help others who are in distress.

For most such persons, it is not only rational to believe those principles; their believing them false would be quite unjustified. Given the understanding that, from daily life and exposure to ordinary moral discourse, most such people would have these or similar principles, they would be justified in believing them. Granted, the notion of the prima facie is not one an ordinary rational person who is exposed to moral principles need use; but such people are justified in believing (e.g.) something to the effect that "in general" or "by and large" or "barring emergencies" one should keep one's promises (avoid lying, and so forth). In part on the basis of beliefs of this kind, such people will often have prima facie reasons to act morally, say where they make a promise or are asked for information. When, moreover, they have overall reason to act morally, their reason for doing so is surely strong enough so that their doing so for that reason is never irrational.

Is there any reason to think that such prima facie moral reasons are always or are typically overridden, say by reasons of self-interest? I doubt this. The point is not that self-interest often favors the same actions as

---

[20] A detailed discussion of motivational internalism and externalism is provided, and a moderate externalism is defended, in my "Moral Judgment and Reasons for Action," in my *Moral Knowledge and Ethical Character* (Oxford University Press, 1997), 217–47.

morality, though this is surely so. Recall the case outlined above for the impersonality of the grounds of reasons. What should rational persons who think clearly about reasons believe about whether their own good is better than that of others or about whether, given the basis of their reasons for action, they always have better reason, in a case of conflict between the two, to advance their own interest than to do what morality calls for? There is no good ground for such persons with anything close to normal human experience to resist thinking that their good is on a par with the good of others and that, accordingly, when the two conflict they do not always have better reason for self-preference than for moral choice.

These points concern cognition. Suppose it is agreed that a rational person with a certain common kind of social experience – say growing up and living in mainly coordinated and often harmonious relations with others – should believe the kinds of moral and normative propositions that, on my view, entail the existence of moral reasons. Without rational desires, they will still not act rationally. This point poses a problem here because we are concerned not just with the cognitive authority of reason but also with its practical authority and its power to ground rational action. Here I have two points.

First, in a globally rational person there is an integration between rational beliefs (especially those with normative content pertinent to what one should do) and rational desires, and it would not be rational to have both the kinds of rational beliefs I have ascribed to "normal" rational persons and, while living in mainly coordinated and often harmonious relations with others, *only* egoistic basic desires. Just what range of non-egoistic desires rationality may call for given this integration, and in what range of cases they must outweigh egoistic desires, will be explored below.

Second, *given* the kinds of social experiences I am assuming for normal adults living in civilized conditions, some degree of altruistic desire is both rational and expectable. To illustrate both this point and the kind of integration between belief and desire characteristic of rational persons, if (1) I believe the moral principles in question (as I should given their self-evidence and an adequate understanding of them), (2) I believe something to the effect that, given our similar experiences of (especially) pain and pleasure, my good is not better than yours, and (3) my desires are integrated with these rational beliefs, then will I not be likely, in our interactions, to have motivation to act morally which is strong enough to lead to my in fact acting so even in a wide range of cases where my own pleasure or other interests are better served by immoral action? This seems so. I do not think the point is empirical, but I must grant that (1)–(3) do not permit assigning definite probabilities to such action. Specific probabilities can be assigned only in the light of facts about the person in question. We must also allow for some cases in which weakness of will or some other interference with the integration blocks moral action that would otherwise occur. What we can say on philosophical grounds is something like this: the stronger the beliefs referred to in (1) and (2) and the greater the integration specified in (3), the greater the likelihood of the kind of moral action (3) describes.

Rationality and reasonableness

This conclusion falls short of the claim that a rational person of the integrated kind in question will *always* act morally. But if moral reasons are not assumed to be supreme, that conclusion is in any case too strong. There may, however, be justification for a stronger conclusion than we have so far argued for, and I want to approach it by bringing in the concept of *reasonableness*. Reasonableness entails rationality, but not conversely. 'Be reasonable', for instance, is an appropriate thing to urge of someone who is biased but perfectly rational or, indeed, is being rational in a given matter but also ruthless in pursuing self-interest. Saying 'Be reasonable' presupposes rationality; it would not be properly said to someone who is not rational. 'Be rational' is quite different; it suggests that the speaker believes the addressee is not thinking competently on the relevant matter. It would not normally be an appeal to specific reasons but an attempt to engender or rekindle a sensitivity to them. If, for instance, it is said to someone who is being irrational in an overall way, it might be an attempt to cause a change, perhaps by calling to mind standards the person respects but has violated on the occasion.[21]

If reasonableness is a stronger normative notion than rationality, we should ask whether, at least under some conditions, it is reasonable to be a moral person and unreasonable not to be, or at least unreasonable to act immorally. The notion of reasonableness is difficult to characterize briefly, but, in preparation for answering these questions, let me indicate some aspects of it that help us see how it is normatively stronger than rationality.

I begin with a comparative point. Reasonableness requires a greater responsiveness to reasons than does mere rationality. Apart from special lapses as may be caused by, say, abnormal fatigue, a reasonable person must actually respond to reasons when they are offered or otherwise encountered.

---

[21] These points on reasonableness are largely drawn from my *Architecture*, ch. 6. Cf. the discussions of it by John Rawls in *Political Liberalism* (New York: Columbia University Press, 1993); and T. M. Scanlon, *What We Owe to Each Other* (Cambridge, Mass.: Harvard University Press, 1998).

Responding to reasons, to be sure, does not always take the form of acting on them. On being given a strong financial reason to break a promise, I may appreciate its bearing on what I should do and, though tempted to act on it, be moved to explain why it is not compelling. This is a response to the reason, but not a case of acting on it.

A second important point is that being a reasonable person requires a measure of good judgment and is incompatible with pervasively bad judgment (though a reasonable person may make some bad judgments in certain cases). An aspect of the required level of good judgment is – in rough terms – a tendency to treat like cases alike and to be prepared to give a reason for doing otherwise. This holds both in the theoretical realm, for instance in scientific matters, and in the practical domain, say in prudent classification of risks and benefits and in the treatment of people. As this point suggests, a track record in judgments about what means will yield desired ends is also relevant.

If reasonable people must, within limits, have good judgment, must they also unfailingly act on it? This would preclude some major kinds of weak-willed conduct; and although such action may be prima facie irrational and, if frequent in people's behaviour, count against their reasonableness, there is room for some weak-willed action even in the lives of reasonable persons – and more room in the lives of merely rational people who are not reasonable.[22] There is no good way to quantify this fourth point; but even as it stands it helps to bring out how reasonableness should be understood.

A related, fifth point helps to clarify the fourth. There are limits to how much a reasonable person may be governed by mere whim, in the sense (roughly) of desire not grounded in one's long-term projects and arising from sudden attractions. These limits are more permissive for merely rational persons, i.e., persons who are rational but not reasonable. One kind of defect that counts against reasonableness is having so many whims that even if they are resisted, their presence causes interference with normal conduct. Another such defect is certain sorts of unresisted whims, say, to dangle for an hour by one's toes.

Nothing said so far entails that a reasonable person must be a social being, in a sense implying ongoing social relations with others. The last person in a dying world would not necessarily cease to be reasonable. If, however, we think of a social being simply as one *capable* of social interaction – and this is the kind to which the question "Why be moral?"

---

[22] That in special cases weak-willed action may be rational, though it *tends* to count against rationality, is argued in detail in my "Weakness of Will and Rational Action," *Australasian Journal of Philosophy* 68 (1990): 270–81.

is chiefly relevant – our conclusion may be different. The concept of a reasonable person does seem to be social in this capacity sense. Since our concern here is with people functioning in the kinds of social contexts that call for moral conduct, we may say more. *When* reasonable people live in human societies of the kind that concern us, they maintain cooperative relations with certain other people.

A stronger point about persons living in societies of the relevant kind is warranted here: reasonable people must, in a suitable proportion of their relations with others, be willing to give reasons to them for certain kinds of conduct and to consider reasons given by them for similar kinds of conduct. Think of the complaint that someone 'won't listen at all'. If this is true, such a person is not reasonable. By and large, neither is someone who, even to intimates, will not give any reasons for significant kinds of conduct. None of this entails highly specific standards of conduct or presupposes that moral reasons have normative authority; and although moral conduct, in calling for respect for persons, implies such reasonableness, that claim is not needed as a premise for the point made here about reasonableness. Moreover, if, as seems plausible, we can presuppose rationality and the kinds of beliefs and desires I have argued are expectable in rational persons given a normal kind of human experience, then we can see how the interpersonal aspects of reasonableness can be expected to lead to a willingness to negotiate and even – in ways to be indicated shortly – to make morally structured agreements. Far more could be said here; there are, for instance, complicated constraints on the ways in which reasonable people must respond to reasons. But perhaps enough has been said to enable us to take another step in understanding reasonableness in relation to morality.

Permissions, demands, and requirements of reason

A useful conception of reasonableness represents it as a *demand* of reason. Meeting this demand is more than a matter of avoiding irrationality, as one does by having minimally rational beliefs and desires, but it is less than a requirement of rationality, as with wanting to stop a raging headache and, in the cognitive domain, believing an obviously self-evident proposition one is comprehendingly considering. The unreasonable are subject to normative criticism; the irrational may instead be candidates for medical help. The question I am now raising is whether a reasonable person must be moral.

A positive answer may not be given without qualification, for people differ greatly in experiences, and, as indicated for hypothetical cases, some may lack the kinds of experiential grounds for beliefs and desires in the light of which one may be expected to believe basic moral principles and is likely to have some measure of altruistic desire. Consider, however, people who, like essentially everyone living in civilized conditions, grow up with nurturing from elders, live in coordinated and often friendly relations with others, and believe other people are much like them in basic physical and psychological needs, in sentience, and in many common beliefs and desires. These include beliefs about the environment, about elementary causal connections, and about human practices; desires corresponding to bodily needs and social standing are also included. We are all different; but, in nearly all of humanity, differences exist against the background of overlapping physical and psychological characteristics, including certain beliefs and desires.

For people in this huge category, it is also reasonable to believe the Rossian moral principles or similar ones, even if (as in the case of certain philosophical skeptics) it is not irrational not to believe them. The same holds for accepting the impersonality of normative grounds. Given that a reasonable person will exhibit a substantial degree of integration – and a higher degree than a merely rational person – between cognition and motivation, it is also reasonable to have strong moral desires. Beyond this, it is reasonable to have a good measure of altruistic desire.

Altruistic desires, moreover, are clearly entailed by *loving* others. Love requires intrinsically wanting the good of the person loved. This is not to claim that a reasonable person who lives among others *must* love someone else; but it is important to see that those who do love must have desires of a kind that support at least some moral conduct. Moreover, if it is both reasonable to want to be loved – something whose value even an egoist will appreciate – and also reasonable to believe that being loved is more likely, and more likely to be stable, if one loves reciprocally, then there is yet another reason to cultivate and maintain the kinds of altruistic desires that support moral conduct.

If everything said so far is correct, we may say that, for at least the ordinary kinds of persons described, it is not only rational but also reasonable to be moral – to some degree. But what degree? Can we show that it is never unreasonable to do something one sees one has an overall moral obligation not to do? Certainly we cannot show that this is always *irrational*. Indeed, the normative power of self-interest is apparently such that it is never irrational to act in its service, even if that is immoral. Having granted this much to the egoist, however, I hasten to add that it seems equally plausible to maintain that it is never irrational to act in the service of morality, even if that violates self-interest.[23] I see no way to show that reasonableness entails always doing what morality requires (at least where one knows what it requires), and here I leave this open. I also leave open whether a reasonable person who is moral in an overall sense must *always* adhere to final moral obligation.[24] Perhaps there are some lapses that entail only moral imperfection but do not sufficiently stain moral character in a way that prevents the person's being moral overall. If being an overall moral person does not require invariably doing what morality requires, then being reasonable does not require it if the moral standard it entails is, as it appears, no stronger than being an overall moral person.[25]

A moral skeptic who grants this last point may insist that nothing said so far *proves* that it is unreasonable to be a moral person in the overall sense. But proof constitutes a perhaps unreasonably high standard here. Could one prove this without showing that being a moral person is rationally required for us, in the sense that implies that failure to be so is *irrational*? I do not claim that one can show this; my point is simply that the weight of evidence favors the view that it is reasonable, and not merely rational, to be moral.

This point is consistent with granting that the question 'Why be reasonable?' has not been shown to be rationally inadmissible. Indeed, I have granted that being merely rational does not entail being reasonable and that, for particular elements such as beliefs and actions, although being reasonable entails being rational, the converse does not hold. A merely rational person could ask what reason there is to be reasonable overall, and it is doubtful that we can show that it is irrational not to be reasonable in an overall way. But, supposing that we cannot show that being so is rationally required categorically, we might be able to show that it is required *given* certain rational beliefs and rational desires that the rational person in question has. Quite apart from that, however, I have indicated how it can be shown that being moral is not irrational and, given certain assumptions

[23] That acting morally is never irrational has been long held by Bernard Gert, e.g., in *Morality: Its Nature and Justification* (Oxford University Press, 1998), and is also held by Parfit, *On What Matters*.

[24] I leave open what constitutes adhering to a moral obligation in this context. The point made here can accommodate the view that it requires true belief, the position that justified belief is enough, and even the view that mere belief is enough. There are limits to how much error moral persons can make about their obligations, but some of what needs to be said on this matter concerns the theory of excusability.

[25] For an account and defense of the kind of reasonable compromise between egoistic and altruistic considerations that morality represents, see James P. Sterba, "Completing the Kantian Project: From Rationality to Equality," *Proceedings and Addresses of the American Philosophical Association* 82 (2008): 47–83.

about the kind of person in question – including the kind most likely to discuss the issue – being moral in an overall way is a demand of reason.

If a strong motivational internalism were true, we could maintain that a person could not knowingly violate an overall moral obligation. But surely weakness of will is possible, and for that and other reasons no strong motivational internalist view should be accepted. What the theory of rationality does enable us to claim is that in a *reasonable* person, there is a high degree of integration between self-addressed normative judgments, such as that one must keep a promise, and conduct. Given this integration and the kinds of beliefs and desires that must be possessed by persons of the normal kind I have described, we can say something rough but capable of fruitful refinement in several directions: for the most part, and in the most important matters, reasonable persons who live with others in a society of the kind we have sketched will act morally.

We now can see the perennial question 'Why should I be moral?' in a new light. To see this, we should first set aside the motivational interpretation on which "should" refers to motivational reasons, as in 'Why should I want to hurt him?' Our concern is normative.[26] The question might then be whether there are non-moral reasons to be moral. One result of our reflections is that this may concern external reasons *there are* for anyone to be moral or external reasons there are *for me* (or some other person) to be moral. A further result is that the existence of reasons, even for me, to do or be a certain way, may be held to render it minimally rational, to make it reasonable, or even to render it rationally required. In any of these three cases, the experiences of the person in question are crucial for providing reasons supporting any of these levels of commitment. What follows is a partial summary of conclusions on this topic warranted by this paper.

VI Conclusion

The perennial question of the relation between morality and rationality is multidimensional. In pursuing it, I have distinguished practical from theoretical rationality, have connected both with the notion of global rationality, and have treated the status of moral reasons as a question in the theory of practical reason. I have also distinguished practical from theoretical reasons and have shown how the latter can have a kind of authority over

---

[26] William K. Frankena distinguishes the motivational and normative sense of "should" in his short instructive discussion of 'Why should I be moral?' in his *Ethics*, second edn. (Englewood Cliffs, NJ: Prentice-Hall, 1973), 113–14. See also his *Thinking about Morality* (Ann Arbor, Mich.: University of Michigan Press, 1980).

the former that the former do not have over the latter. Practical and theoretical rationality are mutually irreducible, but structurally parallel. The
most important analogous element figuring in this paper is the experiential,
non-egoistic grounding of reasons in both realms.

In the light of this conception of the background against which the
relation between morality and rationality should be considered, I have
argued that we cannot presuppose specific beliefs and desires on the part
of all rational persons. What we can do is identify beliefs and desires that
rational persons will have, *given* a certain familiar kind of life. This is a
kind of life known to all who think about the issue before us; and it is for
that kind of life, in which moral reasons can conflict with self-interested
reasons and other kinds of reasons, that the question of the relation between
morality and rationality is best pursued.

For this familiar kind of life, I have argued that, on the theoretical side, a
certain impersonality of the grounds of reasons should be accepted. I have
also maintained (and argued elsewhere) that Rossian moral principles –
though not necessarily Ross's specific formulations – should be accepted,
indeed are self-evident. Although we may not assume (and I reject) the
view that practical rationality requires that agents *must* act in accordance
with their moral judgments, I have affirmed that in rational persons, and
even more in reasonable persons, there must be an integration between
theoretical and practical reason such that there is a tendency to act on what
one takes to be one's practical reasons, particularly where one takes these
to be undefeated.

With the notion of a reasonable person sketched and made a major focus
of inquiry into the relation between morality and rationality, and with a
certain ordinary kind of reasonable person in mind, I considered several
central questions that must be kept distinct. One is the global question
of whether a reasonable person must be unqualifiedly moral. Another is
the invariability question: whether a reasonable person must *always* act
morally. A third is the aretaic question of whether a reasonable person
must, in some overall if minimal way, be moral (morally virtuous). And
the fourth is the proportionality question: whether such a person must,
given appropriate occasions, act morally in a suitably weighted proportion
of cases. Only for the last two have I defended positive answers.

Reasonableness is a demand of rationality. This does not entail that an
unreasonable person is irrational, and we cannot show either this claim or
that an immoral person must be irrational. That impossibility, however,
is of limited significance given how much immorality mere rationality
tolerates, especially in lives in which the route to reasonableness is blocked

by misfortune, obscured by ignorance, or overshadowed by superstition. It is quite enough to show that, in character and conduct, being moral in an overall way is reasonable and is indeed supported by a theory of theoretical and practical rationality that can countenance the initial plausibility of skepticism without granting its conclusions.[27]

[27] Earlier versions of this paper were presented at Dartmouth College, Simon Fraser University, and the Center for Ethics and Culture at Notre Dame. I benefited from vigorous discussion on those occasions, and for helpful comments I particularly want to thank Bernard Gert, Walter Sinnott-Armstrong, James Sterba, Evan Tiffany, and, especially, Sam Black, whose comments were rigorous and detailed.

PART II

Intuition, Obligation, and Virtue

CHAPTER 5

Intuitions, intuitionism, and moral judgment

Ethical intuitionism has now taken a place as a major position in contemporary ethical theory. But there is still a widespread impression that the view depends on concepts and theses that are insufficiently clear for the work they must do or, if clear enough to sustain the view, then not plausible. One question here is what constitutes an intuition. Another is how intuitive cognitions differ from inferential ones. There is also a need to address the question of just how ethical intuitionism depends on the answer. This paper addresses all three questions and, in the light of what we find in pursuing them, explores the resources of intuitionist ethical theory for providing an understanding of how moral judgments may be justified.

I The nature and varieties of intuitions

Intuitions are important not only for intuitionist ethical theories but also for philosophy in general. Indeed, even many philosophers who do not speak of intuitions theorize as if they were in part seeking to provide an account of shared intuitions, say intuitions about knowledge or obligation. They are what we might call *intuitivists*. An intuitivist must be responsive to intuitions, but need not be an intuitionist. The term 'intuition' is, in any case, not crucial for understanding intuitionism. The main point is that philosophy, like any theoretical enterprise, requires data, and intuitions are crucial philosophical data. For Rawls among many others, our data include the "considered judgments" that, when suitably placed in reflective equilibrium with principles of justice, confirm the latter.[1] The judgments

---

[1] Rawls (1971) says that "any ethical theory is bound to depend on intuition to some degree at many points" (40), and that "there is nothing irrational in the appeal to intuitions to settle questions of priority" (41). His later discussion of "considered judgments" and their role in reflective equilibrium (47–8) indicates nothing inconsistent with taking those to be a kind of intuition. They are certainly not represented as premise-dependent. Cf. Tim Mulgen's view that "One primary purpose of a moral theory is to unify and make sense of our considered judgments or intuitions . . . A decisive intuition represents a judgment any acceptable moral theory must accommodate" (2006: 2).

constituting our data at least roughly fit the characterization of (cognitive) intuitions to be given shortly.

I am taking intuitionism as an ethical theory to be, in outline and in a minimal version, the view that there is at least one moral principle that is non-inferentially and intuitively knowable. Historically, intuitionists have also posited what they consider an irreducible plurality of such principles, and I propose to call this stronger view, on which there is a group of at least several such moral principles (such as we find in W. D. Ross and others) *generic intuitionism*.[2] Conceived more fully, an intuitionist ethics also incorporates a particular set of basic moral principles that directly apply to daily life. A specific intuitionist theory that, like Ross's, achieves this is an intuitionism. My intuitionism emphasizes principles expressing obligations of justice and non-injury, of fidelity and veracity, of beneficence and self-improvement, of reparation and gratitude (Ross's list, which I interpret differently at several points), and of liberty and respectfulness – my two additions to Ross's list.[3] More will be said about these ten *Rossian obligations*, as we may call them, when their status has been clarified.

An account of intuitions should clarify at least five related notions. Let me characterize each briefly and then proceed to indicate how some of them figure in ethical intuitionism as I conceive it.

Cognitive intuition. This is the most common kind of intuition considered in ethical literature: it is intuition *that p* (a proposition), say that a student's paper deserves an A or, to take a moral example, that one should not accept a major gift from a salesperson who should be fairly compared with competitors. In the latter case, to be sure, the intuitive proposition could be subsumed under a moral rule; but this need not prevent it from being the object of an intuition, and some who would have it might not accept any such rule – at least antecedently.

---

[2] This characterization can probably include all major intuitionists if we distinguish irreducibility from underivability. Sidgwick, e.g., may have regarded the kinds of principles I call Rossian as derivable (even if not rigorously deducible) from his overall utilitarian formula; but derivability does not entail reducibility, and I do not think he considered them reducible to formulas expressible wholly in utilitarian terms. Indeed, in a general characterization of intuitionism he calls it "the view of ethics which regards as the practically ultimate end of moral actions their conformity to certain rules or dictates of Duty" (1907: 96), using the plural. Moreover, his own view affirms more than one ethical axiom; see e.g. (1907: 382). I leave aside the question of whether strong particularists should count as intuitionists if they countenance non-inferential knowledge of singular but not general moral propositions. If they do not countenance such knowledge of some ethical generalities, I prefer to speak of their being *particularistic intuitivists*. For distinctions among various forms of ethical particularism and criticism of some, see my (2006a).

[3] Chapter 5 of my (2004) introduces and clarifies these last two principles and proposes some improvements in Ross's interpretation of the others.

Objectual intuition. This is roughly direct apprehension of either (a) a concept, such as that of obligation, or (b) a property or relation, such as the property of being a promise, the property of being unjust, or the relation of entailment. As a kind of knowledge, such intuitions are in a sense *epistemic* and may also be considered cognitive, though not propositional, but I prefer to reserve 'cognitive intuition' for intuitions with propositional objects. In a sense to be explored below, these objectual intuitions constitute intellectual perceptions.

Intuitiveness. This is a property primarily of propositions, but is also predicated of concepts, arguments, and other intellectual phenomena. As predicated of a proposition, it is equivalent to the proposition's being *intuitive* – having the property of evoking (under certain conditions) what might be called *the sense of non-inferential credibility* (this notion may be relativized, e.g. to persons of a certain description or to a certain level of understanding needed for the intuitive sense to be manifested). That sense is roughly equivalent to the sense of a proposition's (non-inferentially) seeming true, and it normally produces an inclination to believe.[4] As predicated of arguments, 'intuitive' means roughly *seeming plausible*, a property an argument may have in virtue of being obviously sound, or quite perceptibly valid and having plausible premises, or something quite similar. As applied to concepts, it means roughly *readily understandable* in a sense implying that one can imagine instances or at least what they are like. Far more can be said here, but my aim is simply to sketch the basic idea.

Propositional intuition. This is intuition conceived as a proposition taken to be intuitively known; say that capital punishment is wrong, or that what is colored is extended. Hence, unlike cognitive intuitions, propositional intuitions are abstract, non-psychological elements and (on most uses) include only truths.[5] In a wider use, intuitions might be simply propositions that exhibit intuitiveness, as where someone says, 'Let's begin our inquiry with a range of intuitions we should take into account'.

Apprehensional capacity. This is intuition as a rational capacity – *facultative intuition*, for short – a kind needed for philosophical reflection

---

[4] One might think intuitions are constituted by "a subclass of inclinations to believe," as argued by Erlenbaugh and Molyneux (2009). It seems to me that an entailment here is the most that can be claimed, at least on the plausible assumption that we are speaking of (occurrent) phenomenal states and may take inclinations to believe as dispositional in nature.

[5] Moore said of propositions about the good, for instance, that "when I call such propositions 'Intuitions' I mean merely to assert that they are incapable of proof." See (1903: 36). See Sellars (1968) for his use of 'intuiteds' for intuited propositions (this category is wider than Moore's in that he intended to use 'intuition' as he here characterizes it for propositions that do not meet Moore's strict standard for intuitions.

and manifested in relation to each of the other four cases. It is roughly a non-inferential capacity by whose exercise what is intuitively believed or known is believed or known. Ethical intuition, like logical intuition, is a special case of this capacity (calling it a faculty is simply classificatory as to its scope and implies no implication of modularity of mind or a special kind of intellectual sense). Cognitive and objectual intuition will be my main concern, but the other notions should be kept in mind if only for the clarity we gain by distinguishing them from the former two and connecting them with those when necessary.[6]

There is much to be learned from conceiving facultative intuition as analogous to the 'faculty' of perception and intuitions as analogous to perceptions. Take seeing as a paradigm of perception. Intuitive apprehension is analogous to seeing. First, it has objects, typically, or at least most importantly for our purposes, concepts and properties. (We need not discuss what kinds of objects these are, but I assume they are both abstract and in some way connected with linguistic usage.) Second, in addition to objectual apprehension – apprehension *of* – there is also apprehension as: *aspectual apprehension*. The former, apprehension *simpliciter*, is *de re* and apparently does not entail cognition, as where a small child apprehends the wrongness of smashing a toy but does not believe that this is wrong or see it *as* wrong. Aspectual apprehension entails at least some degree of understanding of the property the object is apprehended as having, say the wrongness of smashing the toy. Third, given an apprehension, it may also intuitively seem to us *that* (for instance) an act is wrong. Fourth, we may, on the basis of this seeming, believe the act is wrong. Fifth, if this belief is true, then we intuitively see (apprehend) that the act is wrong. Such true doxastic intuition, a case of intuitive belief, would at least normally constitute intuitive knowledge. We thus have, with intellectual perception as with sensory perception, simple ('objectual') perception, aspectual perception, and propositional perception: apprehensions *of* the relevant kind of object, apprehensions of the object as something, and apprehensions *that* it is something. Objectual apprehensions have the same kind of veridicality as perceptions of objects; aspectual and propositional apprehensions may or may not embody beliefs, but, when they do, they commonly represent knowledge.

Are there, as the perceptual analogy suggests, apprehensional counterparts of illusion and hallucination? Might someone mistakenly ('illusorily')

---

[6] Most of these notions are discussed in my (2004), e.g. 32–9, 48, and 208 n. 37, but it contains little explicit treatment of intuitive seemings.

apprehend the property of redness as coming in precisely discrete shades in concert with its wavelengths? This would be a misapprehension but could still be *of* red, somewhat as visually misperceiving a glass's round rim as elliptical is still seeing that rim. In neither case, moreover, need the illusion produce false belief. An analogue of hallucination is more difficult to delineate. Mere possibilia, such as chimeras, are apprehensible, so – if we assume that hallucinatory perceptions have no object at all – we must focus on something like thinking of a round square.[7] How could one apprehend "round-squarely," even granting that no false belief is implied? Perhaps someone could apprehend each of the elements with a false sense of their unity and perhaps also a sense of properties consequential on or otherwise closely connected with each. One could perhaps speak here of a hypothetical object, analogous to an object that might be posited for hallucinations, but this is not the place to carry the idea further. It is enough that the analogy between intuition and perception is extensive. Let us now explore its application to justification.

II   The role of intuitions in prima facie justification

It is widely acknowledged that sensory experience justifies beliefs based on it if anything does. If, for instance, I have a steadfast visual experience as of print before me, then I have prima facie justification for believing that there is print there. Is it any less plausible to maintain that when, in the light of understanding a proposition, I have an intuitive sense that it is true (an intuitive seeming), then I have prima facie justification for believing it?[8] In many cases of moral propositions, such intuitions are evoked by instances of general propositions that intuitionists consider self-evident (hence a priori). An intuition that I should not break a certain promise could, for example, be connected with an a priori belief that promise-keeping is prima facie obligatory, and thereby with the proposition that promises should not be broken, a proposition that, on any plausible understanding of 'should', is entailed. Both beliefs might be partly based on a sense of the fittingness of performing a promise to having made it. This is not to suggest that the general proposition is epistemologically more basic than the instantial

---

[7] For detailed discussion of the ontological and other aspects of hallucination (as well as an account of the a priori that supports intuitionism), see Chapters 1, 2, 5, and 6 of my 2010a.

[8] This principle is stronger than phenomenal conservatism as formulated by Huemer (2005: 99) – a principle one might also call phenomenal liberalism given how permissive it is. I have defended principles like this one in several parts of (2004) and will suggest some indications of their plausibility below.

one. That is not implied, nor are intuitions inferentially based on premises. The genetic order may indeed be more "inductive,"[9] with moral intuitions commonly serving as a partial basis for holding the principles under which their content is subsumable. The remainder of this section will develop these ideas.

In describing ethical intuitionism, I have treated cognitive intuitions as a kind of belief (e.g. in 2004). One reason for this is that such intuitionists as Moore, Pritchard, Ross, and many later writers (including Rawls) have spoken of intuitions in a way that presupposes that the cognition in question entails, or is a kind of, belief. One way to see that some intuitions are beliefs is to consider how a person who (sincerely) asserts something may in some cases respond when asked for a reason. One answer is 'I can't give you an argument; it's just a clear intuition'. Similarly, knowledge that an inference is invalid or that a paper deserves an A may be constituted by the kind of intuitive belief sometimes called "intuition."

If, however, one begins not with cases in which beliefs are directly in question, but with an analogy to perception and, somewhat controversially, conceives perceptual deliverances as, in the primitive cases, non-belief-entailing, one may arrive at a non-doxastic conception of intuition. Let us consider this analogy.

Suppose we are asked whether p is true. Then, if we are aware that we do not believe p but it *non-inferentially* seems true – roughly, seems true by virtue of a kind of credibility of its own rather than on the basis of one or more supporting premises – we are likely to say, in careful usage, just that: that it seems true or, in some cases, that it seems intuitive. Indeed, it would in many (though by no means all) contexts be misleading to say that we have an intuition that p but do not believe p. In the intuitional cases of non-inferential credibility, there is a sense of credibility that goes beyond the generic kind of non-inferential seeming true that can also result from a memory impression or other *non*-intuitional source of support, such as a hazy sense-impression that makes it seem to one that a distant shape is a tree. Any cognitive intuition requires *understanding* the content of p and, at least in part on that comprehensional basis, having the impression that it is true. A proposition that is non-inferentially credible on the *basis* of

---

[9] Indeed, in (2004) I noted how intuitive induction could help to explain how we come to understand, and thereby to believe, self-evident moral propositions such as those Ross formulated (e.g. 62–3). I also allowed that property intuitions – apprehensions of properties – might be more basic than propositional intuitions (208 n. 37) and, as will be apparent below, this may help to explain how we gain the concepts whose apprehension is crucial for intuitive justification and knowledge for singular as well as general propositions.

(e.g.) memory, by contrast, need not seem true in part on the basis of its content. Some memories of bare historical facts illustrate this.

The point here, then, is not that there are no non-intuitional sources of non-inferential credibility, such as seeming to remember that *p* or taking *p* to have been told to one by someone reliable. It is that, for cognitive intuitions, the intuitive impression of truth is not based on such sources. Granted, there can be justificatory overdetermination, as where memory impressions support a cognitive intuition. But it is probably the "pure" case, where there is no overdetermination, that has been most important in ethics and indeed in understanding the kinds of singular propositions that are justified by thought experiments and are central in supporting philosophical theories.

Suppose, however, that cognitive attitudes are conceived simply as those with truth-valued objects. Then a proposition that is *not* believed but, in the relevant non-doxastic phenomenal way, seems true to us may also be considered an object of intuition. For some philosophers, this non-doxastic notion of an intuitive sense of the truth of a proposition is the primary concept of an intuition.[10] We can accommodate this terminology by dividing cognitive intuitions into those that are doxastic, i.e. a kind of belief, and those that are not doxastic but have the relevant proposition as their content and embody a disposition to believe it based on a non-inferential impression of its truth. I prefer, however, to call the latter *intuitive seemings* rather than intuitions *simpliciter*, but they may also be called *non-doxastic intuitions*.[11]

This terminology allows us to do justice to the view of intuitions held by most who take seemings to be the primary (or only) cases of cognitive intuitions.[12] More important than which terminology we use is identifying the relation between doxastic intuitions and intuitive seemings. The important point here is that, much as a sensory seeming can be an evidential ground for a perceptual belief, an intuitive seeming that *p* can be an evidential ground for an "intellectual" or other non-perceptual belief that *p*. Intuitionists have typically presupposed this, even when they have

---

[10] See e.g. Bealer (1998), Sosa (1998), and Huemer (2005). Sosa's notion may allow that both beliefs and seemings can count as intuitions (see e.g. 258–9); but for Huemer intuitions are a distinct type of propositional attitude, evidenced when someone admits that *p* is intuitive (e.g. seems to be true), but denies believing it. Cf. Sinnott-Armstrong's definition of 'moral intuition' as "a strong immediate moral belief" (2008: 47).

[11] Intuitive seemings might include such property (*de re*) intuitions as occur when something seems to have a property where there is no proposition in question. This might occur where one person is seen as more sincere than another, though one has not conceptualized the difference in any particular way, say as providing an advantage in leadership.

[12] Tolhurst (1998).

conceived intuitions as beliefs. Some have asserted it, sometimes with the idea that just as a perceptual seeming – say, its visually seeming that there is a light way down the corridor – is evidence for the proposition in question, an intuitive seeming that p is evidence for p.[13] Evidential grounds need not produce overall justification, but they do produce some degree of prima facie justification, and in some cases 'justification' will serve us better than 'evidence'.

III   Intuitive evidence and non-inferential justification

If the analogy between perceptions and intuitive seemings is sound, we have reason to think that the latter have some evidential weight. But not every proposition that intuitively seems true is true, nor are all the true instances self-evident. Moreover, as is often not realized, some self-evident propositions do not seem true upon initial consideration, even if every self-evident proposition *can* seem true to someone who adequately understands it. The latter point can be clarified in the light of an account of the self-evident by appeal to the understanding of concepts as abstract entities, where this understanding includes an apprehension of their relations.[14] On this account, self-evident propositions are conceived as truths such that (a) in virtue of adequately understanding them one is justified in believing them (which does not entail that all who adequately understand them *do* believe them), and (b) believing them on the basis of adequately understanding them entails knowing them.[15] This is not the place for a full-scale extension of that account, but let me clarify it and then proceed to some points concerning intuitive non-self-evident moral judgments.

Take first the kind of self-evident proposition most readily amenable to explication in terms of the proposed account of the self-evident: analytic propositions. Suppose it is analytic that all vixens are female. If so, then an adequate understanding of the concept of a vixen *contains*, in a certain roughly formal way, that of being female. There are many ways to explicate the relevant kind of conceptual containment.[16] I prefer to do it (as will

[13] See e.g. Huemer (2005: 102), who calls "an intuition that p a state of its seeming to one that p."
[14] For a brief account of how the relevant understanding underlies justification and knowledge, see my (2008).
[15] My (1999) contains a more detailed account of self-evidence than (2004), and some extensions of both treatments are made in my (2010a). I should add that we might also speak of full understanding to avoid the suggestion that adequacy implies sufficiency only for some specific purpose. Neither term is ideal, but 'full' may suggest maximality, which is also inappropriate.
[16] There has been much controversy over whether the notion of the analytic is adequately clear for purposes of philosophical analysis. In Chapter 5 of (2010a) I defend the view (e.g. against objections by Quine) that the notion is adequately clear for such modest use as I make of it here.

be apparent) by appeal to abstract entities and their relations, but let us first focus on an account usable even by those who prefer to avoid positing abstract entities.

Consider the phenomenology of conceptualization. Phenomenologically, one way to explicate the containment idea is to say that having a *thought* of a vixen that contains all the elements in the concept – a kind of thought possible in principle for those who adequately understand the concept – also contains the thought of femaleness. To have the former thought entails having the latter, though the point is not as obvious as, say, the thought that someone said that *p* contains the thought that *p* or the thought that if *p*, then *q*, contains the thought that *q*. Even for those who can accept something like this containment aspect of the analytic, it should be clear that moral cases are more difficult to analyze. Take an instance of Rossian principle of "duty" formulated on the assumption that prima facie obligations are grounded in certain kinds of facts (I here use 'obligation' for the deontic notion in question): that hitting a person with a cricket bat would cause excruciating pain is a moral reason – roughly, grounds a prima facie obligation – not to do it. This does not imply that the *concept* of such hitting is moral, but that the kind of fact in question grounds a moral obligation. It is an obligation-making fact, though not itself a moral fact; it grounds the applicability of, but does not contain, a moral concept. Must the concept of a moral reason for action, then, *contain*, say, the notion of avoidance of causing pain if a Rossian principle of non-injury is genuinely self-evident? Intuitionists need not claim that this containment relation holds, but nothing in the major versions of intuitionism commits them to denying the possibility. They certainly have no need to deny it if, as I suggest, the notion of conceptual containment does not presuppose that only concepts admitting of a full *analysis* may be properly said to contain other concepts.

The non-reductivist containment view that I suggest, then, does not presuppose something that at least *Moorean intuitionism* would imply is impossible: a naturalistic *analysis* of moral (prima facie) reasons. It does not presuppose even the weak kind of analysis that would be pluralistic, disjunctive, and non-hierarchical – if we may call that an analysis – a kind on which to be a moral reason is simply to be *either* an obligation of non-injury or an obligation of veracity or an obligation of beneficence . . . where the disjunction contains all the basic prima facie obligations. The possibility of such an analysis would support a conceptual containment view regarding moral reasons, but a Rossian intuitionism does not presuppose this possibility. It may leave the possibility open for prima facie reasons, though almost certainly not for final reasons. To be sure, if we think (as Ross apparently did) that even our most reflectively composed list of basic prima facie obligations may be incomplete, we will doubt that we can achieve even a full description, much less an analysis, of the basic constituents of a would-be naturalistic analysis of the notion of a moral reason.

Let us suppose that no naturalistic analysis of prima facie obligation is possible. What, then, can be said of the basis of intuitive knowledge of our apparently self-evident moral proposition? Does any containment notion apply here? To see how it might, consider an analogy. Much as we can see that certain items of furniture are in a room without seeing everything therein, we can see that a certain concept is contained in another without seeing all that the former contains. The readiest illustrations are at once phenomenological and conceptual. Suppose we are asked whether there is any moral reason to avoid acts of certain types, such as hitting someone with a cricket bat. In entertaining the thought of moral reasons for action – especially in the context of such a question – it is natural, given time to reflect, to think of *paradigms* of moral reasons, such as reasons to avoid injuring or harming persons, to keep promises, and to avoid lying. This is one way to think of how one might construct a Rossian list. The first of the three categories of reasons encompasses avoidance of acts of hitting with a cricket bat, even though neither the proposition that this is a moral reason nor the proposition that moral reasons include reasons to avoid such acts is plausibly considered analytic.

We might also begin at the abstract level. Suppose a conceptually sophis-ticated person is asked what constitutes a moral reason. A natural way to begin is with the uncontroversial idea that a reason gives support to what it is a reason for. A natural second step is to ask what differentiates moral reasons from other kinds. Here nearly anyone familiar with moral dis-course (with uses of 'right', 'wrong', 'obligation', 'morally impermissible', and other terms) is likely to think of reasons as supporting some kind of treatment of or interactions with others. Morality is at least mainly *social*. What kind of treatment, then? Here divergence is likely to occur – some will think of good treatment, others of respect, still others of specific kinds of treatment, say doing good deeds and avoiding lies. But no one with an understanding of morality and reasons would be likely, if even able, to clarify such notions without pointing to Rossian grounds of obligation. Clarity for such abstractions requires discerning the contours of particular-ity. This route to understanding does not automatically preclude reaching a plausible analysis – though that seems unlikely – but my point is that any plausible *beginning* will, once elaborated, contain Rossian grounds. Just as any room in a normally occupied domestic residence will contain one or another item of furniture, any concept of a moral reason that corresponds to the inferences crucial for moral reasoning and ethical discourse will contain at least some of the Rossian grounds. But just as there need be no analytically closed list of the contents of a residential room, there need be none for the contents of the concept of a moral reason.

Granted that, in entertaining the thought of moral reasons, one may think of many considerations other than avoiding injuring and harming, this may well come to mind because the category of avoidance of injury and harm obviously and naturally extends to the avoidance of bludgeoning people, which is the case that (in our example) prompts the thought of moral reasons. This is not to imply that reasons such as to avoid injuring persons, to keep promises, and to abstain from lying *must* come to mind in the imagined context of inquiry about moral reasons. But neither must one, upon looking into a room, see everything that is clearly in it. Reflection is not always sufficiently thorough or comprehensive to find what it seeks, and it is sometimes not guided by adequate understanding of the concepts in question.

Taken by themselves, such phenomenological points have limited evidential weight. But they gain support from two complementary points concerning conceptual explanation. One crucial question is how we can explain what *constitutes* a moral reason. A second important (and related) question is whether, for a correct common-sense explanation of why an act is obligatory (or wrong) that cites one or more obligation-making moral reasons and indicates their application to action, there is any need for an inferential justification of taking them to be reasons. Regarding the first question, I do not see how we can properly explain (as opposed to abstractly characterizing) what constitutes a moral reason except by appeal to examples of the kind just given. Concerning the second question, I have argued that certain moral propositions supported by such examples can be justifiedly believed non-inferentially, though they may *also* be justifiedly believed inferentially. The point is that in such cases justified belief is not premise-dependent and so need not be inferential.

IV The intuitive apprehension of fittingness

Suppose that what has been said gives us a basis for explaining the possibility of non-inferential intuitive knowledge of self-evident moral propositions and indeed does so in a way that makes it plausible to claim that there are such propositions.[17] It is quite another thing to explain the possibility of non-inferential intuitive knowledge of singular, *non*-self-evident propositions, such as the moral judgment that, as I encounter a toddler wandering alone on the sidewalk, I have a moral reason to stop to see if the child is lost. In describing intuitive knowledge, one direction natural for intuitionists is to appeal to fittingness relations (including unfittingness).[18] I take support relations to exhibit a kind of fittingness, and certain relations of incongruity to manifest unfittingness, but here I must be content to clarify these subtle notions mainly with illustrations. In many cases, non-trivial entailment (as opposed to mere strict implication) is a paradigm of fittingness between the entailing and entailed propositions; incompatibility is a paradigm of unfittingness. But entailment is not necessary for the former nor incompatibility for the latter. Surely doing what one promised to do *befits* the promising thereof, whereas lying to a friend *ill* befits the relation of friendship. By contrast, lying to a would-be assassin to prevent mass murder would not ill befit the situation, and might be a fittingly deflective act. What explains such points? I suggest that at least part of the explanation is that we apprehend a relation of support between (for instance) the envisaged instance of promising and the envisaged act of doing the promised deed. Suppose this is so. What is required for a person to *respond* to apprehension of a fittingness relation?

At least three cases should be considered. In the most conceptually complex case, the relation perceived in (e.g.) the promising case is *propositionalized*, i.e. formulated or expressed in a proposition, such as the proposition that one should do the promised deed. The proposition may be only thought or perhaps briefly considered. It need not be believed, though believing it would be normal for a child learning the concept in question; nor need we assume that the proposition is linguistically formulated even if it is believed. The second case is less complex: the envisaged property-instances that figure in fittingness relations are *conceptualized* but not propositionalized. This is like seeing something as having a property, such as being elliptical, without believing that it has it. As indicated in developing the analogy between intuition and perception, however, discrimination is possible without conceptualization. Much as perceiving a

---

[17] It is worth emphasizing that my account of self-evidence does not carry the burden of building in necessity as a further condition, though it leaves room to argue for the necessity of self-evident propositions. This is explained in my (1999) and further in my (2008).

[18] See e.g. Broad (1930: 220–2), Ross (1930), where at least Chapter 2 seems to employ the notion implicitly, and Ross (1939: esp. 79–85) where fittingness is discussed at length in relation to Broad's view; and Ewing (1953: 119).

tree provides raw materials for conceiving it as a tree but does not require doing so, apprehending morally important relations provides raw material for, but does not require, conceptualizing them, as we do when we believe that they obtain between one thing and another.

Consider entailment. With that in mind we can see the same levels of responsiveness in relation to fittingness. I begin with the simplest case, which is closest to sensory perception.

Discrimination of properties. Intellectual perception of at least one kind occurs very early in life. A child learning the logic of the syllogism as a way into understanding entailment does not initially believe, of the premises and conclusion of a valid syllogism, *that* the former entail the latter. We illustrate; we draw diagrams; and the child ultimately grasps the entailment relation *in* those cases. This initial grasp is manifested in a discriminative capacity: the ability to distinguish the good syllogisms (the valid ones) from the invalid, for instance to accept the former as "OK" and to reject the latter. Much as perceiving a tree provides raw materials for conceiving it as a tree but does not require doing so, apprehending logical relations like entailment or morally important relations like promissory obligation provides raw material for, but does not require, conceptualizing them as one does when one believes (or even has the thought) that they obtain between one thing and another. We can thus have discrimination without conceptualization.

Conceptualization: from seeing to a kind of seeing as. Given discrimination of properties (including relations) viewed as a starting point – or in any event an early point – we can understand how, at some time in the intellectual learning process, the child can conceptualize and perhaps name the entailment relation. Conceptualization requires more than discrimination, including understanding a kind of generality. It is analogous to perceptual seeing *as* but is of course not sensory. The idea is this. We can conceive two property-instances and apprehend a relation (*de re*) between them without believing or even thinking (de dicto) something to the effect *that* this relation obtains between them. The properties might be promising to *A* and being obligated to *A*. The relation might be entailment (if the obligation in question is prima facie) or a kind of fittingness. One may be *disposed* to think of or indeed believe some such proposition as that if one promises to *A*, then one should *A* or that *A*-ing befits promising to *A*; but that disposition need not be manifested in thinking or believing them, any more than seeing a difference in height between two buildings on the New York skyline entails believing, or even having the thought, that one is taller than the other.

Propositionalization. Given conceptualization, we can have intentionality – thought with an intentional object – whether or not the thought represents believing the proposition in question. When children are in a position to reach this third, propositional stage, they may believe *that* the entailment relation (*following*) holds for the syllogisms in question.[19] Moreover, its holding will often be intuitive for the child; and given the discriminative capacity at the base of the child's conceptualizing the entailment relation, such logical intuitions, though fallible, will commonly be evidential. Now take the relation perceived in (e.g.) the promising case. It is *propositionalized*, i.e. expressed (and sometimes formulated) in a proposition, such as the proposition that one should do the promised deed. The proposition may be only momentarily thought or perhaps briefly considered. It need not be believed, though believing it would be normal for a child learning the concept in question; nor need we assume that the proposition is formulated even if it is believed.

This developmental pattern, with its three stages, illustrates a kind of epistemological particularism in which discrimination of particular relations grounds conceptualization and conceptualization makes possible (though it does not entail) belief formation. The temporal separation between the stages is contingent; there are fast and slow learners. Moreover, even fast learners do not form beliefs of all the propositions for which, given their newly acquired concepts, their experience provides support.

The suggestion, then, is that the fittingness relations between conceptualized property-instances reflect similar relations between the relevant concepts. Where the fittingness is moral, the corresponding relation between the properties in question, say that of being a causing of excruciating pain and that of being an abstention from doing this, is also moral: roughly, obligation-making. The perception of the instances, *given* appropriate discriminative capacities and sufficient conceptual capability, puts us in a position to conceptualize those instances; we can then readily apprehend fittingness relations between them; and on that basis (though not only on that basis) we can come to believe corresponding general moral propositions and, eventually, to understand those adequately for justified belief and knowledge of them.

This picture accords well with a rationalist intuitionism on which basic moral principles are self-evident. But an empiricist account of the relevant kind of non-inferential justification and knowledge can also be given

---

[19] The idea that we can have a *de re* grasp of relations and can take the relata (e.g. propositions) to stand in them without believing the proposition that they so stand – where this de dicto belief requires conceptualizing the relation – is illustrated and applied in my (1986a).

(one on which such knowledge is either empirical or analytic). My preference is a moderately rationalist intuitionism, but my aim here is to extend and defend intuitionism as an overall position more than to show the superiority of a rationalist version.

V   Intuitions, inferential processes, and inferential beliefs

So far, I have assumed that intuitions are non-inferential. This assumption is natural because (for one thing) they are conceived as direct responses to what is apprehended. The assumption is important because, on the most plausible conceptions of intuitions, they are considered evidentially independent: conceived doxastically, as beliefs, they do not require premises for their (prima facie) justification; conceived non-doxastically, as intuitive seemings, they are akin to sensory experiences and do not admit of justification in the first place, though they can confer some measure of it.[20]

Given that doxastic intuitions do admit of justification, why should they be considered non-inferential? One indication – significant though not conclusive – that they are non-inferential is that, if asked (in an informational as opposed to skeptical way) why we believe the relevant proposition (p), the initial tendency, especially if p is not self-evident, is to point to non-propositional grounds – such as *seeing* that it is true – on which we believe it or, if p is self-evident, to explain what it means or how to see its truth by understanding it. Neither of these responses is a presentation of a premise for p.

To be sure, if we feel challenged by a why-question, we naturally seek to frame an argument. That effort may lead us to adduce premises that were not a basis of the intuition or may indeed have been conceived only as a response to the felt challenge. I suggest that when such a why-question arises, then where our grounds are *non-propositional* and the belief is non-inferential, we do not have the normal tendency that goes with inferential beliefs – to adduce one or more of our premise-beliefs. Granted, a fast thinker may tend to adduce premises on the spot from among propositions not previously believed but quickly conceived as plausible support for p or, if previously believed, not previously a basis of the belief that p. But this facility in supplying rationales manifests a different tendency, though it is easily assimilated to the former.

---

[20] I have made no commitment to cognitive intuitions necessarily being justified, though I believe they are at least very commonly justified.

The role of non-propositional grounds is easily misunderstood. One reason is that *pointing out* a non-propositional ground in explaining or justifying a belief or other cognition – something we commonly do when asked to justify or, sometimes, explain a belief we hold – is itself a *propositional* act. Recall my discovery of a wandering toddler. I immediately lean over and quietly say 'Are you lost?' My sense that the child needs help grounds my judgment that I must inquire. But if someone asks why I spoke to a child who was apparently playing in front of her home, I will readily say that she might have needed help. *Now* I have a belief expressing a premise for my original immediate and intuitive judgment. But such retrospective formation of belief by no means implies that my initial judgment was originally based on believing some such premise. Compare my saying 'I hear it' in answer to 'How do you know that bass note is flat?' My correct response does not imply that I knew (or believed) that proposition (inferentially) on the basis of *believing* that I heard the flatness. My ground is not a belief; it is *hearing* the flatness, which I recognize as I do a familiar kind of dog.

One might now think that *every* ground for a non-inferential moral judgment is articulable as a premise for it and that, since such grounds are 'implicit', judgments that are *psychologically* non-inferential are nonetheless *epistemically* dependent in an inferential way after all.[21] These claims require several comments.

First, even if every ground can in some way be articulated by *someone*, it does not follow that (a) grounds can do their justificatory work only *in* someone capable of articulating them or (b), in such a person, they cannot do that work without articulation or even conceptualization. The three-stage developmental account given above helps to make this clear. Moreover, even for conceptually mature moral agents, (b) seems false in some cases in which we are just becoming aware of a fittingness relation between a ground and what it supports, as where body language and intonation indicate that one person is intimidating another. Discriminating such relations can be temporally prior to our conceptualizing or formulating them, much as it seems developmentally prior even to the ability to conceptualize or formulate them.

Second, the notion of an "implicit" premise is ambiguous between (at least) (a) one that is believed but not *articulated* and (b) one that the person is *disposed* to believe but does not believe. Intuitionists need not deny that, in at least many cases in which we have non-inferential

---

[21] Sellars (1975) probably thought this.

justification for a moral judgment, we can *find* a premise for it that we are justified in believing. This capacity commonly goes with having an (internally accessible) ground in the first place. But none of these points should lead us to assimilate a disposition to *form* a belief of a premise to an already *existing* dispositional belief thereof.[22]

That (doxastic) intuitions are not premise-dependent does not entail that they are not epistemically dependent at all.[23] Like perceptual beliefs, they are *ground-dependent* (the ground being mainly perceiving, for instance seeing, a morally relevant property or understanding of the relevant concepts and certain of their relations), whereas an inferential cognition is mediated by at least one premise and is in that way indirect: it is doxastically, not just epistemically, ground-dependent. The premise-belief must ultimately trace to a (non-doxastic) ground if it is to be justified (I assume a moderate foundationalist view here). Intuitions are thus viewed as epistemically direct responses to something presented.

Functionally, intuitions, whether doxastic or, by contrast, non-doxastic seemings, commonly save us from needing a premise. They do not, however, make premises impossible or protect us from refutation by premises that cogent critics may adduce for a contrary view. In this way, intuitions are analogous to visual beliefs grounded in seeing, which also provides non-inferential but defeasible justification for those beliefs. But the analogy to seeing must be carefully interpreted: much as a mere glance at an unfamiliar tree may not yield justified visual belief or indeed any belief, a mere thought of a proposition or concept may yield no understanding of it, and reflection on it may be needed to see even what, once it is clearly seen, is intuitive.[24]

I have so far spoken of inferential belief, but not of inference. There is wide agreement that a belief which is premise-dependent is inferential, but there is less agreement on what constitutes *an inference*, in the common sense in which inferences are *made* or *drawn* and making or drawing an inference entails *reasoning*. On my view, an inference is roughly a kind of

[22] The distinction between dispositional beliefs (the non-occurrent kind stored in memory and not in consciousness at the time in question) and dispositions to believe is explicated and defended in my (1994).

[23] The non-inferential justification in question here is not "self-justification" – a notion that is misleading. Ground-dependence in fact entails the existence of something *other* than the cognition that justifies it.

[24] The point that what is intuitively known may be knowable only through reflection though still known non-inferentially is defended and developed in my response to Sinnott-Armstrong (2007) in my (2007). Cf. the misleading idea, common among twentieth-century intuitionists (as noted in *The Good in the Right*, my 2004), that we "just see" the truth of self-evident and many other kinds of intuitive true propositions.

passage of thought from one or more propositions to another, in part on the basis of a sense of some support relation between the former and the latter.[25] This leaves open whether an inference is valid and whether it is, at the time it occurs, (a) belief-forming – in which case the conclusion belief is at least characteristically based, wholly or in part, on the premise belief(s) – or (b) proceeds from propositions already believed to another that is already believed, or indeed (c), as with disproofs by deductions of absurdities, from propositions only supposed, to another proposition that may be only considered and quickly rejected. The notion of inference is both psychological and, at least on an objective conception of support-relations, epistemic.

The notion of inference is also *phenomenal*: inference is episodic and manifested in consciousness, though there need be no consciousness *of* the inference under any particular description. The point that inference is phenomenal is easily missed because the related notions of *inferential belief* and of inferential (dispositional) judgment are not phenomenal, though they are psychological. A belief that *p* can be based on a belief that *q* *without* the person's inferring *p* from *q*. I could, for instance, discover *q*, which is evidence for *p*, only after *already* believing *p* (non-inferentially) on testimony. I could then begin to believe *p* inferentially, on the basis of the (non-testimonial) evidence, *q*. There need be nothing phenomenal, such as a sense of forming the belief that *p*, or even my consciously connecting *p* with *q*, as where I have a thought of *q* as supporting *p*. The kinds of phenomenal elements essential in drawing an inference are not required for a belief to acquire the relevant supporting role: the inferentiality in question is not episodic or even phenomenal; it is a *structural relation* between beliefs. It implies nothing about what occurs in consciousness. We often *make* connections between propositions by drawing inferences; but (by the grace of God or evolution or both) the mind is capable of responding to such connections more spontaneously, without our drawing inferences. Precisely because inferential belief need not arise from inference and because inferentiality need not be phenomenal, showing that intuitions are not inferential is difficult.

[25] The notion of inference and related notions, such as inferential belief, are explicated in my (1986b), and especially in Chapters 4 and 8 of (2006b). I should add that I assume that a *belief* that the premises support the conclusion may be taken to be a special (perhaps phenomenally thin) case of the sense of support in question. Unfortunately, my (2004) did not refer to (1986b) or other works in which I have explicated the notion of justified belief and did not reproduce the account. It is understandable, then, that Shafer-Landau (2007) finds such an account needed.

VI The grounds and extent of intuitive knowledge and justification

What kinds of propositions are intuitively knowable is an epistemological question. What kinds are in fact known non-inferentially is not only an epistemological question but also a psychological one and indeed partly relative to the kind of person or social context in question. With at most a few exceptions, anything non-inferentially knowable can, at some time and by some person, be known inferentially; and perhaps anything inferentially knowable at all can be known non-inferentially.[26] Apparent exceptions to the first point arise where there is no suitable premise because of, for instance, the strong axiomatic status of the proposition (say that if $2 \times 2 = 4$, then $4 = 2 \times 2$).

Some of the groundwork for an account of intuitive moral justification and knowledge has been laid. We have seen in outline how an adequate understanding of a self-evident proposition can enable one to see its truth by virtue of apprehending conceptual relations and without relying on premises. I have also offered a partial account of intuitive non-inferential justification and knowledge for a related kind of singular moral judgment: the kind involving ascription of obligatoriness to an action or affirming prima facie moral reasons for it. We should now consider related kinds of moral judgments, both prima facie and final. Let us take these kinds in turn.

An intuitionist, simply as such, has various options for a general epistemology, say rationalist or empiricist; but here I will work from a rationalist perspective, as have Sidgwick, Moore, Ross, Ewing, and other major ethical intuitionists. Let us begin with something that has been in ethical literature at least since Moore: the idea that moral properties are consequential on non-moral ones, in the sense that a thing having moral properties has them in virtue of having certain non-moral properties.[27] An action cannot, then, be brutely obligatory, or brutely wrong. It will be (e.g.) obligatory in virtue

---

[26] I ignore one arguable exception: first-person propositions that only the believer can genuinely understand. As to the clear cases of propositional knowledge, in (1995) I explain why memory beliefs should be considered non-inferential, and in (1997) I make a case for treating testimony-based beliefs as also non-inferential (though they have an operational dependence, as opposed to a premise-dependence, on perception). Kappel (2002) seems unaware of such cases when he says, "For Audi, intuitively known propositions are simply non-inferentially known propositions" (292).

[27] Consequentiality entails supervenience but is stronger. Supervenience is not a determination relation having explanatory power. The consequentiality relations central for the Rossian principles are apparently also, as mere supervenience relations need not be, both a priori and necessary.

of being promised or wrong in virtue of being a lie. Similarly, a just person may be just in virtue of certain intentions and action-tendencies.

Even if we do not take the relevant basis-relations – those expressed by 'in virtue of' here – to be necessary and a priori, they imply grounds for justification and knowledge (to simplify matters I'll consider only knowledge). Intuitionists do not deny the possibility (noted earlier) of inferential knowledge by subsumption, say the possibility of knowing that an act is wrong on the basis of knowing that it creates a conflict of interest and that such acts are prima facie wrong. This is an important point, since some intuitionists may allow the impression that *only* ethical intuition can justify moral judgment or yield moral knowledge. But it is also important to see how moral justification is possible without subsumption. Consider this. I hear someone promise to mail a letter and then see him slip it into a trash can. Is it not possible for my perception of the presence of the base property, that of being promise-breaking, to lead to (and ground) my believing, non-inferentially, that the agent is wronging the promisee? Or, suppose I see an elementary school luncheon server give a visibly smaller portion to a black than to a white child. I may immediately and non-inferentially judge that this is unfair. In part because the disproportion is a prima facie indication of unfittingness, I "see" the unfairness.[28] Seeing the act in its context provides my ground for the judgment and may precede my making that judgment. Do we have knowledge in such cases?

The beliefs in question seem intuitive, justified, and good candidates for knowledge. The descriptions of the cases do not rule out, however, that some overrider is present. We could then know that the act is prima facie unfair but not know that it is unfair all things considered. Suppose we are thinking of *final* (all-things-considered) wrongness or obligation. Must we abandon the claim that these descriptions often yield propositions we can *know*? Certainly skeptics would claim we must. For in my two examples, it is possible that both agents had excuses we did not know of, hence did not violate a final obligation. But surely this possibility may in the context (and in many common contexts) be presupposed to be at best highly unlikely. The intuition may thus be justified. The remaining question is what degree of evidential strength the grounds must have in order to sustain knowledge of a final obligation. Here it is useful to compare the perceptual case. How good a glimpse do we need of a deer grazing in the distance to know that it is a deer? There is no easy answer, but if (with no "Gettier condition") we have a justified true belief based on a ground that is objectively

---

[28] This is a case of moral perception, in a sense explicated in my 2010b.

good – though not entailing – evidence, it is plausible to say that we know this.

On my view, we often have such justified non-inferential beliefs ascribing final obligation. Just as a perceptual belief may be produced by a sensory response to the factual conditions in virtue of which it is true, a judgment of final obligation may be produced by a moral response to the descriptive properties of the action in virtue of which it is obligatory. There is a reliable connection in both cases, and both cognitions may constitute knowledge. To be sure, much depends on the ethical sensitivity of the moral judge. But similarly, for everyday observational knowledge much depends on the perceptual acuity of the observer. In ethical matters, intuitive judgments may require moral acuity, and when they do they are a primary realm of the exercise of practical wisdom.

VII Intuition and moral judgment

Intuitionism in ethics has often seemed to lack a way to unify the plural standards it endorses. It has also been taken to have at best meager resources for explaining how we should resolve conflicts between prima facie obligations. On this resolution problem, W. D. Ross appealed to Aristotelian practical wisdom. He argued that neither Kantian nor utilitarian ethics (the two rival views he considered) offers an adequate alternative.[29] I propose, however, an interpretation of Kant's Humanity Formula of the Categorical Imperative for which this negative assessment does not unqualifiedly hold. If, as I maintain in contrast to Ross, Moore, and others,[30] many self-evident propositions can be evidenced or even proved by other propositions, the way is open both to support Rossian moral principles by appeal to a more comprehensive principle and to characterize the self-evident in a way that makes it easy to see why self-evident propositions may be not only far from obvious but also subject to rational disagreement.

I understand the Humanity Formula along lines that, though they reflect some important elements in Kant's ethical texts, do not presuppose a

[29] See Ross (1930), esp. 18–20. It is noteworthy that Ross evaluated Kantian resources on the assumption that they must accord with Kant's view that "there are certain duties of perfect obligation, such as those of fulfilling promises... which admit of no exception whatever in favour of duties of imperfect obligation, such as that of relieving distress" (18). Whatever the status of Kant's apparent endorsement of this implausible position, no such view is required by a plausible interpretation of the Categorical Imperative framework, as will be shown in this paper.

[30] See Chapters 1 and 2 of my (2004) for references to Pritchard, Moore, and Ross's claims that the self-evident is unprovable and for a detailed account of self-evidence that indicates why this requirement is mistaken. Consider a simple case: If p entails q and q entails r but r is false, then p is false. This is self-evident but readily provable.

specific interpretation of them. In particular, I have sought to show that its negative injunction – which prohibits treating persons merely as means – is explicable in terms of descriptive notions, and its positive injunction, which requires treating persons as ends, is explicable, if not descriptively, then at least without dependence on moral notions.[31] Doing this is important for defending Kantian ethics as well as for providing objective anchors for these notions. If the Humanity Formula is to serve as one of our *basic* guides in making moral judgments, we need a way to understand its requirements that does not depend on prior moral judgments. Otherwise, those judgments would be epistemically prior to it, and in that case it would (in at least some of its applications) lack basic moral force.

Given the detailed development of Kantian intuitionism that I have provided in earlier work, what I will do here is simply clarify the framework sufficiently to indicate how it helps in yielding intuitive resolutions of conflicts of obligation. Suppose I am correct in thinking that treating a person merely as a means is roughly treating the person not just *solely* as a means but (with some qualifications) also with a disposition *not* to be concerned with any *non*-instrumental aspects of the treatment. (This negative disposition is needed to account for the force of "merely.") An example might be ordering a timid and willing employee to do a risky job, with an intention to let the person struggle alone even if the job becomes highly dangerous.

If, as I think plausible, this kind of treatment is prima facie wrong – wrong-making, in another terminology – and prima facie wrong even if the act-*type*, ordering the job done, is not prima facie wrong in the context, then we have a morally relevant factor that can weigh in favor of a Rossian obligation, for instance non-injury.

A different example may help: a conflict between veracity in making a promise and an opportunity for beneficence. Suppose that, in making a promise I do not intend to keep, I would be getting the promisee, who expects to benefit from my keeping my promise, to do a very good thing for a third party. Making such a promise might also manifest the relevant disposition not to be concerned with non-instrumental aspects of the treatment of the promisee, say the person's suffering from the loss

---

[31] I developed Kantian intuitionism in (2001b) and further in (2004), esp. ch 3. Particularly in the latter I appealed to the notion of dignity as adding a dimension to the framework; but, contrary to the suggestion of Gert (2006), I did not depend on the notion for the clarity or defense of the overall view; and I sought to clarify the notion independently, e.g. on 99, 157–8, and 176–7. For a detailed discussion of Kant's conception of duty and of the proper treatment of persons see Stratton-Lake (2000), esp. chs. 2–4.

of an important opportunity when I break the promise. Let us assume this. The point that in making the insincere promise I would be using the promisee merely instrumentally weighs in favor of not making the promise or, if I do make it, of reversing my course and keeping it after all. It also supports the promissory obligation over the obligation of beneficence (though this does not entail that the support is overriding). The decision on whether to keep the promise may still not be easy, though it might be.

In any case, the point is that the added moral ground – that making the insincere, manipulative promise would be treating the promisee merely as a means – is helpful and potentially determinative, not that it makes all the conflict cases easy to resolve. That is something no plausible moral view will achieve.

Consider now treating someone as an end, which is mainly a matter of doing – for its own sake – something that is (and is appropriately conceived by the agent as) for the good of the other person.

Suppose I have to decide whether to punish a child for bad behavior by keeping the child at home or to make do with a reprimand. Assume that I know this punishment is reasonable but will make the child suffer. Suppose the retributive considerations, together with the good the punishment will do for the child in the long run, are just strong enough to make the decision difficult, given the desirability of avoiding the suffering. Now suppose that I consider not just the two act-types in question, punishing and simply reprimanding – types which some other person could token – but how I would be *treating* the child in each case. It could well be that treating the child as an end requires, not a kind of utilitarian calculation, but tolerating the suffering and carrying out the punishment in the appropriate spirit.

These promissory and retributive examples might give the impression that the notions of merely instrumental and end-regarding treatment simply place two more prima facie obligations on a Rossian list and hence are no help either in its unification or in dealing with conflicts of obligations. I have indeed suggested that the non-moral grounds in question – the two kinds of treatment – generate prima facie obligations and seem to do so in their own right. Suppose this were all we could say of them: that there are prima facie obligations to treat persons as ends and to avoid treating them merely as means. This is significant in itself. The obligations would be morally important by virtue of their *instantial*, as opposed to systematizing, uses. They would not only provide a sense of kinds of acts to be avoided – those that *use* people – and a sense of deeds to be aimed at, such as contributing to the well-being of others; they also figure (as illustrated) in many cases that would otherwise be difficult or impossible to decide in an intuitively satisfactory way.[32] They are, however, more comprehensive than the Rossian obligations. One or the other of them is applicable to all (or virtually all) instances of Rossian obligation. For all of the Rossian obligations, many kinds of fulfillments can be cases of treating someone as an end; and violation of the negative obligations, for instance of non-injury, fidelity, and veracity, are the kinds of actions that tend to manifest or at least approach treatment merely as a means.

These considerations indicate how the notions of avoiding merely instrumental treatment and aiming at end-regarding treatment express broad negative and positive aims proper to the institution of morality – a *telos*, as it were. They characterize, in broad strokes, some of the kinds of evils morality opposes and some of the kinds of goods it honors and promotes. This purposive role that the two notions partly represent is a significant unifying element for the Rossian obligations.

These clarifications of Kantian intuitionism do not provide a formula for dealing with conflicts of obligation, but they do show that the notions of merely instrumental and end-regarding treatment of persons can play positive roles both in providing a comprehensive conceptual framework for conceiving the Rossian obligations and for dealing with certain conflicts between those. I do not claim that every such conflict is better dealt with in the light of those notions, but many are. It is also important to realize that even when conflicting obligations present a difficult case, we may not need to appeal to general principles to apprehend our overall obligation. Again, the analogy to perception is useful: confronted with someone who looks like a man I remember, I may have to look a long time to see that he is. My discriminative faculties may be hard at work and may succeed even if I never draw any inferences, say from the premise that he is too young to be the person I remember or from the premise that, given his unusual diction, he must be that person. Such things might indeed occur to me later; but the supportability of a judgment by a premise by no means implies its antecedent role in arriving at the judgment.

VIII   Reasons for action and final obligation

I have been presupposing that a ground of obligation, such as making a promise, is also a reason for action. But not all normative reasons are moral,

---

[32]   I leave open whether it is self-evident that the two kinds of treatment ground prima facie obligations; they can play the indicated role even if this is not self-evident.

and I have taken no position on the (normative) strength of moral reasons relative to other kinds.[33] The possibility of conflict between moral and non-moral reasons, such as reasons of pure self-interest, can make more difficult the overall question of what one ought to do (what *to* do, if that question is understood normatively). Non-moral reasons may not only conflict with moral ones but may also support some moral reasons against other moral reasons. Here it is enough to indicate how, on my theory, we should conceive conflicting moral reasons. Much that is said will apply to conflicts between moral and non-moral reasons.

To begin with, I take it that there is no a priori hierarchy among the moral reasons represented by the Rossian obligations. Thus, there are apparently no two categories of Rossian obligation, say justice and beneficence, such that *every* obligation in one will outweigh *any* (individual) obligation in the other. An implication of this view – a kind of particularism regarding normative hierarchies – is that a moral reason corresponding to such an obligation is not a priori overridden in every case of conflict with a moral reason belonging to a different category of obligation. Note, too, that even on the assumption that a reason of one kind is always overridden in a pairwise conflict with a single reason of some other kind, certain coalitions of reasons on one side might still prevail over any single reason that would always override any one member of the coalition. If, for instance, in conflict cases, any reason of non-injury were to outweigh every reason of gratitude taken by itself, some of the former taken singly might not outweigh every *set* of gratitudinal reasons.

Given these points, might we not formulate some rough generalizations, each rationalizable by, even if not strictly deducible from, the Humanity Formula on my interpretation? Each might be conceived as a kind of *adjunctive principle* that can guide one in dealing with conflicting prima facie obligations, whether between two or more of the ten I have posited or within a single category, as where two promises conflict. (I do not take the list of ten as necessarily complete, but it is highly comprehensive and at present I see no clear need to extend it.) These principles are adjuncts to Rossian principles, but do not have the same moral status and need not be self-evident. They might be considered partially adjudicative, in the sense that they have weight in properly determining moral judgment, even if they apply only where there are already conflicting Rossian considerations.

---

[33] A theory of reasons and of the possible kinds of relations that hold between moral and non-moral reasons is provided in my (2001a), e.g. chs. 5 and 6. To be sure, the notion of a *moral* reason is not sharp. For extensive discussion of the relative weights of practical reasons and, in particular Sidgwick's problem of the dualism of practical reason, see Crisp (2006), esp. ch. 5.

The following are two candidates for partially adjudicative principles that might be plausibly thought to hold when other things are equal in terms of the Rossian obligations.

Treatment of persons. If two options we have are equally well supported by conflicting Rossian obligations, then if one option is favored in terms of our (a) avoiding treating persons merely as a means or (b) treating persons as ends (or both), then that option is preferable, other things equal, with (a) having priority (other things equal) over (b) if (a) supports one option and (b) the other. The punishment case above illustrates the applicability of this principle. It should be added that although it is not clear that Kant viewed the obligation to avoid merely instrumental treatment as, other things equal, weightier than the obligation to treat persons as ends, this view is independently plausible and provides greater determinacy for my interpretation of the overall moral force of the Humanity Formula. Another principle I take to be supported by (but not only by) the Humanity Formula as I interpret it concerns the political domain (counterparts may be formulated with other realms of conduct).

The principle of secular rationale (roughly, of natural reason): citizens in a free democracy have a prima facie obligation not to advocate or support any law or public policy that restricts human conduct, unless they have, and are willing to offer, adequate secular reason (roughly, natural reason) for this advocacy or support (e.g. for a vote).[34]

Here a secular reason for an action (or a belief) is roughly one whose status as a justifier of action (or belief) does not evidentially depend on (but also does not deny) the existence of God; nor does it depend on theological considerations, or on the pronouncements of a person or institution *as* a religious authority. This notion is epistemic, roughly a matter of evidential grounding, not a matter of the content of the reason. We can imagine a case in which a person's reasons for action include commitments based essentially on religious convictions. Consider a (higher-order) promissory obligation grounded in swearing on the Bible that one will keep a promise to one's priest to support outlawing same-sex unions. The secular rationale principle would call for abstaining from coercion (as opposed to persuasion) in this matter apart from having an adequate reason that does not depend in this way on religion or theology. (If, for instance, the welfare of children could be shown to be adversely affected by such unions, there would be a secular reason.) The secular rationale principle is not clearly entailed by

---

[34] This formulation is drawn from Audi (2000: 86), though I published essentially the same version much earlier in (1989).

the Humanity Formula as I understand it; but the role that the principle accords to natural reasons is one we would expect them to play on a non-theological understanding of the formula.

It must be granted that even if the adjudicative principles proposed and others like them help in resolving conflicts of Rossian obligations, they themselves may still leave some conflicts unresolved.

Indeed, they too can generate difficult cases. Consider treatment of persons. Suppose our only way to stop a drunken man from becoming violent is to manipulate his estranged wife into giving him the sense that she has forgiven his excesses. This would be prima facie wrongful instrumental treatment, and it would approach using her merely as a means, but might this prima facie wrongful treatment be preferable to risking violence to several innocent bystanders? In cases of this kind, Ross appealed to Aristotelian practical wisdom and to Aristotle's comment that "the decision rests with perception" (1930: 41; *Nicomachean Ethics* 1126b4). Both have intuitive judgments in mind (rather than sensory perceptions), but neither specifies how these are like judgments grounded in sensory perception. Is there sufficient analogy between sensory perception and intuition as intellectual perception to sustain Ross's terminology here?

Consider how one might decide which of two paintings is a copy, or how one can tell Owen from his fraternal twin when we see him in the half-light. The art expert may simply look at both paintings for a long time and judge on the basis of the complex visual data. And we may need only a closer look to determine which is Owen and which is John. Might art experts tell us how they do it? Perhaps. And might there even be a true generalization linking observable properties of the original painting to its author's work? Certainly. Arguably, if there are, as there surely must be, observable indications that ground ordinary perceptual knowledge, then, in principle, there *must* be a generalization, however complex, linking them to authorship. Think of the distinctive brush strokes of Van Gogh, easily recognizable but difficult to describe in a way that distinguishes them from those a forgery might display. And if I can (visually) tell Owen from John, must there not be observable features, perhaps a multitude of them, by which I do it? The answer seems positive, but it does not follow that our singular judgments are tacitly *subsumptive* or otherwise inferential. On the contrary, it is in part because our intuitive singular judgments are trusted and confirmed that we can arrive at the relevant generalizations in the first place.

The visual perceptions just described are themselves intuitive and apparently rest on a sensory seeming. There is no reason to consider intellectual perception of the kind represented by certain intuitions to be different on this score. My sense that I should not break the promise is a response to the apprehension of the case before me. In the case of the wandering toddler, I may have a moral perception that *embodies* the intuitive sense of what I should do. This sense, which is a kind of moral seeming, yields a judgment that embodies belief and that, leaving skepticism aside, can constitute knowledge.

The intuitions appear, moreover, both prima facie justificatory for the beliefs they support and epistemically prior to knowledge of the generalizations that connect the intuitively discerned elements to the moral attributions these elements ground, say, on the one hand, the disoriented look of the toddler amid the threatening circumstances of the street and, on the other, the attribution of a prima facie obligation to check on the child.

These points are entirely compatible with taking the capacity of intuitions to yield true beliefs to depend on such connections between properties. These are the kinds of connections that, as illustrated by cases like that of the promise and the wandering toddler, the generalizations express. It would indeed be surprising if a discriminative grasp of the connections underlying singular moral truths were not epistemically prior to our knowledge of those connections. There is, then, much to be said for the analogy between sensory and intellectual perception and for the capacity of both to yield justification and knowledge.

* * *

The status of ethical intuitionism depends largely on the power of our rational capacities to perceive truth by certain kinds of non-inferential discernment of properties and propositions. This discernment may or may not be produced by or even accompanied by reflection. On rationalist versions of intuitionism, even general moral principles may be directly (non-inferentially) known – though neither indefeasibly nor, invariably, in a way that is wholly unmediated by reflection.[35] Reflection may be necessary even to see the truth of a self-evident proposition: being self-evident does not entail being obvious, unprovable, or beyond rational dispute. As I have developed intuitionism, the required apprehensional power of reason to ground non-inferential knowledge, and non-inferentially justified belief, of

---

[35] It may be thought that noncognitivism avoids the problem of determining the scope of reason in ethical matters, as suggested by, e.g., Kappel (2002: 411). But any plausible noncognitivist view must account for what constitutes a relevant (and indeed a good) reason for holding a non-cognitive pro or con moral judgment. How we might know or justifiedly believe such an account seems to me a problem in moral epistemology much akin to the kind I have been dealing with here.

general moral principles is essentially like the power needed for knowledge of the a priori in general; and its power regarding the grounding of singular judgments is highly analogous to the epistemic power by which we acquire perceptual knowledge.

In both cases there are evidential grounds, but these need not provide support only in inferential ways. In extending the comprehensive intuitionism constructed in earlier work, this paper shows how my account of intuitions accommodates intuitive seemings and the related phenomenon or apprehending fittingness relations. I have connected both of these notions with doxastic intuitions on the model of the relation between perceptual seemings and the beliefs they justify. I have also clarified the notion of self-evidence, the way in which it makes non-inferential general knowledge possible, and how such knowledge, as well as the adjudicative principles it warrants, can guide intuitions in resolving conflicts of obligation. In the light of the accounts of self-evidence and intuitive justification sketched here, ethical intuitionism can be seen as a plausible framework for understanding justification in ethics.[36]

References

Audi, Robert (1986a) "Acting for Reasons," *Philosophical Review* 95(4): 75–205.

(1986b) "Belief, Reason, and Inference," *Philosophical Topics* 14(1): 27–65.

(1989) "The Separation of Church and State and the Obligation of Citizenship," *Philosophy and Public Affairs* 18(3): 259–96.

(1994) "Dispositional Beliefs and Dispositions to Believe," *Noûs* 28(4): 419–34.

(1995) "Memorial Justification," *Philosophical Topics* 23(1): 31–45.

(1997) "The Place of Testimony in the Fabric of Knowledge and Justification," *American Philosophical Quarterly* 34(4): 404–42.

(1999) "Self-Evidence," *Philosophical Perspectives* 13: 205–28.

(2000) *Religious Commitment and Secular Reason.* Cambridge and New York: Cambridge University Press.

(2001a) *The Architecture of Reason: The Structure and Substance of Rationality.* New York: Oxford University Press.

(2001b) "A Kantian Intuitionism," *Mind* 110(439): 601–35.

---

[36] This essay has benefited from comments by many philosophers and from discussion with various audiences. I would particularly like to thank Jens Timmermann for comments when an earlier version was presented at the University of St. Andrews and Robert Cowan for detailed comments when it was presented at the University of Glasgow. Many of the contributors to Hernandez (2011) have also been of great help to me in thinking the problems through on one occasion or another. I much regret that space does not permit responding to points they raise bearing on my position; but this essay may at least provide an indication of how I might respond, and the future will surely hold many more opportunities for discussions that advance understanding of the issues.

(2004) *The Good in the Right: A Theory of Intuition and Intrinsic Value.* Princeton University Press.

(2006a) "Ethical Generality and Moral Judgment," in James Dreier (ed.), *Contemporary Debates in Ethical Theory.* Oxford: Blackwell, 285–304.

(2006b) *Practical Reasoning and Ethical Decision.* London: Routledge.

(2007) "Intuition, Reflection, and Justification," in Timmons, Greco, and Mele, 201–21.

(2008) "Skepticism about the A Priori," in John Greco (ed.), *The Oxford Handbook of Skepticism.* Oxford University Press, 149–75.

(2010a) *Epistemology: A Contemporary Introduction to the Theory of Knowledge.* London and New York: Routledge.

(2010b) "Moral Perception and Moral Knowledge," *Proceedings of the Aristotelian Society* 84: 79–94.

Bealer, George (1998) "Intuition and the Autonomy of Philosophy," in DePaul and Ramsey, 201–39.

Broad, C. D. (1930) *Five Types of Ethical Theory.* London: Routledge & Kegan Paul.

Crisp, Roger (2006) *Reasons and the Good.* Oxford University Press.

DePaul, Michael, and Ramsey, William (eds.) (1998) *Rethinking Intuition.* Lanham, Md.: Rowman & Littlefield.

Erlenbaugh, Joshua, and Molyneux, Bernard (2009) "Intuitions as Inclinations to Believe," *Philosophical Studies* 145: 89–109.

Ewing, A. C. (1953) *Ethics.* New York: The Free Press.

Gert, Joshua (2006) "Review: Robert Audi's The Good in the Right," *Mind* 115(457): 121–25.

Hernandez, Jill Graper (2011) *The New Intuitionism.* London: Continuum.

Huemer, Michael (2005) *Ethical Intuitionism.* Basingstoke and New York: Palgrave Macmillan.

Kappel, Klemens (2002) "Challenges to Audi's Intuitionism," *Ethical Theory and Moral Practice* 5: 391–413.

Moore, G. E. (1903) *Principia Ethica.* Cambridge University Press.

Mulgan, Tim (2006) *Future People.* Oxford: Clarendon Press.

Rawls, John (1971) *A Theory of Justice.* Cambridge, Mass.: Harvard University Press.

Ross, W. D. (1930) *The Right and the Good.* Oxford University Press.

(1939) *Foundations of Ethics.* Oxford: Clarendon Press.

Sellars, Wilfrid (1956) "Empiricism and the Philosophy of Mind," in H. Feigl and M. Scriven (eds.), *The Foundations of Science and the Concepts of Psychoanalysis, Minnesota Studies in the Philosophy of Science*, vol. i. Minneapolis, Minn.: University of Minnesota Press. Reprinted in Sellars (1963), *Science, Perception and Reality.* London: Routledge and Kegan Paul; reissued in 1991 by Ridgeview Publishing Co., Atascadero, Calif., 127–96.

(1975) "The Structure of Knowledge," in Hector-Neri Castañeda (ed.), *Action, Knowledge and Reality: Essays in Honor of Wilfrid Sellars.* Indianapolis: Bobbs-Merrill, 295–347.

Shafer-Landau, Russ (2007) "Audi's Intuitionism," *Philosophy and Phenomenological Research* 74(1): 250–61.

Sidgwick, Henry (1907) *The Methods of Ethics*. Seventh edn. London: Macmillan; Chicago: University of Chicago Press, 1962.

Sinnott-Armstrong, Walter (2007) "Reflections on Reflection in Robert Audi's Moral Intuitionism," in Timmons, Greco, and Mele, 19–30.

(ed.) (2008) *Moral Psychology*, vol. ii. *The Cognitive Science of Morality: Intuition and Diversity*. Cambridge, Mass.: The MIT Press.

Sosa, Ernest (1998) "Minimal Intuitionism," in DePaul and Ramsey, 257–69.

Stratton-Lake, Philip (2000) *Kant, Duty and Moral Worth*. London: Routledge.

Timmons, Mark, Greco, John, and Mele, Alfred R. (eds.) (2007) *Rationality and the Good: Critical Essays on the Ethics and Epistemology of Robert Audi*. Oxford: Oxford University Press.

Tolhurst, William (1998) "Seemings," *American Philosophical Quarterly* 35: 293–302.

CHAPTER 6

Kantian intuitionism as a framework for the justification of moral judgments

Intuitionism in ethics has often been thought to lack a way to unify the plural standards it endorses. It has also been taken to have at best meager resources for explaining how we should resolve conflicts between prima facie obligations. On this resolution problem, W. D. Ross appealed to Aristotelian practical wisdom. He argued that neither Kantian nor utilitarian ethics (the two most promising rival views he considered) offers an adequate alternative.[1] There is, however, an interpretation of Kant's Humanity Formula of the Categorical Imperative for which this negative assessment is unduly pessimistic. This paper will show why. I am not implying, however, that dependence on Aristotelian practical wisdom in certain cases is a fatal defect in a Rossian intuitionism. There are, moreover, many cases of conflicting obligations for which, even if practical wisdom is required for their resolution, there is no reasonable doubt about what should be done. In any event, no plausible ethical theory makes dealing with conflicts of obligation easy or uncontroversial; and dependence on practical wisdom is a central element in any virtue ethics and, in some ways, indispensable for practical ethics even when it is guided by a plausible moral theory of some other kind. My aim, then, is not to eliminate dependence on practical wisdom but to construct a broadly intuitionist ethical theory that helps us to enhance both the unity and the applicability of the intuitively acceptable moral principles it provides. Doing this will bring more resources to guide practical wisdom than Ross and later Rossian intuitionists have provided.

---

[1] See Ross (1930), esp. 18–20. It is noteworthy that Ross evaluated Kantian resources on the assumption that they must accord with Kant's view that "there are certain duties of perfect obligation, such as those of fulfilling promises...which admit of no exception whatever in favour of duties of imperfect obligation, such as that of relieving distress" (p. 18). Whatever the status of Kant's apparent endorsement of this implausible position, no such view is required by every plausible interpretation of the Categorical Imperative framework, as will be indicated by this paper.

I   Kantian intuitionism as an integrated view

In early twentieth-century intuitionism, as in much earlier intuitionist writings, three ideas have been salient. First, basic moral principles have been held to be self-evident. Second, self-evident propositions have been claimed to be unprovable. Third, as suggested by the unprovability claim – which brings to mind the idea of propositions so basic as to be Aristotelian indemonstrables – the self-evident has been represented as a category of propositions whose truth a mature rational person can "just see" and can know only by such immediate insight. All three of these views have led to criticism of intuitionist ethics. But if, as I hold in contrast to Ross, Moore, and others, many self-evident propositions can be evidenced or even proved by other propositions, the way is open both to support Rossian moral principles by appeal to a more comprehensive principle or set of principles and to characterize the self-evident in a way that makes it easy to see why self-evident propositions may be not only far from obvious but also subject to rational disagreement.[2] Ross's list of apparently basic moral principles consists of eight: they posit prima facie obligations of (1) justice, (2) non-injury, (3) veracity, (4) fidelity to promises, (5) beneficence, (6) self-improvement, (7) reparation (e.g. for injuries to others), and (8) gratitude.[3] In earlier work (2004) I have represented a modified Rossian intuitionism, including two additional principles, as a good ethical theory, but have argued that a Kantian intuitionism that integrates it with a version of the Categorical Imperative is still better.

The version I have mainly appealed to is the Formula of Humanity. This might also be called the personhood formula or, alternatively, the intrinsic end formulation. I understand it along lines that, though they reflect some important elements in Kant's ethical texts, do not presuppose a specific interpretation of Kant. In particular, I have sought to show that its negative injunction – which prohibits treating persons merely as means – is explicable in terms of "descriptive" notions, and its positive injunction, which requires treating persons as ends, is explicable, if not descriptively,

---

[2] See chapters 1 and 2 of my (2004) for references to Prichard, Moore, and Ross's claims that the self-evident is unprovable and for a detailed account of self-evidence that indicates why this requirement is mistaken. Consider a simple case: If p entails q and q entails r but r is false, then p is false. This is self-evident but readily provable. The self-evident is justifiably believable without dependence on premises, but not (in general) incapable of receiving support from them.

[3] See Ross (1930), ch. 2. In ch. 5 of my (2004) I proposed adding two further Rossian principles that express prima facie obligations of two other kinds: those of respectfulness (understood in terms of the *manner* of action as opposed to its type) and of protection and enhancement of liberty. Both are elements in the Kantian intuitionism defended in this paper and their content will be clarified by examples and other aspects of the discussion below.

then at least without dependence on moral notions.[4] Showing this is important for defending Kantian ethics as well as for providing objective anchors for these notions. If the Humanity Formula is to serve as one of our *basic* guides in making moral judgments, we need a way to understand its requirements that does not depend on prior moral judgments.

A proponent of Kantian ethics might accept this constraint but still object that, first, if we adequately understand the Categorical Imperative, it will suffice by itself to lead us to correct moral judgments in any sufficiently well described case, and, second, that as a principle of final (overall) obligation, it cannot have prima facie principles (such as Rossian ones) as consequences.[5] Regarding the first, suppose the Categorical Imperative can lead us to correct (overall) moral judgments. This could be because it enables us to weight and take adequate account of the Rossian principles and thereby the considerations that ground prima facie obligation – something people with practical wisdom would do in any case. This point indicates why the second objection fails: the Categorical Imperative could be so interpreted as to imply the Rossian principles conceived as each indicating at least one moral element crucial for applying the imperative. In applying it to determine our final obligations, we must, for example, take into account promises, human needs, and potential harms. Indeed, I doubt that the Categorical Imperative can adequately guide moral decision *apart* from taking account of such factors, and, on the positive side, deeds that enhance non-moral goodness. Even if it could, it would surely do so better as integrated with principles according prima facie obligating force to those and other factors.

Given the detailed development of Kantian intuitionism that I have provided in earlier work, my aim here is to extend and clarify the framework in new ways. Addressing further objections will help in this. One objection is to the effect that the Categorical Imperative framework is no help in deciding what to do when, as is common, there is a conflict of prima facie obligations and we need to determine what obligation is final,[6] say

---

[4] I developed Kantian intuitionism in (2001b) and further in (2004), esp. ch. 3. Particularly in the latter I appealed to the notion of dignity as adding a dimension to the framework; but, contrary to the suggestion of Gert (2006), I did not depend on the notion for the clarity or defense of the overall view; and I sought to clarify the notion independently, e.g. on p. 99, pp. 157–8, and pp. 176–7. For a detailed discussion of Kant's conception of duty and of the proper treatment of persons see Stratton-Lake (2002), esp. chs. 2–4.

[5] One might take act-utilitarianism to provide such a principle; e.g., one ought to do what optimizes well-being (where overriders are ruled out). On some readings of Kant, the Categorical Imperative yields such final obligations. Ross was at least doubtful that any such principles are sound.

[6] This is suggested by Hurka (2007), and I have responded in detail in Audi (2007). Ross (1930) implies something similar in ch. 2.

an obligation to keep a promise to protect property and an obligation not to harm a person who is fleeing with stolen goods. A related objection is that Kantian intuitionism leaves unclear how *close* we may come to treating persons merely as means and that, without an account of this, the Humanity Formula cannot provide grounds for the Rossian obligations.[7] I take these objections in turn. The response to the first partly deals with the second.

Suppose I am correct in thinking that treating a person merely as a means is roughly treating the person not just *solely* as a means but (with some qualifications) also with a disposition *not* to be concerned with any *non*-instrumental aspects of the treatment. (This negative disposition is needed to account for the force of "merely.") An example of such merely instrumental treatment might be ordering a timid and willing employee to do a risky job, with an intention to let the person struggle alone even if the job becomes highly dangerous. If, as I think plausible, such treatment is prima facie wrong – wrong-making, in another terminology – and prima facie wrong even if the act-type, ordering the job done, is not prima facie wrong in the context, then we have a morally relevant factor that supports fulfilling a Rossian obligation: roughly, a prima facie obligation of sufficient weight to yield overall obligation in the absence of conflicting considerations.

A different example may help: a conflict between the obligation of veracity in making a promise and an opportunity for beneficence. Suppose that, by making a promise I do not intend to keep, I would be getting the promisee, who expects to benefit from my keeping it, to do a very good thing for a third party. Making such a promise might also manifest the relevant disposition not to be concerned with non-instrumental aspects of the treatment of the promisee, say the person's suffering from the loss of an important opportunity when I break the promise. Let us assume this. The point that in making the insincere promise one would be using the promisee merely instrumentally weighs against making the promise or, if one does make it, favors reversing one's course and keeping it after all. It also supports the promissory obligation over the obligation of beneficence (though the support may not be overriding). The decision on whether to keep the promise may still not be easy, though it might be. In any case,

---

7 This objection was formulated by Peter Wicks in correspondence. The terminology to which he reacted had "negative ideal" where I now have "negative standard" and the objection indicated that the former could create the impression that there is a prima facie obligation to *maximize* distance from merely instrumental treatment of persons. This would be both misleadingly quantitative and too strong.

the point is that the added moral ground – that making the insincere, manipulative promise would be, or would at least approach, treating the promisee merely as a means – is helpful and potentially determinative; the point is not that it makes all the conflict cases easy to resolve. That is something no plausible moral view will achieve.

Consider now treating someone as an end, which is mainly a matter of doing – for its own sake – something that is (and is appropriately conceived by the agent as) for the good of the other person. Suppose I have to decide whether to punish a child for bad behavior by keeping the child at home and I know this punishment is reasonable but will make the child suffer. Suppose the retributive considerations, together with the good the punishment will do for the child in the long run, are just strong enough to make the choice between punishing and simply reprimanding difficult, given the desirability of avoiding the suffering. Now suppose that I consider, prospectively, as is appropriate to making a moral decision, not just the two act-types in question – which some other person could realize – but also how I would be *treating* the child in each case. *Treatment* is a matter of my *conduct*, in a sense in which that term expresses a three-dimensional concept encompassing these diverse elements: first, the act-type I would instantiate; second, the reasons(s) for which I would perform the act; and third, the manner in which I would perform it. There are two significantly different questions here. On the question of whether giving the punishment is justified by the disobedience, the answer might be positive. On the question of whether I, as opposed to someone less emotionally involved, should give it, the answer might be negative. The explanation of this difference requires analysis.

II Thick and thin moral questions

I propose that we conceive the question of what my conduct should be as morally thicker than the question of what act-type I should perform. One difference is this. The thicker question partly concerns the fittingness of my expectable motivation in performing the prospective act of punishment to the context in which I envisage performing it, whereas the thin question concerns not that, but mainly the fittingness of the act-type to the factors that ground the basic prima facie obligations. The latter question is roughly a first-person application of 'What should *be done?*' whereas the former is a conduct-specific version of 'What should *I do?*' Suppose my concern is guided by a sense of the thick conduct question. Here are two possibilities.

First, I might see that, in punishing, I would be acting mainly *from* intrinsic motivation to contribute to the overall good of the child, whereas in simply reprimanding I would be avoiding temporary suffering on the child's part and would be motivated mainly by avoidance of this painful consequence and to some extent by a desire to avoid having to hear the anticipated screams of protest. The realization that one action would be treating the child as an end and the other would not (which is not to say it would be treating the child merely as a means) might properly tip the balance in favor of punishing.

The second possibility also concerns treatment conceived as conduct but might be such as to favor either the reprimand or yielding the decision itself to someone else. Suppose I know that I am very angry with the child. I may still think the punishment is required but may believe that I would be administering it partly out of anger, perhaps mainly so. I think, then, that I would be doing the right thing but at least not mainly for the right reason. Here one might be reminded of what Socrates is believed to have said to a slave boy: I would beat you if I were not angry. In addition to thinking I would not be acting mainly for the right reason, I might also believe I would punish *angrily*, and this expectation about the manner of my act is a further significant consideration. My conduct, then, might well not be an instance of treating the child as an end. If it would not be, then on that count it would be morally deficient.

Prospective and retrospective conduct questions

The punishment case illustrates the important point that treating persons as ends goes beyond fulfilling the obligation of beneficence, which requires, chiefly, bringing about the relevant good with an appropriate connection to an awareness of the obligation to do so (this does not entail acting from the *virtue* of beneficence, which requires that the action be based on certain elements in one's character). The obligation of general beneficence is *already* taken into account in my weighing of the overall good that the act of punishment will do in comparison with the good of avoiding the suffering it would cause. The point here (which a plausible virtue ethics might also stress) is that there is additional moral reason to treat the person with a kind of goodwill *and* in a manner that manifests it. There is a good in the *doing* of the right, conceived as conduct; this conduct is not just something done that *is* right.

The case does not imply that in making moral decisions, even where treatment of persons is in question, we must *always* reflect on or even attend to how we would be treating whoever is in question. Often we see clearly what we ought to do, and even how we would do it, without any need for scrutiny or reflection. There is often no need to raise the thick question. Moreover, in many cases of conflicting obligations there would be no difference of the kind in question, on any of the competing options. Nonetheless, the kind of treatment of persons we would instantiate in doing one thing rather than another is morally important. Its importance is not an element in Rossian intuitionism but is compatible with the core of that position. Taking account of the difference, moreover – and of what might be called the kind of *aretaic good* that my view thereby accounts for (a kind of good in the doing of the right) – does not require either direct voluntary control over motivation or any greater knowledge of our own motivation than we may be plausibly thought to have.[8]

The conduct question, then, is three-dimensional. It takes account of the moral assessment not just of the act-type in prospect when we make a moral decision but also of the kind of treatment of persons that we would instantiate in doing one or another thing in question; that in turn is partly a matter of our motivation and our manner of action. The thin moral question concerns simply what act-type is morally appropriate for an agent in the relevant circumstances. I am of course assuming that the same act-type, such as requiring a child to stay home, can be tokened for different reasons. This should be uncontroversial but must be stressed; for there are also *conduct-types*. Conduct is not just instantiating an act-type; it is (roughly) instantiating it for a particular set of reasons and in a particular way. But, in part because we have indirect control over why we do things – if only through our power to abstain from or delay doing them – conduct is subject to moral evaluation as part of our record.

Conduct, then, is richer than action narrowly considered, but it is also an element in our manifest accomplishments in a way traits of character are not. This places it between elements of character on the dispositional side and overt performances on the behavioral side. It tends to reveal character, but is not an element in character. It requires action, but is not a matter simply of the type of act the treatment embodies. Granted, we can give a behavioral name to an act-type instantiated in a certain way, and many act-describing terms apparently reflect a sense of the importance of some of these double-barreled types. To yell, for instance, is to speak very loudly; to pace is to walk in a certain repetitive way. But yelling and pacing can

---

[8] The kind and degree of our voluntary control of our reasons for acting is explored in detail in my (2009a).

be done in different ways. There are limits to the number of ways we can control the manner of our actions, but for a huge range of act-types we can consider realizing, *how* we should do the thing in question is morally significant.

The significance of thick questions can easily be missed. Ethics is easily taken to concern just what we ought to do. It certainly concerns that. But it also concerns the kinds of reasons for which we should do what we ought to do; and, as is less widely noted and sometimes ignored, it concerns *how* – in what manner – we should do what we ought to do. The manner of an obligatory action is not fixed even by a specification of both the obligatory act-type it tokens *and* the reason(s) for which the agent realizes it. A person of moral virtue naturally tends to do the right thing for the right reason and in the right manner; but one need not be a virtue ethicist to acknowledge the value of singling out the three dimensions of conduct as I have.

The scope and comprehensiveness of prima facie obligation

These promissory and retributive examples might give the impression that the notions of merely instrumental and end-regarding treatment simply place two more prima facie obligations on a Rossian list and hence are no help either in its unification or in dealing with conflicts of obligations. I have indeed suggested that the non-moral grounds in question – the two kinds of treatment – generate prima facie obligations and seem to do so "in their own right." Suppose this were all we could say of these grounds: that there are prima facie obligations to treat persons as ends and to avoid treating them merely as means. This is significant in itself. The obligations would be morally important by virtue of their *instantial*, as opposed to systematizing, aspects. They would figure (as illustrated) in many cases that would otherwise be difficult or impossible to decide in an intuitively satisfactory way.[9] They are, however, both different in kind from Rossian obligations, since they concern conduct rather than act-types. They are also more comprehensive than Rossian obligations. One or the other of them can be seen as applicable in all (or virtually all) instances of Rossian obligation. For all of the Rossian obligations, many kinds of fulfillments can be cases of treating someone as an end; and violations of the "negative" obligations, for instance of non-injury, fidelity, and veracity, are the kinds of actions that tend to approach treatment merely as a means.

---

[9] I leave open whether it is self-evident that the two kinds of treatment ground prima facie obligations; they can play the indicated role even if this point is not self-evident.

A further point is that the notions of avoiding merely instrumental treatment and aiming at end-regarding treatment express broad negative and positive aims proper to the *institution* of morality – a *telos* of morality, as it were. They characterize, in broad strokes, some of the kinds of evils morality opposes and some of the kinds of goods it supports. This purposive role that the two notions partly represent is a significant unifying element for the Rossian obligations.

Regarding the second line of objection, I begin with a clarification. In speaking of the Categorical Imperative as usable in systematizing the Rossian obligations, I have in mind at least this minimal kind of systematization: on my interpretation of it, the imperative provides three kinds of understanding: first, a way of conceiving the obligations as partially explained in terms of the wider obligations to avoid treating persons merely as means and to treat them as ends; second, a way to view the Rossian obligations as in some way derivable from it (at least with some regimentation); and third, a way of interpreting and comparing those obligations in concrete cases (as will be illustrated especially in Section IV). I have not implied (and do not hold) that the Rossian obligations are ontically *grounded* in the obligations to treat persons as ends and never merely as means, i.e., possessed in virtue of the fulfillment of those obligations being ways of meeting the deeper, treatment obligations. Rossian principles can be true "in their own right" even if they gain support from elsewhere. This brings us to a different kind of grounding, the epistemological. I have argued for the epistemological (and axiological) *groundability* of Rossian principles: roughly, for their being *justifiable* on the basis of the Categorical Imperative framework I have sketched or (consistently with this) of a certain theory of value, or by integrating the two (2004, pp. 149–50). Their justifiability (and knowability), however, does not depend on the imperative or on such a theory; and their epistemic groundability in these sources does not entail (and I do not assert) the ontic point that their *truth* depends on the Categorical Imperative or on axiological propositions (2004, pp. 141–2).

III   The treatment of persons and the Rossian prima facie obligations

As to the particular epistemic relations I take to exist between the Humanity Formula as I interpret it and the Rossian obligations, the weakest is that of providing a "justificatory rationale" (2004, esp. pp. 102–3). The idea is roughly that in the light of the former, the latter can be seen as reasonable. One might argue that wherever one set of propositions provides a justificatory rationale for another set, there is a regimentation of the former which *entails* the latter or a regimented version thereof. I have left this entailment possibility open and with it the possibility of a stronger epistemic relation than providing a justificatory rationale; but I do not think that such an entailment must be presupposed in order for the rationale to yield a significant degree of justification for what it rationalizes. It should be stressed that the possibility that self-evident Rossian propositions can receive justification from other propositions does not entail that they stand in need of it: justificatory overdetermination is a possibility even for the self-evident; and, for both self-evident and other kinds of propositions, it is realized in ethics as elsewhere.

It should also be emphasized that one can take each set of propositions to provide support for the other without holding (as a coherentist might but I do not) that each justifies (or explains) the other. I do hold the conceptual thesis that each may help to clarify the other, but the kind of mutual clarification in question does not imply mutual entailment and is consistent with various epistemic and explanatory connections.[10] My epistemological thesis here is that insofar as the Humanity Formula (correctly) explains, or is an essential explanatory element in what best explains, the Rossian principles, it receives support. This is because a proposition's having a certain kind of explanatory power in accounting for what is justifiably believable and true provides some degree of justification for it – a kind of abductive justification. The Rossian principles thus play a justificatory role regarding the Humanity Formula, even though they themselves are rationalizable by appeal to it. But this role is not that of *justifying* or directly supporting the formula; it is that of constituting truths whose explanation yields justificatory support for what explains them. Explaining what is true confirms the explainer.

A remaining question is what work the notion of treating merely as a means can do when it serves (as I intend) as a negative standard which we should avoid even approaching. The idea to be clarified is, in part, that we have reasons not only to avoid actually treating people merely as means but to avoid approaching this. There are at least four cases of such approach, for a given kind of instrumental act *A* whose performance would constitute

---

[10] Olson (2006) raises (though he does not pursue) the question of how all the relations I posit between the intrinsic end formulation and the Rossian obligations can obtain together. He is especially suspicious regarding the compatibility of the specification relation between the latter and the former and the explanation and (overdetermining) justification relations between the former and the latter (p. 542). This section should help to justify the overall integration between the two elements that my Kantian intuitionism maintains.

treatment of some person. 1. There is *approaching A*-ing, as in taking preparatory steps to send someone on a dangerous mission for a minimal payment, while aware that one is disposed not to be concerned with any non-instrumental aspects of sending the person, such as physical injuries. 2. A second case is *continuing to A*, say continuing to keep an employee working on an increasingly dangerous task, when one is approaching such an indisposition, as where the prospect of monetary gains fills consciousness and crowds out moral scruples. 3. A third case is less directly at odds with avoiding merely instrumental treatment. It is failing to avoid conduct that foreseeably strengthens one's motivation to exploit someone. This might occur with one's employees or in close personal relationships, as where a man employs a female assistant he knows he is likely to seduce and then abandon. 4. Similarly, a fourth case is failing to take opportunities to nurture or develop motivation that enhances the likelihood of treating as ends persons one interacts with. Refusing to hear about suffering friends one could easily help might be an instance of this.

Both 3 and 4 also bear on character development. One should resist conduct that makes one callous in such a way as to incline one to act with the disposition to treat people merely as means (such conduct might include doing something that tends to cause treating persons merely as means to cover up wrong-doing). One should, by contrast, enhance one's tendency to treat persons partly as ends, and we should do this even where they must be treated *partly* as means, as is common in much of normal life. (Treating someone merely as a means may be uncommon and presumably *is* quite uncommon among decent persons, and it is ruled out by treating someone even *partly* as an end, which we may hope is common.)

Taking account of cases 1 and 2 helps in deciding overall obligation, both by adding independent support to certain options and by clarifying the moral status of certain prospective conduct. This has been illustrated above in the punishment and promising examples. Cases 3 and 4 reflect the secondary obligation to support fulfillment of a primary one (the obligation to avoid treating persons merely as means). Moreover, since treating a person even *partly* as an end entails that one is not treating the person merely as a means, developing a tendency to treat persons even partly as ends, which 4 enjoins, reduces the likelihood of treating them merely as means.

These clarifications of Kantian intuitionism do not provide a formula for dealing with conflicts of obligation, but they do show that the notions of merely instrumental and end-regarding treatment of persons can play positive roles both in providing a comprehensive conceptual framework for understanding the Rossian obligations and for dealing with certain conflicts between those. I do not claim that every such conflict is better dealt with in the light of those notions, but many are. A main reason for this is that in dealing with these conflicts, we may often benefit from asking thick moral questions rather than just thin ones aimed at determining what is to be done (other reasons will emerge in Section IV). This enables us to do a fuller evaluation and, often, to conduct ourselves better.

IV Reasons for action and final obligation

I have been presupposing that a ground of obligation, such as making a promise, is also a reason for action, but not all normative reasons are moral. I have also taken no position on the (normative) strength of moral reasons relative to other kinds.[11] The possibility of conflict between moral and non-moral reasons, such as reasons of pure self-interest, can make more difficult the overall question of what one ought to do (what *to* do, if that question is understood normatively). Non-moral reasons may not only conflict with moral ones but may also support some moral reasons against other moral reasons. Here it is enough to indicate how, on my theory, we should conceive conflicting moral reasons. Some of what is said will apply to conflicts between moral and non-moral reasons.

To begin with, I take it that there is no a priori hierarchy among the moral reasons represented by the Rossian obligations. Thus, there are apparently no two categories of obligation, say justice and beneficence, such that *every* obligation in one will outweigh *any* (individual) obligation in the other. An implication of this view – a kind of particularism regarding normative ethical hierarchies – is that a moral reason corresponding to such an obligation is not a priori overridden in every case of conflict with a moral reason belonging to a different category of obligation. Note, too, that even on the assumption that a reason of one kind is always overridden in a pairwise conflict with a single reason of some other kind, certain coalitions of reasons on one side might still prevail over any single reason that would always override any one member of the coalition. If, for instance, in conflict cases, any reason of non-injury were to outweigh every reason of gratitude taken by itself, some of the former taken singly might not outweigh every set of the latter.

---

[11] A theory of reasons and of the possible kinds of relations that hold between moral and non-moral reasons is provided in my (2001a), e.g. chs. 5 and 6. To be sure, the notion of a *moral* reason is not sharp. For extensive discussion of the relative weights of practical reasons and, in particular, Sidgwick's problem of the dualism of practical reason, see Crisp (2006), esp. ch. 5.

Weighting principles

Given the ethical theory so far outlined, we might formulate some rough generalizations which might be conceived as *weighting principles* that can guide one in dealing with conflicting prima facie obligations, whether between two or more of the ten I have posited or within a single category, as where two promises conflict. (I do not take the list of ten Rossian obligations I have formulated – Ross's and the two mentioned in note 3 – as necessarily complete, but it is highly comprehensive and at present I see no clear need to extend it.) What follows are several candidates for weighting principles that might be plausibly thought to hold when other things are equal in terms of these Rossian obligations. The formulations are tentative, but seem defensible on some plausible reading. I do not claim, however, that any of these principles is self-evident or even broadly a priori; nor do I claim that all are implicit in my interpretation of the Humanity Formula. Not all are, but each is at least harmonious with that principle. They might be viewed as *adjunctive* relative to both that and the Rossian principles. I will illustrate these weighting principles in terms of choice among singular acts, but the formulations also apply where our options are certain principles of action. They are all forward-looking, formulated with making moral decisions in mind, but their application is not limited to prospective action. They can also be used in appraising deeds already done.

The first weighting principle indicates one way in which the Categorical Imperative bears on Rossian obligations:

> 1. *Treatment of persons.* If two options we have are equally well supported by conflicting Rossian obligations, then if one option is favored in terms of our (a) avoiding treating persons merely as a means or (b) treating persons as ends (or both), then that option is preferable, other things equal, with (a) having priority (other things equal) over (b) if (a) supports one option and (b) the other.[12]

---

[12] Two points should be noted here. First, although the obligations to treat persons as ends and never merely as means overlap the obligations of manner (a wide category of Rossian obligation introduced in ch. 5 of Audi 2004), the two sets are not equivalent, and an account of the latter is helpful in clarifying the former. The obligations of manner are *performative*; the others are largely *motivational*. This is why one could be treating someone nicely in manner, even nursing injuries, yet still treating the person merely as a means, say to preserve for later enslavement. Second, it may be true that whenever obligations of manner – *adverbial obligations*, as I called these in ch. 5 of Audi (2004) – are violated, so is some value represented among the obligations of matter (including the other nine Rossian obligations). Might obligations of manner, then, reduce to those of matter? Imagine that, e.g., being beneficent covers most of the former. Still, *being beneficent* is not an

The punishment case above illustrates this principle. The thick moral question concerning appropriate conduct is central for 1; and because the focus of the principle is on conduct-types rather than act-types, it differs from Rossian principles. It is also plausible, however, even as applied only to the relevant alternatives conceived as act-types *insofar as* identifying them is a reliable guide to the kind of treatment one will engage in. It should be added that although it is perhaps not obvious that Kant viewed the obligation to avoid merely instrumental treatment as, other things equal, weightier than the obligation to treat persons as ends, this view is independently plausible and provides greater determinacy for my interpretation of the overall moral force of the Humanity Formula.

For some of the same kinds of reasons why it is desirable to give more than one argument for a thesis, it may be desirable, in moral matters, to have (and act on) more than one reason. In this light one might give some weight to diversity of moral considerations, as follows:

> 2. *Moral diversity.* If two options we have are equally well supported by the conflicting Rossian obligations, but the number of distinct obliga-tions or of types of obligations favoring one option is greater, that option is preferable, other things equal.

The degree of preferability in question may be slight, but taking number of obligations or of types of obligations into account seems reasonable. In part, this is a matter of always giving some weight to the variety of *kinds* of considerations favoring an action; but it leaves open whether, other things being equal, number of types of obligations is more important than the number of individual obligations. One among other considerations here is that the number of obligations corresponds to the number of moral considerations that can be cited in support of an action. It seems reasonable to give the number of such reasons some weight, in part because error is less likely and because each kind of moral reason for an act is at once a pathway to understanding why it is obligatory, a potential motivational support for it and, if it is performed for that reason, at least a partial explanation of why it is performed.

The awarding of grants and fellowships might illustrate this principle. If *A* and *B* are approximately equally good candidates for the same award,

act-type, and I am construing the other nine Rossian principles as designating obligatory act-types, and have stressed (esp. in 2004, pp. 179–82) that any act-type can be performed in various *ways*, and that the manner of our performances is often morally important. (Treating merely as a means and treating as an end are not act-types, however – at least not behavioral act-types – a point that goes with their comprehensiveness.) The problem of specifying the connection between the adverbial obligations and the others was posed to me by Paul Audi.

then if the number of the criteria on which A merits the award is larger than the number on which B does, then – other things equal – choosing A tends to be slightly preferable. This is not to say one is required to prefer A. I take preferability to render the relevant choice rational and morally better, but not necessarily to render every competing alternative irrational or morally wrong.

It is uncontroversial that the number of people (even other sentient beings) affected by an act is relevant to its moral appraisal. This suggests the following principle:

> 3. *Distributive scope: number of affected people.* If one of two options equally well supported by the conflicting Rossian obligations negatively affects a smaller number of people than another, or positively affects a larger number of people than the other option, then the first is preferable, other things equal.

This has clear application to legislative and administrative decisions. A choice between healthcare plans might illustrate the principle regarding distribution of goods; a choice between plans for wartime military conscription might illustrate it for distribution of "bads." The principle might indicate one kind of respect for what Rawls has called the "separateness of persons." Everyone matters – we are all "ends." It is not just the collective human good that is morally important. Principle 3 is also supported by some of the considerations cited in rationalizing 2. In positively affecting more people, for instance, we may in some cases tend to fulfill a larger number of types of obligations.

Still another weighting principle reflects the moral importance of equal treatment of persons:

> 4. *Equality.* If one of two options equally supported by the Rossian obligations treats the persons who would be affected more nearly equally, it is preferable, other things equal.

It must be granted that since promoting justice and eliminating injustice may be matters of equality, this adds nothing to the obligation of justice where that standard calls for pursuing equal treatment. But this rule would apply even where justice is not at stake, as where two needy groups of people compete for help not *owed* to either. If, moreover, we countenance *indirect* treatment, then where two sets of charities compete for one's donation (as a fulfillment of the obligation of beneficence), and one charity distributes its benefits in a more nearly equal fashion than the other, this principle would provide a basis for preference of the former.

A sound ethics should give some kind of priority to reducing suffering over enhancing positive well-being.[13] This suggests a principle like the following:

5. *Priority of the worse off.* If one of two options equally supported by the Rossian obligations benefits one or more persons who are worse off than the person(s) benefited by the other option, then, other things equal, it is preferable, and the more so the greater the disparity in well-being, or the worse off the latter set of persons is in absolute terms.

There are many prioritarian principles that reflect what might be called the stronger moral "claim" of the worse off, and the priorities may be specified more quantitatively. This principle may be less controversial than more quantitative versions. Once again, an illustration might come from choices between serving two groups of people or between choosing between two charities or grant applicants.[14] The principle reflects the plausible idea that the relief of pain or suffering is, other things equal, morally more important than the provision of positive benefits.

One could regard 5 as implicit in a proper understanding of beneficence, but that claim is probably controversial, and some theorists might give it a different interpretation that is incompatible with 5. It should also be noted that pain often impedes autonomy in our conduct, and the importance of that point is better, or at least differently, accounted for by the value of treating persons as ends than by considerations of beneficence. In any event, explicitness is best served by including this principle separately from that of beneficence.

It is natural to regard ethics as centrally concerned with how we should conduct ourselves as social beings. In this light, the following seems to be a natural weighting principle:

6. *Reducing alienation.* If one of two options equally supported by the Rossian obligations would be alienating to one or more persons affected, or would be more so than the other, or would reduce alienation less than the other, then the latter is preferable, other things equal.

---

[13] This priority of the worse off is related to the positive and negative aspects of beneficence discussed in my (2004), esp. pp. 175–7.

[14] Insofar as equal treatment is considered in some way *proportionate*, for instance to need or effort, the intuitive importance of equality gives some support to the priority principle, which has results similar to those of the equality principle interpreted to require proportionate equality. But the moral importance of preference of the worse off is an independent consideration.

This principle might apply to a choice between two government policies or two healthcare plans for a company. Alienation need not be a kind of injury, so this principle goes beyond emphasizing non-injury. Arguably, the principle exhibits an instance of according weight to giving people the sense of being treated as ends or at least of a disposition to avoid treating them merely as means. Providing this sense may be a kind of beneficence but it is not usually considered under that heading and is plausibly taken to go beyond beneficence. To be sure, if *A*-ing is morally positive, the sense of being treated as a target of the act tends to be positive; but that point does not imply that the treatment in question is a case of, or in any event nothing more than, beneficence.

Here is a plausible counterpart of 6:

7. *Coordination values.* If one of two options equally supported by the Rossian obligations would be superior to the other in reinforcing or enhancing coordination among persons, it is preferable, other things equal.

No doubt enhancing coordination, for example by instituting car pooling or a grievance policy to reduce conflicts, is by and large a way of doing good for people; but whether it actually achieves this is a contingent matter, and this rule is not simply reducible to according additional weight to beneficence. Given both our social nature and our interdependence as a condition of success in much that matters to us, coordination is an indispensable element in human flourishing taken to be essentially social. Abiding by this principle seems warranted even by its instrumental value in contributing to flourishing. A certain kind of coordination among persons also has inherent value, as where a team wins a game by mutually supporting plays. Such inherent value would provide further rationale for treating the principle as a distinctive element in certain moral decisions.

Higher-order normative principles

The last two principles I want to suggest are different in being higher order than 1–7. Both can be rationalized by appeal to the Humanity Formula, but they are better understood and can be better justified if that principle is interpreted in relation to the determinate prima facie requirements, such as equal treatment, liberty, and beneficence, that are explicit in the Rossian principles. Both principles concern the sorts of reasons appropriate for a kind of action or the apparent level of one's justification for action relative to that of someone (possibly hypothetical) who disagrees. Both are particularly important in political contexts in which, as with legislative decisions, interpersonal discussion is crucial in the process of determination and justification of policy.

Legislative and public policy decisions often imply coercion and should be justifiable in a way appropriate to both the idea that liberty is important in its own right as a morally desirable good and the idea that interpersonal conduct should be justifiable in broadly moral terms. Particularly in the often difficult task of balancing religious considerations and "natural reasons" – which are such that any normal rational person can accord them some degree of normative authority (which implies their secularity) – we need a principle that indicates what kind of reason is needed.[15] Here I suggest a principle that goes beyond those so far articulated in applying where reasons not singled out by them, mainly religious ones, might otherwise be thought to have sufficient weight to justify a coercive action:

8. *The principle of secular rationale* (roughly, of natural reason). Citizens in a free democracy have a prima facie obligation not to advocate or support any law or public policy that restricts human conduct, unless they have, and are willing to offer, adequate secular reason (roughly, natural reason) for this advocacy or support (e.g. for a vote).[16]

Here a secular reason for an action (or for a belief) is roughly one whose status as a justifier of action (or of belief) does not evidentially depend on (but also does not deny) the existence of God; nor does it depend on theological considerations, or on the pronouncements of a person or institution *as* a religious authority. This notion is epistemic, roughly a matter of evidential grounding, not a matter of the content of the reason. We can imagine a case in which a person's reasons for action include commitments based essentially on religious convictions. Consider a promissory obligation grounded in swearing on the Bible that one will keep a promise to one's priest to oppose same-sex unions. The secular rationale principle would call for abstaining from coercion (as opposed to persuasion) in this matter apart from having an adequate reason that does not depend in this way on religion or theology. If the material welfare of children could be shown to be adversely affected by such unions, there would be a secular reason. (The adequacy condition rules out the appropriateness of certain

---

[15] The notion of natural reason needs explication, and I have outlined an analysis, and in doing so taken account of Aquinas's notion of natural reason, in (2009b).

[16] This formulation is drawn from Audi (2000), p. 86, though I published essentially the same version in (1989).

non-religious reasons, e.g. racist ones; but the prominence and special importance of religious reasons calls for a principle like 8.)

The principle of secular rationale can be supported by a very broad one that also applies to coercion even outside the political realm:

> 9. *The principle of tolerance.* If it is not reasonable for proponents of coercion in a certain matter to consider themselves epistemically superior in that matter to proponents of the corresponding liberty, the former have a prima facie obligation to tolerate rather than coerce.[17]

The principle is meant to apply where there is an actual or hypothetical disputant who is, in the matter(s) at hand, an apparent *epistemic peer* of the person, i.e. (roughly) equally rational, possessed of the same relevant evidence, and equally conscientious in assessing that evidence. This principle reflects the value of liberty – respecting which is a partly constitutive element in treating persons as ends – but it is not entailed by simply taking some degree of protection of liberty to be, like promoting the well-being of persons, an object of prima facie moral obligation. Imagine someone's making a case that certain apparent harms justify coercion, whether institutional or in personal relations, to prevent them. The principle of tolerance would call for restraint if it is not reasonable for the would-be coercer to consider the proponent of liberty epistemically inferior in relation to the issue at hand. Thus, in what might otherwise be a case in which coercion is justifiable by the balance of conflicting obligations, this principle might determine that liberty should prevail.

Each of the weighting principles may conflict with at least one other, but they may still serve to reduce the difficulty of dealing with conflicts between Rossian obligations, and in any case conflicts at the level of weighting principles may be less common or (at least often) less serious, or both. As with the Rossian obligations, I see no a priori hierarchy. In any plausible ethic, judgment on the basis of practical wisdom of a kind that need not be a matter of applying *any* principle may at some point be needed. My aim is not to eliminate the need for practical wisdom but to assist it as much as possible by formulating principles congenial to it.

Might we also have a principle framed in terms of negative and positive obligations? Might we say that where a "negative" obligation – for example one of non-injury, fidelity, or veracity – conflicts with a positive one, say an

---

17 I cannot explicate the notion of the reasonable here, but I take it to be stronger than the concept of the rational: what is reasonable is rational but not conversely. Detailed defense of this view is provided in my (2001a), esp. pp. 149–53.

obligation of beneficence or self-improvement, the former takes priority, other things equal? I suspect this is too broad to be helpful (I leave open whether some other formulation in this range might be sustained). Here the problem of deciding what has to be equal is even more difficult than in the case of the other rough generalizations.

The obligation of beneficence is particularly troublesome. In a world with as much suffering as this one has and with as good means as now exist for relieving some of it by charitable contributions, it looks as if the beneficence obligations of the prosperous are very weighty. Can they be weakened by making promises to one's children and friends to commit large proportions of one's resources to them? As these cases apparently show, a blanket preference for negative obligations, even when other things are equal, does not take account of the voluntary character of many of them. It is not plausible, for instance, to regard a prosperous person's obligations of beneficence as substantially reduced by promises of support which, with a view to rationalizing the reduction of charitable contributions, are made (but not owed) to already flourishing children. This is not to say that promises made with such an evasive aim generate no prima facie obligations; but acting for that kind of reason is morally criticizable conduct, and (as in other cases) the resulting obligations may or may not be overridden. Nor should we deny that some promises, and certain other commitments, that it is morally reasonable to make to those close to us foreseeably limit our capacity for general beneficence. The problem here may not be soluble by any single principle of the kind just illustrated, and it remains a challenge to any ethical theory.[18]

* * *

The status of ethical intuitionism depends largely on our power to perceive truth by certain kinds of non-inferential discernment. This discernment may be intuitive and may or may not be accompanied by or even based on reflection. On rationalist versions of intuitionism, even general moral principles may be directly (non-inferentially) known – though neither indefeasibly nor in a way that is wholly unmediated by reflection.[19] As

---

[18] In (2004, pp. 94–101) I have dubbed this demandingness problem *the beneficence problem* and argued that the prohibition of treating persons merely as means indicates an important element in dealing with it.

[19] It may be thought that noncognitivism avoids the problem of determining the scope of reason in ethical matters, as suggested by, e.g., Kappel (2002), p. 411. But any plausible noncognitivist view must provide an account of what constitutes a relevant (and indeed a good) reason for holding a non-cognitive pro or con moral judgment. How we might know or justifiedly believe such an account seems to me a problem in moral epistemology much akin to the kind I have been dealing with here.

I have developed intuitionism, the required power of reason to ground non-inferential knowledge of certain moral principles is essentially like the power needed for knowledge of the a priori in general; and the power of reason regarding singular judgments is highly analogous to the epistemic powers by virtue of which we acquire perceptual knowledge. These points hold for a modified Rossian intuitionism, which I consider a good theory even when not strengthened by integration with an interpretation of the Humanity Formula or some other comprehensive principle.

The integration achievable by Kantian intuitionism is supported in part by axiological considerations. The comprehensive theory that reflects this further unification of ethical considerations is developed in *The Good in the Right* (2004). Even apart from that theory, this paper enables us to see how the injunction to avoid treating persons merely as means and to treat them as ends figures both in systematizing Rossian obligations and in dealing with conflicts between them. The notions of merely instrumental and end-regarding treatment help us to take account not just of act-types appropriate to a situation of choice but also of conduct and of a related distinction between thick and thin moral questions. The notion of conduct is complex, and the question of what our conduct should be has both behavioral and motivational dimensions. Answering it requires more than considering options conceived as act-types or even act-types and the consequences of instantiating them. The normative framework of the overall view is also enhanced by the formulation of certain weighting principles that can often help in resolving conflicts of prima facie obligations and connect these diverse obligations with such ethically important notions as scope of distribution, equality, and social coordination. Further clarification is needed, but it should now at least be clear how incommensurable moral considerations can be rationally compared in a way that facilitates making justified singular moral judgments.[20]

References

Audi, Robert (1989) "The Separation of Church and State and the Obligations of Citizenship," *Philosophy and Public Affairs* 18(3), 259–96.
(2000) *Religious Commitment and Secular Reason* (Cambridge University Press).

[20] Earlier, quite different versions of this paper have been presented to the Philosophical Society in Oxford, at the University of Münster, at Wake Forest University, and at the Arizona Workshop on Normative Ethics. I have benefited from discussion on all those occasions and, for helpful comments, would particularly like to thank Mark Timmons and two anonymous readers for the Press.

(2001a) *The Architecture of Reason* (Oxford University Press).

(2001b) "A Kantian Intuitionism," *Mind* 110(439), 601–35.

(2004) *The Good in the Right: A Theory of Intuition and Intrinsic Value* (Princeton University Press).

(2007) "Kantian Intuitionism and Ethical Pluralism," in Timmons, Greco, and Mele, 213–18.

(2009a) "Moral Virtue and Reasons for Action," *Philosophical Issues* 19, 1–20.

(2009b) "Natural Reason, Secularity, and Neutrality Toward Religion," *Religion and Human Rights* 4, 1–20.

Crisp, Roger (2006) *Reasons and the Good* (Oxford University Press).

Gert, Joshua (2006) "Review of Audi, *The Good in the Right*," *Mind* 497(15), 121–5.

Hurka, Thomas (2007) "Audi's Marriage of Ross and Kant," in Timmons, Greco, and Mele, 64–72.

Kappel, Klemens (2002) "Challenges to Audi's Intuitionism," *Ethical Theory and Moral Practice* 5, 391–413.

Olson, Jonas (2006) "Review of Audi, *The Good in the Right*," *Philosophical Review* 115(4), 540–2.

Ross, W. D. (1930) *The Right and the Good* (Oxford University Press).

Stratton-Lake, Philip (2002) *Ethical Intuitionism: Re-evaluations* (Oxford University Press).

Timmons, Mark, John Greco, and Alfred R. Mele (eds.) (2007) *Rationality and the Good: Critical Essays on the Ethics and Epistemology of Robert Audi* (Oxford University Press).

CHAPTER 7

Moral virtue and reasons for action

Moral virtue is a central notion in ethics, and understanding it is a challenge for action theory and moral psychology. It is no easy task to provide an account of it, but even a plausible account of what moral virtue is leaves largely open the difficult question of what it is to act virtuously and the related question of how we can ensure that we do so act. To see the problem that I want to address, consider two points. First, although we can fulfill our obligations by doing the right things – call this *behavioral fulfillment of obligation* – we deserve little or no credit for doing them if we do not do them for one or more reasons of the right kind. Such creditworthiness is a necessary condition for *virtuous fulfillment of obligation.* Second, given that acting virtuously is in part a matter of acting for the right kind of reason, and that (as I shall argue) we cannot at will determine for what reasons we act, we cannot act virtuously at will. This holds even when the act that virtue calls for, such as apologizing, is one we can perform at will. Apologizing can be done for a reason of mere self-protection, which is inappropriate to virtue – at least to the kind of virtue, such as respectfulness, which an apology should express. This limitation on acting virtuously is disturbing, perhaps even paradoxical. We think of ourselves as having the voluntary power to conduct ourselves in morally admirable ways. Do we not have that power after all? I shall argue that, in certain ways and under certain conditions, we do. The theory to be presented here will indicate those ways and conditions. It will also bear on the extent to which Aristotle was right in thinking that virtue itself is up to us.[1]

---

[1] Aristotle says, e.g., "virtue is also up to us, and so also, in the same way, is vice" (*Nicomachean Ethics* 1113b7–8), and "being decent or base is up to us" (1113b14); but he does not imply that what is up to us is always under direct voluntary control (or that it never is). References to *Nicomachean Ethics* (*NE*) will be hereafter included in the text. The translation is by Terence E. Irwin (Indianapolis: Hackett, 1989).

I Moral virtue as an element in character

My purposes do not require a full-scale account of moral virtue. I shall simply presuppose (drawing on earlier work)[2] that to have a virtue of character is to have a certain kind of trait, one appropriate to pursuing the particular good with respect to which the virtue counts as such. I shall also presuppose that moral virtues include justice, veracity, fidelity, respectfulness (toward persons), beneficence, and some related character traits. A concern with the well-being of others, for instance, is essential for moral virtue and, more specifically, for determining what counts as respectfulness or, especially, beneficence. In what follows, moral virtue will be my central concern, though much of what emerges will hold for other "practical" virtues and some of the points will also hold for intellectual virtues. I will not, however, provide an analysis of moral as opposed to other virtues of character, but that difficult task need not be undertaken for our purposes here.[3]

A trait constituting a virtue may be more or less deeply rooted; it may be more or less dominating in the person's behavior; and it may be variable in many other ways. We want our virtues to be inseparable from our very nature, but this is not always how it is.[4] However deeply rooted a virtue is, both cognitive and motivational elements are central. A virtuous person, say owing to veracity, must have certain beliefs; some would say, indeed, that a weighted proportion of these beliefs must constitute knowledge, for instance knowledge of when it is appropriate to avoid an unjustified question rather than either answer it truthfully or lie. Knowing *how* as well as knowing *that* is important for the cognitive elements in virtues. Virtuous agents must also have desires (or other motivational elements, such as intentions) that are appropriate to the virtue. Fidelity, for example, requires a constituent desire (even if not always a preponderant desire) to stand by family and friends.

The analysis of the notion of a virtue of character should cover at least six conceptually important dimensions.[5] (Virtues of character overlap those

---

[2] In this sketch of virtue and acting from it I draw on my "Acting from Virtue," *Mind* 104 (1995), 449–71.

[3] There is no easy way to distinguish the moral from the simply normative elements in the domain of practical reason. I have addressed this problem, in part in relation to the distinction between the moral and the prudential, and sketched an approach to the problem, in *Practical Reasoning and Ethical Decision* (London: Routledge, 2006), ch. 9.

[4] As someone (probably the great critic A. C. Bradley) said of Emilia in Shakespeare's *Othello*, "She wears her virtue loosely, but never quite casts it off."

[5] Here and in the next few paragraphs I develop ideas in "Acting from Virtue." My interest is mainly in moral virtues, but much of what is said applies to intellectual and other virtues.

of intellect but I will not here try to distinguish the two kinds, beyond noting that for some intellectual virtues, say for insightfulness, motivation and other elements connected with action, as opposed to cognitive elements as constitutive manifestations, need not play the same kind of role, if any essential role at all.) These dimensions correspond to situational, conceptual, cognitive, motivational, behavioral, and teleological aspects of the trait in relation to the actions proper to it – actions from virtue, as I shall call them. Let us consider these in turn.

The first dimension is the *field* (or domain) of a virtue, roughly the kind of human situation in which it characteristically operates, such as, for fidelity, standing by friends when they are under attack. The field for beneficence is even more open-ended and encompasses the wide range of actions affecting others, particularly as they bear on reducing others' pain, enhancing their pleasure, or providing something else that is broadly rewarding.

The second dimension is a matter of the characteristic *targets* the virtue leads the agent to aim at. For beneficence, the major target is the well-being of others. In the case of honesty, there is avoidance of deceit. For humility, there is appropriate restraint about describing one's accomplishments. And so forth. If there is a single overarching target, say the good of others, we might speak of the *telos* of the virtue, as do some writers on Aristotelian virtue ethics.[6]

The third dimension of analysis of virtue as an element of character is the agent's *understanding* of the field of the virtue, for instance of criteria for benefiting others. Virtue is enhanced by a wide and deep understanding of this field, but having a virtue is consistent with limited understanding of the field. Still, one can hardly find a target with no sense of where it is or what means will lead to it. There are, then, objective limits on what range of actions can express a virtue of character or even be of a virtuous kind.

Fourth, there is the agent's *motivation* to act in that field in a certain way, where that way is appropriate to the virtue, say a desire to contribute to the well-being of refugees, as opposed to wanting just one's own enrichment

---

[6] There are alternative views about how to determine targets, e.g. the functionalist position of Edmund L. Pincoffs in *Quandaries and Virtues* (Lawrence, Kan.: University Press of Kansas, 1986). For critical discussion of this view see Alasdair MacIntyre, "*Sophrosune*: How a Virtue Can Become Socially Disruptive," *Midwest Studies in Philosophy* 13 (1988), 1–11. MacIntyre argues that "Pincoffs' thesis about the virtues denies their teleological character. But on an Aristotelian account the only way in which a virtue such as *sophrosune* can be characterized adequately . . . is by relating it to the *telos*, both directly and through its relationship to *phronesis*" (7). The sixfold scheme I present is an effort to give a partial explication of this relation. For further discussion of virtue ethics in general and in particular of the teleological aspects of virtue, see William J. Prior, *Virtue and Knowledge* (London: Routledge, 1991).

(the former but not the latter desire is appropriate to beneficence). Having a moral virtue requires not just doing good deeds or being suitably disposed to do them, but having certain good intentions.

Fifth, there is the agent's disposition to act on the *basis* of the constituent understanding and motivation, for instance on the basis of a concern with justice to others rather than with one's own personal projects. The strength of this disposition is an indication of the strength of tendency for acts of the right type to be attached in the right way to the relevant aretaic, cognitive and motivational elements in the agent. This notion is important for distinguishing actions merely in conformity with virtue from those performed *from* it, in the sense implying that they *bespeak* an element of good character.

The sixth dimension of analysis we must take into account is the *beneficiaries* of the virtue, above all (and perhaps solely) the person(s) who properly benefit from our realizing it: for veracity, our interlocutors in general; for fidelity, family, friends, or larger groups such as one's community or country; for self-discipline, oneself; and so forth.[7] (For intellectual virtue, say being logical, there may be no beneficiaries in this sense; but I am taking such traits to be virtues of intellect, not of character.)

II Acting virtuously

These six dimensions of virtues of character are particularly appropriate to explicating virtuous action and the richer notion of acting from virtue. Let us first consider the field of a virtue, with moral virtue as our main concern. The field of, say, the virtue of justice – which is a trait possessed in some measure by any person of moral virtue – might be roughly retribution and, more important, the distribution of goods and evils; that of fidelity might be conduct required by explicit or implicit promises; and so forth. Such fields may overlap other aretaic fields, but each has some distinctive features.

There is no way to characterize moral virtue without a measure of vagueness. One reason for this is that the notion of morality itself is both vague and, even apart from that, subject to rational disagreement about

---

[7] Special problems are created by such groups as religious communities and military units, particularly in times of crisis or war. Here there may be explicit promises of obedience that make fidelity more far-reaching than it would otherwise be, and in extreme cases, such as war service, conduct that would ordinarily be required by one virtue, such as beneficence or compassion, may be prohibited by another, say fidelity to the war effort. The latter, however, should not be understood so as to license atrocities.

its scope. Here I propose to represent it largely in relation to the Rossian obligations – those of justice and non-injury, of veracity and fidelity, of beneficence and self-improvement, and of reparation and gratitude[8] – taken in reflective equilibrium with Kant's Categorical Imperative. But note that one of these obligations is self-improvement, and this may be plausibly argued to be a matter of prudence rather than morality (an obligation can, to be sure, be both one of beneficence and a requirement of prudence).[9] Nothing major in this paper turns on how this classificatory question is decided. Certainly anyone who has internalized the Rossian principles in a suitably balanced way has moral virtue, even if one could have it without internalizing all of them – though all correspond to virtues of some kind (e.g., self-improvement to pride, in the good sense of that term, in which it implies concern with maintaining some high standard).

To understand acting virtuously, consider how a beneficent person understands the field of, say, charity. The appropriate understanding naturally manifests itself in believing that wartime medical emergencies create a prima facie obligation to contribute to relief efforts, to support initiatives for a ceasefire, and to replace hatreds by understanding. But suppose someone did not use the concepts of duty or obligation (at least here) and thought simply that it is *good* to do these things. We need not require of virtuous agents that they approach the domains of virtue with any specific normative concepts, only that they operate with any of a range of acceptable concepts and commitments. Beneficence, like most other virtues of character, represents a kind of *practical success*, not a theoretical achievement; its cognitive requirements are quite latitudinarian and can be met by a self-conscious rule-theorist, by a spontaneously good person, or even by a moral skeptic who is suspicious of ethical concepts.

To be sure, a moral field cannot be understood without a sense of its (moral) normativity, but that sense is not restricted to either virtue concepts or hedonic ones (as a utilitarian might perhaps think) or deontological principles (as Kantians may tend to think). There *are* some general requirements for understanding any moral field, for example that a kind of impartiality be recognized as necessary[10] and that the well-being of people must be

---

[8] See W. D. Ross, *The Right and the Good* (Oxford University Press, 1930), esp. ch. 2.

[9] Bernard Gert argues that what Ross and others (including me) consider an obligation of self-improvement is simply one of prudence. See his essay, "Two Conceptions of Morality" (54–63), and my response to it, "Intuition, Reflection, and Justification" (210–13), in Mark Timmons, John Greco, and Alfred R. Mele, eds., *Rationality and the Good: Critical Essays on the Ethics and Epistemology of Robert Audi* (Oxford University Press, 2007).

[10] This is a subtle matter. As Bernard Gert points out in *Morality*, second edn. (Oxford University Press, 2005), in certain cases – those he calls matters of moral ideals (as opposed to strict duties) –

given some weight. Beneficence, for instance, requires a sense of when to act to relieve someone's anxiety. A strong pattern of well-intentioned failures in such attempts is not sufficient for the virtue of beneficence, even if it might suffice for a measure of *benevolence* as a psychological disposition. This requirement expresses part of what it is to understand the field of a virtue, and – more broadly – to have practical wisdom.

Particularly from the point of view of the theory of action, it is useful to conceive the relevant traits – at least traits of broadly *moral* character – as constituted by fairly stable and normally long-standing wants and beliefs, or at least beliefs, provided they carry sufficient motivation.[11] Surely beneficence, for instance, requires appropriate wants, such as desires to help others, and certain beliefs, say the belief that the suffering of others is a reason to try to render aid, at least indirectly. The more self-consciously virtuous an agent is, the greater the moral content of the appropriate wants and beliefs tends to be, or at least the greater the tendency for the agent to entertain the relevant content; but even being spontaneously virtuous is more than a matter of simply doing the relevant kinds of deeds. The deeds must be appropriately aimed, in terms of what the agent wants and believes, or they are not moral – in the sense of morally performed – but at best merely consistent with morality.

We have now implicitly described acting virtuously. It is acting on the basis of motivation and beliefs whose content has a sufficiently close relation to the elements essential in the trait constituting the virtue in question. But although acting *virtuously* is necessary for acting *from* virtue, it is not sufficient. The point is not that one can do what virtue requires for a reason that, like self-aggrandizement, is inappropriate to virtuous action. This is merely *acting in conformity with virtue.* To be sure, it is important to see that acting virtuously is not entailed by acting in conformity with virtue; but the point here is that, creditworthy though it is, acting virtuously does not entail acting from virtue. Consider a person who is often generous but could not be said to have the virtue of generosity. In Aristotelian terms, generosity is not a "firm and unchanging" element in the person's character. (See *NE* 1105a30–5.) Generous feelings and beneficent giving

---

such as which of several deserving charities to give to, one need not be impartial and can choose as one simply prefers. Notice, however, that one could not permissibly exaggerate the merits of one charity in order to justify preferring it over another.

[11] Two points are in order here. First, this formulation is intentionally vague, but should serve our purposes. Second, I do not think beliefs can carry all the motivation required; but for this paper, as opposed to a full-scale analysis of traits, what is essential to the point is only that traits require both a cognitive and a motivational dimension. It is at least more perspicuous to separate these as I do in the text.

might, in people with a certain character, be sufficient to indicate acting generously; but this pattern does not always yield such action, and if a generous action is not rooted in character, it would not imply *having* the trait, generosity. Granted, as with most kinds of virtuous actions, regularly acting generously is likely to lead to developing the trait in question; but the possession of the trait is not a condition for acting in ways that are characteristic of it.

In speaking of motivation as I have, I do not mean to imply that there are not also external constraints on acting virtuously. There are limits to how far from a sound normative view one can get and still qualify as acting virtuously.[12] But here I presuppose no specific normative view. The main idea is that acting virtuously implies acting for a reason appropriate to the virtue, whether or not one *has* the virtue. The question, then, is how we can act virtuously as often as possible and at least in important things. This brings us to the question of the kind of control we have over our reasons for action.

III   The nature and scope of motivational self-control

There are many kinds of control we might have regarding our reasons for action. One kind of control over such reasons is *generative*: an ability to produce (as opposed to simply recalling) such a reason at will or, if the power in question is indirect, to produce it by doing something else. Another main kind of control is an ability, given that we have a reason to do something, either to *harness* it to the action, i.e., bring it about that the action is performed at least in part *for* that reason, or to *unharness* it, i.e., bring it about that the action is not performed even in part for that reason. My main concern will be harnessing of motivational elements and its implications for moral virtue.

The importance of harnessing can be seen by reflecting on the point that myriad reasons for action are always with us, and our practical challenge is largely to see *how* to do, or to bring about our doing (in the right way), the deeds for which they (or a properly weighted subset of them) are reasons. To see this clearly we should distinguish two cases. There are (1) motivational reasons, paradigmatically desires, which, together with instrumental beliefs, generate actions and action tendencies, and (2) normative reasons for action: roughly reasons that support it, in the sense that they count toward

---

[12] It is very difficult to specify in general what these limits are. This is discussed in some detail in my "Acting from Virtue." That there are objective limits does not entail that there can be *no* kind of moral credit for an act that misses them where one has excellent reason for it.

its rationality, as do its reducing pain and its promoting pleasure. Since moral reasons are normative, it is easy to see why we always have them. Even if we should have no personal relationships that ground obligations, we have obligations of beneficence (given a world at all like this). In my view, moreover, one has obligations of self-improvement (or at least self-maintenance) quite apart from obligations to others.

Normative reasons are also generated by a certain kind of *need.* I refer to *normative need,* the kind that, like avoiding pain and remaining healthy, there is reason to fulfill. Normative needs are of course pervasive. Whether or not we take avoiding pain and remaining healthy to be *basic* normative needs, i.e., those that (prima facie) ought to be fulfilled independently of their role in bringing about anything else, it is nonetheless true that failing to do what is needed for continued life would cause pain and reduce enjoyments and satisfactions. *Norm-based* desires – desires based on a normative ground, paradigmatically a moral one, but including desires normatively need-based in the way just illustrated – are pervasive. They include many involving comfort and bodily needs. At any moment in a normal life, then, an agent has desires that provide both normative and motivational reasons for action.

Some major types of control of reasons for action

To see a main question confronting us here, consider six kinds of case, each of which can be fruitfully viewed in relation to the virtue of beneficence. In each, *S already* wants to help a colleague, Sanja, and the question is what *S* can do *at will* in relation to grounds for the beneficent deed in question – call it *A*-ing. I refer both (1) to normative grounds, whether propositional or not and whether potential – hence not a psychological basis of desire or belief – or actual, and (2) to psychological grounds, whether normative (as in the case of a justified belief that supports *A*, e.g. believing that it is obligatory) or not, as with an irrational desire that is a causal basis of *A*-ing but provides no normative support for *A*-ing. A normative ground may be practical, say a moral reason to do a particular deed, or epistemic, as in the case of perceptual evidence for a proposition. The analogy between the practical and the epistemic is illuminating and will be considered, but practical grounds (and especially moral ones) are our main concern here.[13]

---

[13] A detailed theory of psychological grounds and of normative grounds, practical and epistemic, is provided in my *Architecture of Reason: The Structure and Substance of Rationality* (Oxford University Press, 2001), esp. Part I.

First, suppose we have in consciousness a normative ground for *A*-ing, as where we want to help Sanja with a report and are aware that helping her is a good thing to do. May we at will act *on* it? We would then act *virtuously* if our beneficent desire were a sufficient motivational ground (adequate by itself, given a suitable instrumental belief, to yield a motivational explanation of the act). But suppose we also have a selfish reason for the act, say, to curry favor with Sanja as an influential person; we might then think we acted for the beneficent reason when we did not. Call the view that we can achieve motivational grounding at will the *direct harnessability thesis*. I am not aware of any sustained case for it; but that it is sometimes presupposed is suggested by certain uses of the phrase 'Do it because', as in 'Do it because it's your duty, not because you will be paid for it'.

Consider a case in which one spouse offers to do for the other something that is burdensome. A natural response might be 'I don't want you to do it because you have to; do it because you love me'. This is a request to act for a kind of reason. Can one fulfill it? If so, how? A person can also be urged *not* to do a thing for a given reason, as where I say that I am going to disallow a student's appeal owing to a late paper (and am told that I should not do it for this reason, since many with late papers were allowed the privilege this student asks for). Such locutions as 'Do it because' and 'Don't do it for that reason' create the impression that their users think it is sometimes *up to us* what to base an action on. If decision is considered an action, as it should be in certain instances, there is no question that we may sometimes think we can at will bring it about that we can decide on a given reason.

Second, suppose a reason for action is expressed by a belief and that the self-control question concerns whether we can act at will on this belief. Consider the testimony of someone we respect yet think unreliable on the subject of what we should do now. The person says that we should *A*, but we have independent, if limited, evidence supporting *A*-ing and we see that it is good. May we at will bring it about that we *A only* on the latter ground and not on the basis of the unreliable testimony? The view that we can might be called the *direct selective harnessability thesis*. This thesis is suggested by teachers' saying to their students such things as 'You're welcome to write on a topic not listed, but please don't do it just to show how inventive you are'. The students are supposed to consider their grounds and avoid basing their action on any grounds that do not pass muster.

Third, suppose we have a merely motivational reason to *A*, hence not a normative ground at all, but only a reason which, if we act on it, is a psychological basis of action, as envy may be.[14] We can sometimes be quite tempted by a bad reason. Someone in the grip of the gambler's fallacy, for example, might, after six successive appearances of heads on a coin toss, bet heavily on tails, thinking it now more likely. May we, at will, block our inclination to act on such a basis? Call this direct *veto power* over a would-be ground of action.

The fourth case emerges when we see that we could have veto power and thereby *prevent* a potential reason from becoming an actual one – one *for which* we act – even if, given that we are *A*-ing for some other reason, *r*, we do not have the power to cease, at will, to have *r* as an actual reason for our present action. Call this "detachment" power the *power to unharness at will.* The point here is that detachment power need not accompany veto power. There could be reasons such that one can prevent their becoming reasons for which one acts but, once they are not vetoed and are operative in determining action, they become like a glue too strong to overcome. The ability to prevent a glue from joining two pieces of wood does not imply the power to separate them once glued.

The fifth case to be considered concerns the possibility of enhancing or reducing the psychological support that a reason gives to an action based on that ground, whether wholly or in part. (The latter case occurs where the ground is only part of what sustains the belief, which is also partly sustained either by another ground or by a causal factor, such as wishful thinking or post-hypnotic suggestion, which is not a normative reason for acting, though it may produce action, if only by producing desire or belief.) Call this power *sustenance control of a ground.* Where it is positive, one can enhance the sustaining support of a ground; where it is negative, one can reduce that support. As with harnessability, sustenance control admits of a distinction between direct and indirect forms. One might think that sustenance control is implied by harnessability or unharnessability; but this is not self-evident. Our psychological make-up could be such that we might be able, say, to harness a ground to an activity we are engaging in, or to unharness it, without being able to affect what degree of psychological support it adds or subtracts.

Even if we cannot affect the degree of psychological support a reason gives to an action performed at least partly for that reason, there should be no doubt that the harnessing of an additional reason adds *some* degree of such support, hence one kind of strength. One would expect, for instance,

---

[14] See John Rawls, *A Theory of Justice* (Cambridge, Mass.: Harvard University Press, 1971), 143 for a plausible indication of why a rational person does not suffer from envy (momentary envious impulses are presumably an exception).

that an action actually based on an additional ground gains at least some resistance to being stopped by contrary motivation. There is, after all, one more "foundation" to be crushed. This is a kind of motivational strength. Another kind of strength is broadly memorial: a matter of resisting the tendency to forget, as some might resist forgetting desires to make amends for a wrong. Whether the addition of a reason to act might also enhance this kind of strength is not a philosophical question (I would think adding a motivational reason would be enhancing); but there is a normative contrast here: whereas the addition of a normative reason to one's basis for A-ing does not imply that one is less likely to fail to A, it does imply that, other things equal, one *ought* to be less likely to fail, even under the pressure of counter-reasons.

A sixth case, closely related to the fifth, concerns *intensity control.* Here the relevant variable is the degree of felt commitment to an action with which that action is performed. This variable differs from strength of motivation, understood as resistance to cessation of the action in question, say by intimidation or fatigue. An activity might be engaged in with only moderate energy or resolution yet be highly resistant to foreshortening or prevention; an activity engaged in with the great resolution of an enthusiastic new convert may be readily abandoned by exposure to a charismatic speaker who urges something different. With intensity as with strength, one might expect harnessing an additional ground to produce an increase. But it need not. The case might be like that of a siren that, having no volume control, cannot be made louder or softer, but only turned on or off. The possibility of unalterable intensity does not imply that the relevant motivation must be *maximally* strong (a notion that, to be sure, needs analysis). Some people might simply reach a point of motivational fixity at which, barring new considerations that call for additional thinking, they simply store new evidence alongside the foundation(s) of their belief. It may add potential resistance to ceasing to be motivated to A yet leave the level of motivational attraction, conceived as a kind of psychological determination, as it is.[15]

All six of the theses that have emerged – the two harnessability ones, the veto thesis, the unharnessability thesis, and the sustenance and intensity

---

[15] Some readers may wonder why what Bayesians call degree of belief is not mentioned here, where this is given by the probability the believer attributes (or would, under certain conditions, attribute) to p. I distinguish this variable from degree of strength, but much of what I say in this paper bears on our voluntary control of the former. Still, even persons who have the concept of probability *need* not attribute a probability to every proposition they believe (and tiny children can lack that concept altogether), whereas every belief does have one or another degree of strength. The universal applicability of the latter variable by contrast with the former in part explains why I do not discuss the former.

control theses – are important. We are told by philosophers and others not only that we ought to do the right things, for instance those morality requires, but also that we ought not to act *for* selfish reasons and ought to act *for* good reasons. This sounds like an imperative applying to actions, but, taken literally, it is not: expressions of the form of '*A*-ing for reason *r*' do not simply designate acting. They are double-barreled: they designate *both* what is done and an explanation of *why* it is done. These are quite different; '*A*-ing' is an answer to '*What* is *S* doing?' whereas 'For *r*' is an answer to '*Why* is *S* doing that?' It is true, however, that one's intellectual responsibilities extend to "doing" such things as acting for appropriate reasons. Partly for this reason, one might think that harnessing, vetoing, and unharnessing of grounds *are* actions; but I doubt this and will shortly explain how the relevant intellectual responsibilities can be understood without granting it.

There are, then, at least six positions to be considered regarding voluntary control of reasons for action: harnessability, both selective and non-selective, veto power over grounds, *un*harnessability, and sustenance and intensity control.[16] In each case we must distinguish direct from indirect control; and, as with control of belief, indirect control over motivational grounding seems more nearly within our reach than direct control. The two dimensions of control – one concerning action itself and the other reasons for action – are logically independent, though surely psychologically connected. The same holds for the positive and negative direct theses: it could be, for instance, that we can unharness directly but cannot harness directly.

Five dimensions of moral responsibility regarding practical reasons

Given the tentative conclusions so far reached concerning control of our reasons for action, much can be said about how moral responsibility – a major element in moral virtue – applies to our conduct and attitudes toward our own reasons for action. Let me suggest five general points.

First, in regulating our conduct we should in many instances seek reasons and counter-reasons for actions relevant to whatever matter is at hand. This is not something we need to do, or can do, for every action, even

---

[16] It is worth emphasizing that I find *at least* six needing exploration. Even using only the categories I have introduced, one could identify further theses. We might also use other terminology that might facilitate discussion, as does Nikolaj Nottelmann in "The Present and Future State of Epistemic Deontologism," in V. Hendricks and D. Pritchard, eds., *New Waves in Epistemology* (Basingstoke: Palgrave Macmillan, 2008), 75–105.

every important one. It is sometimes obvious what should be done and why. But some actions are particularly important. Some are also credibly challenged; and at least for important actions, credible challenges should be taken seriously, and a good response typically requires seeking reasons and counter-reasons.[17] Some categories of people, moreover – for instance philosophers – tend to have a greater obligation to seek reasons and counter-reasons. Rational persons tend to be responsive to reasons for action that they are aware of, for instance to be motivated to act accordingly (at least where they see the reasons as sufficiently strong); and, in explaining or justifying their conduct, they tend to appeal to reasons they think they have or had for the action(s) in question. The search for reasons and counter-reasons, then, can give wider scope to nature in regulating conduct and richer content to our discourse in explaining or justifying our actions.

Second, as rational persons, we should seek a kind of reflective equilibrium, both in our overall view of the world and in important aspects of that view. We should try to achieve a view of the world and, if we are virtuous, of our responsibilities, that has a high degree of unity and minimal internal tension. We should periodically review our outlook on important matters. Some are ethical, some political, some personal, and some, of course, intellectual.

Third, even apart from direct voluntary control over our reasons, *identifying* and *focusing* on reasons with the aim of clearly assessing them is salutary. Focusing on reasons may result in automatic adjustments that enable moral virtue to manifest itself. We may, for example, see by reflection that a reason is unclear or not supportive of *A*-ing to the extent we might have presupposed. It is useful in any case to identify our actual reasons for action. We can then explain ourselves better and are less likely to miss some basis of action or, worse, to rationalize by seeking reasons we might have had (or mistakenly think we did have) and then view them, or even offer them, as an actual basis of something we have done. We may then adduce considerations that we do not even accept (which would be at best self-deceptive) or on which our action is not based (which would be a case of offering a rationalization rather than an explanation). We should know what ground we are really standing on, lest we unwittingly stand on shaky foundations.

Fourth, with reasons for action as with actions themselves, interpersonal comparison is often desirable. Particularly on realist assumptions, this

---

[17] For a response to the skepticism supported by the frequency of rational disagreement, see Thomas Kelly, "The Epistemic Significance of Disagreement," *Oxford Studies in Epistemology* 1 (2005), 167–96.

is a good idea; we share the same world, but normative truth is often elusive. Someone else may have evidence we lack or may be less biased about evidence we share. And suppose we agree with someone else on the desirability of *A*-ing. Our agreement is likely to be more stable, and our communication better, if we agree on at least some of the grounds that support *A*-ing and, if possible, on how strong they are.

Fifth, we may have reason to rid ourselves of a degree of motivation disproportional to the normative strength of our grounds. Just as one may believe a proposition with unjustified confidence or with undue diffidence, we may perform an action with an exaggerated sense of the normative strength of our reason or with an insufficient appreciation of that strength. Since it may well be possible to determine such normative facts about ourselves, we may be justly criticized if we do nothing to rectify these disproportions. A parallel point holds for the case in which a reason is in some way underestimated and merits not reduced influence, but an enhanced role.

In many cases of the kinds we have been considering, morally virtuous persons may form beliefs about the status of their reasons or of the relation between these and their actions. Much moral virtue, however, does not require forming such higher-order beliefs. But the self-scrutiny that goes with identifying and appraising reasons for one's actions encourages and sometimes simply produces such higher-order beliefs. A good measure of unselfconscious natural moral virtue seems possible without higher-order beliefs, but they are natural for most self-critical persons. Being self-critical is one kind of virtue, and if it is by its nature an intellectual virtue, it nonetheless supports moral virtue in the ways just noted (among others). Some people may, to be sure, be blessed with an ability to assess reasons and actions and to respond appropriately without forming beliefs about their own reasons; but this ability is apparently not common, and in a world in which our reasons are sometimes challenged we usually cannot help forming beliefs about them and, under some description, beliefs about our grounds for accepting them.

It should be clear that in making these normative points I am not presupposing that we have direct control of our reasons for action, even negative direct control. But we surely have some indirect control over our reasons-responsiveness. Most people can enhance it, and for most people moral virtue requires regular efforts in that direction. How these efforts may be carried out is suggested by some of what has been said here, but much psychological knowledge is needed for a detailed account, and a full account requires empirical inquiry.

The deontological analogue of the conception of acting virtuously

Kant's ethics, as well as virtue ethics, is clarified by the points that have emerged. In the *Groundwork* he held that an action not done "from duty" has no moral worth and that when we have a motive of inclination supporting an action that is also a duty, we cannot in general tell whether we acted *from* (the motive of) duty.[18] He does not in this context raise the question of whether we can veto a motive at will or unharness it at will, but it seems reasonable to take him to be committed, if not to unharnessability, then to our being unable to know that unharnessing has occurred.

This paper generally supports Kant's apparent epistemological position on veto power and unharnessability, but I am not here concerned with the scope of self-knowledge in these matters. I must also leave to the reader the formulation of the implications for theoretical reason of what emerges here concerning practical reason.[19] I take it, however, that we should consider preservation of the parallel to theoretical reason to be a constraint in this sense: if the theoretical analogue of a view about our power over grounds of action is not plausible, this is some reason to doubt the counterpart of that view for the domain of practical reason.

One clear parallel to be stressed is this: just as a belief held over time can be held on one set of grounds at one time and on another set at a different time, an action that takes time, such as assisting someone in preparing a meal, can be performed for one set of reasons at one time and for another set at a different time. The role of a given set of grounds, moreover, can intensify or diminish as the action (or activity) proceeds. There is, however, at least one significant disanalogy here: whereas the notion of completion does not apply to beliefs, it does apply to actions and activities that require time for their (full) performance. Let us pursue the comparison between action for reasons and belief for reasons.

Although one can do something – for instance teach a person how to drive a new kind of vehicle – for an admirable reason initially and lapse from this into doing the deed for a selfish reason, one cannot count as *simply* doing the thing for an admirable reason where there is such an admixture, any more than one can count as simply believing a proposition for a good reason when another reason for which one believes it is not

---

[18] See, e.g., the *Groundwork* sections 397 and 406.

[19] For informative discussion of the similarities and differences between belief and action in relation to the will see J. Montmarquet, *Epistemic Virtue and Doxastic Responsibility* (Lanham, Md.: Rowman & Littlefield, 1993) and Bruce Russell, "Epistemic and Moral Duty," in Matthias Steup, ed., *Knowledge, Truth, and Duty: Essays on Epistemic Justification, Responsibility, and Virtue* (Oxford University Press, 2001), 34–62.

good. One could do the deed *mainly* for an admirable reason, but not unqualifiedly. This point implies a major complication in the appraisal of actions and agents themselves. Some reasons are more important than others in a given context; some deeds may be admirably done even if a reason of self-interest is one basis, as where, mainly from beneficence, one is effectively helping a person with a hard task, but is also to some extent motivated by the monetary reward. We may also excuse a change from admirable motivating reasons to selfish ones when the task becomes unpleasant in certain ways or another person involved in its performance ceases to merit support. Similar points hold for belief, since some reasons for belief are more important than others, and believing for a bad reason may sometimes be excusable, as where irresistible psychological manipulation produces unjustified inferences.

Action contrasts with belief, however, in this. Unlike beliefs, actions are not dispositional in nature (which is not to imply that the possession of a belief admits of a full analysis in subjunctive conditionals); actions are occurrences. In part because of the way we are engaged in their performance, we are commonly aware of performing them while we do so, and we can and sometimes do monitor our reasons for so acting and, in some cases, can cease acting or change the manner of our acting if we see or come to believe that we are acting on an inappropriate reason. To be sure, we are not always aware of our reasons for acting or always able (in practice) to see what they are. But what we do is, as it were, in the foreground of our lives at the time we do it; what we believe may never come before the mind or, quite often, do so for only a small proportion of the time we hold it.

Another disanalogy is that one can fully believe *p* when one has no reason for it at all, even if one did once, whereas, unless behavior is sustained by one or more appropriate reasons, it is not action at all, as opposed to moving in the way the action requires on a kind of momentum. If I wave in order to greet you and then become preoccupied with a problem and cease to have the relevant motivation, I may go on moving my arm, but this is merely hospitable movement. It is no longer my action of greeting a friend. Just as we must keep in causal contact with a path if we are to *follow* it rather than fortuitously continue on it, our behavior must remain in causal contact with our reasons if it is to count as action rather than fortuitously coincident movement. Since acting virtuously requires causal grounding in appropriate reasons, it cannot, like belief, occur in a full-blooded form when detached from them. Fortunately, this causal connection between actions and the reasons that ground them is often both sturdy and readily discerned by the agent. The agent may therefore be considered responsible for reattachment where necessary and redirection of behavior where no adequate ground remains.

Can virtue be up to us?

The harnessability and unharnessability theses are important in a perhaps unexpected way. Their status bears directly on the extent to which virtue is up to us. Indeed, if even the indirect harnessability thesis holds, it can be up to us whether something we are doing or will do is (or will be) a case of acting virtuously. This can hold even if what we do to promote acting virtuously is entirely *internal* and does not entail acquiring new basic desires. Let me first note some uncontroversial cases for comparison and contrast.

To some extent, control of reasons for action is a matter of control of grounds for *beliefs* about the action and indeed of control of how vividly these or other grounds supporting the action are held in consciousness. This is because what we believe, especially in normative matters, tends (if we are rational) to affect our actions, and is (other things equal) more likely to do so if vividly in consciousness. A (believed) moral principle requiring promise-keeping, for instance, seems more likely to yield an operative desire to do the promised deed if the principle is brought to mind. Certainly it is up to us whether we know the kinds of things we can find out by observation that is within our power. The observation may be external or internal; we can acquire knowledge or new information simply by, for instance, looking around us or searching our memory and forming new beliefs about, or making inferences from facts about, things and events we remember. As this indicates, inference is another potential source of new knowledge or new motivation and, thereby, new reasons for action. There is no fixed limit to how much can be known on the basis of inferential extension from what is already known. An analogous point holds for practical as well as for theoretical reasoning. If, for example, I intend to *A* and I realize that a precondition is *B*-ing, I often thereby come to want to *B* and (if this want is rational) come to have a reason to do things required for achieving *B*. To be sure, we can end up subtracting as well as adding beliefs, desires, or intentions. Modus tollens and its practical analogue (in which an intention or other practical attitude is relinquished) are as easily performed as modus ponens.

Suppose, however, that we could harness or unharness reasons at will. Given the pervasiveness of normative reasons to act, we could often, by a purely internal volitional effort, bring it about that we act virtuously where we would otherwise have simply done the same thing – the thing supported by a normative reason – for a reason of self-interest. What we would be doing, in many such cases, is altering the *role* of an existing reason. Suppose, for instance, that I am inclined to A for a bad reason but have a good reason to A. If I can bring it about at will that either (1) I believe I should A for the good reason or (2) I want (strongly enough) to A for a good reason, I can thereby act virtuously at will, i.e., at will *A-for-r*, where r is a good reason to A and of a kind appropriate to some virtue. This would mean we could sometimes act virtuously, and perhaps contribute to becoming virtuous or to strengthening our virtuous character if we already have it, just by a kind of mental exertion: what some would call a volition.[20]

It is doubtful that we have the kind of direct voluntary power just illustrated. Imagine that I am helping someone in a task for a selfish reason, though I also have an unselfish, moral reason. If thinking about my moral reason in the right way brings it about that I am now acting (just) *for* that reason, my conduct will now have moral worth, in the sense that I am morally creditworthy for performing it, and I will be acting virtuously. Beliefs may have, and may acquire, intellectual worth in a similar sense: they can come to be held on a justificatory basis. Then, just as a believer deserves intellectual credit for holding the belief on a justificatory basis (as opposed to, say, wishful thinking), an agent deserves moral credit for performing an action for an appropriate kind of good reason, such as an adequate moral reason. The credit might of course be minor, especially in the intellectual case. But the point is simply that moral character is properly evaluated both on the basis of how well-grounded a person's actions are in practical reasons and on the basis of what the person does to see to it that they are thus well-grounded.

Achieving the kind of good grounding in question may not be possible at will; but it apparently is at least possible given the right kind of effort, and the attempt to bring it about is worth while. It is particularly significant that some of the relevant efforts can be made entirely *in foro interno*. The proportion of our acts that are virtuous certainly depends partly on our efforts of will, and the proportion can be increased by the kind of reflection that enhances the power of the kinds of reasons for which we should act and thus increases the likelihood that we will both do what they call for and do it on the basis of those reasons.

---

[20] For a detailed account of volition see Hugh J. McCann, *The Works of Agency: On Human Action, Will, and Freedom* (Ithaca, NY: Cornell University Press, 1998).

Much of what this paper says about questions of the harnessability of reasons for action also holds for certain causal factors that do not count as reasons. I have in mind particularly psychological elements, such as certain emotions, that can lead to desire formation or intention formation, or affect a desire or intention already formed, without having any normative bearing on the action in question or counting as reasons *for* acting, as opposed to reasons *why* one does act. Consider a case in which a driver kills a child. A juror is supposed to be impartial in deciding whether there is, say, negligence in the case. But suppose the juror has seen films of the child lying crushed and bloody on the pavement and happens to know the bereaved family. This information might cause anger. That emotion could incline or even cause the juror to want to punish the defendant. Suppose this is an emotional desire not based at all on evidence of guilt. What can a juror do to keep the desire from biasing the vote on the verdict? Is there any kind of veto power for such non-evidential pressures on action? Here we face questions similar to those already considered. Many are empirical, but a number of philosophical points the case suggests are not. Here are two. First, if, *just* out of anger, one wants to punish the driver, one does not have the kind of reason that would ground virtuously declaring guilt. Second, even if, on adequate grounds, we do know the driver is guilty, our intention to vote for a verdict of guilt should (normatively speaking) be uninfluenced by the angry desire.

We may hope that there are ways to cultivate and sustain moral virtue so that one's actions are not influenced by such normatively irrelevant elements. The point is closely connected, of course, with intellectual virtue: if the belief that the driver is guilty is contrary to intellectual virtue, then (other things equal), acting on it by declaring the driver guilty is contrary to moral virtue. Here as elsewhere in this paper we can see how philosophical analysis points toward a range of empirical questions whose answers may be eminently useful both in the quest for knowledge and in the effort to fulfill the standards of morality.

Achieving actions of the kinds characteristic of moral virtue is of course not sufficient for achieving that virtue itself; but developing the kinds of critical habits that may result from regularly scrutinizing our reasons for action and from internalizing the appropriate normative standards may, over time, yield that achievement. In any case, *trying* to achieve good grounding of our actions may itself be quite creditable. This is not to suggest that even persistent efforts to achieve moral virtue are either sufficient or necessary for that accomplishment: they are not necessary because one might, for example, be a natural who, with good fortune and good role models, has simply grown up to have the right kind of reasons-responsive behavioral constitution; they are not sufficient because, whatever our high marks for conscientiously trying, there are objective standards to be met, and they may sometimes evade even serious attempts to meet them.[21]

IV The possibility of autonomy and the sustenance of virtue

Autonomy, I take it, is roughly self-government. Autonomy contrasts both with the tyranny of dictators one must obey and with the arbitrariness of whim. It is self-government under a set of guiding aims or principles with a certain minimal unity.[22] Have we perhaps undermined the presumption of autonomy for normal persons by arguing that their direct control of our reasons is severely limited? Are we victims of the desires we happen to have, even if no one else imposes them?

Here we must remember two things. First, our governing motives are often both need-based and norm-based. Given the benignity of nature, many of our natural desires provide good reasons to act, in that their objects are worth realizing. Second, we can have a high degree of *indirect* control of our motivational grounds. We can learn to resist motivational tendencies on which we should not act; this indicates a kind of negative control – a veto, if you like: if we cannot at will eliminate a motive, we often can at will resist acting on it. We can also do things to make it likely that when we have more than one reason to act, where at least one is good and at least one is bad, if we do act, it is at least sufficiently for a good reason, in roughly the sense that the reason exercises enough influence to bring about the action even without the support of any other motivator. This kind of control is positive; its result (where we have it) is to empower certain reasons, not to disempower others – even if their relative force is diminished.

In the light of these and earlier points, we can see how the achievement of virtue turns out to be a result of a cooperation between nature and nurture. By nature we acquire the capacity for both action and the kind of learning needed to direct it. Through nurture we acquire concepts, learn truths in which they figure, and develop both motivational structure and behavioral capacities. We need not be passive in these developmental

---

[21] On the kind of intellectual make-up that constitutes intellectual virtue see Ernest Sosa, *Knowledge in Perspective* (Cambridge University Press, 1991) and his response to critics in John Greco, *Ernest Sosa and His Critics* (Oxford: Blackwell, 2004). My own paper in that volume ("Intellectual Power and Epistemic Virtue," 3–16) is in part a response to the (generally non-voluntaristic) virtue epistemology developed by both Sosa and Greco.

[22] This broad conception of autonomy is elaborated and defended in my "Autonomy, Reason, and Desire," *Pacific Philosophical Quarterly* 72 (1992), 247–71.

processes. Self-cultivation is possible. Indeed, on the wide view of morality that Kant, Ross, and many others have taken, there is an obligation of self-improvement which encompasses seeking to achieve and maintain virtues of character.

* * *

Given the structural and functional parallels between practical and theoretical reason, it should be expected that voluntary control of reasons for action is similar to that of reasons for belief. We apparently do not have (and probably cannot have) direct positive control over either kind of reason. We apparently have only quite limited direct negative control over them. We do, however, have many kinds of indirect control in all these cases. So far as I can see regarding the relevant empirical questions, the direct harnessability views, then, should be rejected; the direct vetoability thesis is doubtful; the direct unharnessability view is still less plausible; and there is little reason to hold the direct sustenance control or the direct intensity control theses concerning grounds of action. But surely none of these types of control is beyond the possible reach of *indirect* motivational power. In part for this reason, moral virtue requires monitoring both one's actions and one's consciousness and, in a certain range of cases, exercising the best control one has over the reasons for which one acts. This applies both to desires and to beliefs – especially those desires and beliefs partly constitutive of virtues of character.

The morally virtuous agent not only seeks to find good reasons for action – roughly, desirable states of affairs one should try to realize – and, on the intellectual side, sound moral principles, but also seeks to do what is required to enable those reasons to play the kinds of roles they should play in yielding action. At least in rational agents, nature assists in the effort to find good reasons and harness them to action; but it can be hindered by self-deception, wishful thinking, inattentiveness, and other sources of error. How morally virtuous we are is in part up to us and in part a matter of the contingencies of our heredity and environment; how virtuous our actions are – once we have a modicum of moral virtue – can be very largely up to us.[23]

---

[23] Earlier versions of this paper have benefited from audience discussions at Biola University, the Institute for Cognitive Sciences and Technologies (in Rome), and the University of Cologne. For helpful comments I would particularly like to thank Roger Crisp, Mario De Caro, Alexander Jech, Hugh McCann, Michael Quante, and Andreas Speer.

CHAPTER 8

Virtue ethics in theory and practice

Virtue ethics provides unique resources for moral thinking, and some writers and teachers in ethics consider it superior to rule theories. The most notable rule theories with which it is commonly contrasted are Kantianism, utilitarianism, and intuitionism. This paper will not systematically compare any virtue-ethical position with any rule theory in ethics, but it will bring out some resources of virtue ethics – or at least certain uses of virtue-theoretic (aretaic) concepts – in both ethical theory and moral practice. Its concern extends both to enriching rule theories and to enhancing their uses in professional ethics. This extension represents an important territory, and skillfully navigating it requires both guidance by general moral standards and a capacity to make particular moral judgments.

I Virtues as traits of character

We might begin with a quite general characterization of virtues. They are traits of character that constitute praiseworthy elements in a person's psychology; specifically, praiseworthy character traits appropriate to pursuing the particular good or kind of good with respect to which the trait counts as such.[1] Take justice and generosity as examples. The former virtue might be viewed as deontic, in that the good in question concerns what is obligatory or permissible in a moral sense, as in the case of a fair distribution of benefits to co-workers. The latter might be viewed as axiological, since the good a generous person properly aims at is characteristically

---

[1] This characterization is quite generic and seems compatible with a number of conceptions of virtues of character. See, e.g., the detailed account given by Alasdair MacIntyre in *After Virtue*, second edn. (University of Notre Dame Press, 1984), ch. 14 and pp. 218–20; and Christine Swanton, *Virtue Ethics: A Pluralistic View* (Oxford University Press, 2003). She offers, as a widely shared conception of a virtue, "a good quality of character, more specifically a disposition to respond to, or acknowledge, items within its field or fields in an excellent or good enough way" (p. 19).

enhancement of well-being, understood non-morally, as are pain and pleasure. Virtues vary along many quite different kinds of dimensions. They may be more or less deeply rooted; more or less dominating in behavior; more or less integrated with other traits the person has, including non-virtues; and variable in many other ways. Moreover, in any virtue, both cognitive and motivational elements are central.[2] A virtuous person, say one with veracity, must have certain beliefs. Some theorists would say that at least a high proportion of these must constitute knowledge, such as knowledge of when it is appropriate to avoid an unjustified question rather than choose between answering it truthfully and lying. But such cognitive knowledge – knowing *that* – is not the only significant kind here: behavioral knowledge – knowing *how* – is also important. Virtuous persons must also have desires (or other motivational elements, e.g. intentions) appropriate to the virtue, such as, in the case of fidelity, a desire to stand by friends.[3]

The analysis of the notion of a virtue of character should include at least six conceptually important dimensions. These correspond to situational, conceptual, cognitive, motivational, behavioral, and teleological aspects of virtues in relation to the actions proper to them – *actions from virtue*, as I shall call them. Let us consider these dimensions in turn.[4]

Field. The first dimension is the field (or domain) of a virtue, roughly the kind of human situation, such as distributing year-end bonuses to

---

[2] The explanatory power of virtue ascriptions, such as it is, is largely dependent on that of sets of desires and beliefs that are elements in, or appropriately related to, the trait(s) in question. This paper presupposes no particular degree of descriptive or explanatory power on the part of traits constituting virtues, but I do not believe that these traits should be taken to have none at all. A skeptical treatment of the explanatory power of traits has been provided by John Doris, *Lack of Character: Personality and Moral Behavior* (Cambridge University Press, 2002). For critical discussion see the symposium on this book in *Philosophy and Phenomenological Research* 71, 3 (2005), 632–77.

[3] For discussions of many aspects of virtue ethics see Roger Crisp, ed., *How Should One Live: Essays on the Virtues* (Oxford: Clarendon Press, 1996) and *Midwest Studies in Philosophy* 13 (1988), an issue devoted to the topic of character and virtue. Its studies by Robert C. Solomon, on love, and Gabriele Taylor, on envy and jealousy, are helpful investigations of specific virtues; the papers by Marcia Baron ("Remorse and Agent-Regret"), Amelie Rorty ("Virtues and Their Vicissitudes"), Nancy Sherman ("Common-sense and Uncommon Virtue"), and James D. Wallace ("Ethics and the Craft Analogy") are among the helpful studies of more general aspects of virtue ethics. For a detailed treatment of virtue ethics that contrasts it with common sense and Kantian ethics and stresses its elements of continuity with utilitarianism, see Michael Slote, *From Morality to Virtue* (Oxford University Press, 1992).

[4] Here and in the next few paragraphs I develop ideas in my "Acting from Virtue," *Mind* 104 (1995), 449–71. Swanton makes heavy use of the metaphor of the target of a virtue and elaborates on other elements among the six I characterize; see, e.g., *Virtue Ethics*, pp. 231–9. This paper concerns mainly moral virtues, but what is said about virtue in general applies to a large extent to intellectual and other virtues.

employees, in which it characteristically operates. The field of, for example, beneficence is open-ended, as is that of loyalty. Both fields encompass opportunities for actions affecting others, particularly as these bear on reducing pain or enhancing pleasure. This field is *external.* By contrast, the field of self-discipline is *internal.* Many virtues, such as prudence, have both internal and external fields.

Target. The second dimension is specified by the characteristic aims the virtue leads the agent to have (though the targets need not be aimed at under any specific description). For beneficence, the major target is others' well-being. In this "aim" faithfulness as a character trait – global faithfulness – is similar. Religious faithfulness is commonly focused centrally on God, but the well-being of other people may also figure in its target (a virtue may have multiple targets). For humility, there is restraint about describing one's accomplishments and openness to criticism. And so forth. A virtue having a single overarching target, say the good of others, may be said to have what writers on Aristotelian ethics call a *telos* (arguably, every virtue has a *telos*).[5] Such a target may, however, be internally pluralistic. Thus, if the target of beneficence is the well-being of others, this by no means implies that beneficent persons as such have a monolithic aim. Again, loyalty as a trait is similar.

Beneficiaries. The third dimension of aretaic analysis is the beneficiaries of the virtue, above all (and perhaps solely) the person(s) who properly benefit from our realizing it: for veracity, interlocutors; for loyalty, family, friends, or larger groups; and so forth. (For intellectual virtue, say logicality, there may be no external beneficiaries; but I take such traits to be virtues of intellect, not of character and am not addressing them here.)

Agential understanding. The fourth dimension of analysis is intellectual: the agent's understanding of the field of the virtue, for instance of criteria for benefiting others. Possessing the virtue is consistent with limited understanding of this field not requiring conceptual sophistication. This is why generosity and even fidelity can occur in quite young children. But one cannot hit a target without a good sense of where it is or how to hit it. There are, then, objective (though inexact) limits on what range of actions can express a virtue of character or even be of a virtuous kind.

---

[5] There are alternative views about how to determine targets, e.g. the functionalist position of Edmund L. Pincoffs in *Quandaries and Virtues* (Lawrence, Kan.: University Press of Kansas, 1986). For critical discussion of this view see Alasdair MacIntyre, "*Sophrosune*: How a Virtue Can Become Socially Disruptive," *Midwest Studies in Philosophy* 13 (1988), 1–11.

Motivation. Fifth, there is the agent's motivation to act appropriately in a way befitting the virtue. An appropriate motive for beneficence might be a desire to contribute to the well-being of refugees, as gaining approbation. Realizing virtue requires not just good deeds, but good motives, particularly intentions, which are in part a kind of dominant motive. Even if a person has a settled tendency, rooted in enduring motivation and cognition, to do the kinds of things appropriate to the virtue, if the person's only reasons for so acting are instrumental, then even if some trait of character underlies the actions, it is not a virtue. Faithfulness illustrates this: just as honest persons cannot be truthful simply to promote their own interests, so, where loyalty is a virtue, it must embody a sufficiently strong and deep set of desires to be loyal to (or to protect or support or advance, and so forth) the person or object toward which it is directed.

Grounding. Sixth, there is the psychological grounding of the relevant action tendencies. This is largely a matter of the nature and depth of the agent's disposition to act on the *basis* of the constituent understanding and motivation, for instance a concern with justice to others rather than with one's own personal projects. Such grounding is important for distinguishing actions merely in conformity with virtue from those performed *from* it, the truly virtuous ones that *bespeak* an element of good character. As Kant saw, motivation to keep a promise (for instance) does not entail that keeping the promise will be *based* on that desire rather than some self-regarding motive the act also serves. We can imagine someone who has the right kind of motivation for beneficence and does the right deeds; but the deeds may still be based on self-interest. Virtue requires not just the right combination between motive and deed, but an integration between them.

I have already noted that the field of a virtue may be internal or external or some combination of the two. In this case the internal–external contrast parallels the difference between a broadly self-regarding virtue and a broadly other-regarding one. But we may also draw a contrast between the internal and the external in regard to dimensions of a virtue, as opposed to drawing it within a dimension. Thus, the first three dimensions are plausibly conceived as external. To be sure, with, for instance, temperance the field can be internal and both the beneficiary and the target can be oneself; but none of these is an element *of* the virtue. By contrast, the fourth, fifth, and sixth dimensions of aretaic analysis are naturally considered internal, and they represent elements partly constitutive of possessing the trait. They concern not only conditions for understanding virtues of character but for having them at all, whereas the first dimension concerns circumstances appropriate to its exercise, the second the kind of aim appropriate to its behavioral manifestations, and the third the objects of its successful exercise.

These six aspects of virtue are useful in explicating action from virtue. Let us first consider the field of a virtue of character and the agent's understanding of it.

Take justice and fidelity as paradigmatic virtues. The field of justice might be roughly retribution and the distribution of goods and evils, that of fidelity behavior required by explicit or implicit promises. Such fields may overlap other aretaic fields, but each has distinctive features. Consider how a just person understands the field of justice. It would be natural for the appropriate understanding to manifest itself in believing that distributions, say of salary or bonuses, create a duty to identify relevant merits and to proportion one's outlays to them, and that sharp deviations from this pattern in the behavior of others provide a reason to try to institute it. But suppose someone did not use the concepts of duty or obligation (at least here) and thought simply that it is *good* to vote (and to criticize people who do not). A virtuous person could be skeptical about moral concepts or might think them indistinguishable from aretaic concepts. Moral goodness is compatible with various kinds of metaethical skepticism. People may have virtuous character even if they do not approach the relevant tasks with any normative convictions and perhaps even if they are not guided by any normative concepts. It is sufficient if, say as citizens or colleagues, they operate with concepts and commitments lying within a certain range. Metaethical skepticism might make it very difficult to defend standards of justice, beneficence, and veracity, but it need not prevent its proponents from having those virtues.

A moral field cannot be understood without a sense of its (moral) normativity, but that sense is not restricted to either virtue concepts (as Aristotle may seem to imply) or hedonic ones (as some utilitarians may tend to think) or deontological principles (as Kantians may tend to think). There do seem, however, to be *some* general requirements for understanding any moral field. Take justice. Here a kind of impartiality must be recognized as necessary,[6] and the well-being of people must be given some weight.

---

[6] This is a subtle matter. As Bernard Gert points out in *Morality*, second edn. (Oxford University Press, 2005), in certain cases, those he calls matters of moral ideals (as opposed to strict duties), such as which of several deserving charities to give to, one need not be impartial and can choose as one simply prefers. Notice, however, that one could not permissibly exaggerate the merits of one in order to justify preferring it over another.

More broadly, the relevant norms must be, if not "designed" to overrule self-interest, then capable of conflicting with it.

It may be, then, that action from virtue requires an exercise of some normative concept, if only of some appropriateness-concept, say being in some way good or in some way bad. Certainly the possession of a virtue entails a *recognitional capacity* regarding the appropriate occasions for the exercise of the virtue. A conscientious colleague, for instance, must have a sense of when to act to promote a common project that will relieve stress and when to oppose one that will lead to institutional collapse. This is part of what it is to understand the field of a virtue, and without that understanding one would not act from virtue.

It is useful to conceive the relevant traits – at least traits of broadly *moral* character – as constituted by fairly stable and normally long-standing wants and beliefs, or at least beliefs, provided they carry sufficient motivation.[7] Consider fairness. Surely it requires both appropriate wants, such as desires to treat people equally, and also certain beliefs, say a belief to the effect that one must provide the same opportunities and rewards for people in the same circumstances. These wants and beliefs do not rule out spontaneity. But even being spontaneously fair is more than a matter of simply doing the relevant kinds of deeds. The deeds must be appropriately aimed, in terms of what the agent wants and believes, or they are not morally performed but at most merely consistent with what morality requires. If I give my students the same grade only because I like them equally well, then even if they all deserve that grade, I am not exhibiting fairness in my grading; the fairness of my resulting grades is quite coincidental.[8]

Two further points should be taken into account before we proceed. First, virtues as traits of persons must be distinguished from even their wide-ranging desirable powers. Every virtue implies certain powers, but not every desirable wide-ranging power is a virtue. A person might have extraordinarily great powers of arithmetical calculation or extreme athletic

[7] Two points are in order here. First, this formulation is intentionally vague, but should serve our purposes. Second, I do not think beliefs can carry all the motivation required; but for this paper, as opposed to a full-scale analysis of traits, what is essential to the point is only that traits require both a cognitive and a motivational dimension. It is at least more perspicuous to separate these as I do in the text.

[8] The importance of cognitive and motivational elements in virtues of character may in part underlie Thomas Hurka's attitudinal definition (which he considers "to some extent" stipulative). He says, "The moral virtues are those attitudes to goods and evils that are intrinsically good, and the vices are those attitudes to goods and evils that are intrinsically evil." See *Virtue, Vice, and Value* (Oxford University Press, 2001), p. 20. As I characterize moral virtue, it would at least tend to embody such an attitude; but I differ from Hurka in not treating vice as a precise counterpart of virtue.

prowess. These good traits are not properly considered virtues of character.[9] Second, there are virtues that are non-moral and better conceived as virtues of *personality* than of *character* (a distinction that is significant but far from sharp). Consider wittiness and good taste. These can be *personality traits*, and they can be considered traits of character in a broad sense of that term, though not as traits of *moral* character. They do not by their nature contribute to or even affect good character and are not required for having it.

If virtues of character (at least of moral character) are conceived as cognitively and motivationally constituted in the way I have illustrated, then we each normally have a measure of indirect control over certain of our own traits, by virtue of the kind of indirect control we have over our wants and beliefs. This point is central both for moral education and for institutional practices that are intended to support ethical conduct. To be sure, normal agents are not directly responsible for producing either their beliefs or their wants. We can produce them *by* doing certain things, but normally we cannot produce them except through indirect and often arduous means. This does not imply, however, that we are not indirectly responsible for having produced certain of our traits. A selfish person who, as a foreseeable and avoidable result of the selfishness, is unfair but wants to reform, can, through repeated self-discipline, become unselfish and fair. In this way, one could both recognize indirect responsibility for a bad trait and successfully take responsibility for replacing it with good ones. With sufficient commitment to moral standards, it is sometimes possible to become to a significant extent morally self-made.

Here I find a remarkably Aristotelian passage in Shakespeare's *Hamlet* quite apt. Hamlet says to his mother, regarding her marriage to his murderous uncle:

> Assume a virtue if you have it not.
> That monster, custom, who all sense doth eat,
> Of habits, devil, is angel yet in this,
> That to the use of actions fair and good
> He likewise gives a frock or livery
> That aptly is put on. Refrain tonight
> And that shall lend a kind of easiness
> To the next abstinence, the next more easy.
> For use almost can change the stamp of nature.
>   (Act III, Scene iv, 160–7)

---

[9] This distinction is developed in some detail in my "Intellectual Virtue and Epistemic Power," in John Greco, ed., *Ernest Sosa and His Critics* (Oxford: Blackwell, 2004), pp. 3–16.

Not only does this suggest that a (certain kind of) virtue can be acquired; it also indicates how habituation can be a route to developing virtue. If Aristotle stressed the development of virtue in education from childhood rather than later in life, nothing in his virtue ethics precludes countenancing Hamlet's suggested route to its apparent acquisition. Shakespeare leaves us wondering whether a habitual pattern of conduct so acquired can be a genuine virtue. Perhaps, however, if habit cannot change the "stamp of nature," it can change the nature of the agent's character. This leaves room for deep-seated moral improvement whatever we call the result.

II   Virtue ethics as moral theory

Given the understanding of virtue expressed in Section I, it should be clear that the notion is morally significant and that the range of virtues is wide enough to provide raw material, and at least a partial basis, for comprehensive ethical theory. Aristotle set out such a theory and is a good point of departure. He apparently took moral traits of character to be ethically more basic than moral acts. He said, for instance, regarding the types of acts that are right, "Actions are called just or temperate when they are the sort that a just or temperate person would do" (*NE* 1105b5ff.). It is virtues, such as justice and temperance, rather than acts, that are ethically central for Aristotle. He says, for instance, "Virtue makes us aim at the right target, and practical wisdom makes us use the right means" (1144a).[10]

For a thoroughgoing virtue ethics, agents and their traits, as opposed to rules of action, are morally basic. The idea is that we are to understand what it is to behave justly through studying the nature and tendencies of the just person, not the other way around. We do not, for instance, construct a notion of just deeds as those that, say, treat people equally, and,

---

[10] The idea that traits rather than acts are ethically central for Aristotle should not be accepted unqualifiedly. In addition to taking certain acts and emotions to be by their nature base (1107a), he stressed the development of virtue by habituation. To be sure, on the one hand, we might think that it is only because of being counter-virtuous in a trait-theoretic sense that the relevant acts are base, and one might claim that it is only a contingent fact that the kinds of acts we stress to children in aiding their moral development – say, truth-telling, promise-keeping, and rendering aid – are appropriate to the relevant virtues. But a case can also be made that Aristotle took traits to have a two-way conceptual connection with act-types: perhaps he might have viewed the virtues as essentially leading to certain act-types under favorable conditions, while taking at least some of those types to be crucial for understanding the virtue concepts in question. See, e.g., 1129a, in which he says that "everyone means by justice the same kind of state, namely, that which disposes people to do just actions, act justly, and wish for what is just" (p. 81 in Roger Crisp's translation, Cambridge University Press, 2000). Note too that virtues can be ethically central for the notion of moral worth even if they are not central – or not the only element ethically central – for the notion of moral obligation.

on this basis, define a just person as one who characteristically does deeds of this sort. Thus, for adults as well as for children, role models are crucial for moral learning. The person of practical wisdom is the chief role model in ethics, exemplifying all of the moral virtues and tending to give good advice on ethical decisions.

Aristotle understood the virtues in the context of his theory of the good for human beings. He says, "the best good must be something complete," and he takes only happiness (*flourishing* in some translations) to meet this condition:

> Now happiness more than anything else seems complete [since "choicewor-thy in its own right"] without qualification. For we always choose it because of itself, never because of something else. Honor, pleasure, understanding and every virtue we certainly choose because of themselves, since we would choose each of them even if it had no further result, but we also choose them for the sake of happiness. (1097b2–5)

Happiness, then, stands as our final unifying end: although we do seek other things for their own sake, it is only when "through them" we can achieve happiness. Happiness is not, however, a passive state; it requires a life in which "actions and activities . . . that involve reason" (which is our distinctive characteristic) are central; the "human good," then, proves to be "activity of the soul [roughly, mind] in accord with virtue" (1098a14–17).

If, however, we take traits as ethically more basic than acts, we face a problem: how does a virtue theory enable us to determine what to *do*? Ethics largely concerns *conduct*. How do we figure out what counts as, for instance, acting generously or honorably? Virtue ethics has resources for answering this, including the appeal to practical wisdom as applied to the context of decision. A person of practical wisdom is a paradigm of one having virtue, and in a famous passage Aristotle calls virtue "a state that decides, consisting of a mean, the mean relative to us, which is defined by reason . . . It is a mean between two vices, one of excess and one of deficiency" (1107a1–4). Consider beneficence. If, relative to my resources, I am selfish and ignore others' needs, this is a deficiency; if, today, I contribute so much to charity that I am prevented from doing much greater good through contributing later, I am excessive. Good ethical decisions, on this view, may be seen in the light of such comparisons.

Instrumental rationality – taken to be a matter of a certain kind of efficiency in desire satisfaction – is another partial basis for determining what counts as virtuous without presupposing prior normative notions. The point is not that maximizing desire-satisfaction is by itself a *basic* standard of rationality. It is that *given* what might be considered normal basic desires in human beings, for instance to avoid pain and achieve pleasurable experiences, instrumental success counts positively toward at least the virtue of prudence and, more important, failure to avoid what is aversive counts toward folly. To be sure, success and failure here are themselves partly relative to the rationality of the agent's beliefs. A fully excusable failure, for instance, need not count toward folly. If one holds a virtue epistemology, a similar problem arises with beliefs in relation to intellectual virtues, but similar resources are also available to theorists who take the trait notions to be normatively basic.[11]

In the light of the broad conception of virtue ethics outlined here, we can distinguish strong and weak versions. Two theoretical dimensions of comparison are particularly important. The first concerns whether aretaic concepts are considered more basic than axiological, deontic, or other kinds. The second concerns whether the theory in question is an account of moral obligation or of moral worth or both. Read in one way (probably the most common way), Aristotle's virtue ethics is strong on both counts.

Consider first whether aretaic concepts are considered basic. Here a comparison with hedonistic utilitarianism, such as Mill's, is instructive. For this view (whether or not Mill would have acknowledged the implication), a trait is a virtue provided its possession tends (through its normal expression in behavior) to increase the balance of pleasure to pain in the relevant population.[12] For Aristotle, by contrast, happiness, which is the good for human beings, is itself understood in terms of the exercise of virtue; there is no axiologically more basic non-aretaic conception of the good. Similarly (and again in a rough formulation), on a classical utilitarian view, the rightness of an act is determined by what *it causes*, whereas on a virtue-ethical view the rightness of an act is chiefly a matter of what causes *it*.

---

[11] For discussion of whether a truly naturalized theory of practical reason can succeed with desires as the basis of reasons for action, see my "Prospects for a Naturalization of Practical Reason: Humean Instrumentalism and the Normative Authority of Desire," *International Journal of Philosophical Studies* 10, 3, 2002, 235–63. This paper notes the dependency (suggested in the text) of this project on naturalization of the notion of rational belief. The prospects for developing a "pure" virtue epistemology are explored in detail in my "Epistemic Virtue and Justified Belief," in Abrol Fairweather and Linda Zagzebski, eds., *Virtue Epistemology* (Oxford University Press, 2001), pp. 82–97.

[12] I have developed the distinction between internalist and externalist conceptions of moral virtue in "Internalism and Externalism in Moral Epistemology," *Logos* 10 (1989), reprinted in my *Moral Knowledge and Ethical Character* (Oxford University Press, 1997), pp. 11–31. For related discussion of how virtue is to be conceived in a consequentialist framework, see Julia Driver, *Uneasy Virtue* (Cambridge University Press, 2001).

The second contrast corresponds to the distinction between act-types and act-tokens. A virtue ethics may, like any plausible ethics, distinguish between actions that, by virtue of their type – say, as promise-keeping – are in conformity with what morality requires and those that are performed *from* virtue, duty, or some other morally appropriate ground, as opposed to self-interest. These are act-tokens, particular actions by a given agent at a specific time and place. In Kantian terms, among actions only tokens, and only those of the latter kind, have "moral worth," since types are abstract and not grounded in the agent at all and tokens that are grounded non-morally are not a basis of moral credit. It should be apparent that an ethical theory could take virtue to be basic in the theory of moral worth without taking it to be basic in the theory of moral obligation.

I am leaving open whether aretaic concepts are basic in the way a strong virtue ethics requires. I have doubts about this, but have argued that in any case virtue concepts are essential in the theory of moral worth.[13] It is important to see, however, that even if virtue concepts are not conceptually basic, virtue ethics can provide *criteria* for right action, by providing either necessary conditions or sufficient conditions or conditions that are both necessary and sufficient. Right action can be equivalent to action in conformity with virtue, and acting rightly – doing the right thing for an appropriate reason and in the right way – can be equivalent to virtuous action, even if the concept of virtue cannot be explicated apart from other kinds of concepts, such as those of the plurality of obligations posited by intuitionist ethics.

The point that providing criteria for right action does not require an analysis of the notion of right action, much less an account of it in any particular set of concepts, is important. It is especially important for normative ethics, though a similar point holds for the application of other important notions. For even if it should be true that the concept of right action is explicable only in terms of, say, maximizing the good or conforming to the Categorical Imperative, the analytic accounts available through these routes might not provide illuminating criteria for the right, the wrong, and the obligatory. These are criteria that enable their ready identification or at least their identification in terms of properties of behavior and context that facilitate moral education and, for morally mature agents, moral exhortation and guidance. Given that an account of rightness is not sufficient for an account of moral worth, virtue concepts would be ethically important

[13] In, e.g., "Acting from Virtue."

for their indispensable role in clarifying that notion even if they did not provide a basis for plausible criteria of rightness.

III Normative virtue ethics

So far, my concern has been mainly metaethical. But virtue ethics has particular strengths in the normative domain. For one thing, any ethical theory should help us identify morally good persons. Doing this is, for practical purposes, impossible without relying on virtue concepts, for instance honesty, fairness, and loyalty. Indeed, if we cannot identify and describe morally good persons in fairly simple terms, moral education is at best stymied; and overall moral evaluation of persons, as opposed to their actions, is largely confined to crediting one action at a time and, given suitably unified patterns of behavior, descriptively and predictively generalizing as best we can.[14]

I take the notion of a morally good person to be roughly equivalent to that of a person of moral virtue. (The equivalence is only rough because virtue implies both a minimal range of virtues of character and a related stability not entailed by being morally good: a morally good person could be so without the required constitution and could alternate among responses to different kinds of basic grounds for moral conduct in ways a virtuous person could not.) Both notions admit of degree, and both allow for certain lapses, though neither is subjective, even in the qualified sense of entailing that actual normative status is a construct from justified beliefs ascribing it to the thing in question. Thus, not even a justified belief to the effect that something is (say) obligatory makes it so. Moral virtue requires a good measure of objective success relative to opportunities.

I have presupposed that there is a rough notion of moral virtue that helps us in understanding what constitutes a morally good person, but I have not meant to imply that the notion of *moral* virtue, as opposed to other kinds of practical virtue, is entirely clear. This need not be a problem in practice, so long as we have certain paradigms and sufficient clarity concerning normative appraisal of persons. If we can achieve sufficient clarity regarding the notion of a good person, this is perhaps more important, both for practical evaluation and for moral education, than achieving clarity on the

---

[14] Even my moderate claim about identifying morally good persons is controversial. For a case against it see Mark Alfano, *Character as Moral Fiction* (Cambridge University Press, 2013), and for a response to that case see Christian Miller, *Moral Character: An Empirical Theory* (Oxford University Press, 2013).

notion of a *morally* good person. Still, we should explore the extent to which that notion can be clarified.

We should immediately distinguish what might be called *omnibus traits* from virtues of character. Omnibus traits need not be moral. Consider goodness and rectitude and, on the opposite side, badness and turpitude. These are *overall* characteristics possessed on the basis of a weighted combination of traits or qualities. A person of rectitude, for instance, is morally good, but no particular moral trait is specified in the ascription. By contrast justice, fairness, honesty, loyalty, and benevolence are specifically moral traits. This is not because a person who has them must exercise moral concepts. To be sure, without seeing the importance of the corresponding moral properties for being a moral person, and without seeing the morally relevant grounds of action they indicate as partly constitutive of moral appraisal of action, one would exhibit some deficiency in understanding morality. If, for instance, someone said that being honest had no relevance to being a moral person, or that promising to help someone never provides a moral reason for doing it, this would be strong prima facie reason to question whether the person grasps the moral concepts apparently figuring in the statements. The kind of intellectual grasp of morality in question, however, is not a requirement for simply being a moral person.

A central point here is that although none of these traits – justice, fairness, honesty, loyalty, and benevolence – is sufficient for being morally good overall, each counts toward its possessor's being moral, at least in the sense that by its very nature it is a moral merit. Similarly, for the negative case: being unjust, unfair, dishonest, disloyal, and malevolent are by their nature moral defects.

It should be clarifying to consider two other cases of virtue. What of courage and that favorite in business ethics, integrity? Let us consider courage first, in the light of a distinction between two kinds of virtues important in ethics but rarely distinguished.[15]

Substantive moral virtues, such as honesty, fairness, and beneficence, are traits that are *morally* good in themselves. Having them normally implies a significant measure of success both in internalizing and in living up to sound moral standards. To have these traits requires (among other things) certain attitudes toward others, certain kinds of intentions in interpersonal relations, a sensitivity to the difference between right and wrong, and a tendency to act toward others for an appropriate range of reasons, for

---

[15] Here I draw on Robert Audi and Patrick E. Murphy, "The Many Faces of Integrity," *Business Ethics Quarterly* 16, 1 (2006), 3–21.

instance out of a sense of obligation as opposed to self-interest. But there are other virtues, such as courage and one kind of conscientiousness – roughly, a thoroughness and steadfastness in doing what one is committed to – of which these points do not hold. Courage and the kind of conscientiousness in question are not morally good in themselves. What is good about them need imply no commitment to moral standards, and their possession is consistent with gross immorality. They can exist in thoroughly unethical people: people of whom it would be wrong to say that they have *any* morally good traits of character. This does not hold for moral virtues.

Such non-moral traits as courage and conscientiousness can also contribute to success in immoral projects in a way moral virtues cannot. It is true that in special circumstances a person who is (say) honest but otherwise immoral might succeed better because of the virtue, say because of the confidence honesty can inspire. But this would require a great deal of luck. Asked the right questions, such people would be hampered in their immoral projects if they did not lie about themselves. Honest people can of course refuse to answer questions about their intentions, but an immoral person's silence might well give away some nasty truth or put the questioner on guard. Courage, by contrast, is non-accidentally contributory to the success of almost any kind of substantial project, whether moral or not. One might think that in people of strong *conscience*, courage and other non-moral virtues would conduce to overall moral goodness. But conscience (as understood generically and apart from some special theory of its function such as Kant's) is a faculty that has no moral standards of its own. Conscience takes from elsewhere the standards it reinforces. Like a commanding officer, it can be misguided, bigoted, and even corrupt.

In most people, however, and probably in all who are basically ethical, the qualities of courage and conscientiousness strengthen moral character. From the moral point of view, it is natural to call these qualities *adjunctive virtues*. They are important for achieving overall moral uprightness (as well as for prudence and for other non-moral traits that are not of direct concern here). In a *good* person, courage and conscientiousness are important in realizing good intentions. Without courage and at least enough conscientiousness to remember one's promises and carry out cooperative projects, one could be morally good only if this is compatible with a serious kind of weakness. But this does not imply that these traits are moral virtues. A structure of bricks cannot be strong without cement, but this does not entail that cement is a building block.

Now consider integrity. In one sense, 'integrity' is an omnibus term roughly equivalent to 'rectitude' – an overall moral soundness in a person.

The term may also be used equivalently with some specific virtue term. The most common is 'honesty'. But the wide use in question here is the distinctive one in which integrity is a kind of integration in character. Hypocrisy is an example of a failure in integrity precisely because it exhibits a lack of integration between word and deed; so does dishonesty, which may in part account for why honesty is the virtue most often thought of when integrity is ascribed to someone. My suggestion about integrity – in this distinctive, integrational sense – is that it belongs to this second category of virtues. Integrity in both senses is important for understanding human conduct in general and ethical behavior in particular. But in its integrational sense, as opposed to its aretaic sense, integrity does not entail any self-sufficient ethical standard and, like courage, is an adjunctive rather than a substantive virtue.

IV Virtuous persons, action from virtue, and virtuous action

We have distinguished between acting from virtue and acting merely in conformity with it. Central to the former is acting for a kind of reason that is appropriate to the virtue. In addition, such action entails the possession of the virtue that grounds the action. It should be noticed that (putting the point in terms reminiscent of Kant's reference to doing things "from duty"), although every action from virtue is a virtuous action, cases of the latter need not be cases of the former. This is not because there are virtuous actions in what we might call the thin sense of actions merely in conformity with virtue. It is because one can act for the right sort of reason even without *having* a virtue appropriate to acting for that reason. This may occur during moral education, in which one can do things for good reasons along the way to developing a virtue, but before succeeding. Virtues are not normally acquired instantaneously the first time an agent performs an aretaically required action for the right reason. A pattern of such acts is normally required.

This point is one that Aristotle could grant. For surely the kind of habituation he took to be crucial for developing virtue is not mere habitual performance of acts of the right type – actions in conformity with virtue – the acts of the right type may, and perhaps must, include some that are performed for an appropriate reason. These, however, can be performed in developing virtue; they do not require its prior development.[16] Action

---

[16] Swanton, *Virtue Ethics*, also distinguishes acting virtuously from acting from virtue; and although she does not make just the point I make here, her contrast is informative and supports it. See, e.g., pp. 238–9.

from virtue merits more credit for the agent (other things equal) than virtuous action that is not from virtue. This is not a matter of the act-type – the contrast is indeed intended to apply to tokens of the same type. The point holds mainly because the *doing* of the deed bespeaks the character of the agent; it does not represent just motivation and cognition appropriate to the deed but not rooted in a virtue. To be sure, virtuous action is still creditworthy and is to be aimed at by those self-consciously guiding conduct – their own or, especially, that of children they are morally educating. People *having* virtue will naturally act virtuously, though their doing so is by no means automatic; those trying to develop virtue should be urged to act virtuously and reinforced when they do.

How, in practice, should someone whose moral orientation is primarily a virtue ethics decide what to do? In practice, this decision may be spontaneous, but it may also have much in common with the decision-making practices of conscientious theorists with other orientations, say intuitionist, or rule consequentialist. Those practices may allow for spontaneous decisions. Consider four cases that suggest more overlap between virtue and rule orientations than is often recognized.

Ethical decision

This is crucial for practical and professional ethics. One might think that a virtue-ethical perspective would commit one to guiding difficult cases (the kind that most need discussion and are of chief interest here) by the question, *What would a virtuous person do in this case?*[17] But this is not the only way to proceed, whether we adhere to a virtue ethics or simply operate with a sense of the importance of virtue in guiding conduct. For one thing, the problems of evaluating subjunctives are difficult, and the guidance they provide is limited by our ability to anticipate how agents would be affected by changes of kinds that may never have occurred. These changes range from angry passions, to threats of embarrassment, to proposed bribes. For another thing, this hypothetical question invites one to proceed from an abstract understanding of the notion of a virtuous person or at least of some virtue. That may or may not be illuminating.

In contrast with this abstract approach is what might be called a *narrative approach*. Here one considers imaginary or historically relevant cases,

---

[17] Rosalind Hursthouse, e.g., who provides a subjunctive characterization of what constitutes a right act as "what a virtuous agent would characteristically (i.e. acting in character) do in the circumstances." See "Normative Virtue Ethics," in Crisp, *How Should One Live*, pp. 19–36. This kind of account is critically discussed by Robert Johnson in "Virtue and Rights," *Ethics* 113, 4 (2003), 810–34.

whether from actual life or from fiction, and one imagines a role model's resolution. The abstract and narrative approaches may be combined, and both are also available to at least some rule theorists. Ross, for instance, thought that where a conflict between prima facie duties is difficult to resolve, we should use Aristotelian practical wisdom. He approvingly quoted Aristotle's dictum that "The decision rests with perception."[18] The reference includes what might be called moral perception. Whether moral properties are literally perceptible or not, in part because moral perception is based on ordinary perception of the observable properties on which moral properties are consequential, it may be veridical. Like ordinary perception, it is non-inferential and intuitive, but it may still be quite reflective, as where one must listen carefully to a person explaining something to another to see that the first is being unfair to the second. Surely possession of a capacity for discerning moral perception is a requirement of moral virtue in a mature person; and in giving it so large a role Ross may be plausibly seen as granting that, whatever the order of dependency between aretaic and deontic or other moral concepts, virtue is indispensable in practical ethics. Even if moral behavior may be sound without grounding in virtue, credit for it depends in part upon virtue. Practical ethics as a set of standards for a morally good life must take account of this: both the evaluation of persons and the guidance of their conduct are inadequate apart from a discriminating use of aretaic concepts.

Rules of action

If Ross as a rule theorist makes room for the kind of moral perception often needed for ethical decision, might virtue ethics also make a place for the kinds of rules Ross and others have taken to be partly constitutive of morality? A strong virtue ethics will take virtues to be epistemically more basic than moral rules, in the sense that such moral rules as we can know or justifiedly believe are discoverable only by generalizing from sufficiently discerning observations of virtuous persons. But suppose this is so. A virtuous person may still rely on rules in many cases. These might include some cases that are of a largely unfamiliar kind on which the agent has been given a credible argument supporting some rule for generally dealing with them; but any ethical person may want to formulate and be guided by a rule or principle implicit in a precedential case. Such a case

---

[18] See W. D. Ross, *The Right and the Good* (Oxford University Press, 1930), p. 42. This translation is Ross's; he cites *NE* 1109b23 and 1126b4.

may or may not have been originally resolved through using rules. That is an independent matter.

Given the generality of moral judgments that is implicit in the consequentiality of moral properties on non-moral ones, it is at best difficult to teach virtue without at least implicitly affirming certain rules. Imagine saying to a child (as any ethical parents may, regardless of whether they are virtue ethicists) things like: 'Tell the truth', 'Don't lie', and 'We must be honest'. How is the child to develop the virtue of honesty without both habitually telling the truth and an awareness that this is generally to be done? But this practice does not by itself seem sufficient: to develop honesty the child must also see that truth-telling – and avoiding lies – is not only to be done, but a *good* thing, and that lying is generally *bad* (to be avoided, wrong, not done).

Once it is realized that (as I have argued elsewhere)[19] the only plausible moral rules and principles – certainly the only plausible everyday ones, by contrast with, say, the principle of utility or the Categorical Imperative – express prima facie rather than absolute obligations, the practical contrast between virtue ethics and rule ethics is greatly diminished. This is not to say that 'prima facie' or any such qualification need come into practical formulations of everyday moral principles or rules; the point is that the relevant types of obligations are not absolutely indefeasible. In any case, the differences that remain between rule and aretaic standards of action allow even strong virtue ethicists to countenance, as initial guidelines in much of our conduct, moral rules *discovered* aretaically from observations of the virtuous.

Traits of character and grounds of action

Given the points made so far and some of our examples, it may be evident that there is a correspondence between many major virtue concepts and at least the majority of the plausible moral principles that Ross and other moral philosophers have defended. Consider the obligations Ross singled out: those of justice and non-injury, fidelity and veracity, beneficence and self-improvement, and reparation and gratitude. Of these terms, only 'non-injury', 'self-improvement', and 'reparation' fail to indicate a virtue with the same name. But this is not because they indicate none; it is because they either indicate more than one virtue or because the action called

[19] In my "Ethical Generality and Moral Judgment," in James Dreier, ed., *Contemporary Debates in Ethical Theory* (Oxford: Blackwell, 2006), pp. 285–304.

for is indicated by an indefinite range of virtues or varying combinations of the effects of their exercise. To non-injury there corresponds (among other things) gentleness, kindness, and respectfulness. To self-improvement there corresponds (among other things) being self-critical and being proud. To reparation there corresponds fairness (of a certain positive kind); the paradigm ground of the obligation to make reparation is harming someone without excuse. To do nothing is unfair.

The correspondence indicated here is significant for understanding virtue concepts. For one thing, in the morally crucial cases just cited, to have the virtue is in part to be both perceptually sensitive to the relevant grounds – which is a cognitive receptivity – and behaviorally responsive to them in the right way, which is a matter of conduct. A just person, for example (one with the virtue of justice), is (other things equal) more likely than someone who lacks this virtue to *see* cheating that occurs in a competition and, certainly, to *respond* to it with action or at least disapproval sufficiently strong to yield action if a suitable opportunity arises. Similarly, a person who lives by the rules central for just action is more likely, other things equal, to internalize them in a way that achieves or at least supports development of the corresponding virtue. There is, however, a vast range of trait terms that are relevant to the moral appraisal of persons and their deeds, and here virtue and rule ethicists alike can refine both their perceptual capacities and their systems of rules.

Aretaic and deontic conflicts

The most common example of conflict for rule theories is conflict between promissory obligation and beneficence. It should be emphasized that there are counterpart conflicts for virtues: not because the relevant virtues are incompatible – this is no more plausible than treating conflicts of prima facie duties as entailing contradictions – but because they pull the agent in different directions. Clearly a virtuous person will have traits of fidelity and beneficence and so can face similar hard decisions.

A different kind of hard case might arise for someone who is both just and forgiving. Justice might call for punishment, forgiveness for waiving it, at least given repentance in the offender. The case is different because, although forgiveness is a strength of character and a good trait, it is not clear that it is a moral virtue rather than, say, a theological one. A person of overall virtue, however, will be competent to decide the matter in a reasonable way. In doing so, it may be appropriate to seek a reflective equilibrium among the inclinations that go with all of the relevant virtues.

It is also reasonable to take any hypothesized resolution in a conflict case as precedential.

One might note that virtues can be clarified by contrast with their polar opposites. Take forgiveness again. Granted, its polar opposite (roughly, rancorous resentfulness) is a vice. But virtues cannot be defined as the polar opposites of contrary vices: the extreme opposite of the vice of stinginess is lavishness, not generosity. Polar opposites are, however, guides to finding a virtuous middle. They indicate some of the raw material of the relevant virtue, as stinginess indicates a dimension of conduct crucial for understanding generosity; but the analysis of vice is not a sufficient basis for the analysis of virtue.

In these hard cases of conflicting normative forces, formulating a generalization that covers them is pertinent, and any conscientious ethical thinking is likely to seek a reflective equilibrium between a promising general formulation and intuitions about particular cases it is intended to cover. For the virtue ethicist, the rule does not have independent authority as, say, the Categorical Imperative does for a Kantian; but the availability of a plausible *ex post facto* rule may still be a reasonable constraint for agents guided by a virtue ethics. A virtuous person will tend to treat like cases alike; this does not require following or formulating a rule, but responding to the relevant similarities does imply a capacity to cite them on adequate reflection and that in turn implies an ability to frame a rough generalization. Similarly, following a moral rule requires a capacity to discern a range of cases falling under it. Whether or not we think one of these processes has higher epistemic authority than the other, we may agree that both singular judgments and commitments to rules should be harmonized and may require adjustments on each side as a result of a search for reflective equilibrium. A mature reflective moral agent will doubt both singular judgments that cannot be subsumed under an intuitively plausible, non-trivial prima facie principle and principles that cannot be supported by intuitively plausible judgments or by actual or hypothetical cases.

The same considerations hold for rule theorists confronted with decisions not resolved by appeal to the principles they take as basic. But rule theorists will have fewer resources if they do not appeal to aretaic notions. It turns out, then, that just as aretaically determined decisions have a kind of responsibility to principles, decisions made by rule theorists may need or benefit from reflection on the relevant virtues. Virtue in practice leads to patterns of conduct that the rule-oriented will seek to codify; the conscientious following of the intuitively most plausible moral rules bespeaks conduct that virtue ethicists will seek to anchor in traits of moral character.

V   Some major uses of aretaic concepts

If, in making ethical decisions, so much overlap between virtue and rule approaches is possible, why do we need virtue ethics? I have said that we need a moderate version of it in the theory of moral worth. This is significant even if virtue ethics is not needed in the theory of moral obligation. But there is another dimension of ethics of equally great concern in this paper: normative ethics, including applied and practical ethics.

To appreciate the full value of aretaic concepts in ethics, it is essential to keep in mind that 'aretaic' implicitly covers vices as well as virtues. To be sure, vices are not in general precise counterparts of virtues. For one thing, they are in the main motivationally less restrictive. The veracious must tell the truth in part because they care about it; the loyal must cleave to agreements in part from respect for them; and so forth. But, for any of a huge range of types of reasons, the dishonest may lie or cheat, the unjust may discriminate, and the cruel may cause pain. The reasons for such acts need not even be selfish. Granted, there are exceptions to the disanalogy in question: perhaps maleficence is a virtually perfect counterpart (and polar opposite) of beneficence, or at least malevolence is of benevolence, and intemperance of temperance. But many morally bad traits are not vices in this aretaic sense.

One could, then, distinguish a vice from a *moral defect* and hold that genuine vices are counterparts of virtues but have the bad (or some aspect of it), as opposed to the good, as their *telos*. In any case, for a full picture of the value of virtue ethics we must explore pejorative and condemnatory terms as well as the laudatory epithets that dominate much discussion of virtue ethics. The former, negative terms are crucial in moral education and in providing incentives to avoid wrong-doing. There are at least four kinds of contexts that should be considered here. I begin with the pejoratives.

The context of prohibition. The power of pejoratives is not to be underestimated, especially in their noun forms, in which their application suggests a vice or serious defect of character. It is at best a rare person who does not have a deep aversion to being called a liar, cheat, coward, brute, bully, thief, turncoat, fraud, or phony. People seem particularly averse to being conceived in pejorative terms by those they care about, such as their children. These terms express negative standards and have considerable rhetorical power. They should be given an appropriate role in both moral education and moral reinforcement. In educating children, we can clarify positive standards by contrast with the deeds or patterns these pejoratives designate, and we can use those terms to discourage immoral conduct.

In reinforcing adults, we can point to the vices or defects in question as negative standards, and we can reinforce motivation by ascribing them, with perceptible aversion, to people who exemplify them.

The context of exhortation. Nearly everyone wants to be considered (for instance) honest, fair, loyal, just, kind, and generous. These traits should be developed in moral education, and some of them figure in major moral principles, such as the kind Ross formulated. Such principles are especially useful in teaching ethics and in critically appraising actions. They are also appropriate to institutional mission statements, which is a quite different thing. They have considerable exhortatory power. It is an interesting question why they do not have quite the rhetorical or emotive power of the pejoratives cited above. One hypothesis is that we know we must be on guard against those who are bad (the vicious, in extreme cases), whereas we tend to think we may generally be comfortable with the virtuous. Another is that there is more condemnation in applying one of these pejoratives than praise in ascription of a virtue. A related hypothesis, which helps to explain the second, is that whereas overall virtue requires at least several of these virtues, overall badness of character is implied by possession of any of the bad traits mentioned above. Commendation is much harder to deserve than condemnation. It takes much to weave the fabric of good character, but little to stain it.

The context of discovery. The heuristic value of aretaic concepts is evident in many points in this paper. We can reflect on what it is to have a given virtue. We can ask how various role models who have a virtue have acted or would act in a given situation calling for moral decision. We can look to narratives, historical or fictional, for insight into the virtues. All of these modes of discovery, moreover, apply to deciding what kind of person we want to be. That existential question is not as well approached from the perspective of any rule theory that is not integrated with a good grasp of aretaic concepts and their bearing on human life. To be sure, as adults we have only limited control of our character, but even adults can alter themselves for the better; and certainly parents can have much influence on the character of their children.

The context of justification. When it comes to justifying moral judgments and moral decisions, such aretaic statements as 'It was the just solution' and 'Loyalty demands standing by her even though she made the wrong decision' have a kind of incompleteness. In part for this reason, although making such statements is often a good opening for a justification, anyone who doubts what is said or does not see the basis of the statement will want specific facts. Justification, by contrast with discovery, commonly requires citing facts that can be put together into at least a rough generalization. This is not a surprise if we take normative properties, such as being obligatory, being justified, or indeed being wrong, to be not only consequential on non-normative properties but *also* epistemically dependent on them in the sense that (normally) knowledge of a person's or action's having a normative property depends on knowledge of its having (or at least an appropriately justified true belief that it has) certain non-normative properties, such as being an equal distribution of money or being a promised gesture of support for a colleague. Consequentiality implies that no two persons or actions can differ in their normative properties if they are alike in their non-normative ones.

One idea underlying the plausibility of the view – present in Aristotle's account of justice but also reflected in any plausible interpretation of Kant's Categorical Imperative – that like cases should be treated alike is that what morally justifies a kind of action is one or more discernible properties possessed by it or by the relevant person(s) in the context. When these properties are adequately described, it is usually possible to formulate at least a rough generalization with non-trivial applications to similar cases. Even if virtue leads in a quite spontaneous way to *discovering* what action should be taken, justifying the action usually requires formulating a general description that is a basis for a rule or principle that applies to the action. The properties crucial for such a rule or principle are, of course, just the kind to which the virtuous agent tends to be perceptually sensitive and behaviorally responsive. In some cases, what virtuous agents notice and respond to is a basic for formulating generalizations that they do not ordinarily need but, on reflection, can accept.

* * *

On the view presented here, a virtue is a praiseworthy trait of character with a significant capacity to influence conduct. A virtue supplies its possessor both with normatively adequate reasons indicating, for diverse contexts, what sort of thing should be done and with motivation to do such things for a reason of the right kind. Virtue is not a mere capacity for good deeds, but a settled, internally rooted tendency to do them for an appropriate reason. Although vices are not in general close counterparts of virtues, a good account of the ethical importance of character traits should take account of vices and the moral defects associated with them. Avoiding vices and moral defects may be, if not a constitutive aim of a mature virtuous agent, then a guiding indication of the excesses and deficiencies whose identification helps us to understand virtue. In the light of the partial account of moral virtues provided here, it is evident that their ethical importance is incalculable and must be acknowledged by proponents of rule ethics. Indeed, the contrast between virtue and rule theories is often drawn too sharply, even where a strong virtue ethics is in question. For even theories in this range make room for both theoretical and practical uses of rules. If the inherent goodness of persons themselves and the moral worth of their deeds is the central focus, virtue concepts and the insights of virtue ethics are essential for a good account of these notions. If the question of what types of act are obligatory is the central focus, then moral appraisal of act-types in relation to the properties on which their normative character is consequential is indispensable, and principles of conduct are essential. A comprehensive ethics needs both a theory of moral worth and a theory of obligation. Even if aretaic concepts are not more basic than deontic notions, they are essential in this task.[20]

[20] This essay has benefited from comments by Jason Baldwin, Anne Margaret Baxley, Roger Crisp, Edwin Hartman, and Robert C. Solomon, as well as from discussions with the participants in a conference at the University of Gdansk and in presentations at New York University and the University of Notre Dame.

PART III

Religion, Politics, and the Obligations of Citizenship

CHAPTER 9

Wrongs within rights

Appeals to rights are common and influential both in everyday life and in public affairs. Legal as well as moral rights are important in guiding conduct, but the latter are my main concern. The notion of a moral right presents a challenge. On the one hand, it does not seem morally basic, and no major kind of ethical theory – even the major deontological ones, Kantian and intuitionist – takes it as such. On the other hand, it is not readily accounted for in terms of the concepts provided by the major ethical theories – or by any others. This would be less disturbing if it were clear just what our moral rights *are*. In the widest usage, illustrated by the breadth of the Universal Declaration of Human Rights,[1] rights include what some would regard as simply morally reasonable aspirations.

This paper will not provide a full-scale account of rights. My aim is chiefly to examine a question important for understanding morality in general as well as rights in particular: the relation between violations of moral rights and other moral wrongs. It is clear that whatever the moral rights we have, violation of them is a moral wrong. This is central for rights discourse. But may we also say that an act which does *not* violate rights is not wrong? It may be natural to think so. It is especially common to presuppose something similar: that if you have a right to *A*, then in *A*-ing, you do not act wrongly.[2] I will question this. Our rights imply much about

---

[1] For a valuable short discussion of the Universal Declaration of Human Rights (adopted by the UN General Assembly in 1948), see William A. Edmundson, *An Introduction to Rights* (Cambridge University Press, 2004), esp. 105–7. Some of these illustrate what Joel Feinberg has called rights in a "manifesto" sense.

[2] In discussing John Courtney Murray, Paul J. Weithman suggests that Murray may have held a view of this kind. Explicating Murray, he writes, "If someone has a moral right to do something, then she violates no obligation by doing it" (where there is no indication that doing a wrong does not entail violating an obligation). See Weithman's "The Privatization of Religion," *Journal of Religious Ethics* 22 (1994), 15. In "A Right to Do Wrong," *Ethics* 92 (1981), Jeremy Waldron quotes William Godwin as holding that "There cannot be a more absurd proposition than that which affirms a right of doing wrong" (Waldron's 23). My view is not that there is a *right to do wrong*, but that there are *some* wrongs there is a right to do. Godwin and probably also Murray implicitly deny this.

what should *not* be done, but they tell us far less about what should be done. First, however, we must consider what, in general, constitutes a right.

I Sketch of a conception of moral rights

On any conception of rights, they are the sorts of things of which we may predicate (among other things) being claimed, asserted, denied, respected, violated, forfeited, and transferred. Perhaps some rights, such as the right not to be enslaved, are "inalienable" and hence cannot be transferred; some may also be plausibly held to be incapable of forfeit. But the ascriptions just indicated are intelligible, even if, for some rights, never true. An adequate theory of rights should be consistent with that point. It should also distinguish between *claiming a right*, which commits one to adhering to a normative standard and puts that standard forward as governing the context, and claiming *that* one has it, which may be a metaethical (or a legal) assertion. The former is at least implicitly interpersonal, the latter not. Rights are appropriately claimed *against* violators or someone seen by the claimant as a potential violator; they may also be appropriately claimed as a reminder or indication of the right, say where negotiations are in view. A similar distinction may be made between asserting a right and asserting that someone has it. These and other constraints will be observed in what follows.

I want to begin by exploring a view applicable to (moral) rights *to do*, an important group that might be called basic liberty rights (basic because they are "natural" rights, the kind we have in virtue of being persons rather than because of such special circumstances as being parents, friends, or citizens). On this view, a right is (roughly) a defeasible normative protection from a certain kind of coercive conduct, such as suppression of free speech.[3] In saying this I presuppose the common view that rights entail corresponding duties; in part, the point of pursuing the protectiveness conception is to specify the *kinds* of duties that are largely constitutive of rights. Not all duties entail correlative rights (as will be illustrated). Moreover, we should understand rights in terms of what their holders *have*, not just in terms of what others are obligated to do toward them.

---

[3] The overall conception of rights offered here is based largely on the sketch of rights I present in *The Good in the Right: A Theory of Intuition and Intrinsic Value* (Princeton University Press, 2004), ch. 5. One clarification is important for the formulation just given (and even then it remains rough). Provided we distinguish eradication from other kinds of elimination, such as forfeiture and alienation, we might consider moral rights ineradicable. (This leaves open that some rights *cannot* be forfeited or alienated, such as, perhaps, the right not to be enslaved.)

Two qualifications are essential. First, I take a normative protection to be a (defeasible) but strong justification for prohibiting the conduct in question – morally prohibiting it, in the cases that concern me. Second, we must take the notion of coercive conduct broadly if we are to do justice to the full range of liberty rights. Freedom of speech can be forcibly limited by a machine that drowns us out as well as by threats that prevent our uttering any words at all. One important idea that goes with liberty rights is that by and large, violations of these rights limit our options and force us to act within a narrower range than is available to us when the right in question is observed. Coercive conduct in the relevant sense, then, need not produce a specific action (as on the most common use of 'coercion') but may be constituted by forcibly limiting options, thereby reducing the scope of someone's agency or even impairing it. The qualification 'by and large' is essential in reference to limiting the rights-holder's options because in some cases a rights violation can liberate. Someone intending to wound a prisoner bound by ropes could unintentionally cut through them, causing no injury, and thereby enable an escape. In the usual case, however, there would be a wound that impairs agency.

Although the broad notion of protection from coercive conduct applies most clearly to rights *to do*, by contrast with rights *against*, say against being physically harmed, the notion is nonetheless clarifying for these other cases. This is so particularly if, as I assume, rights are above all a kind of protection of our agency (though this is not all they are). Physical harms tend to impair agency and thereby to force us to perform compensatory actions and forgo others. It is true that a rights violation need not compel the victim to perform some particular act; the idea is rather that rights violations characteristically force one either to choose among a range of options that, from the moral point of view, is inappropriately narrow or at any rate to do something in a way that, at least given the right, is morally objectionable. Thus, lies might put desirable options out of consideration and, in that way, beyond one's reach; and (to illustrate the second case) a broken promise might force me to do a mission without the promised provisions, though I am still able to do it. Similarly, violations of my privacy might force me to listen to music louder than I would like because of the blare of a neighbor's television. This last case also shows that a rights violation need not cause what is ordinarily considered harm, except insofar as reducing one's options is a kind of harm in itself.[4]

---

[4] Cf. Amartya Sen: "A pronouncement of human rights includes an assertion of the corresponding freedoms – the freedoms that are identified and privileged in the formulation of the rights in

Privacy rights are a special challenge to the conception of rights I am exploring, and these among other cases may show that, without some regimentation, it cannot provide a necessary and sufficient condition for the possession of a right. Not every violation of privacy rights even affects the rights-holder, at least directly. A peeping Tom pathetically enamored of a woman he spies on through her office window might never interact with her. Nonetheless, the *characteristic* violations of privacy either impose limits on people's agency or provide a means to do so. We should thus regard the notion of normative protection from coercive conduct as applicable to conduct that, like privacy violations, is *characteristically* of this kind or provides a means to limit agency, even if it need not affect agency in every case.

It is special rights, such as those conferred by people who make promises, that are least readily accommodated by the normative protection conception of rights. Consider a friend's promising to care for my child or the government's promising to provide healthcare. I might manage these failures well and could also remain a "free agent." Still, breaking these promises tends to force me to do things, such as impose on relatives or give up savings, that would not otherwise be necessary. Indeed, in the relevant circumstances I apparently have a freedom right *not* to do them.

There are two further points that connect the conception of rights as normative protections from coercion with special rights. First, special rights – like liberty rights – carry a strong (though defeasible) justification against being prevented from *claiming* the right, or having it claimed by a suitable proxy, say a parent, where claiming is understood as making a moral *demand* that the relevant duties be fulfilled. The point is important in part because the ability to claim rights is an essential element in (unimpaired) *moral agency* and justification for having them claimed on one's behalf is an essential element in *moral status*. Second, special rights are also like liberty rights in carrying a strong justification against third parties' preventing those who have the duties from fulfilling them. This justification does not require *making* such claims or seeking such prevention; but it does entail that one should not be forced to give up or abstain from pressing these claims or from seeking appropriate prevention. Again, a normative protection from coercion is a major element in the right.

question – and is indeed motivated by that importance." See "Elements of a Theory of Human Rights," *Philosophy and Public Affairs* 32 (2004), 321. Sen associates human rights (which he apparently construes as moral) even more closely with freedom than I do, e.g. in tying them to the very "formulation" of rights. Below I address some difficulties with this freedom-centered conception that he does not consider.

If special rights are like liberty rights in the two respects just described, they are unlike the latter in another significant respect. Liberty rights apparently imply, or are in any case supported by, "public" third party rights to assert them on behalf of their holders and even to take certain actions in defense of those rights where they are abridged or threatened. If a stranger is being oppressed, I have a *second-order right* to take appropriate action in defense of the abridged liberty right. The counterpart claim for a stranger's breaking a promise to another stranger does not hold. Liberty rights – and arguably natural rights of any kind – thus have a kind of publicity that special rights need not have.[5] (Special rights may be, in *one* important way, a private matter.) This public character is reflected in the idea that the normative protection from coercive conduct that liberty rights carry may be properly undertaken by anyone appropriately positioned (adequately informed, not engaging in overkill, and so forth).

We can see other elements entailed by the normative protection view by considering how, where clarity and explicitness are sought, rights should be specified. Regardless of our theory of what constitutes *having* a right, in order to specify what a given right amounts to we must indicate at least four kinds of fact. First, its possessor(s): who has the right. This is whoever is protected by it and may justifiedly claim it (or have it claimed by proxy). Second, the addressee – the person(s) against whom a right is held – should be indicated. Addressees, though they may never be explicitly spoken to or even mentioned in describing the conduct within the scope of the right, are those *bound* by it.[6] Third, the content of the right – the conduct it protects (or prohibits) and concerning which the addressee

---

[5] If there are such second-order rights, they are presumably a kind of natural right. They may also have the special property of being *deontically iterative*: there is presumably a parallel third-order protective right regarding the second-order one, a parallel fourth-order right protecting that one, up to some unspecifiable finite limit.

[6] To say that rights must have addressees does not entail that *knowledge* that someone has a right requires knowing who its addressees are. This is supported by the distinction (in the text) between claiming a right and claiming that one has it. One cannot claim a right without a general sense of who has the correlative obligation; but, on the conception I am exploring (as on others) one might know that one has a right, on the basis of knowing what *sorts* of coercions one has a strong justification against, yet be unable to specify any particular addressee. The most basic rights, to be sure, such as liberty rights, are addressed to everyone (or at least everyone *else*). But given the wide scope of the human rights many would posit, and given even certain welfare rights, it may be argued that we can have an adequate basis for positing rights without specifying who has the correlative obligations. In "The Moral Reality of Human Rights," in Thomas Pogge, ed., *Freedom from Poverty as a Human Right: Who Owes What to the Very Poor?* (Oxford University Press; Paris: UNESCO, 2007), 75–101, John Tasioulas argues for this possibility regarding certain human rights. Cf. Onora O'Neill, *Toward Justice and Virtue: A Constructive Account of Practical Reasoning* (Cambridge University Press, 1996) and *Bounds of Justice* (Cambridge University Press, 1999), to which Tasioulas's paper replies on this point.

(and possibly others) owe the possessor(s) non-interference – must be indicated. Fourth, understanding a right requires knowing its domain, for instance moral or legal – the normative realm in which criticism or sanctions or both are (prima facie) in order for non-performance of the relevant conduct.[7]

This conception of rights is akin to a Rossian conception of prima facie duties. I have argued elsewhere[8] that these duties ('obligations' may be preferable in contemporary parlance) are ineradicable *given* their grounds. But they remain defeasible, as where even a right not to be killed is defeated by lethally attacking others. Moreover, their grounds are cancelable or otherwise eliminable, as where someone I have promised to assist asks me not to proceed or dies. For certain ascriptions of rights, say a general right to free speech, it is arguable, as it is for certain principles of prima facie duty, that these ascriptions are self-evident (this does not entail that they are obvious or even compel assent in all who understand them). As in the case of duties, this self-evidence does not preclude rights' being grounded (or groundable) in something else, including principles. I take the self-evident to be knowable without epistemic reliance on independent evidence; this does not preclude there *being* such evidence.[9]

Consider rights not to be harmed, not to be lied to or given insincere promises, and not to be treated unjustly. Granting that the notion of justice is multi-faceted and difficult to characterize in simple terms, insofar as an act is clearly an injustice to someone, it is plain that it violates a right, even if that right is most clearly specified without appeal to 'injustice' and its cognates, say as the right to be treated as innocent unless "proven" guilty. Similar points hold for rights against being harmed, lied to, and being betrayed by broken promises, even if violations of these rights need not constitute injustice. Moreover, insofar as the conception of rights as normative protections against coercive conduct is sound, coercive conduct

---

[7] The view of rights presented here takes account of Ronald Dworkin's distinction between abstract and concrete rights: "An abstract right is a general political aim the statement of which does not indicate how that particular aim is to be weighed . . . against other political aims . . . Concrete rights, on the other hand, are political aims that are more precisely defined so as to express more definitely the weight they have . . . [e.g.] a newspaper has a right to publish defense plans classified as secret provided this publication will not create an immediate physical danger to troops." See "Hard Cases," in Dworkin, *Taking Rights Seriously* (Cambridge, Mass.: Harvard University Press, 1978), 93. I grant the suggested difference in abstractness vs. concreteness, but I am distinguishing the stringency of a right from the specificity of its content. However specifically we indicate content – even if we do so in a way that indicates that some other rights have lesser stringency – on the assumption that there are no (non-trivially specifiable) absolute rights, there can still be conflicts of rights in which the original one is overridden by one or more other rights.

[8] In *The Good in the Right*, e.g. ch. 1, 23–4.

[9] This conception of the self-evident is defended in *The Good in the Right*, ch. 2 (where the conception is contrasted with that of Moore and Ross in their works cited in note 12).

against which the person in question has a strong justification is also a violation of rights. Since there are liberty rights against coercion, this claim has some plausibility.

Any right can in principle be claimed. Claiming a right, however, does not require *naming* it. For instance, we can claim a right not to have a promise to us broken, implicitly, by citing not the right but the promise, as where someone refuses to do something promised. We can also say (e.g.) 'I have a right to your help'; but that explicit way of claiming a right is usually less natural: more often, rights are most appropriately claimed not by citing *them*, but by indicating their *ground*. Such an implicit claim is not only less likely to seem adversarial; it also cites a *reason* why the person addressed should do the thing in question.

Many less general rights fall under the headings I have specified. Consider the diversity of harms. Many are physical, but some are psychological. There are even more rights in the category of rights not to be harmed or be treated unjustly if *omission* of reparations for harms and for certain other wrongs constitutes a kind of injustice or harm or both. There will then be as many kinds of rights as there are kinds of wrongs that give rise to duties of reparation.

Given the number of rights that must be countenanced on the protectiveness conception, one might think that rights cover all possible human conduct, i.e., that all such conduct is in their *scope*, in the sense that for any person, P, and act-type, A, either P has a right to A or someone has a right against P that precludes P's A-ing. But there are possible deeds, such as claiming an abandoned fifty-dollar bill on the street, that none of us has a right to do or a right to prevent others from doing.[10] There *is* a right not to be prevented *by force* from picking up the bill; but this is a special case of some other right, such as the right to freedom of movement. This is not a right to be protected against others' taking the bill if they arrive first. Others have the same rights.

The case illustrates that some permissible acts are neither protected by rights to perform them nor forbidden by rights against performing them. This should be no surprise: morality itself does not cover all acts – at least in the sense that all come under an *ought* or *ought not*. Having some coffee is discretionary, hence permissible in the sense that it is not wrong: though I do not have a right to have it on demand, no one has a right to prevent my having some, and I am neither obligated to have it nor obligated not to have it. We should distinguish being protected by a right not to be forcibly

---

[10] In the terminology of Wesley Hohfeld, this is a privilege or a "no-right," where (in line with the text) the *absence* of a right is on the part of the other party. For a brief discussion of the Hohfeldian conception of rights, see Edmundson, *An Introduction to Rights*, esp. 88–95.

prevented from *A*-ing, as I am here, in that no one may coerce me in the matter, and, on the other hand, *having* a right to *A*. If I have a right to *A*, others are obligated ("bound" or have a duty) not only not to force me to abstain (say, by threats), but also not to do certain other things that would prevent my *A*-ing.

These points hold only if rights are (perhaps with special exceptions) defeasible. If my right not to be forced to have coffee were indefeasible, then no one would be justified in forcibly preventing me from doing so if the coffee contained cyanide. *If* there are exceptions to this defeasibility claim, they may occur where conduct both violates a right and is, on balance, unjustified. Consider treating *P* in a brutally inhumane way simply for pleasure. Even in administering capital punishment, such conduct is unwarranted. True, brutally inhumane treatment could be required to prevent an ill-considered suicide in a disturbed masochist; but even then, the relevant deed could not be justifiedly performed simply for pleasure.[11]

The partial account of rights now sketched is meant to supply a conception that, though incomplete, suffices for my normative purpose: to show how moral criticism may be applicable where, on some views, it would be unexpected or even precluded. This aim cannot be fully accomplished, however, apart from an understanding of how rights may be grounded. In exploring (very briefly) the grounding of rights, I assume (as is standard in ethics) that moral properties, say having rights or duties, are under the control of non-moral facts. An act may, for instance, be a violation of rights because it is an assault, or obligatory because it is promised.

The point here is reflected in the virtually uncontroversial view that two things identical in their non-moral properties cannot differ in moral ones. Suppose, as this suggests, that moral properties are consequential on natural properties (roughly, descriptive, hence non-normative, properties).[12] Then we have rights in virtue of having such properties as rationality (or the natural properties it is consequential on) combined with agency and a capacity for joy and suffering. If natural properties of these sorts ground

---

[11]   This possible exception is stated in terms of *conduct* rather than act-type, where conduct includes motivational grounding. *A*-ing for pleasure is not a different act-type from *A*-ing but differs as conduct. Explication of the distinction between action *simpliciter* and conduct is provided in my "Treating Persons as Ends," in progress.

[12]   The idea that moral properties are consequential on natural ones is given early formulations by G. E. Moore in *Principia Ethica* (Cambridge University Press, 1903) and W. D. Ross in *The Right and the Good* (Oxford University Press, 1930). I explicate it in "Ethical Naturalism and the Explanatory Power of Moral Concepts," in Steven Wagner and Richard Wagner, eds., *Naturalism: A Critical Appraisal* (University of Notre Dame Press, 1993), 95–115; reprinted in my *Moral Knowledge and Ethical Character* (Oxford University Press, 1997), 112–28.

rights, there is a *general grounding* of rights. It is general because it does not indicate how any particular right is grounded. If, however, some such general thesis is correct, then any particular right should be grounded on properties in the indicated range. A right to freedom of movement, for example, would be grounded (partly) in some property of our agency or in our tendency to suffer from certain restrictions in it.[13]

Take Kantianism first. Consider an intrinsic end formulation of the Categorical Imperative: We must never treat people merely as means but always as ends in themselves. It is natural to think of this as normatively grounded in the "intrinsic" worth of persons,[14] which Kant roughly equates with their dignity. If this Imperative is the basic principle we must obey in order to respect our dignity, rights should be understandable at least partly through the Imperative. Let us explore this.

Presumably, *if* we treat persons as ends, we respect their rights. But *failure* to treat persons as ends need not violate their rights. I presuppose that treating people merely as means violates some 'perfect' duty, such as the duty not to lie, and *merely* failing to treat them as ends (which implies *not* treating them merely as means) violates some 'imperfect' duty, such as the duty of beneficence, but *not* a perfect one.[15] Granted, Kant might have thought that we have a right to *criticize* people for failure to be beneficent. But a right to beneficent treatment implies more: it justifies a kind of *demand*, one specifying a duty owed to the rights-holder. One reason to resist positing a natural right to beneficent treatment is that not assisting needy people is not coercive, even if it fails to *facilitate* agency. I doubt that Kant took all such failures to entail violations of rights, but perhaps violations of perfect duties – not to kill, injure, steal, or lie, for instance – do entail them. In any case, this is one broadly Kantian position.[16]

---

[13] It is noteworthy, and perhaps a merit of the protectiveness conception, that it incorporates rationales commonly associated with two different theories of the basis of rights: the "interest theory," on which rights function to protect their holder's interests, and "choice theory," on which rights function to protect their holder's freedom of choice. For critical discussion of these two conceptions, see Edmundson, *An Introduction to Rights*, 120–32, and John Tasioulas, "Human Rights, Universality and the Values of Personhood: Retracing Griffin's Steps," *European Journal of Philosophy* 10 (2002), 79–100.

[14] Kant himself suggests such a grounding of the Categorical Imperative: "Suppose there were something *whose existence* has *in itself* an absolute value, something which *as an end in itself* could be a ground of determinate laws; then . . . in it alone, would there be the ground of a possible categorical imperative." See *Groundwork of the Metaphysics of Morals*, trans. H. J. Paton (New York: Harper and Row, 1956), sec. 428.

[15] This view is defended in some detail in my "Treating Persons as Ends."

[16] I offer no definition of 'perfect duty' or 'imperfect duty'. I rely on examples to suggest the distinction and am taking the intrinsic end formulation of the Categorical Imperative, given sufficient interpretation, to provide one good way to clarify it.

As to utilitarianism, even an act-utilitarian can distinguish acts that merely fail to maximize (say) welfare from acts that do this *and* are punishable or at least (soundly) criticizable. It is open to utilitarians, then, to distinguish perfect and imperfect duties along these lines and to argue that their overall view supports some kind of punishment for violations of the former but not the latter. My point is simply that even utilitarians who take maximization of a single basic value as their standard can distinguish wrongs that violate rights from wrongs that do not.[17]

In virtue ethics, rights apparently have at most a minor role. But consider Aristotle. Although there is apparently no equivalent of the notion of a right in the *Nicomachean Ethics*, he did say that some acts do not admit of a mean between excess and deficiency, for instance murder and adultery.[18] Could he not have consistently held that such unqualified wrongs violate a right? And might he have used the distinction between an act's being wrong and its calling for punishment to clarify the notion of a right further?

Granting, then, that *reliance* on the notion of a right goes against the grain of virtue ethics, virtue theories are not without resources for accounting for rights.[19] They also have resources for showing the normative thesis that – as I shall argue – moral standards call on us to do far more than observe rights.

II   The plurality of rights

Kantian, utilitarian, and virtue-theoretic approaches to understanding rights may each capture part of the truth about them. Dignity can be a basis of rights even if its capacity to ground them depends on something else. This might be Kantian autonomy; but, as utilitarians would stress, our capacity for joy and suffering is also important in explaining why certain kinds of acts violate our rights. Suppose, on the other hand, that rights can

[17]   Mill says, e.g., "duties of perfect obligation are those duties in virtue of which a correlative *right* exists in some person or persons; duties of imperfect obligation are those moral obligations which do not give birth to any right." See ch. 5 of *Utilitarianism*, 61 in the Oscar Piest edn. (Indianapolis: Bobbs-Merrill, 1957). Mill also says, "We do not call anything wrong unless we mean to imply that a person ought to be punished in some way or another for doing it – if not by law, by the opinion of his fellow creatures; if not by opinion, by the reproaches of his own conscience" (60). This broad notion of punishability as a necessary condition for wrong-doing accommodates not only the possibility that one may do a wrong though one has a right to do it, but also the possibility – which Mill might not have countenanced – that one ought to do something that is not even an imperfect duty.

[18]   *Nicomachean Ethics* bk. 2, 1107a9ff.

[19]   For critical discussion of how one notion of natural rights should be viewed, see Alasdair MacIntyre, *After Virtue*, second edn. (University of Notre Dame Press, 1984), esp. 68–71.

be seen as based on the moral centrality of virtue; rights violations might be acts that are in sharp *opposition* to certain virtues: they characteristically bespeak vice. These approaches can be combined. Even if, say, the dignity of persons is taken to be the basis of rights, and that in turn is grounded in rationality, in a capacity for agency, and in the capacity for joy and suffering (arguably natural properties of persons), other notions may play a grounding role, including even theological notions such as that of being created by God. This theological property can be considered a basis of dignity and so, indirectly, of rights.

It may be that the idea that rights are normative protections from violations of the dignity of persons is the best global unifying conception of rights. The kinds of coercive conduct I have described as prohibited by rights constitute such violations, even if there are other kinds of rights violations that cannot be included under the wide notion of coercive conduct in question. Dignity can be grounded in a number of ways, and it can be understood partly as a status of persons that is undermined by coercive conduct toward them. Some of these have been suggested; but rather than develop those ideas, I want to proceed toward a normative view concerning the role of rights in relation to moral appraisal in general.

One of the first things to notice is that some rights protect us from treatment that is not *instrumental* (in using us as a means) but nonetheless limits our agency. Consider knocking people over as one rushes to make a plane, or laughing loudly at a cartoon one is reading during a formal lecture. Even the latter abridges the freedom to speak without undue interruptions. The rights violation here may be minor; but, like knocking people over in a rush for a plane, it is inconsistent with respecting the dignity of persons. Both cases, then, show that the grounding of rights in dignity is broader than grounding it in the instrumental prohibition central to the Categorical Imperative.

Once it is clear that disrespectful treatment need not be instrumental, we can see that there are not only duties to do certain deeds, but, even in treating people in ways that are obligatory, there are (further) duties of *manner*.[20] These need not have correlative rights. Suppose I am obligated to disengage a co-worker from a wild rosebush. To do it with resentful curses and in a hasty way that disregards the possible scratches would violate the right to be treated decently that goes with our cooperative relationship. I fulfill my duty to liberate; but I do it in a way that is wrong and – whether or not there is a particular virtue I fail to manifest – my conduct is not what is expectable from a *virtuous person*.

---

[20] Duties of manner are explicated in *The Good in the Right*, esp. 179–82.

If we use the notion of disrespectful treatment, understood by contrast with treating persons as befits their dignity, we can say that many rights may be seen as normative protections against disrespectful treatment. We may also use the notion of treating people merely as means – or in ways that approach that negative ideal – to capture part of the idea of a right. A related notion is that of *degrading* conduct toward someone. This is disrespectful, though not everything disrespectful is degrading. Suppose we also posited a right to be treated as an end. If we then took the Categorical Imperative to provide a complete basis for duties, we might conclude that moral obligation is *equivalent* to the obligation to observe moral rights. This view has a surface plausibility, but I want to show that it is mistaken.

III Morally protected moral failures: reprehensible exercises of rights

Do persons have a general right to be treated as ends? Surely not. Suppose the heat goes off in a hotel. One other guest and I are in the lobby. I have no coat and am shivering. The other guest could treat me as an end by lending me a coat. Still, I have no right to this loan. If the cold is just as serious for the other guest, I do not even have a ground for complaint, though I might have a reasonable *expectation* of cooperation in a protective strategy, such as building a fire.

Suppose, however, that the other person has a heavy sweater under the coat and is not even cold. This would give me better reason to expect a loan of the coat. If the person is a friend, it might make it clearly wrong not to lend it. I do not see, however, that this implies my having a right to the loan. The friend's right to keep the coat is compatible with an obligation of friendship that calls for lending it. Indeed, the friend could correctly reply, 'I'm sorry you're cold, but I have a perfect right to keep my coat on'. The same friend, however, might properly feel guilty about declining and might later think that it was wrong not to lend the coat, at least for a limited time.[21] This point implies that the friend *ought* to have lent it.

---

[21] The idea that one might do something one ought not to do, despite having a right to do it, appears at least as early as Judith Jarvis Thomson's "A Defense of Abortion," *Philosophy and Public Affairs* (1971), 47–66. For a later, detailed discussion containing many plausible examples of such cases, see Waldron, "A Right to Do Wrong." See also Thomson's *The Realm of Rights* (Cambridge, Mass.: Harvard University Press, 1990), in which she criticizes the view that "whenever you ought to do a thing, you are under a duty to do it" (61). Another pertinent discussion is Michael J. Meyer, "When Not to Claim Your Rights: The Abuse and Virtuous Use of Rights," *Journal of Political Philosophy* 5, 2 (1997), 149–62. Here and in "Rights Between Friends," *Journal of Philosophy* 89 (1992), 467–83, Meyer shows how one might have a right to claim a right in a case where one should not do so.

A natural reply makes use of the claim that if one has a right to do something, one is *justified* in doing it. If one is justified in doing something, how can it be wrong? Compare belief. If you have a justified belief that *p*, how can you be wrong – roughly, unreasonable – in believing *p*? (You might have a false belief, but truth is not the relevant basis of comparison.) Note that there are degrees of justification. Consider a lottery in which I hold just over half the tickets. Perhaps I may (in a marginal way) justifiedly believe I will win. But here justification would be something like mere intellectual permissibility. Reasonableness is a different notion.[22] It may be *more* reasonable to suspend judgment and, in an important matter, it might be quite unreasonable to believe a proposition whose probability of truth one takes to be barely better than even.

In the rights case, however, there is strong justification in the vicinity: the guest has strong justification for claiming that the coat should not be taken *by force*. But that point leaves ample room for criticism of retaining it. The point may not leave room for *punishability*; but we have already seen that, on any of the major theories of the grounds of rights we have considered, wrong-doing does not entail punishability. The doxastic analogy might be this: believing on marginally satisfactory evidence cannot be positively irrational, but it can be unreasonable, injudicious, or in other ways criticizable.

The doxastic analogy is misleading in one way. Even a minimal justification for believing something implies *some* reason to believe it. By contrast, a right to do something does not imply any reason whatever to do it. I have no reason to exercise my right to telephone a friend to ask for help in thinking about rights; indeed, I have some reason not to do so, including its being an awkward time of day. Rights do, of course, entail reasons for action that *accords* them; but the point here concerns reasons for their *exercise*. I leave open whether, in addition to entailing reasons for accordance, rights partly or wholly *ground* such reasons. If their moral force entirely derives from some kind of "external" grounding, the entailment claim is consistent with the absence of any "internal" grounding. A plausible intermediate view is that, even if rights are not ultimate grounds of (moral) reasons to accord them, they have at least the indirect grounding role implied by serving as a *justification* to do this.

My examples are not of isolated kinds. Indeed, supposing there are ("imperfect") duties of beneficence, they clearly represent prima facie

---

[22] I have provided an account of reasonableness, by contrast with rationality, in *The Architecture of Reason* (Oxford University Press, 2001), esp. 149–53.

obligations whose existence does not entail that anyone has a right to our performing them, whereas that does not seem to hold for the ("perfect") duties, such as non-injury and fidelity. Consider first the duty of benefi- cence and ask whether the following are such that there must be someone who has a correlative right: saving life, relieving suffering, and giving to charity. Take the duty of self-improvement and consider reading good arti- cles that go beyond one's interests, or doing regular exercise. Granted, one can have *other* grounds, such as promises, for doing these things; but others do not have a right to our doing them simply in virtue of our having the relevant duties.

There may even be perfect duties whose exercise, say in a self-sacrificial way, is not something to which their addressees have a right. Consider the duty of fidelity. Would friends automatically have a right to one's risking injurious reprisals in defending them against hecklers? Take the duty of reparation. Do victims have a right to more than the minimum needed for rectification? Nonetheless, one may fail to do what one ought to do in such cases even if one does not fail in a way that violates the rights of the addressee. One may, for instance, have resources that make it easy to do more to compensate the victim than the right to reparation entails. This is akin to the case in which one ought to fulfill a duty of beneficence though no one has a right to one's doing so and one has a right not to. For the duties of fidelity and reparation, however, there are correlative rights to their performance; thus, the point that one may fail to do something one ought to do even where no one has a right to it cuts across the distinction between duties that entail rights to their performance and duties that do not. Even where one has a duty of, say, fidelity, not *everything* one ought to do in fulfilling it need be included in the "core" of deeds to which the beneficiary has a correlative right.

One reply to this line of argument is to claim that the contrast between an imperfect duty and a perfect one is that the former is disjunctive and the latter conjunctive. Thus, there is no particular good deed that, to be beneficent, I must do; I may, for instance, either lend my coat to a shivering guest or do something comparably good; whereas, for, say, the duty not to kill, it is true of all other persons and all types of killing, that (with exceptions such as self-defense) I must not fatally shoot them, must not fatally stab them, must not fatally poison them, and so forth.

Assume this disjunctivist view of imperfect duties for the sake of argu- ment. First, it does not follow that anyone has a right even to one's realizing the disjunction. Second, it does not follow that realizing just *any* disjunct is morally acceptable: I should not leave someone to bleed to death even if I can instead serve in a soup kitchen (another beneficent deed). The former omission would be a serious wrong. Granting that, however, does not require positing a right on the part of the bleeding subject to have me stop to help. Indeed, suppose there is only one person in the world I can help. Does that contingent fact turn a duty that does not entail a right on the beneficiary's part into one that does? On the disjunctivist view, then what we have is a degenerate case with one disjunct, rather than a case in which the strength of the duty must rise with a contingency.

These conclusions are expectable if a moral right is a normative protection from a certain kind of coercive conduct. For there is no reason to think that this protection implies the rightness of doing the (non-coercive) deeds in question, much less protection from sound moral criticism for doing them. That conception of rights, then, has at least the benefit of this much explanatory power. It is an interesting question whether legal rights differ in this respect. Perhaps you cannot do something legally *wrong* if acting within your legal rights. One could, however, do something legally *unwise* even if not legally wrong. There might also be acts that, at a given time, are legally permissible but constitutionally wrong. Perhaps moral rights are, as it were, articulations of something analogous to statutes, whereas moral appraisal derives from a wider set of standards.

IV Ideals, oughts, and duties

It might be thought that it is only *ideals* that form the basis of the criticisms I claim to be possible regarding actions that do not constitute rights violations and show that there can be wrongs within rights. I doubt this, but there are different kinds of ideals, and some kinds may be invoked to clarify how morality goes beyond rights and why rights do not exhaust oughts.

Consider forgiveness as an ideal. It can be both difficult to achieve and a good thing for both forgiver and forgiven. It is not an ideal for everyone, though it must be for some, say Christians. The same holds for gentleness, which differs from forgiveness in governing the manner of action more than its *content*, which, in my terminology, is the act-type to which it belongs. By contrast, sincerity and veracity are ideals for moral agents in general. This point is not utopian; but if 'ideal' suggests the utopian, 'standard' could also be used for the points that follow.

The sense in which these positive elements constitute ideals is partly captured by their goodness together with their difficulty of attainment. I take an ideal for conduct to be at least this: a standard that can in principle be met by varying kinds of conduct and at varying levels of closeness to perfect realization. But there is something more. There is no general right on the part of others to our *complete* sincerity or even our complete honesty, and so for ideals in general. If we are asked highly intrusive questions that ought not to be asked, we may be indirect or, in some special cases, less than veracious, without violating the questioner's rights (or going beyond ours). This is not to say that we *should* be so, only that our being so does not violate others' rights.

It would be a mistake, however, to treat the ideals of veracity and sincerity as just discretionary. They correspond to virtues of character that moral agents as such should have and should try to cultivate. The associated virtues (which here bear the same names) may be possessed by people who do not completely fulfill the ideals, but there are limits to how far below complete fulfillment a truly virtuous person may fall. My point, however, concerns all moral agents, virtuous or not. I am particularly interested in what such ideals show about the relation between acting within one's rights and doing what one should. I hold that moral agents, even when they meet minimally satisfactory standards of sincerity and veracity – and so act within their rights in these domains – may not be indifferent to sincerity and veracity as ideals appropriate to judging them. That in some cases one has a right to tell only part of the wanted truth does not imply that one may not be morally criticized by being less veracious and sincere than one ought to be.

By contrast, the ideals of generosity and, even more, of conversational charm or athletic prowess, are, from the moral point of view, *voluntary ideals*: morally optional standards. Moral agents need not have athletic prowess, conversational charm, or even generosity as goals. Again, we can see that there are things we ought to do that we have a right not to do and that, correspondingly, no one has a right to demand. We ought to be sincere and veracious, and we are criticizable for failure to achieve these ideals at a rather high level even if this level cannot be demanded of us as moral agents, as non-injury can be. But, insofar as one can lack generosity without lacking beneficence, generosity cannot be demanded of us simply as moral agents. Conversational charm certainly may not be.

More specifically, there is a level of sincerity and veracity – which may be higher or lower in different circumstances – such that we *ought* to achieve it even though we have a right to fall short of it. Granted, close friends talking to each other is one thing; defense attorneys speaking for their clients is another. Still, there is *also* a level of attainment of these and other standards – a minimal level of moral acceptability – that we have no right to fall below. If moral rights are a kind of normative protection, it should be no surprise that, on the one hand, they warrant opposition to conduct that falls far enough below a moral standard to be a danger, and, on the other hand, they do not warrant demands for conduct that goes beyond satisfying moral standards to a minimally acceptable level.

If I am correct in holding that rights do not exhaust oughts, it is a short step to the conclusion that duties *also* do not exhaust oughts, at least not if duties are conceived as Rossian prima facie moral obligations. We can be morally criticized for failure to meet certain standards even if we had nothing naturally called a duty to do what is in question or indeed a moral obligation (if that notion is associated with conduct that may be demanded of us even in a way that does not rise to claiming we would be violating a right by non-performance).

Among the ways that help to mark the threefold distinction in question is a contrast of terms appropriate to different kinds of moral failure. If I fail to accord someone a right, the act(s) in question may be *demanded* of me. If I fail to fulfill a duty of beneficence, as where I quickly pass a distressed stranger who has fallen and is alone and in pain, I am subject to moral *reprimand* (or *complaint*): not only to disapproval but to moral pressure to do my duty. If I fail to fulfill an involuntary ideal that does not coincide with a duty (as where I make charitable donations to the extent that is my obligation but can afford much more), I am subject to moral criticism, but not reprimand; I am subject to disapproval but not necessarily to moral pressure to meet the standard. The wrongs in question differ, in turn, in that the first category of wrongs entails a duty of reparation, whereas the second and third do not, though they differ in what they imply about the agent's morality at the time. Both kinds of deed are contrary to what good character requires. The distinction between them is not sharp, but the third characteristically counts less than the second against one's having good character.[23]

Take as an example something akin to sincerity: forthrightness. This is a candidate for an involuntary ideal, but it is in any case a *domain-specific*

---

[23] If this is right, then Ross's view that a "wrongful act" (*The Right and the Good*, 21) creates a duty of reparation should be understood to apply to a certain kind of wrong, not to just any case in which we do the (morally) wrong thing and ought to have done something else. It is plausible to take the view to hold only where the agent has done a wrong *to* someone (or "wronged" someone). The paradigms of such wrongs will be coercive in the broad sense sketched in this paper, including restrictions of freedom by, e.g., threats, physical injuries, lies, and broken promises. If we consider apology a minimal case of reparation, we may perhaps say that violations of the duty of beneficence characteristically generate *that* duty of reparation but not the same duties of reparation as unjustified coercive conduct.

ideal. For friendship, it is not optional, whereas some ideals, such as excellence of style, which is voluntary, and respect for persons, which is involuntary, apply so pervasively that they bear on any domain of life. Now, I am morally obligated to be minimally forthright in speaking with a friend. But I have some discretion as to how forthright to be on delicate matters, such as the private life of a friend of both of us. I (normally) must not lie or be entirely evasive, but I can be brief and highly selective in what I say. It is possible here to be as forthright as obligation demands but not as forthright as fully befits the friendship in the context. I may later think that in saying what I did I was not being a good friend, even if I was also not being a bad one. The deed merits disapproval but not reprimand. I should have done better, in a sense of 'should' that goes with virtues of character rather than with fulfillment of duty.[24]

It is a mistake, then, to think that *whenever* an act justifies moral criticism there is at least an imperfect duty to perform it. Some things we ought to do are at least not happily described as duties or, even more broadly, as obligations. An involuntary ideal whose satisfaction in a given context is readily within my reach does not (or certainly need not) create a duty, but I should meet it as closely as is possible for me. We could use 'duty' in a broad sense in which anything we do that warrants moral criticism violates a duty; but although this broad usage is perhaps defensible, it is less clarifying than maintaining that some involuntary ideals, such as ideals of sincerity, provide a rationale for moral criticism that does not entail violation of a duty.

---

[24] In a critique of my position on the balance between religious and secular reasons, Philip L. Quinn says, regarding a use I made of the distinction between duties and certain *oughts* that go with involuntary ideals, "[S]omeone who merely fails to live up to an ideal only deserves criticism for not reaching some lofty level of excellence . . . Ideals of citizenship specify what only the citizen of outstanding virtue will normally do, even if, when they are not optional for citizens on account of being involuntary, every citizen must endorse them." See "Religion and Politics, Fear and Duty," in Jeremiah Haskett and Jerald Wallulis, eds., *Philosophy of Religion for a New Century* (Dordrecht: Kluwer, 2004), 314. I agree that properly acknowledging an involuntary ideal does not imply that one morally ought to fulfill it at the highest level, but the claim neglects a distinction between achieving *the ideal* in a given spectrum, say, the communication situations to which sincerity is relevant, and achieving, to *some* degree, one or more *ideals of* that spectrum, where the degree might be lower than this but higher than the minimal level one has a *right* to take as normatively adequate. The former is normally understood as implying a pinnacle, a point of excellence leaving nothing to be desired, and I nowhere imply that one is criticizable for not reaching that level. I conceive ideals as achievable to different degrees and have emphasized – in, e.g., *Religious Commitment and Secular Reason* (Cambridge University Press, 2000), the work Quinn is discussing – that there are degrees of fulfillment of ideals that, in certain cases, one ought to achieve though one has a right not to. In this paper I suggest that in some such cases one might not be properly said to have a duty to reach this degree either.

On my view, we can say that although there is a duty of beneficence, there are *also* ideals of beneficence. There is an involuntary ideal of beneficence by which we may be properly judged as morally deficient even if we do not violate our duties of beneficence; and there is a higher, voluntary ideal of beneficence, a kind appropriate to saints and not such that ordinary people's failure to live up to it is morally criticizable. This illustrates that in saying that we ought to be beneficent in a given situation of choice, the 'ought' may express any of at least three different things: (1) an ascription of duty, with no implication that someone has a correlative right to its fulfillment (as would be so with, e.g., duties of non-injury) but with the implication that non-performance subjects one to reprimand and moral pressure to conform; (2) a moral standard we should fulfill and are criticizable for not fulfilling, though fulfilling it is not strictly a duty or our moral obligation and non-fulfillment need not subject us to moral pressure to meet the standard; and (3) an ideal that it is admirable to fulfill even though we are not criticizable for failing to do so. The last case is naturally called *supererogation*; but a wider use of the term would apply to at least some cases of (2).

Perhaps one reason why ideals – especially but not only involuntary ones – are so easily assimilated to duties (or obligations) is that often the same term, such as 'beneficence', 'fidelity', or 'sincerity', can be used to refer to either duties or ideals. The distinction between involuntary ideals and prima facie duties is in any case not sharp. There are not only duties of (for instance) beneficence which we have a right not to fulfill yet ought to fulfill; there are also beneficent deeds we ought to perform that are not properly considered duties. These satisfy involuntary ideals. And there are stronger duties, including those of non-injury, that we have no right not to fulfill and others have a right to demand we fulfill.

* * *

I have explored the idea that general moral rights may be broadly conceived as normative protections from a certain kind of coercive conduct. This presupposes that rights entail duties, and it applies most clearly to liberty rights, though it can be illuminatingly applied to other kinds of moral rights, such as special rights, provided coercive conduct is understood with suitable breadth. Even if the normative protections that rights provide have greater breadth than this conception can accommodate, rights are certainly normative protections from *some* kinds of conduct by others and provide a basis for demands that they be accorded to their bearers. As normative protections, rights play an important role in moral discourse and moral reasoning. But they need not be taken as basic moral notions. They may be grounded, and their force largely explained, by a number of moral theories. I favor a partly Kantian grounding that stresses the dignity of persons as a unifying notion and emphasizes rationality, the capacity for agency, and (though this is perhaps not prominent in Kant) the capacity for joy and suffering as major elements underlying dignity.

In the light of this perspective on rights, I have argued that although there are many rights governing many domains of conduct, rights do not encompass all human conduct. There are acts that are neither protected by a right to perform them nor prohibited by a right against performing them; there are also deeds that we have a right to perform but would be morally criticizable for doing. Some but by no means all of these acts are objects of "imperfect" duties, say of beneficence. Others are objects of involuntary ideals. These ideals show a major point about morality: the protection from coercion that rights represent does not carry protection from sound moral criticism.

We can do the wrong thing even when we are exercising a right. Rights, then, cannot be the basis of morality. They may, however, be indispensable in stating certain moral facts; even if there are normative statements that are necessarily equivalent to rights ascriptions, they differ both in conceptual content and in pragmatic role. Whether there are equivalent statements depends on how rights are grounded. I have shown that they can be non-reductively grounded, but not that no reductive grounding can succeed. Even if none can succeed, there are still reasons to hold that, as effective as claiming rights can be in calling attention to wrong-doing, our moral conduct cannot be adequately described, appraised, and guided without appeal to obligations, virtues, and moral ideals.[25]

[25] This paper has benefited from discussion at a colloquium on Reasons, Freedom, and Responsibility held at the University of Helsinki in 2004 and from presentations at the University of Notre Dame and Wake Forest University. For comments on earlier versions I am also grateful to Brad Hooker, Alasdair MacIntyre, Hugh McCann, David Solomon, John Tasioulas, and Nicholas Wolterstorff.

CHAPTER 10

Religion and the politics of science
Can evolutionary biology be religiously neutral?

Political decisions should be appropriately informed, and in much of the world the information that legislators and voters rely on is based on the results of scientific inquiry. If that inquiry is not itself free of political and other biases, then its role in providing a kind of neutral common ground between opposing political forces is threatened. Skepticism about the 'value-neutrality' of science is not new, but the striking advances and wider teaching of evolutionary biology have brought out both more writings and more protests by those who consider it biased against certain religious views and have made the question of its role in scientific education politically controversial. Evolutionary biology is a standard topic in scientific education in much of the world; but at least in the USA it remains a focus of controversy, and the growth of fundamentalist populations may be reason to think that it may become similarly controversial in other countries. This article explores the question whether evolutionary biology – and particularly the teaching of it – can be religiously neutral. The article will also have a wider bearing: it will argue for a general conception of scientific inquiry in relation to both religion and ethics, and it will outline a notion of religious neutrality that may be useful for both political theory and science policy.

In the USA many people who reject the religious neutrality of scientific inquiry have insisted that creationism be taught side by side with evolutionary theory, and the name 'creation science' has been used to suggest that this curricular demand does not imply that science instructors should endorse any religious position. The name 'intelligent design' (ID) is also intended to imply that science teachers introducing that perspective need not be committed to a religious position. The courts in the USA will likely continue to examine this issue.[1] A major focus of their considerations has

---

[1] For recent discussion of the Supreme Court's decisions on the kind of neutrality in question, as well as for analysis of what constitutes such neutrality, see Kent Greenawalt, *Does God Belong in Public*

been what constitutes neutrality toward religion. One of my aims is to clarify the issue and to propose a framework for guiding public policy regarding science and religion and, especially, for structuring science education. One of my hopes is to help in reducing the tensions now causing difficulties both for education in science and for civic harmony.

I   The scope and methodology of science

There is no need here to define 'science', but I will assume that paradigms are the natural sciences, especially physics, chemistry, and biology. The term 'science' applies, however, to psychology and the other 'human sciences', different though they are from the natural sciences. What all of these disciplines have in common that is particularly relevant to our topic is a use of scientific method and a tendency to foster what has been called *a scientific habit of mind*.

Scientific method is the subject of a huge literature. Here I can discuss only three important elements that bear on the status and teaching of evolutionary biology – and religiously motivated theoretical challenges to it – in pluralistic societies.

Testability

First, it is widely believed that a scientific hypothesis (indeed any statement belonging to science) must be observationally testable, in the sense that in principle some observations could confirm or disconfirm it. Testability in principle is more than the mere logical possibility of testing but less than its technological feasibility. The notion cannot be precisely defined; but we may say that scientists tend to demand of a proposed hypothesis that those competent in the relevant field at least see what kinds of empirically possible observations would tend to confirm or disconfirm it.

Testability has been identified with falsifiability.[2] There is such a thing as falsification of a hypothesis to the satisfaction of competent judges; but falsifiability is not equivalent to testability. *Logically* speaking, apart from special exceptions unlikely to be important for understanding scientific method, existential claims (those asserting the existence of something)

Schools? (Princeton University Press, 2005). For further discussion on neutrality and particularly on non-establishment and on the related ethics appropriate to a liberal democracy, see Michael J. Perry, *Under God: Religious Faith and Liberal Democracy* (Cambridge University Press, 2003).

[2] Karl Popper is the most widely known proponent of the falsifiability criterion. See especially *The Logic of Scientific Discovery* (London: Hutchinson, 1959), originally published in German in 1934.

can be verified and disconfirmed, but not falsified.[3] Suppose it is claimed that human beings will ultimately be found elsewhere in the universe. This is in principle verifiable but it cannot be strictly falsified. There might be experiments that disconfirm it and well-confirmed theoretical grounds to consider it improbable, but such results would at most render it highly improbable. Similarly, logically speaking, universal propositions (of a scientific kind), say that all metals conduct electricity, can be falsified (by counter-example) but not verified – in the strong sense entailing that they are decisively established.[4]

Consider also what counts as observability. Take a psychological hypothesis to the effect that if I have a certain sequence of thoughts, I will next have a certain mental image. The entire test could be conducted mentally. Contrary to the usual assumption that observability must be through the five senses, here we have *experienceability* but not, strictly speaking, observability. Must we say that the experiment is not scientific? I doubt that; but in any case there is something crucial for scientific inquiry that the example does not challenge, namely that the confirmatory relevance of experience is crucial for scientific status.

Publicity

I have assumed both that mental phenomena are of scientific interest and that our mental lives are in a certain way private. To see how the latter assumption can be squared with the idea that science is "public," we might generalize our psychological hypothesis to the claim that *anyone* who has the relevant sequence of thoughts will have a certain image, where the thoughts are abstract but the image is of, say, Jesus. This generalization meets a kind of *publicity test*: any competent person could run the experiment and give publicly observable testimony as to its outcome. Publicity is in fact the second element in a very common conception of scientific method, perhaps the standard conception of it if there is one. In part, this requirement is needed both to rule out epistemically prejudicial idiosyncrasy and to

---

[3] This has reference mainly to existential claims likely to be of scientific interest, such as that there is an as yet undiscovered planet. If we think of artificially simple cases, e.g. that there is a purple patch in my visual field, then my considering this introspectively and *not* finding one would in some good sense falsify the claim. But the solar system is not so easily scanned, and a planet could escape discovery in a way a colored patch in consciousness apparently cannot.

[4] This is not quite the same as the point that general ('scientific') propositions cannot be *proved*, in a sense implying a valid argument for them from premises that are at least beyond reasonable doubt. It is consistent with holding that they may be validly deduced from more comprehensive principles. For one thing, the relevant ones may not be beyond reasonable doubt; for another, this is not normally considered a kind of verification.

accommodate the cooperative character of scientific endeavor. If I discover a connection between silent utterance of certain sequences of words and the formation of certain mental images, this should be a publicly testable result even if each person seeking direct confirmation must ascertain the connection internally.

To be sure, if *reports* of the results could not be publicly produced and made accessible to competent observers, we would not regard the experiment as meeting the publicity condition. It may be true that we cannot directly verify someone's report of an inner experience, such as imaging a person; but even to check on someone's perceptions of what is experienced in the public domain (such as the color of a precipitate), we have to rely on other perceptions, and here we count on sensory experiences to reveal properties of external objects. Those experiences are no less interior than any other mental phenomena. Publicity implies a kind of intersubjectivity, but it does not require either perceptual infallibility or exclusive reliance on non-mental phenomena.

Empiricality

A third element important in understanding scientific method is its restriction to empirical matters. This restriction may be argued to follow from testability. Perhaps, but it does not obviously follow. The idea underlying the restriction is, in part, to set aside inquiries in logic or pure mathematics. These fields may be regarded as non-empirical without being considered *un*scientific, nor are they. Still, however competent in these fields some scientists may be, the claims of logic and mathematics are not usually considered the kinds science investigates.[5] A major contrast here is between the empirical and the a priori. At one time many would have said, following Kant, that the a priori is equivalent to the necessary and hence science must be concerned with what is both empirical and contingent. It seems clear, however, that what is necessary, say that water is H_2O, need not be a priori.[6] A necessary truth, then, can be discovered empirically, even if the higher-order fact that it *is* necessary is not itself an empirical matter.

---

[5] To be sure, the well-known work of W. V. Quine challenges the distinction made here and would instead simply provide distinctions among degrees of generality. Some such distinctions might serve my purposes here, but I have defended a stronger distinction in, for example, ch. 4 of my *Epistemology* (London: Routledge, 2003).

[6] The work of Saul Kripke and others, however, has apparently shown this. See especially his *Naming and Necessity* (Cambridge, Mass.: Harvard University Press, 1980). Cf. Aristotle's view that *scientia*, which includes knowledge of natural patterns, has the necessary as its object.

Suppose that necessary propositions are not ruled out of the domain of scientific confirmability. An important consequence is that certain necessary theological propositions might be scientifically confirmable. That God's existence is empirically confirmable has long been held by proponents of the argument from design (by which I mean, roughly, the argument from the order in nature to the existence of God as needed to explain it – or at least as what best explains it). To be sure, theists need not take the existence of God to be necessary. In that case, an empiricality requirement alone would be plainly compatible with the scientific confirmability of theism.

Fallibilism

In addition to testability, publicity, and empiricality, fallibilism as a procedural attitude has also been thought essential to scientific method. I call it procedural because the point is about scientific *practice* and the epistemic claims made in assessing it; the actual psychological disposition of scientists engaging in the practice is of secondary importance. In my view, procedural fallibilism is a better candidate for a requirement on proper *use* of scientific method than partly definitory of scientific method itself. A dogmatic person could successfully use scientific method to confirm hypotheses and could even acquire knowledge through using it. But given the fallibility of both the procedures used and those who use them, the person would have an inappropriate attitude. If fallibilism as a procedural attitude is above all (roughly) an openness to the possibility of one's being mistaken even in what seems obvious or established, it is indeed necessary for a scientific attitude. But clearly fallibilism is also appropriate in theology and other fields.

If we now note that the occurrence of religious experiences can be both predicted from theological assertions and also experienced, we can begin to see that the kinds of demarcation criteria we have been considering do not strictly show that no theological hypothesis is experimentally, or at least observationally, testable. To be sure, theologians and lay religious people have rarely staked their faith on predictions. But consider an example of a religiously significant prediction: that ardent believers who pray wholeheartedly will more often than not feel better immediately afterwards. This can actually be confirmed or disconfirmed. Suppose it is true. Its truth does not, of course, entail the existence of God, and skeptical scientists will likely say that the explanation of the pattern lies in secular psychology. Let us grant this for the sake of argument. It should be balanced by the point that it is common for clearly scientific hypotheses to be explainable in more than one way; so, just as different scientists may retain conflicting theories to explain data they agree on, theists may claim that the confirmation of this hypothesis would constitute *some* evidence for divine action in the world.

The demarcation problem and theological testability

Suppose we set aside these difficulties of analysis and conceive scientific method in relation to the three criteria that, in some form, can withstand scrutiny: observational testability, publicity, and empiricality. We might then partly characterize a scientific claim (a hypothesis or a full-scale theory) as one that can in principle be confirmed or disconfirmed using this method. The problem – *the demarcation problem* – is to distinguish scientific claims, in the broad sense of claims appropriately assessable by using scientific method, from others, such as those of logic on one side and theology on another side. A great deal has been written on this problem.[7] All I need to do here is further indicate the difficulty of ruling out certain kinds of claims, including some by creationists or intelligent design theorists, as non-scientific. In the light of that, we can better assess how those views should be treated in (among other important areas) public education and governmental funding of scientific inquiry.

It is commonly thought that theological claims are intrinsically un-testable empirically.[8] But consider the claim that God will produce hail at noon. This cannot be *established* by observation, since the occurrence would only confirm it but would leave open what *caused* the hail. Yet it is empirically confirmable and, more obviously, empirically disconfirmable (when no hail falls). Still, what of human origins? It could be claimed that we can confirm 'God created the earth in 4004 BC' if this implies that

---

[7] Some philosophers believe that the demarcation problem is probably insoluble: "The prospects for this [drawing a line between science and non-science] are dim. Twentieth-century philosophy of science is littered with the smoldering remains of attempts to do just that." See Alexander George, "What's Wrong with Intelligent Design, and with Its Critics," *Christian Science Monitor*, 22 December, 2005, p. 9. In his view, then, "either we should find alternatives to the courts to protect our curricula from bad science [as opposed to non-science] or we should start arguing in court that the separation of church and state would be violated by intelligent design's injection into the science curriculum on account of its predominantly religious motivation" ("What's Wrong with Intelligent Design," p. 9). Though slightly less pessimistic than George about the possibility of determining a reasonable demarcation, I agree (as will be evident in the text) that doing so is not the best way to proceed; but it will also be evident that I would put little weight on motivation.

[8] In the post-positivist era unfalsifiability was a common charge against theistic claims. See, for example, Anthony Flew's challenge replied to in detail by John Hick in "Theology and Verification," *Theology Today* 17 (1960), 12–31.

we will both find faults in, say, carbon dating and develop a new dating system that confirms this time of origin. I do not see how this scenario can be shown inconceivable.[9]

Let us leave creationism aside for the present. The intelligent design view is more modest. In principle *some* version of it might yield predictions about how human brains are constructed or how human beings would adjust to certain changes, predictions that could be confirmed or disconfirmed in months or a few years.[10] We do not (to my knowledge) find such predictions emerging from ID theorists. Some critics would hold that the positions are not even clear enough for predictions of these sorts to be said to follow from them (even with high probability), in which case their observationally bearing out is not confirmatory. Even if this is so, there remains the idea that only what *best* (or well) explains observable phenomena is thereby confirmed. This idea raises more questions than can be pursued here. One is what counts as a good explanation; another is whether predictive power is a condition for qualifying as one. Still another is whether being best is enough: why should the best of a number of *poor* explanations be supported at all by what it explains? (I here assume for the sake of argument the legitimacy of a loose usage that may be controversial: that we can properly speak of explanations that are not wholly *factive*, i.e. contain only true explaining and explained propositions.)

Methodological vs. metaphysical questions

The elements of scientific method so far emphasized are methodological, not ontological. Neither the testability nor the publicity nor the empirical character of scientific hypotheses entails any substantive ontological conclusion, such as that only natural events can be causes or that there cannot be an infinite chain of causes extending into the past. But it is commonly and plausibly held that a commitment to scientific method presupposes a commitment to *methodological naturalism* (MN): roughly, the view that causes and explanations of natural phenomena should be sought in the natural world, paradigmatically in terms of what meets the other three

---

[9] It has been argued that theism, indeed Christian theism, is testable *eschatologically*, i.e. by experiences one could have after bodily death in what would be reasonably considered a resurrection world. For the original statement of the case see Hick, "Theology and Verification."

[10] There are many versions of ID, and considering any of them in detail is beyond my scope here. But note the latitudinarianism of this general formula is: "Intelligent Design is the hypothesis that in order to explain life it is necessary to suppose the action of an unevolved intelligence." See William A. Dembski and Michael Ruse (eds.), *Debating Design: From Darwin to DNA* (Cambridge University Press, 2004), p. 3. This volume contains informative papers on both sides of the debate.

criteria (testability, publicity, and empiricality) *and* does not presuppose supernatural agency. Granted, this view is no clearer than the notion of the natural (a problem addressed below), but a standard assumption is that the physical is paradigmatically natural and that God as understood in any major monotheistic religion is supernatural.

Methodological naturalism neither affirms nor denies theism. In this, it is like liberal democracy itself, which is the kind of society that provides the context of our discussion. MN constrains the conduct of scientific inquiry but implies no substantive conclusions of either science or, especially, metaphysics.

My formulation of methodological naturalism allows that scientific inquiry might posit causal elements, such as the Big Bang, which may be argued to *require* (in a non-formal sense of 'require') a supernatural cause. The point is that, methodologically and epistemically, one would need no evidence of any supernatural proposition in order to conduct scientific inquiry and confirm scientific hypotheses. One might, then, qualify as using scientific method to understand the world even if one takes the Big Bang to have a supernatural cause, provided one does not treat such a factor as essential in the content or confirmation of one's scientific work.[11] A methodological naturalist might even hold that *every* natural event, whether mental or physical, has a natural cause and even a sufficient naturalistic – indeed perhaps physicalistic – explanation, *as well as* a theistic explanation, provided that the latter, supernaturalist claim is no part of one's scientific account.[12]

Given this conception of MN, the best response to the demarcation problem for the purposes of this article is to draw four tentative conclusions:

1   There very well may be no way to show that theological hypotheses are intrinsically untestable by observation or experience.[13]

---

[11] This requirement needs discussion. A scientist could, for instance, argue in a theological paper that the scientific findings imply divine action or even that proper confirmation of them presupposes that God guarantees the reliability of our sense-perception. But these points, even if true, are not part of the scientific account and would not prevent an atheist from understanding and confirming the scientific theory developed within methodological naturalist constraints.

[12] The suggestion that there might be theistic as well as naturalistic explanations of the same events is not uncontroversial. Jaegwon Kim, for example, has proposed the idea (which many scientifically minded thinkers find plausible) of the 'causal closure' of the physical domain (entailing that every physical event has a causally sufficient physical condition), and he has argued that overdetermination (the presence of two independent causally sufficient conditions) cannot be posited between the mental (which would include divine fiats) and the physical. See, for example, his *Mind in a Physical World* (Cambridge, Mass.: MIT Press, 1999). It should be added that even naturalistic explainability of all events in physical terms need not be understood so as to imply *determinism*; the explanatory laws in question need not be considered deterministic rather than statistical.

[13] Cf. Daniel C. Dennett: "The postulation of invisible, undetectable effects that (unlike atoms and germs) are *systematically* immune to confirmation or disconfirmation is so common that such effects

2 It does not follow (and is not true) that, if they *are* observationally testable, they thereby represent good scientific hypotheses (or scientific hypotheses of any sort).

3 There is no good reason to think that every significant scientific hypothesis or theory in a given domain should be introduced into science teaching in that domain, especially at the pre-college level.

4 The common and not unreasonable commitment to MN in the moderate form described above implies that any creationist or ID view that presupposes or self-evidently entails a supernaturalistic proposition is not a proper object of scientific appraisal. (This is not to say that scientific evidence cannot be in some way *relevant* to such a view.)

In the light of what we have so far seen, I believe that although there apparently are plausible methodological criteria of demarcation that many creationist or ID views do not satisfy, those criteria do not warrant wholesale rejection of all possible hypotheses from those domains as non-scientific. Why, then, should some of them not be included in even pre-college courses seriously treating evolution?

II Is the scientific habit of mind theologically neutral?

The point that a theological hypothesis is not intrinsically insusceptible of observational confirmation should be balanced by two others. One is that such hypotheses are not normally put forward in a way that makes it clear *how* they might be observationally confirmed. A second is that scientists working as such are commonly committed, even if tacitly, to methodological naturalism and hence view their work as concerned with understanding and predicting natural phenomena in terms of laws and phenomena in the natural world. This is perhaps implicit in the standard use of the term 'natural science' as contrasted with 'the humanities', 'theology', or 'pure mathematics'. Might we go further and say that the scientific habit of mind is naturalistic as opposed to supernaturalistic? The question is important for philosophy in general and scientific education in particular because an affirmative answer would imply that the teaching of science is by its very nature not entirely neutral toward the truth of religious views.

In speaking of the scientific habit of mind I refer not just to an intellectual orientation but also to a practical commitment to using scientific methods

are sometimes taken as definitive. No religion lacks them, and anything that lacks them is not really a religion, however much it is like a religion in other regards." See *Breaking the Spell: Religion as a Natural Phenomenon* (New York: Viking, 2006), p. 164. We have already seen reason to doubt these strong claims, and, on the plausible nine-point characterization of religion given below, nothing in the concept of a religion implies them.

in the pursuit of empirical questions. Defining this idea would take much space, but the idea is sufficiently clear for my use of it here. I would add, however, that I take the scientific habit of mind to imply a tendency, even in non-empirical matters, to seek data, to try to explain them by appeal to theoretical notions, and to be willing to revise theory in the light of data and – sometimes – to reinterpret data in the light of theory. (I am also taking questions of logic and pure mathematics and, more controversially, ethics, to be non-empirical.)

It may seem that even scientific *method* sets science at odds with religious commitment. For scientific method is easily taken to entail not only using experimentation as a central way of achieving knowledge, but also taking the view that science alone can yield general knowledge, or at least any general knowledge outside logic and mathematics. Assessing this controversial view is not possible here.[14] Surely the sound point in this vicinity is that scientific method is *applicable in principle* to any kind of empirical question about the world, probably *relevant* to all such questions, and *needed* for some of them. This point is in no tension with classical theism, on which the physical universe is a creation of an omniscient, omnipotent, omnibenevolent God.

Indeed, for many religious traditions, including at least Christianity and Judaism, the scientific study of nature is readily viewed as an attempt to understand God's creation. One can view scientific inquiry as a use of reason conceived as a natural endowment from God. What about the theory of evolution? The theory is clearly inconsistent with the account of creation given in Genesis interpreted *literally*. But literal interpretation of scripture is not a requirement of a reasonable theology and is increasingly rejected by educated biblical interpreters. This is not to suggest that there can be no tension between scientific results and some scripturally based beliefs on the part of a religiously committed person. The point is that it is theologically implausible to think of scripture as competing with scientific inquiry with respect to answering the same questions. One possibility, for instance, is to take the account in Genesis to be affirming (among other things, to be sure) the creative action and the sovereignty of God. These generic attributions are compatible with the theory of evolution.[15]

---

[14] I have defended the possibility of substantive a priori knowledge in "Skepticism about the A Priori: Self-Evidence, Defeasibility, and *Cogito* Propositions," in John Greco (ed.), *The Oxford Handbook of Skepticism* (Oxford University Press, 2008), pp. 149–75.

[15] Eliott Sober uses the term 'theistic evolutionism' for the view that "evolution is God's way of making organisms." See *Evidence and Evolution* (Cambridge University Press, 2008), p. 110. In the main his position in the book is consistent with the view taken here of the demarcation problem and the metaphysical neutrality of evolutionary theory. See, for example, ch. 2, "Intelligent Design."

But, one might reply, isn't the evolutionary account of our genesis physicalistic, and doesn't the physicalism in question entail a conception of human beings that is at odds with the dualistic view that some find in the Bible, or at least in the Christian tradition? I do not see that the evolutionary account is inconsistent with dualism, particularly the modest *property dualism* on which mental properties are irreducible to physical ones even if – as on substance monism – there is only one kind of *substance*. For all that, I suspect that the closer biological science comes to explaining the origin and development of human beings, the more it will seem to some people that a physicalistic view of the human person is receiving confirmation. I find this association understandable, and its strength is part of what underlies some religious people's hostility to evolutionary biology. Nonetheless, the evolutionary account of human origins is genetic and biological, not metaphysical. Above all, providing physicalistic conditions (such as biochemical ones) for the genesis of biologically identified human beings leaves open whether or not they are wholly physical in *constitution*.

Evolutionary science also leaves open two other important views. The first is that *normative* properties, such as being intrinsically good, being virtuous, and being obligatory, are not physical or even "natural." The second is that survival of bodily death does not have to be either rejected or understood in terms of, say, a resurrection body with physical properties appropriate to sustain personhood.[16]

If evolutionary science is neutral with respect to physicalism about our ultimate psychological constitution, presumably the scientific enterprise as a whole is too. For plainly psychology and the other social sciences can be scientifically pursued without the assumption of physicalism about the human person; and the physical sciences certainly are pursued without this assumption.

III Philosophical naturalism as a worldview

Many who have the scientific habit of mind are committed to something more: philosophical naturalism. Often the term 'philosophical' is omitted, but I think it will soon be clear that naturalism in a commonly accepted form, and in a version in which it is widely considered a worldview incompatible with theism, is a philosophical position.

---

[16] Hick, in "Theology and Verification," argues for the possibility of a resurrection body that sustains both personhood and individuality. I have critically assessed his case in "Eschatological Verification and Personal Identity," *International Journal for Philosophy of Religion* 7 (4) (1976), 393–408.

There is no consensus about just what constitutes philosophical naturalism. In metaphysics, naturalism is both a reaction against supernaturalism (especially theism) and, in some versions, a rejection of mind–body dualism. Philosophical naturalists certainly reject Cartesian dualism and tend to favor materialism about even mental properties, even if they countenance non-material abstract entities. In ethics, naturalism forswears irreducible concepts of value and obligation, or, in more cautious versions, irreducible moral and axiological *properties*. And in epistemology, naturalism is above all the attempt to account for knowledge and justification using notions amenable to scientific treatment, particularly common-sense observation concepts and concepts of physics and psychology. Epistemological naturalists tend to be more friendly than metaphysical naturalists toward countenancing a property dualism on which mental properties are distinct from physical ones. But, although property dualism is not incompatible with either kind of naturalism, nearly all naturalists consider some kind of materialism or, perhaps more broadly, physicalism, to comport with their ideals better than does property dualism.

Is there a unifying conception of naturalism in all these realms? One could be a naturalist in denying the existence of transcendent beings, but a non-naturalist in the philosophy of mind, ethics, or epistemology. Indeed, holding a form of naturalism in any one of these domains may well leave one free to reject it in all the others. Perhaps philosophical naturalism in the main overall sense – a sense that might unify naturalism in these several domains – is roughly the view that nature is all there is, and the only basic truths are truths of nature. But what is nature? The notion does not encompass an omniscient, omnipotent, omnibenevolent God, but perhaps it can include mental phenomena, at least mental properties even if not minds conceived as non-embodied substances.

It will best serve our purposes to assume that philosophical naturalism is not committed to physicalism about the mental, at least regarding mental properties as opposed to mental substances, though philosophical naturalists do consider a physicalistic ontology to be an ideal we should try to achieve.[17] I also assume that philosophical naturalism is not committed to empiricism, even if most of its proponents tend to be empiricists. Modern philosophical naturalists generally are committed, however, to what we

---

[17] Cf. Alan Donagan: "Naturalism can take as many forms as there are conceptions of nature . . . it has come to be accepted that, if there is nothing but nature, then there is nothing but matter in space-time. Naturalism has become materialism." See "Can Anybody in a Post-Christian Culture Really Believe in the Nicene Creed?," in *Reflections on Philosophy and Religion*, ed. Anthony N. Perovitch, Jr. (Oxford University Press, 1999), p. 24.

might call *the epistemological sovereignty of science*: roughly the view that (1) scientific method, broadly understood to include the use of logic and mathematics, is the paradigm of a rational way to seek general knowledge and (2) the sciences are the only authoritative source of general empirical knowledge, where empirical knowledge is understood to include any knowledge (or, loosely, justified true belief) concerning 'the world', particularly the 'external world' but on some views even the inner domain of consciousness. The associated metaphysical view would have as a major element a commitment to countenancing entities as real only if knowledge of them is possible in principle on the epistemological standard just formulated. Wilfrid Sellars may have had in mind both epistemological and metaphysical sovereignty when he said "science is the measure of all things, of what is that it is and of what is not that it is not."[18] For many naturalists, this is an apt slogan.

It is ideas like this that easily create the impression that the teaching of science and, especially, of scientific method as a model of intellectual inquiry, implies a 'religion of secular humanism' or at least some kind of secular religion. For it is God who, in monotheistic religions, is 'the measure of all things'. Even secular humanists, however, need not hold the strong version of philosophical naturalism suggested by Sellars (if any version). For they may certainly take normative questions, such as questions of what constitutes justice, to be non-scientific. Secularity does not even imply empiricality.

It should also be plain that one need not be a philosophical naturalist to be committed to scientific inquiry in answering the kinds of questions that are within the purview of science. (This commitment is compatible with granting that there could be another route, say, through theology, to some of the same truths.) But scientific inquiry has limitations even apart from the normative domain. I do not think that such inquiry extends to the question of why there is any universe at all. It is concerned with understanding patterns *in* the universe and, especially, with articulating laws and associated models that enable us to explain and predict events.

---

[18] Wilfrid Sellars, "Empiricism and the Philosophy of Mind," in Sellars, *Science, Perception and Reality* (London: Routledge & Kegan Paul, 1963), p. 173 (originally published in *Minnesota Studies in the Philosophy of Science* 1 [1956], 253–329). Cf. Jürgen Habermas' reference to "the institutionalized monopoly of scientific experts." See "Religion in the Public Square," *European Journal of Philosophy* 14(1) (2006), 1–25 (14). In this paragraph and the previous ones on naturalism, I draw on my "Philosophical Naturalism at the Turn of the Century," *Journal of Philosophical Research* 25 (2000), 27–45.

IV   The religious, the secular, and secularism

So far, I have argued that neither a commitment to scientific method nor the scientific habit of mind entails a commitment either to philosophical naturalism or to considering every theological statement intrinsically untestable by observations. This is certainly not to claim that, as usually pursued, creation science or even ID is indeed scientific, but I will use other grounds in arguing for conclusions about their position in the broad area of science policy. One concern is of course whether a commitment to them entails a commitment to religion.

What to count as religion presents a demarcation problem similar to the one confronted by trying to determine what counts as science. We do not need a definition; it should suffice to note nine criterial features, each relevant, though not strictly necessary, to a social institution's constituting a religion or to an individual's having a religion: (1) appropriately internalized belief in one or more supernatural beings; (2) observance of a distinction between sacred and profane objects; (3) ritual acts focused on those objects; (4) a moral code believed to be sanctioned by the god(s); (5) religious feelings (awe, mystery, etc.) that tend to be aroused by the sacred objects and during rituals; (6) prayer and other communicative forms concerning the god(s); (7) a worldview according the individual a significant place in the universe; (8) a more or less comprehensive organization of life based on the worldview; and (9) a social organization bound together by (1)–(8).[19]

The richest paradigms of religion, such as Christianity, Judaism, and Islam, exhibit all these features. In virtue of that, they are especially good cases to consider in relation to separation of church and state. They are also good cases in that they take God to be omniscient, omnipotent, and omnibenevolent and hence, in their different ways, claim (or at least hold that there exists) a special authority in human life. It is these three divine attributes that I shall mainly have in mind in speaking of God

[19] These features are stressed by William P. Alston in *Philosophy of Language* (Englewood Cliffs, NJ: Prentice-Hall, 1964), p. 88 (I have abbreviated and slightly revised his list). This characterization does not entail that a religion must be theistic, but theistic religions are my main concern (even in non-theistic religions, the relevant moral code tends to be given a somewhat similar privileged status in relation to appropriate items on this list, such as the worldview, the sacred and profane, and certain rituals, such as marriage). It is noteworthy that in *United States* v. *Seeger*, 380 US 163 (1965) the Supreme Court ruled that religious belief need not be theistic; but, for reasons that will become increasingly apparent, theistic religions raise the most important church–state issues, at least for societies like those in the western world. For discussion of the significance of *Seeger* in relation to church–state aspects of the foundations of liberalism see Abner S. Greene, "Uncommon Ground," a review essay on John Rawls' *Political Liberalism* and on Ronald Dworkin's *Life's Dominion*, in *George Washington Law Review* 62(4) (1994), 646–73.

in what follows, and a paradigm of a religious proposition is one self-evidently entailing the existence of God so conceived. Less clear cases of such propositions are affirmations that (or self-evidently entailing that) a religion in the sense characterized is true, right, "the way" for humanity, or the like. The notion of a religious proposition is at least as vague as that of religion itself, but given such clarity as these notions have and in the light of what has been said here, the points made in this article about the relation between the religious and the political and about education in science should be sustainable.

Should we countenance what has been called the 'religion of secular humanism'? Clearly it lacks many of (1)–(9). This is not to say that a religion must be theistic, but I will restrict my attention to theistic religions. Doing so will not prevent our seeing – in relation to some of the nine criteria – why secular humanism is objectionable to many religious people. Much depends, to be sure, on what kind of view goes by that name. A crucial question is whether 'secular' denotes the 'non-religious', in a sense implying a certain kind of *independence* of religion, or the '*anti*-religious' in the sense of 'incompatible with religion', where 'religion' is understood to embody theism.[20]

Philosophical naturalism is secular in the strong sense, not just the neutrality sense. Moreover, many who consider themselves humanistic and *non*-theistic are also philosophical naturalists. Since a strong association exists between naturalism and the scientific habit of mind, it is to be expected that unsophisticated science teachers and certainly unsophisticated conservatively religious parents of schoolchildren will suspect many science teachers of being philosophical naturalists – or at any rate atheists – and of bringing secularism in the strong sense into their teaching of certain subjects.[21] I have stressed that the scientific habit of mind does not require philosophical naturalism. This is not a point too subtle to incorporate into the teaching (and governmental funding) of science. But how should it be incorporated into the teaching of science – and indeed, of certain other subjects – in the public schools of a free democracy?

---

[20] For a detailed discussion of secularity applied to both political and educational issues in a European context, see Cécile Laborde, "Secular Philosophy and Muslim Headscarves in Schools," *Journal of Political Philosophy* 13(3) (2005), 305–29.

[21] For an indication of why 'secular humanism' is objectionable to many theists, see Greenawalt, *Does God Belong in Public Schools?*, esp. pp. 81–4. Extensive related discussion of how liberal democracy should regard religious citizens and theocratic communities is provided by Lucas Swaine in *The Liberal Conscience: Politics and Principle in a World of Religious Pluralism* (New York: Columbia University Press, 2006).

V   A framework for resolution

Since my concern is with pluralistic democracies, I presuppose a significant degree of separation of church and state as part of a constitutional
framework. Since preservation of religious liberty is a main concern of
free democracies, the state should not interfere with 'churches' (religious
institutions).

Three institutional principles of church–state separation

Here I endorse three principles: first, a *liberty principle*, which says that
(within limits) the government should permit the free exercise of religion;
second, an *equality principle*, which says that government should give no
preference to one religion (or denomination) over another; and third, a
neutrality principle, which says that government should be neutral with
respect to religion.[22]

All three principles are multidimensional and must be interpreted with
great care. The neutrality principle especially needs comment here. Its
most important aim is to prevent governmental *favoritism* of the religious
over the non-religious. Favoritism can occur even if the equality principle is satisfied and no one religion is preferred over any other. Indeed,
even if there is no discrimination (at least of a certain highly invidious
kind) against the non-religious, a measure of favoritism of the religious is
possible. Suppose there is no established church. Those who have some
religion could still be given preference in governmental appointments provided other things are equal. Thus, if a religious person is as well qualified
for such an appointment as a non-religious person, the former would be
appointed. Then competition may be free and – some would argue – in a
certain sense not unfair, since a non-religious person would never fail to be
appointed if *better* qualified than a religious competitor who was appointed.
Still, the former would not have an *equal chance* of appointment, and this
seems unfair relative to the non-religious qualifications for the appointment that we are assuming. The point holds, if with less force, even if
the favoritism given to a particular religious group ceases when a limited
proportion of the appointments are filled by religious people (say, the proportion they represent in the population).[23] (Similar issues arise for certain

---

[22]   These three principles are explicated and defended in my *Religious Commitment and Secular Reason*
(Cambridge University Press, 2000), esp. ch. 2, which discusses all three principles in the context
of the theory of the basis of free democracy.

[23]   This point is supported in my *Religious Commitment and Secular Reason*, esp. ch. 2.

affirmative action policies, but I do not have space to pursue that issue separately.)[24]

As to the liberty and equality principles, these (but apparently not the neutrality principle) are reflected in the First Amendment to the US Constitution. The former is essentially stated therein; the latter is arguably the main underlying standard supporting its Establishment Clause.[25] I shall here assume that the founders were wise to prohibit an established church; and although this prohibition apparently does not entail endorsing state neutrality toward religion, it does indirectly support such a principle.

Political constraints in a free democracy

The three institutional principles are plausible on the basis of the governing norms of free democracy – norms of freedom and of basic political equality (entailing one person, one vote). But they gain additional support from a principle that applies to individual citizens and can be supported by any of a number of ethical theories.

In liberal democracies, citizens have a prima facie obligation not to advocate or support any law or public policy that restricts human conduct, unless they have, and are willing to offer, adequate secular reason for this advocacy or support.[26]

This 'principle of secular rationale' (PSR) is intended to apply to *coercive* laws and public policies, but so few are non-coercive that these need no special attention here. A second point is that since the obligation is prima facie, there can be exceptions (as where only religious appeals can prevent the rise of a fascist regime). A subtler point is that a prima facie obligation *not* to do something is consistent with a moral right *to* do it and, in free societies, plainly with a legal right to do it. Exercises of free speech provide examples in both cases; so do many instances of *toleration*.[27]

To see the application of the principle in science education, consider a case in which a science teacher introduces criticisms of evolutionary biology

---

[24] I have provided a detailed discussion of affirmative action in my *Business Ethics and Ethical Business* (Oxford University Press, 2009), pp. 69–75.

[25] We cannot plausibly hold that preference for some one denomination entails establishment of it; but it tends in that direction and would be objectionable on similar grounds, such as encouraging discrimination against religions or denominations not favored by the government.

[26] Audi, *Religious Commitment and Secular Reason*, ch. 4, p. 86. Votes are included, of course, and the principle applies differently to people depending on their roles (e.g. as governmental officials or ordinary citizens) and on the degree of coercion involved. A prima facie obligation is of course defeasible.

[27] This is confirmed by a detailed study of toleration by Rainer Forst. See *Toleration in Conflict: Past and Present* (Cambridge University Press, 2013).

that are inextricably mixed with a case for biblical theism. Under academic freedom there might be both moral and legal rights to do this. The PSR, however, implies that there is a prima facie obligation not to do it in a state school unless (e.g.) there is good scientific reason to do it. It could be, for instance, that the criticisms are intellectually valuable, that they are not elsewhere well stated, that the related case for theism can be bracketed, and that the course is elective. This combination of factors is, however, not easily achieved. It is especially unlikely that plausible criticisms of a scientific theory cannot be abstracted from a case for theism. This is not to say that an instructor should not point out, for some of them, that whatever strength they might independently have given theism – and certainly the status of theism itself – are matters to be pursued outside the science curriculum. This is likely to be what an instructor committed both to MN and the PSR would point out.

Would the latter principle *alone* yield the same conclusion? Suppose state schools have no prohibition of introducing materials arguing for a religious position. A conscientious instructor in a high school with a pluralistic student body still has an obligation not to introduce materials in a coercive way without having adequate secular reason for doing so. Apart from commitment to MN, a *philosophy* instructor could require readings arguing for theism even in a required course *provided* this is done in an intellectually competent and balanced way. That may require teaching at a level too high for most students in state schools, but this is a contingent matter. The point for political philosophy is that there often *is* secular reason to consider (in a competent and balanced way) arguments for a theistic position, as for other important positions.

This overall point holds for a history or literature instructor *given* the appropriate intellectual competence. Neither the separation of church and state nor the PSR requires abstention from treating theistic arguments *and* criticisms thereof in state schools. But either standard may preclude doing it in certain ways – particularly as proselytizing. In science education, however, if instruction is governed by MN, then apart from special cases in which science teachers are both appropriately competent and have adequate secular reason for appraising theistic arguments, these arguments should not be evaluated in science courses.

The principle of secular rationale has recently been challenged in a wide-ranging paper by Habermas that contains important points about the relation between religion and democracy.[28] A brief assessment of three

---

[28] Habermas, "Religion in the Public Square"; later references to this paper are given parenthetically in the text.

major points concerning the PSR will advance discussion of the issues in this paper.

First, Habermas maintains that the "demand [of the PSR] is countered by the objection that many religious citizens would not be able to undertake such an artificial division within their own minds without jeopardizing their existence as pious persons . . . A devout person pursues her daily rounds by *drawing* on belief" (p. 8). Call this *the artificial division objection*.

The second, related objection (drawn from Nicholas Wolterstorff) is that "This totalizing mode of believing that infuses the very pores of daily life runs counter . . . to any flimsy switchover of religiously rooted convictions onto a *different* cognitive basis" (p. 8). Moreover, as to how devout persons see their religion, it "is not, for them, about *something other* than their social and political existence" (p. 8). This might be called *the totalizing mode of belief objection*.

The third objection concerns the relation between the PSR and what a free democracy may do: "[t]he liberal state, which expressly protects such forms of life in terms of a basic right, cannot at the same time expect of *all* citizens that they also justify their political convictions independently of their religious convictions" (p. 8). Call this *the freedom rights objection*.

Regarding the artificial division objection, there are two elements in the relevant passage: the suggestion that the distinction between the religious and the secular is artificial and the idea that religious citizens' making the distinction jeopardizes their identity. Regarding the first element, without denying that there are borderline cases I want to stress that there are many clear ones. Public health rationales for inoculations are clearly secular; the view that duty to God requires opening school days with prayer is clearly religious. Requiring inclusion of evolutionary biology in the high-school science curriculum on the ground that it is respected by the vast majority of biological scientists is a secular rationale; by contrast, *some* rationales for requiring that creationism be included are clearly not secular, for instance arguing that respect for God's sovereignty requires endorsingly teaching creationism. I grant, however, that a case can be made for the secularity of the contention that intellectual responsibility and respect for religious perspectives requires, in such a science curriculum, *recognizing* creationism (or ID) as possible accounts, at least where the question of their status cannot be avoided by the teacher. The contention involves the *concept* of religion, but it makes no appeal to any religious truth or authority.

In the light of these examples, we can address the jeopardized identity idea. Why would trying to make the kind of distinction in question be a threat to a devout person's identity? The PSR does not imply that religious reasons are not *good*, nor even that secular ones are better in terms of truth-conduciveness. It is also put forward with the specific understanding that religious people can *view* the former as better and can be motivated more by them.

It may help here to consider the power of the Golden Rule: any normal adult can understand the revulsion of being compelled to do something (such as to kneel and recite prayers many times a day) on the basis of someone *else's* religious convictions. If we can rationally want others to abstain from coercing us on the basis of religious reasons, we can understand religious reasons well enough to abide by the PSR.

It is interesting to note that Habermas himself suggests that "religious citizens must develop an epistemic stance toward the priority that secular reasons enjoy in the political arena" (p. 14). In my view, this injunction presupposes the conceptual abilities needed for the principle of secular rationale. One could not follow it unless one had the ability to identify secular reasons and to compare them with other kinds. But suppose we also assume what Habermas calls a "requirement of [secular] translation" – that "The truth content of religious contributions can only enter into the institutional practice of deliberation and decision-making if the necessary translation [of "convictions in a religious language"] already occurs in . . . the political public sphere itself" (p. 10).[29] This requirement implies not only that in general, religious citizens can *understand* secular as well as religious discourse but also that they can find an appropriately strong *correspondence* between the two. Both points support the conclusion that the (rather loose) suggestion of the PSR's jeopardizing identity is at best exaggerated. This conclusion will receive further support from my response to the second, totalizing mode of belief objection.

Two crucial elements in the totalizing mode of belief objection are that the PSR (1) calls for a "switchover of religiously rooted convictions onto a *different* cognitive basis" and (2) overlooks the point that, as devout persons see their religion, it "is not, for them, about *something other* than their social and political existence." Point (1) correctly implies that we cannot at will simply switch the *basis* of (or on which we hold) a belief; but the PSR does not require any particular *basis* of an adequate secular reason: the requirement is (where coercion of other citizens is in prospect) to *have* and be willing to offer adequate secular reason. From his overall text, I doubt

---

[29] It should be noted that Habermas rarely if ever uses 'translation' in the sense requiring synonymy and indeed works with more than one notion of translation. For clarification of at least three notions see Thomas M. Schmidt, "The Semantic Contents of Religious Beliefs and Their Secular Translation: Jürgen Habermas' Concept of Religious Experience," in Hans-Günter Heimbrock and Christopher P. Scholtz (ed.), *Religion: Immediate Experience and the Mediacy of Research, Interdisciplinary Studies in the Objectives, Concepts and Methodology of Empirical Research in Religion* (Göttingen: Vandenhoeck & Ruprecht, 2007), pp. 118–75.

that Habermas would deny that this is a proper understanding of the PSR; but some people have missed the point, and in following Wolterstorff in the way he has here Habermas makes his position look less consonant with the PSR than it is. As to (2), it is surely consistent with the PSR: I can see my religion as *concerning* my whole existence and still think – possibly on religious grounds involving respect for others – that I should have reasons that are both adequate and secular. In a central Roman Catholic tradition, this is simply to give 'natural reason' a major role.

The third, freedom rights objection, calls for a quite different reply. The point that a free democracy recognizes a *right* to vote on any conscientiously chosen basis is not in dispute. The PSR allows for this, *both* by positing a prima facie rather than always final obligation and by distinguishing obligations attached to rights from other kinds of obligations. A *right* to do something, such as vote for a candidate solely because it furthers my religious ideals, does not entail a *reason* to do it and is compatible with having some obligation not to do it. The important point here is that the PSR does not imply that government or anyone else should "expect of *all* citizens that they also justify their political convictions independently of their religious convictions." This is about *discourse*; the PSR is about *reasons* and a *willingness* to offer them. First, it posits only a prima facie obligation even to have them; second, it allows that there are sometimes reasons (such as avoiding reprisals) for not offering them (or even formulating them) hence not engaging in any 'justification'; and third, it allows that a religious person offering secular reasons may *also* offer religious ones. A citizen's approach to public expression or interpersonal persuasion is left quite open. One reason is the centrality of the liberty principle in free democracies and its concomitant commitment to toleration.

Given the clarification brought to the PSR by these responses to Habermas, the appropriate conclusion is that no major element in his position (in the article in question) is inconsistent with the PSR and that, overall, his position supports the view defended in this paper on religion and politics in relation to evolutionary biology. The PSR receives additional support from the three institutional separation principles introduced above. But the neutrality principle is more controversial than the others, and certainly the idea of governmental religious neutrality important for political philosophy needs clarification.

Neutrality in education touching on religion

The neutrality principle must not be given either of two (perhaps tempting) over-broad interpretations. First, neutrality toward the truth of religious doctrines does not imply that the state must view religion as unimportant. Not to teach *about religion* would be a drastic mistake, but one can teach about its content, development, and influence in, say, a history or literature class without endorsing or denying religious propositions. To be sure, doctrinal neutrality is compatible with attitudinal hostility. That hostile stance toward religion is offensive to many citizens and inappropriate to teaching about religion in a free democracy. Second, despite the close association between religion and ethics and despite many people's thinking that ethical principles depend for their "validity" on religion (or at least on the existence of God), teaching ethics need not violate the neutrality principle. I have in mind teaching the kind of common-sense ethical principles that are expressed in the major ethical theories and indeed in the ethical (and non-theological) Ten Commandments, including the prohibitions of killing, stealing, and lying.[30]

By contrast, neutrality does preclude public schools' teaching creationism, which explicitly says that God created human beings, as a true position, since that would endorse a religious view. The equality principle would preclude teaching that God created the world, since otherwise one could teach it without favoring any one religion over any other. The neutrality principle does not, however, preclude noncommittally mentioning creationism; but doing this is neither necessary for good science teaching nor likely to be welcome to students and parents who wish the view to be presented as credible.

If neutrality precludes teaching creationism, it also precludes *denying* such religious propositions as that God created the world. Doing this might also be precluded by the liberty principle on the ground that it tends to reduce religious liberty, but certain kinds of denial need not have this tendency. In any case, to see the scope of neutrality, we need a good understanding of what constitutes denial. I take the basic case of denial of a proposition – *direct denial* – to be either asserting that it is false or affirming its negation. We should also recognize a notion of *indirect denial*; this might be equivalent to an assertion that is not a denial but does self-evidently and obviously entail a denial. Suppose a teacher said that if God created humanity, people would be less prone to evil than they are. Any normal

---

[30] The common-sense ethical framework I refer to is set out and defended in my *The Good in the Right: A Theory of Intuition and Intrinsic Value* (Princeton University Press, 2004), in which I also argue (consistently with Thomas Aquinas' position) for basic moral principles having an a priori status of a kind appropriate to their being elements in the divine mind, rather than established by divine will.

adolescent could see this to imply that God did not create humanity. It would not be a religiously neutral assertion.

The issue becomes more complex, however, when the non-neutral implication is not obvious or self-evident, but is ascertainable by reflection on the part of a normal adult with the level of education reasonably aimed at for students in (say) the tenth grade or above. Imagine that a teacher considers a version of ID theory and composes a list of 'evidences of divine action' in the genesis of humanity. The teacher indicates that the list includes all the possible kinds of evidence and then presents data in such a way as to yield a series of arguments, one marshaling each kind of evidence, and each concluding that the relevant evidence is missing. At the end of this process – for instance, after half a dozen arguments are mounted – the teacher might say that we cannot rationally believe a view for which there is no relevant evidence. Doing this may seem an *implicit denial* of the religious proposition in question (in this case, the proposition that there has been divine action in the genesis of humanity); but it does not carry a commitment to deeming the proposition *false*. It is, however, an *implicit rejection* of the proposition – representing it as unworthy of belief. It might also be plausibly considered a failure of neutrality toward religion.

It will be no surprise that there are borderline cases. Suppose the teacher had concluded instead that there is no evidence of divine creation of humanity and that the probability of such creation is very low. This is not neutral toward religion but is not a clear case of denying the religious view in question. If the teacher had simply said there is no evidence, we would not have denial, but would still have what would, in most contexts, be a breach of neutrality. Breach of neutrality, then, does not entail denial of a religious view. This makes neutrality more difficult to achieve. Two points must be added immediately.

First, just as breach of neutrality does not entail denial of a religious view, the latter – for one broad and common notion of a religious view – does not entail breach of neutrality toward religion. There are many statements in the Bible that are denied – if taken literally as descriptions of fact – by religious people whose mode of biblical interpretation makes frequent appeal to symbolism, metaphor, and the ways of narrative. Some people may think that any serious cosmic or ethical pronouncements by certain religious authorities are religious statements. The second point, then, is that it would be a mistake to define neutrality toward religion so broadly that denial of any of these statements entails breaching neutrality.

Here methodological naturalism is again a useful standard: if clerics or religious texts assert propositions properly assessed scientifically under the assumption of preservation of MN, then neither critical treatment nor denial need be considered a breach of neutrality toward religion. This is not quite to say that religion is best practiced in a way that is *scientifically neutral*; but many educated religious people would endorse a qualified version of such a view, on the ground that religious truths – or at least the deepest ones – are of a different order from the kind appropriately assessed scientifically and that claims distinctive of religion should not compete with the kind appropriately assessed in scientific inquiry.

State neutrality toward religion in the sense in which it is a sound political ideal, then, does not entail neutrality regarding every possible religion or every statement deemed religious. Given that almost any statement can be deemed religious by someone and that religious institutions can be built around indefinitely many sets of statements and practices, to require such sweeping neutrality would be to make an unreasonable demand on both government in general and education in particular. It would thus be going too far to say that the "neutrality required of a liberal democracy is not neutrality with respect to the reasonable religions present in society but neutrality with respect to the religions present in society, period."[31] Consider human sacrifice and the oppression of women. These practices have actually been religiously sanctioned, but a free democracy should not protect them. Even the liberty principle does not obligate the state to protect every possible freedom.

Neutrality has two aspects, applying to affirmation as well as to denial of that to which it applies. Although the examples just given concern what we might call anti-religious breaches of neutrality, they may all be adapted to make similar points about pro-religious breaches. In neither case is it possible to characterize neutrality precisely. Practical wisdom is needed both in identifying it and in abiding by its demands. The notion of neutrality is, however, clear enough to enable us to see that a commitment to scientific method does not entail violating it. It does not even entail denying that God created the universe and humanity within it; hence it does not oppose that minimal kind of creationism. If creationism is understood, as it usually is, in a way that renders it insusceptible of confirmation by scientific method understood to incorporate methodological naturalism, then the neutrality principle does preclude teaching creationism *as science*. This is not to say that *nothing* a creationist holds may be considered a scientific hypothesis, but the hypothesis that God created human beings is surely not such a hypothesis.

---

[31] Nicholas Wolterstorff, commentary on an earlier version of part of this paper.

The preparation of science teachers

May a liberal democracy, then, simply ask science teachers to point all this out – to distinguish (in their own words) methodological from philosophical naturalism and explain the demarcation problem and why a socio-political rationale rather than a narrow conception of science must be brought to bear in designing pre-college education in science? Some science teachers could competently do this without saying or conveying anything objectionable to reasonable religious citizens. Would saying it, however, be needed for good science teaching? As formulated, these points might be an important element in teaching science and indeed some other subjects; but the points do not address intellectual and related learning concerns that students may have. What more might science teachers say?

I believe that those capable of teaching science competently at the level of evolutionary theory are also capable of saying something about the question of demarcation. They need not use that term or even try to distinguish science from other kinds of inquiry in any systematic way. They could, however, explain the empirical character of scientific inquiry and the role of testability and publicity. They could also distinguish methodological naturalism from the metaphysical view that natural phenomena exhaust reality and could then note that a commitment, in doing science, to scientific method as including methodological naturalism is not anti-theistic but neutral with respect to theism. Doing this does not entail any substantive teaching about religion. This can be pointed out. It can also be noted that even teaching about religion, as distinct from teaching theology, is not appropriate in the science curriculum though it is often desirable in, for instance, teaching history.[32] In either kind of teaching, it may or may not be desirable for teachers (in government schools) to note that, in courses required of all students, endorsingly teaching religion is not appropriate.[33]

Beyond this, science teachers – especially below the college level, though much of what is said here applies also to college teaching – might note that evolutionary science does not require a physicalistic conception of the human person. Evolutionary science is compatible with dualism about mental and physical properties and even with Cartesian dualism, which views human beings as a kind of unity of mental and bodily substances.

---

[32] In many parts of Greenawalt, *Does God Belong in Public Schools?*, there are points and examples that indicate the difficulty of even teaching about religion in a neutral way.

[33] The emphasis on required courses is to acknowledge that, as in certain European and Nordic countries, a state school may have required courses in religion *adapted* to the religious preferences of students, say Catholic, Jewish, or Protestant courses as well as non-denominational or secular (e.g. historical) ones.

That view, in turn, need not be combined with theism, though it easily leads to speculation about whether Cartesian minds are souls and have religious significance. Perhaps, then, these points in the philosophy of mind are, in most high schools, best left in readiness and not presented if they need not come up. But my sense is that part of the resistance by conservative theists to the teaching of evolutionary biology is the belief, or at least the sense, that it implies – or that endorsing it conveys the impression – that human beings are simply biological, hence in some sense physical, systems. This view is not incompatible with the possibility of resurrection, but it does imply the falsity of traditional dualistic conceptions of how resurrection may occur.

High-school science teachers can also point to non-empirical disciplines and note that they are legitimate domains of inquiry with standards of genuine knowledge. I recommend that at least three in particular be noted: logic, pure mathematics, and ethics. This can be done without mentioning theology, but there is no reason why that cannot be mentioned with an indication that it is not a subject for discussion in a science class. To be sure, most science teachers cannot be easily prepared to explain the possibility of theological knowledge or to consider whether any of it might be a priori. But that may apply almost as much to ethics, and in any case the main point to be conveyed is that *knowledge* need not be empirical or, even if it is empirical in the way some think ethical knowledge is, it need not depend on scientific inquiry.[34]

I have so far not considered intelligent design, understood as the view that such design best explains the empirical data concerning the history and biology of the human species. There is an ambiguity here which should be immediately exposed: the claim may be that (1) our history and biology exhibit a biological pattern of a *kind* that an intelligent designer might rationally choose or that (2) it is of a kind that *has* been designed by an agent. Though (2) does not entail that this agent is God, proponents of ID surely have God in mind; (1) may be more naturally interpreted philosophically than scientifically, but it is true that the needed description of our history and biology requires scientific inquiry; (2) is not scientific (assuming MN) if the agent referred to is taken to be supernatural. However, (2) can be argued to be, metaphysically, the best explanation of (1). A science teacher could point this argument out both without endorsement and with an indication that it is not an appropriate subject for discussion in a science

---

[34] Another case is the aesthetic. At least certain statements about literary works are either not empirical at all or empirical in a way that does not make knowledge of them depend on scientific inquiry.

class. Granted, pointing it out at all would be difficult to do without evincing a positive or negative attitude. For that reason among others (including facts about the students in attendance), some teachers should resist mentioning it.

A science teacher may also preface certain examination questions with such phrases as 'according to the theory of evolution'. This need not be presented as expressing suspended judgment on the theory, but it allows students for whom the theory is religiously unacceptable to succeed in their exams without feeling that they are asserting religiously offensive falsehoods.

This cautionary suggestion does not imply that evolution is to be taught as 'theory, not fact'. That is a dangerous false contrast: a theory may be true, hence factual. The sound point that may be made about theories here is that they are confirmed or disconfirmed to some degree short of *proof*, where proof is understood rigorously, as in logic and mathematics, to require a deductively valid argument from clearly known premises. In science teaching, as indeed in the humanities and social sciences, distinguishing proof from confirmation and from establishing high probability is a good thing to try to get across to students.

There is no reason why suitably trained science teachers cannot distinguish creationism from ID and explain how scientific method is apparently applicable to at most one of them. But for some teachers, such essentially philosophical discussion may be uncomfortable or impossible. Suppose that it is sometimes inevitable, if only because students insist on bringing up methodological or ontological issues raised by evolutionary biology (and, if less often, by other branches of science). A useful corrective to one kind of misunderstanding is to point out to students that not all legitimate questions or disciplines are scientific and that only scientific questions are the business of instruction in science. As I have suggested, logic is not; pure mathematics is not; and ethics is not. Scientific activity *depends on* the former two; and it should be *constrained* by the latter. Once students see that science is not the only source of knowledge and is not needed to legitimize every kind of question, they need not view the idea that theology is non-scientific as disparaging.

The implication of all this is that education for teaching science should be enhanced and in a way that conduces both to better scientific understanding and to the capacity to discuss evidence and theories in ways that are important in politics as well as education. Philosophy might be a requirement, especially philosophy of science or epistemology or, preferably, both. It is also desirable that teachers be aware of the need to use their coercive power over students in accord with something like the principle of secular rationale. Should we be disturbed about giving philosophy this significant a role in educating teachers? In my view, it should be welcome, especially as things now seem in at least the USA, where pre-college education in science and, more broadly, in critical thinking, is generally (and I think plausibly) regarded as usually inadequate.

Conclusion

I have suggested that there is apparently no plausible way to demarcate science from all of the non-scientific disciplines except by positing a commitment by scientists to a moderate methodological naturalism. Even this approach does not yield a sharp distinction. The more important point here, however, is that methodological naturalism is neutral with respect to theism and thus with respect to what is perhaps the core element in the kinds of religions that raise the most pressing problems for the teaching of science and indeed for the separation of church and state.

Even given the proposed methodological demarcation, we cannot say that no *claims* important for creationism or, especially, intelligent design, are scientifically appraisable. But the overall positions motivating most such claims would be readily seen by students as belonging to a theistic worldview; and their connection to such a view would typically appear sufficiently tight to create the impression that teaching these claims as true or plausible is an endorsement of theism. The theistic worldview, and, similarly, propositions perceptibly presupposing it or self-evidently entailing it, are not appropriate for discussion in science classes – at least as part of the science curriculum.

On the political neutrality of science issue, naturally the practice of science and its funding are political *issues*. But given methodological naturalism and the centrality of systematic observation and controlled experiments, it is not unreasonable to hope that scientific inquiry can yield findings that provide common ground for opposing political positions. The rigor and appropriate neutrality are not automatic, but they are worth preserving. Toward that end, in pre-college science teaching, given my theory of the appropriate separation of church and state and of secular and religious considerations in supporting laws and public policies, we should seek to develop a sensitivity by science teachers – and, so far as possible, citizens in general – to what constitutes science, to the existence of non-scientific disciplines that are genuine fields of inquiry, and to the need to confine discussion to scientific issues in an atmosphere in which it is understood that doing so is neutral with respect to religion rather than hostile to it. The appropriate neutrality toward religion, both in science education and in politics, is entirely compatible with a sense of the historical importance of religion and of its position in contemporary culture. It is also compatible with profound religious faith on one side or, on the other, deep dislike of religion. Good teaching in secular institutions calls on us to transcend commitments to either of these positions, especially in teaching the young. This ideal is related to ethical citizenship in general, which requires a related capacity for balance in political conduct. There is no call to abandon one's religious or metaphysical commitments, even in one's scientific life, and achieving the kind of neutrality portrayed in this article can be an implicit affirmation of values of mutual respect that are shareable by us all.[35]

[35] Parts of this article derive from others of mine and from my lectures and conference presentations during 2006 through 2008. I have benefited from discussions with many colleagues and audiences and especially with Kent Greenawalt, Paul Weithman, and Nicholas Wolterstorff.

CHAPTER 11

Nationalism, patriotism, and cosmopolitanism in an age of globalization

In one way, we live in a shrinking world. The human population is expanding but important natural resources are being depleted and the environment is being degraded. At the same time, information is rapidly increasing and becoming more readily available. Partly through the Internet, we are also becoming more and more conscious of what is happening far away. Distances are shorter. International trade and technology transfer are expanding. These and other factors have increased the pressure for industrialization among historically agrarian societies. People in poor nations are increasingly aware of what people in rich nations have. Their aspirations contribute to competition and, potentially, to hostility. International justice is more urgent than ever – in part because terrorism and war are increasingly dangerous.

Globalization, then, is with us; it is on the rise; and it poses special challenges to the powerful prosperous nations, especially the USA. Approaches to it range from extreme nationalism, embodying patriotism as a characteristic attitude, to extreme cosmopolitanism. This paper will characterize those two poles and proceed to address a set of related problems and ideas. My aim is twofold: conceptually, to clarify both nationalism and cosmopolitanism, and normatively, to propose some guiding standards for their mutual adjustment and their applications to the activities that are central in globalization.

I Nationalism

Nationalist views fall on a spectrum from minimal to extreme. There are too many possible versions to describe here. The same holds for cosmopolitanism, which in many ways is the converse of nationalism. To minimize complexity in both cases, I will characterize extreme, moderate, and minimal forms. I will do this, however, in relation to important variables that, when appropriately assessed, enable us to identify and order nationalist and cosmopolitan positions of many more kinds than we can now address.

The main variable that, in my view, determines the strength of a nationalism is the relative importance it ascribes to national vs. human concerns. Other significant variables are policy considerations under this heading. Nationalists tend to give priority to specifically *national* concerns, cosmopolitans to specifically *human* concerns. Human concerns are such things as the elements of physical and psychological well-being on the part of persons. These properly motivate policy decisions independently of the welfare of any particular nation. Human concerns would be important for people even in a "state of nature." It should be noted that although those concerns have high priority in the ethical frameworks of the world's major religions, the human concerns central for understanding the contrast between nationalism and cosmopolitanism do not normatively depend on values that are intrinsically religious.

In appraising a person or nation in relation to the contrast between national and human concerns, we should consider at least the following dimensions of policy: (1) uses of the military, say in self-defense as opposed to preventive warfare (the kind that may be plausibly argued to be necessary to prevent great danger to one's own country or to other countries); (2) material promotion, for example distribution of economic resources nationally as opposed to internationally; (3) healthcare and preventive health, say in reference to use of funds to deal with cancer at home vs. AIDS worldwide; and (4) cultural matters, for example promoting English as an international language as opposed to having two or more international languages or none. There is, however, a fifth variable, one that clearly connects the contrast between nationalism and cosmopolitanism with ethics: the status of patriotism.

Extreme nationalism

Let us start with an extreme form of nationalism: the kind encapsulated in the phrase, 'my country right or wrong'. Roughly, this view is that where national interest calls for an action, citizens have an overriding obligation to act accordingly.[1] Note that national interests can be distinct from any governmental order purporting to advance or protect them. This distinction is not always easy to make in practice; and making it can be

---

[1] In the interest of space I omit consideration of how permanent residents and other residents of a country should figure in nationalism.

especially troublesome for the military, who are characteristically sworn both to obey orders and to uphold the constitution.[2]

What we can say with some confidence is this. *Given* a view on what is in the national interest, wherever there is a conflict between it and the interest of one or more other countries or peoples in relation to any of the variables in question, for example economic prosperity, national interests are considered overriding. Thus, even when a policy will cause much suffering for one nation and advance my own only slightly, extreme nationalism requires that I prefer my own, except where nationalistic prudence dictates otherwise.

It is important for understanding nationalism to see what it implies for the status of patriotism. The term 'patriotism' may be used to designate at least three different kinds of things: a trait of character, as where we speak of a person who is patriotic to the core; an emotion, as where people are described as glowing with patriotism or bursting with pride in their country; and (perhaps by extension from these more basic cases) a position, such as the view that one owes loyalty to one's country. I assume here that the trait is conceptually more basic than the emotion or the position and that our conceptions of the latter two can be most fruitfully developed if they are largely derived from an adequate conception of the trait. In rough terms, I take patriotism as a trait to be a feature of character that entails a significant degree of loyalty to one's country and an associated disposition to take pride in it, to be subject to emotions closely connected with one's perception of its well-being, and to give some degree of preference to its needs and interests over the needs and interests of other countries. Patriotism, like other traits, admits of degrees and can manifest itself in quite different ways depending on both the other traits of the person in question and the context in which the trait is, as it were, "activated." Much more should be said to fill out this characterization (and below I note the significance of the point that countries *need* not be identified with nations), but given

---

[2] In this connection, I find it of great interest that in the Oath of Allegiance rendered on R-Day at the US Military Academy (West Point), the Constitution of the United States is cited first, before allegiance to the "National Government"; and in the Commissioning Oath Rendered at Graduation, it is the Constitution that one swears to support and defend, and the National Government is not mentioned. We know well that a national government may go in a direction different from any indicated or even permitted by its legitimating constitution. This possibility is of major importance for leaders in the military who swear allegiance to both. My effort here is partly to cast light on how conscientious members of the military may reasonably and ethically deal with the kind of tension that can emerge between constitutional and governmental obligations. See Annex C – "Oaths and the Officer of Commission," USMA (United States Military Academy) Circular 1–101–1, 2007. It is also noteworthy that the Officer Commission statement, announcing appointment to the US Army, does not mention the Constitution at all and stresses following orders of the president of the USA.

the mainly normative concerns of this paper it will suffice for our main question about patriotism, namely what status it has on the kinds of views we are considering.

For extreme nationalism – or at least for a virtue-theoretic version of it – patriotism, as just characterized, is a *basic* virtue. Roughly, to call patriotism a virtue is to say that the degree of goodness of a person's character is in part a matter of whether that person is patriotic.[3] A *basic* virtue is one that, independently of supporting one or more other virtues, has inherent value in a person (at least for persons living in a social context such as a nation). It should be said immediately that whether or not patriotism is a basic virtue or even a virtue at all, it may be a *valuable trait*.[4] Compare a sense of humor. This may help a person to do good deeds and it is a *merit* in a person, but it is not a basic virtue. A person lacking it might be outstandingly good. This is not to deny that a positively *bad*-humored person might for that reason fail to be outstandingly good. But being an opposite of a bad trait does not automatically make a characteristic a virtue. The absence of a black streak across its center is compatible with the beauty of a painting of a tree, but its presence might still be a spoiler.

Patriotism is commonly enlisted in the service of nationalism, but it can also be a force in the opposite direction. It can indeed be a lever that redirects nationalism. The patriot may see, for instance, that a war that nationalists would wage goes against the ideals of the country.[5] Patriotism can produce national self-criticism or national embarrassment as well as national pride.

Extreme nationalism cannot be plausibly claimed to be morally groundable overall, in the sense that a morally good person (who is sufficiently informed of the relevant facts and adequately rational) must embrace it.

---

[3] To be sure a person may be without a country, and we might argue that a basic virtue should be possible for a person independently of contingent circumstances. One reaction is that such a virtue is *possible* for a countryless person. Another is that it is a contingent matter whether one makes any promises, so promissory virtue would not be basic either, if we insisted that virtues be such that good persons must possess them independently of their life circumstances.

[4] As I characterize patriotism, it is in its most basic form a trait of character, though arguably the trait may be a suitably stable attitude rather than a structural feature of character. By contrast, David McCabe calls it "the doctrine that co-nationality is a morally significant relationship that may impose special duties and sanction special treatment" (1997, p. 203). I am inclined to think that the trait tends to carry acceptance of this doctrine, and the doctrine is important in any case. Some of this paper bears on the doctrine, but see McCabe's paper for a careful analysis of the doctrine in comparison with liberal universalism – a view closer to what I call moderate cosmopolitanism.

[5] For a richly illustrated and informative discussion of nationalism and patriotism – one quite different from, if mainly compatible with, mine – see George Orwell's "Notes on Nationalism," originally published in *Polemic* (London, October 1945) and reprinted in his *England Your England and Other Essays* (1953).

Indeed, the very phrase 'my country right *or wrong*' suggests that the extreme nationalist – at least one who adheres to this motto – is aware that morality may pull the other way. Still, as will be evident, basic ethics does allow citizens to be minimal nationalists and, in some cases, moderate nationalists.

Suppose, however, that ethics does not support extreme nationalism. It might still allow that patriotism is a basic virtue. I leave this possibility open. Basic virtues may, however, make conflicting behavioral demands on us. The demands of one virtue, say justice, can conflict with those of another, say patriotism. Justice might prohibit torturing a terrorist's innocent twelve-year-old daughter to discover his hiding place; patriotism might call for it.

To fix ideas, let us ask whether virtues might fall into a strict hierarchy such that (1) no two virtues rank equally and (2) in *every* possible case of conflict (in a decision context) between a higher and a lower virtue, action in accordance with the higher one takes priority over action in accordance with the lower one.[6] I do not think virtues are hierarchical in this way, any more than types of obligation are. But this does not imply that no generalizations are possible, say that *by and large* considerations of justice take priority over those of patriotism. One might, then, hold that although patriotism is a basic virtue, it is not as high in the rough priority ordering of virtues as is justice or, say, non-injury. (A morally sound person would not, e.g., be willing to kill an innocent person solely for a patriotic reason, say in order to show the managers of a corrupt competing foreign company one is infiltrating that one can be trusted to do their bidding.) The general point here for appraising the bearing of patriotism on nationalism is this: the more virtues one thinks are behaviorally dominant over patriotism, the less far-reaching is one's nationalism, other things equal.

Moderate nationalism

We might now consider a moderate form of nationalism and, to keep our eye on societies of the kind that concern me most, go to the context of a liberal democracy. For moderate nationalism, one's country has high priority over others – but not absolute priority. A moderate nationalism

---

[6] An interesting implication of the strict hierarchy conception is that every virtue must be capable of conflicting with some other; else we could have a virtue of an indeterminate level: it could not even be said to be of the same level of any other, since location in a level requires dominance relations. One might think, however, that the notion of two virtues being at the same level is not definable on the hierarchy picture, but that is not so. Two could differ conceptually, but each bear the same dominance relations (positive or negative) to the same other virtues. Loyalty and steadfastness might in some forms be an example.

could hold, for example, that if the numbers of people affected by a decision favor one or more other countries, then in any issue not involving vital interests, such as essential defense of the realm, the interests of one's own country are overridden. It is common for this kind of restraint to be due in part to recognition of moral standards.

We should consider more closely how a moderate nationalist might conceive various issues. Priority in international conflict has been covered: one's own country is favored. Priority in material promotion, for example in economic resources, however, is a different matter. Here moderate nationalists would favor their own country up to a significant point. This is not precisely definable; but whereas an extreme nationalist would tend to allow millions abroad to starve to death, a moderate nationalist would, if saving them required it, sacrifice some national convenience – say, by allowing grain exports that substantially raise the domestic price of bread. Priority in healthcare and preventive health may be understood similarly.

Priority in cultural matters is rather different. Consider promoting English for the convenience of Americans. Here a moderate American nationalist would be willing to do much of what a prudent extreme nationalist would do, for instance push for the status of English as *the* international language, export American and English-language cultural products, and economically penalize countries that do not cooperate. The reason a moderate can do this is twofold. First, the harm done, if any, is arguably minor. Second, much good, in terms of international communication, can be plausibly argued to come from success in establishing an international language.

For moderate nationalism, patriotism can be a virtue, but moderate nationalists who so conceive it would place it lower in the "hierarchy" of virtues than would extreme nationalists. This does not entail, however, that the overall view is morally groundable. Can a moderate nationalism be morally grounded? The answer depends in part on what grounds political obligation itself. If we have obligations to obey the law and, by implication, obligations to a legitimate government that passes laws, does this imply that we should be nationalists of some kind? Not *automatically*; for there may be no laws connecting our country with people outside it. Nationalism, if grounded solely in political obligation of this legal kind, would then require nothing that bears on one's own country in relation to any other. But normally there will be such laws, as with treaties, trade restrictions, and the like. If political obligation is morally groundable, then, by implication, so is some degree of obligation to support our own nation: we owe prima facie support to its duly enacted laws, and this implies at least a minimal degree of nationalism.

In my view, political obligation *can* be morally grounded.[7] One element in its basis is relationships among citizens. As citizens, we operate in relationships in which we mutually presuppose that we and others will abide by the laws. We commonly express a commitment to this by tending (non-hypocritically) to criticize people who do not abide by the duly enacted laws. Some of us, of course, take oaths that commit us to what the law calls for, and here the basic moral obligation to keep promises supports political obligation. Consider the (American) Pledge of Allegiance ("I pledge allegiance to the flag of the United States and to the Republic for which it stands, one nation, under God, with liberty and justice for all").

One question here is whether the Pledge and similar oaths are always taken voluntarily; another is the status of ceremonial pledges of this kind in the first place. However those questions are answered, the phrase 'liberty and justice for all' is striking. This surely does not mean all *citizens* or perhaps even all residents. It presumably applies to all people the USA deals with and conceivably to all the people on earth. If so, it can support some degree of cosmopolitanism as well as a kind of nationalism.

Minimal nationalism

By now, it will be clear that nationalist views come in many different strengths. What might constitute a minimal nationalism? Suppose one holds that the interests of one's country have only non-basic moral status and have only limited priority over those of other nations. For minimal nationalism, in matters of national defense we might prefer our interests over those of allies, other things being equal. But minimal nationalists would not hold that other nations' interests are always overridden by ours when the two sets of interests conflict. Similarly, on the other counts, namely economic factors, healthcare elements, and cultural variables, minimal nationalists would accord lower status than moderate nationalists to the interests of their own country. If, however, they are nationalists at all, then when other things are equal, say where the suffering from a given policy would be equally bad for their own nation as for others, they would give priority to their own.

As to patriotism, for minimal nationalism it would not likely be a *basic* virtue, even one lower in priority than for moderate nationalism. I say 'not likely' rather than 'could not' because it is possible, though unlikely, that one take a virtue to be basic but not *major*, as justice, veracity, and fidelity clearly are. But here we must remember that not being a basic virtue does not imply not being a virtue *at all*. For one thing, strong

---

[7] For a case that free democracy is morally grounded, see Audi (2005).

support of a country with just and sufficiently beneficent policies might promote many values that are universal. These include human flourishing, conceived in terms of happiness on the positive side and suffering on the negative. Whether a given action in expression of patriotism is morally right depends on the moral status of the values of both the individual and the country in question.

Positional vs. attitudinal forms of nationalism

I have so far been discussing nationalism as a position on the status of national interests and how they should be weighted against those of humanity in general. Nationalism is not necessarily a moral position, but it does imply normative standards of some kind, since it entails a view on what in some sense ought to be done, particularly at the level of national policy. One could hold such a position for moral reasons or simply from self-interest or from a kind of identification with one's co-nationals that leads to a protective stance.

Commonly, attitudes match policies in the domain of national vs. human concerns. Thus, extreme nationalists are likely to have evaluative attitudes favoring their own country over others, say a sense that their culture or industry is superior. It is possible, however, for attitudes to be quite disparate from intellectual positions. One might be a minimal nationalist from a sense of moral obligation to humanity, even though one has attitudes of a much more positive kind toward one's own nation than toward others. This disparity could be associated with a kind of *noblesse oblige,* but I am not concerned with a causal account here. My point is that, for clarity, we should make explicit what kind of nationalism is in question. The same distinction between the positional and the attitudinal applies to cosmopolitanism. In both cases, my concern is far more with the positions than with the attitudes. Despite the differences and possible divergence between the positions and the attitudes, what justifies the positions should at least largely overlap what justifies the attitudes.

II Cosmopolitanism

Given the way in which nationalism and cosmopolitanism are counterparts of each other, I can be briefer in describing cosmopolitanism.[8] In this case,

---

[8] For detailed discussion of cosmopolitanism and a case for a strong kind leading to world government, see Pojman (2006). An indication of some of the problems and prospects for international governmental institutions is provided by David Copp in his wide-ranging "International Justice and the Basic Needs Principle" (2005).

I want to start with the valuational position that underlies the plausible forms of cosmopolitanism.

Cosmopolitan values

It is both natural and plausible to assume that the value of nations and other social structures is *derivative*. Nations and other institutional structures derive their value from their role in serving people. This is certainly how cosmopolitans tend to see the matter. On the plausible versions of cosmopolitanism, it is people who have *basic* moral status; nations have derivative moral status. In Kant's language, persons are ends in themselves; they can never be properly treated merely as means to the glory of nations. On a still wider view likely to be held by cosmopolitans, all non-personal values are subordinate to personal ones. Nations, for instance, properly exist for the benefit of persons, not the other way around. Broadly speaking, then, cosmopolitanism gives some degree of priority to the interests of humanity over those of nations, and the stronger the priority, the stronger the cosmopolitanism. The term may designate either a view stating some degree of such priority or an attitude incorporating the view.[9]

Extreme cosmopolitanism

It is easy to see how, starting from the perspective of the values underlying cosmopolitanism in general, we can characterize an extreme cosmopolitanism. For extreme cosmopolitanism, interests of humanity come first in any conflict between them and national interests (other things equal). Second, for extreme cosmopolitanism, patriotism is not a virtue, and loyalty to one's country is valuable only insofar as it promotes the interests of humanity. It would be permissible as an emotional attitude, but it would be discouraged insofar as it has any tendency to create preference for the interests of one's own nation over those of other peoples. Nationality, on this extreme view, has only pragmatic status. Indeed, there would be no nations, though there might be *countries*, roughly geographically and

---

[9] This characterization contrasts with the kind described by Gillian Brock and Harry Brighouse (and attributed to various others), on which "Weak cosmopolitanism just says that there are *some* extranational obligations that have some moral weight. Strong cosmopolitanism, by contrast, claims that . . . there are no society-wide principles of distributive justice that are not also global principles of distributive justice; and that . . . we have no right to use nationality (in contrast with friendship, or familial love) as a trigger for discretionary behavior" (2005, p. 3). I find both characterizations usefully suggestive; but the first characterization is too indefinite in specifying neither what kinds of obligations are in question nor any limit on their weight, and the second is indefinite in its first clause and highly vague in its second, negative clause.

culturally defined groups of people which do not necessarily coincide with nations as understood under international law or by eligibility for United Nations membership. International standards should govern us all, with world government having authority over quasi-national standards in international disputes.

What is the ethical case for world government? I know of no one who has put it better than Louis Pojman in his posthumous book, *Terrorism, Human Rights, and the Case for World Government*:

1 The moral point of view entails universal human rights;
2 Human rights require institutionalization for their full realization;
3 Because of the Hobbesian state of nature, institutional cosmopolitanism (world government) offers the best opportunity for supporting human rights;
4 Therefore, the moral point of view leads to support of institutional cosmopolitanism (world government) (2006, p. 69).

I would stress that (as Pojman need not deny) national – or at least patriotic – aspirations could be allowed enough status to tip the balance in favor of a given country in many cases.[10] (I here assume that world government is compatible with the existence of countries and, in principle, with nations provided their legal status is subordinate to the central authority.) This is mainly because national interests can have high instrumental value for humanity. Suppose the USA were subordinated to a world government that had authority over all nations, and suppose the USA were to be a supplier of food and material goods. American resentment and resistance might rise to the point that US productivity would decline and the needy nations would be less well served than under a cosmopolitanism tempered by the aspirations that underlie a beneficent nationalism.

One may wonder why, in characterizing an extreme cosmopolitanism, I have not imagined someone's saying, 'Humanity right or wrong'. Suppose someone did say this. What would be the intended contrast with the interests of humanity? Not the interests of countries or even nations, for they represent significant elements in *humanity*. Not even the interests of beings from outer space if they are of similar constitution in terms of rationality, motivation, and sentience.[11] The kinds of values that underlie

---

[10] For an informative discussion of the elements that must be considered to achieve a proper balance between patriotic and cosmopolitan concerns, see Richard Miller's "Cosmopolitan Respect and Patriotic Concern" (2005). Another valuable discussion of the requirements for a proper balance here is Soniewicka (2011).

[11] The importance of rationality, motivation, and sentience for grounding moral status is considered in some detail in Audi (2001).

cosmopolitanism tend to support taking the well-being of high-level living beings of any kind seriously. A kind of speciesism might be possible for cosmopolitans – with high preference for human interests over those of any animals – but even in relation to "lower" animals they would be *disposed* to be kind. The values that underlie cosmopolitanism tend to rule out anthropocentrism.

Moderate cosmopolitanism

A version of cosmopolitanism could be strong without being extreme, and the case Pojman makes in support of cosmopolitanism may be argued to give stronger support for moderate cosmopolitanism, with limited world government, than for the extreme version. We might call a cosmopolitan view strong if it differs from the extreme form only in limiting world government to international concerns and allowing nation states to have both international legal status and autonomy over matters concerning only their own people. Depending on how the relevant concerns are defined, there might be little difference between this view and the extreme version, but the difference would still be significant.

What, then, would constitute a moderate cosmopolitanism? It would mirror moderate nationalism; it would give high but not absolute priority to *human* interests. It would differ from moderate nationalism in putting more emphasis on human than on national interests and putting *more* of the former over the latter than moderate nationalism does. It would also differ from extreme cosmopolitanism in allowing patriotism to be a virtue, though not a basic virtue. A moderate cosmopolitan would tend to favor the interests of (enough) other peoples over those of one's own country – the opposite of the preference of moderate nationalists – but one could still care about one's own country in special ways and could devote much energy to promoting its interests where these do not conflict with those of other people.

Moderate cosmopolitans could, for instance, give preference to their own country in, say, a matter of economic policy if the number of people affected in their own country is much larger than those affected elsewhere. But if, as with global warming, doing what is best for humanity as a whole implies that the burden would fall differentially on one's own country, the moderate cosmopolitan would still have to favor humanity.[12]

---

[12] An interesting comparison might be made between moderate cosmopolitanism as characterized here and the position of Thomas Pogge, who argues, regarding the prosperous industrialized nations, that "by shaping and enforcing the social conditions that, foreseeably and avoidably, cause

Minimal cosmopolitanism

When it comes to what may be reasonably called a minimal cosmopolitanism, I suggest that, given the possibility of certain cosmopolitan and certain nationalistic elements being combined in a person's worldview, minimal cosmopolitanism should be characterized so that it is consistent with minimal nationalism but differs from it in *emphasis*. Minimal nationalists need not take any positive interest in the welfare of the rest of the world, but can do so consistently with their position, in which concern for the national interest is an essential element and will of course tend to do so insofar as they are committed to taking the well-being of persons everywhere as a good. Different ethical positions give greater or lesser weight to the prima facie obligation to promote this good; and the extent to which minimal patriots will care about the interests of persons outside the preferred group will depend on their general ethical orientation and other variables. Minimal cosmopolitans, by contrast, must care about the world as a whole. They may have special feelings for their own country, as minimal nationalists may have such feelings – say, of a generally altruistic kind – for people in other nations. But cosmopolitans need not have special feelings toward their own country, though some special national obligations, including national service, may be required by their political obligations. On many issues, then, the two groups might agree, even if for different reasons.

How would minimal cosmopolitanism differ from moderate cosmopolitanism? Whereas moderate cosmopolitans must prefer the interests of humanity over those of their country when other things are *not* equal (though there may be limits to the degree of preference required), the minimal cosmopolitan need only prefer the interests of humanity when other things *are* equal. The difference, then, is a matter of degree, but in practice things are so often not equal that defenders of moderate cosmopolitanism would quite commonly tend to have disputes with nationalists.

Resistance to sectarianism as common to cosmopolitanism and nationalism

The interests of humanity may be plausibly thought to transcend the special interests of any particular religious sect or denomination. Moreover, insofar

the monumental suffering of global poverty, we are *harming* the global poor" (2005, p. 93). The upshot is that we have violated negative moral duties toward them and are not merely failing to fulfill positive ones. This view does not entail what I call extreme cosmopolitanism; and given the desirable institutional reforms he describes (e.g. on p. 103), it appears that his position does not commit him to that.

as sectarian loyalties go against the interests of a nation, nationalism opposes them. In Iraq, for instance, the conflict between Shiite and Sunni Muslims is an obstacle to the success of any national government. Patriotism is like nationalism in opposing at least intra-national sectarianism – and similarly intra-national *tribalism*; what divides nations also tends to divide any country that is at least the major constituent in that nation. If, however, a nation, such as the former Yugoslavia, is composed by (on one plausible view) more than one country, there.is a possibility that patriotism and sectarianism will align in *support* of a constituent country, but against the nation which represents that country internationally. We saw this in the case of Kosovo.

Sectarianism, whether in a cultural form or in its most common, religious form, contrasts with cosmopolitanism in much the way extreme nationalism does. But sectarian positions, unlike most nationalistic ones, are usually taken to be warranted by divine preference. This view can readily make them virulent and can render negotiation with other sects or denominations difficult. Even in nations with democratically elected governments, sectarian aims may be in tension with policies that are in the interest of the nation as a whole. A possible example is the case of Israel, where, partly on sectarian scriptural grounds, some citizens support retaining settlements in the occupied Palestinian territories. Many in Israel and elsewhere consider this kind of appeal to scripture a major obstacle to peace and to statehood for the Palestinians.

American democracy is partly based on a constitutional separation between church and state, expressed in the First Amendment to the US Constitution, which both prohibits establishing a state religion and guarantees the free exercise of religion to all. Separation of church and state is widely believed to be not only consistent with Christianity but called for by it. Here Christianity differs from Islam and certain other religions. Separation of church and state is an important element in democracy, and a major challenge for achieving world peace may be promoting a form of it that is workable in the Middle East and elsewhere. On this point cosmopolitan and nationalist elements can join forces. This could be a coalition that patriotism can applaud.

III   Domains of institutional authority

The contrast between nationalism and cosmopolitanism applies in various domains of human life. One could be a nationalist in, for instance, military and economic matters, but cosmopolitan in other areas, say in public health, where one would endorse taxes for a worldwide inoculation program. These nationalistic views can be held by sector, and one need not hold any one view in this spectrum across all sectors. Indeed, a person need not be either a nationalist or a cosmopolitan of any sort, though thoughtful people tend to take positions somewhere on the spectra we have outlined between these two ranges of positions.

As a matter of contingent fact, there is probably a tendency for extreme nationalists to be nationalistic across all the relevant domains of human life. The same may hold for extreme cosmopolitanism. But for purposes of developing a position on institutional policies – especially governmental policies – we should consider one domain at a time. The case for a given nation to favor nationalism or cosmopolitanism may be quite different from one domain to another. A nation with a rich culture may plausibly favor it for international activities, in which case it is being to some extent nationalistic; but if the same nation is economically rich it may have to favor the interests of poor nations in some of its agricultural policies, in which case it is being to some extent cosmopolitan.

A related point is that as support grows for individual nations' ceding authority to international bodies, the case for doing this may be stronger in one domain than in another. International standards for healthcare and labor might be justly imposed on individual nations with their acquiescence; such standards for the content of the required educational curriculum are much less likely to be universally acceptable, at least above the level of the basic skills of reading, writing, and mathematics.

We might identify indefinitely many domains in which governments and organizations such as businesses make decisions affected by nationalistic vs. cosmopolitan values. To keep my points focused and manageably short, I have singled out four domains: first, the *economic realm*, including tariffs; second, the realm of *military activity*, especially defense; third, the domain of *public health*; and fourth, that of *culture*.

IV The multiple manifestations of globalization

Globalization occurs in all four of these realms, at least if (as seems reasonable) we may count military activity abroad described as protective or preventive as an indication of a nation's global activities.

Military globalization

The first Iraq War would be a case of UN-backed international global military activity; the second Iraq War is an instance of the global military activity of the USA and certain supporting allies. One might think that given the mainly American initiative in the second case, the rationale would be almost entirely nationalistic, but in fact the Bush Administration has sought to justify its action in Iraq partly on the cosmopolitan ground that it protects all peaceful nations from terrorism and promotes democracy for the Iraqis. Here we find an apparently strongly nationalistic administration attributing some weight to the interests of humanity in general.

The more common rationale for the second Iraq War presented to the US citizenry, however, is in terms of a mandate to protect the American people. This is a clearly nationalistic rationale. There is nothing inherently objectionable about emphasizing different (mutually consistent) rationales to different audiences. As we have already seen, some actions by nations or institutions can be justified on *either* nationalistic or cosmopolitan grounds.

There is a further consideration regarding military activity. Much depends on whether it is defensive, corrective, or preventive. For defensive military activity, as with military resistance to the Nazis, a nationalistic rationale is pertinent. There may be no need for cosmopolitan argument appealing to the interests of humanity, though in this case such an argument was clearly available. But consider a UN-sponsored corrective action in the Darfur region of Sudan, where, with government complicity, the Janjeweed militia has slaughtered innocent people. This injustice provides a possible cosmopolitan rationale for corrective intervention, perhaps even military intervention. But there may be no nation that can mount a plausible nationalistic rationale for intervention. If we consider a preventive war, such as – on some views – the second Iraq War, the same point holds. But in this case the loss of life by innocent people before the War was different, and the likely loss (say, through terrorism outside Iraq) if no war was mounted was more difficult to predict. The need for a cosmopolitan rationale, then, and the difficulty of constructing one, seems greater.

Economic globalization

Consider now the economic domain. Two of the important issues raised by globalization are depletion of natural resources and quality of working conditions, particularly as indicated by the extent of child labor and of sweatshops. First take an extreme nationalistic point of view. If domestic industry needs raw materials from abroad, a nationalistic government would tend to allow their import even if they come from mines that employ large numbers of children in dangerous conditions and even if depleting the supply in some small country would have disastrous consequences for its well-being.

If, moreover, cheap but satisfactory products may be made available by purchasing from companies abroad that run sweatshops or use young children as laborers, extremely nationalistic governments would allow their import and sale, and nationalistic (as well as simply greedy) companies would import and market them. A moderate nationalism, by contrast, even if it would not require boycotts, might allow or even encourage negotiating to reduce the harm abroad. A minimal nationalism would allow a boycott. Certainly a government that combined a minimal nationalism with a minimal cosmopolitanism would support a boycott if negotiation failed to improve the working conditions sufficiently. An extreme cosmopolitanism would support major efforts to create reforms abroad and would call for sacrifices by rich nations if these are needed to achieve those reforms.

Healthcare and preventive medicine

The realm of healthcare and preventive medicine is similar, but two points provide a contrast with the economic case. First, there is often the chance that an epidemic, such as bird flu, will spread to one's own country. Second, the resulting suffering that cries out for help can rarely be attributed to lack of economic energy. Epidemics can occur even in rich nations, and they often kill. By contrast, damage from, say, protectionism in an importing nation, can lead to poverty in an exporting nation. For all that, the spectrum of positions from extreme nationalism to extreme cosmopolitanism is similar.

When it comes to preventive medicine and other protections of health, there are perhaps even more borderline cases than for other sectors where the contrast between nationalism and cosmopolitanism comes into play. What of drug trafficking? Certainly addiction is a health hazard; it would threaten the health of addicts even apart from the risks of sharing needles. It is obvious that international *cooperation* is needed here, but what of international requirements? One question is whether there should be an international force that monitors production and export of drugs or even establishes international standards for treatment of addicts. Even if each country has different penalties, there might be medical cooperation affecting rehabilitation.

Globalization at the cultural level

When we consider the area of cultural globalization, we often find a variable that does not affect the other realms in the same way, if at all: pride. People often take pride in their national literature, in the paintings by artists of their nationality, and indeed in their language. Extreme nationalists would be willing to engage in at least some measure of "cultural imperialism" and to resist cultural influence from abroad. It may be a short step from 'my country right or wrong' to 'my culture right or wrong'. Even moderate nationalists would be willing to push hard in either of these directions, though they would be less likely to think that any kind of coercion is warranted, as where learning American culture and history is made a condition for a managerial position in an American company operating abroad.

In the realm of culture, the contrast between nationalism and cosmopolitanism plays out differently than with the other domains we have considered. The point is not that the human interests involved are less clear, though this may be true: it is utterly clear that poverty and disease are to be eliminated, but it is not as clear that English literature and western philosophy should be introduced in educational systems where they are absent. Still, some cosmopolitans, like some American or English nationalists, could well think this curricular policy is desirable; but they would think it partly for different reasons. Cosmopolitans might think western philosophy and English literature have universal value; nationalists could believe this as well but, *as* nationalists, their support of the policy would not depend on this view. The point is important because it shows that things characteristic of a nation or region need not be limited in value or meaning to the people of that region. One kind of provinciality is excessive suspicion of cultural imperialism, for instance thinking that something originating in another culture should not be universally used in one's own simply because it is not native. Here I must admit to ascribing cross-cultural, universal value to – among many other things – western philosophy, English literature, and American initiative, inventiveness, generosity, and civil liberties. (This is of course not to suggest that these elements are not prominent elsewhere as well or to deny universal value to kinds of philosophy and literature.)

To be sure, cosmopolitans would likely think that the exporting culture should also import some of the culturally significant elements from the recipient culture. But this can be a result of the open-mindedness that accompanies any good cosmopolitanism, together with a commitment to reciprocity as a benefit to international harmony. Exporting culture need not come from a view on which there are no objective differences in value. On that naive view, we cannot hold that some values and institutional arrangements serve human interests better than others. There are ethical values – some well expressed in the Declaration of Independence and the US Constitution – that can serve many different cultures despite their many differences.

Is there an intrinsically international realm?

In concluding this section, I want to stress that although there are realms that constitute only part of the life of a nation in which nationalism and cosmopolitanism operate, there are also realms that are *intrinsically international* and in a sense larger than the life of any one nation, even if they play a role in it. Think of international law and of the Internet as an international mode of communication.

Nationalism may lead a given country to try to exercise a large self-interested influence in these areas. But in part because international laws are intended for the fair regulation of all nations, this is prima facie objectionable. As to the Internet, given its shared character, there is at least some presumption that the fairest approach incorporates at least a moderate cosmopolitanism. In both cases, at least for resolution of disputes between nations, it is desirable to have a body, such as the UN, with some authority to impose duties on individual nations. Achieving this would not go as far as the rather strong cosmopolitanism proposed by Pojman, but it would be a significant step in that direction.

* * *

We have seen that both nationalism and cosmopolitanism come in many forms and that they are largely converse positions. Each also applies to realms that are part of the life of a nation – its military or economic system, for instance. The contrast between them is especially important for globalization, since the expanding activities that accompany globalization are prime territory for the conflict between nationalism and cosmopolitanism. Do sound ethical standards call for preferring one or the other in such conflicts?

As we saw with the cultural realm, there is no perfectly general answer to the question of whether ethics requires us to prefer either nationalism or cosmopolitanism. Giving some degree of priority to one's own culture or, for that matter, one's own technology, need not oppose optimal promotion of human interests. It may be quite consonant with doing that in a way sanctioned by good ethics. This is not to deny that giving preference to things characteristic of one's own country *just because* they are characteristic of it is generally a bad thing and may give rise to wrong-doing. But nationalism, at least of weak or moderate kinds, does not entail wrong-doing, though many nationalists have been guilty of it. Commonly nationalists give priority to their own nation because they think that it is superior or because, consistent with that view though not required by it, they believe that they have a patriotic duty to give it. That may or may not lead them to wrong-doing.

Suppose there is no perfectly general answer to the question of whether ethics calls for giving some degree of preference, even if very weak preference, to one's own nation in cases of conflicting interests. We may still say that *by and large* extreme nationalism tends to pay too little attention to obligations of beneficence toward other peoples – a kind of obligation most major ethical views acknowledge. But moderate nationalism need not do this. Moderate cosmopolitanism, however, tends not to do it. It is, as it were, pledged to seek the well-being of all peoples. A high degree of effort in this transnational, cosmopolitan quest is endorsed by at least the major ethical views and probably by all of the major religions as well, including Christianity, Judaism, and Islam. The rise of the modern nation state has spurred extreme nationalism in many quarters; globalization invites – and perhaps is forcing – us to reconsider our historical commitment to this outlook. Most nations still need some measure of patriotism for optimal flourishing, but the only kind of patriotism that is morally justifiable is one leavened by loyalty to the community of all peoples.[13]

References

Audi, R. 2001. *The Architecture of Reason*. Oxford University Press.
    2005. "Moral Foundations of Liberal Democracy, Secular Reasons, and Liberal Neutrality Toward the Good." *Notre Dame Journal of Law, Ethics and Public Policy*, 19, 1, 197–218.
Brock, G. and H. Brighouse, 2005. *The Political Philosophy of Cosmopolitanism*. Cambridge University Press.
Copp, D. 2005. "International Justice and the Basic Needs Principle." In Brock and Brighouse, 39–54.
McCabe, D. 1997. "Patriotic Gore, Again." *Southern Journal of Philosophy*, 35, 203–23.
Miller, R. W. 2005. "Cosmopolitan Respect and Patriotic Concern." In Brock and Brighouse, 127–47.
Orwell, G. 1945. "Notes on Nationalism." *Polemic* (London), 1 (October).

[13] An earlier draft of this essay was written for presentation at the US Military Academy, West Point, in memory of Louis P. Pojman, who taught there from 1986 through the spring of 1995. It has benefited from discussion with that audience and the audience at the Helsinki School of Economics and from comments by Igor Primoratz and Marta Soniewicka. The essay is dedicated to the memory of Louis Pojman.

Pogge, T. 2005. "A Cosmopolitan Perspective on the Global Economic Order." In Brock and Brighouse, 92–109.

Pojman, L. P. 2006. *Terrorism, Human Rights, and the Case for World Government.* Lanham, Md.: Rowman & Littlefield.

Soniewicka, M. 2011. "Patriotism and Justice in the Global Dimension: A Conflict of Virtues?" *Eidos*, 14, 50–71.

Index